Explosion!

ALSO BY MARK GALLAGHER

The Yankee Encyclopedia
Day by Day in New York Yankees History
Fifty Years of Yankee All-Stars

EXPLOSION!
Mickey Mantle's
Legendary Home Runs

by Mark Gallagher
Research Associate: Paul E. Susman

Arbor House New York

Manufactured in the United States of America

10 9 8 7 6 5 4 3 2 1

Library of Congress Cataloging in Publication Data

Gallagher, Mark.
  Explosion!: Mickey Mantle's legendary home runs.

  1. Mantle, Mickey, 1931–   . 2. Baseball players—
United States—Biography. 3. New York Yankees
(Baseball team)—History. 4. Baseball—United States—
Records. I. Title.
GV865.M33G35   1987   796.357′092′4 [B]   86-22281
ISBN: 0-87795-853-X

*To the Bobbys, Huber and Neeb,
the older guys, who in the magi-
cal summer of 1961 were kind
enough to take me along to
Yankee Stadium, where we
watched Mickey Mantle and
Roger Maris chase the Babe's
shadow*

Contents

Acknowledgments

First off, my research associate, Paul E. Susman of Skokie, Illinois, deserves a special thank you. He was with me from Day One and he kept on the trail of any baseball people willing to talk about Mantle, as well as assisting with research of newspapers, periodicals, and books. He was assisted by Robert H. Schiewe, a neighbor of Paul Susman's who, besides doing research, figured the lengths of Mantle's long home runs at USC in 1951 and at Detroit in 1960.

Special thanks also to Fred Chase, my editor, who believed in this book, nurtured it, and put up with my delays, and to Gail E. Ross, who introduced Fred to the book's concept.

As with my previous three books on the Yankees, my mom and dad, Louise and Neil Gallagher, made important research, editing and manuscript preparation contributions, and I'm extremely grateful for these.

In the course of our research, begun in March 1984, many books, periodicals, and newspapers were reviewed. I am indebted to all of these publications and offer a special thanks to the flagship of American journalism and record keeping, the *New York Times*.

The work of several members of the Society for American Baseball Research (SABR), including Bob Davids, Bill James, Pete Palmer, and Raymond Gonzalez, was drawn from for this book. Bob Davids and Pete Palmer were also kind enough to give direct assistance, the former toward the Mantle home-run table and the latter toward the switch-hitting statistics on the Mick. All are also thanked for their unique contributions to the store of baseball knowledge.

Paul and I interviewed or corresponded with hundreds of baseball contemporaries of Mantle. They're too numerous to single out individually, but many of them—Gil McDougald, for one—gave us valued information. To Gil—and all the others—thank you for your invaluable help.

Mark Gallagher
Rockville, Maryland
July 1986

Introduction

Mickey Mantle. A Hall of Fame name. Born and reared to be a ballplayer. Destined to be a Yankee.

Nineteen-year-old Mantle joined the Yankees in 1951. Yankee outfielder Cliff Mapes remembers observing Mickey as an innocent, unsure rookie, "standing in the outfield watching a plane going over and blowing bubbles."

Mantle. A muscular, blond Oklahoman. Promising much. Becoming one of the Yankee greats. The center-field successor to Joe DiMaggio. Number 7. His baseball card the treasure of every kid.

Mantle. Arriving when television was in its infancy and becoming one of the medium's first stars. Leading the Yankees. Playing in the World Series almost every fall. Becoming the greatest American League drawing card since Ruth and having as center-field counterparts in New York Willie Mays and Duke Snider.

Mantle. Burning—explosive—speed. A natural who had everything. Playing in pain most of his career.

Mantle. Switch-hitter. From either side hitting the ball long distances. Long distances? When Mickey Mantle hit a baseball solidly, it sounded like an EXPLOSION!

The Home Runs of Baseball's Most Promising Player

1951

March 26, 1951—Bovard Field, Los Angeles. He was more than a 19-year-old baseball player with a world of promise now. Mickey Mantle was something of a celebrity, and for good reason. He added shine to his star on this date by leading the New York Yankees' assault on the University of Southern California nine with a seven-RBI day, a day that included two legendary homers, a booming triple, and a leg single.

As Mantle tried to board the team bus afterward, he was mobbed by USC students, some seeking autographs, others reaching out to him, and all treating young Mickey as though he were a Hollywood film idol. The boy hadn't played one major-league game, but he was the most talked about ballplayer in the nation! As the Yankees concluded a golden California tour, Mickey was batting .432.

The Yankees may have beaten the collegians in a 15–1 rout, but these were the same Trojans who beat the Pittsburgh Pirates and the tough Pacific Coast League's Hollywood Stars. The same Trojans the Yankees went after, plucking 20 or so off the USC campus and giving big bonus money to several hot-shot kids who never made it. And here was Mickey, who was signed for next to nothing, *exploding*, of all places, on this very same campus.

Mantle hit eye-popping homers from each side of the plate. The left-handed homer was astonishing. Gil McDougald believes this was the longest ball he saw Mantle hit in their 10 seasons together with the Yankees. It was, he says, "certainly farther than the one he hit in Washington in 1953" (a 565-footer). Tommy Henrich says the ball "landed as far away from the fence as it was from the plate to the wall." USC Coach Rod Dedeaux says it "was like a golf ball going into orbit. It was hit so far it was like it wasn't real."

Dedeaux, who has turned out major leaguers by the bushel at USC, cites a football field that paralleled the outfield fence running from the right foul line to dead-center field; Mickey's ball left the baseball field near the 439-foot mark in right-center, Dedeaux says, sailed over the

3

football field (160 feet wide with sidelines of some 40 feet each), and hit a fence on one hop.

According to Dedeaux, USC's center fielder Tom Riach "virtually climbed the fence and hung on to the top, observing where the ball hit. Other people sitting in the stands confirmed the location." No doubt about it, says Dedeaux, "It was a superhuman feat."

Riach recalls shading the Mick to right and running to the right of the 439-foot sign as the ball headed his way. "I jumped up on the fence and watched the ball cross the football field and short-hop the fence to the north of the football field." On a scale drawing of the baseball and football fields, Riach puts the landing spot a shade longer than Dedeaux's point of impact, but the two landing spots are essentially side by side.

Researcher Paul Susman's friend and counselor in things mathematical, Robert H. Schiewe, on the basis of the Dedeaux and Riach accounts, calculates a travel distance of 645 feet from home plate to the Dedeaux dot and, incredibly, of 654 to 660 feet to the Riach dot.

The right-handed Mantle homer also witnessed by the record Bovard crowd of some 3,000 cannot be overlooked either. It soared over the fence in left at about the 351-foot mark, cleared a street and several houses, and landed on the top of a three-story house. This one had to exceed 500 feet.

On the day of Mickey's USC performance, Arch Murray of the *New York Post* did what every other New York sportswriter did; he reflected on Mantle's once-improbable chances of sticking with the Yankees for the regular season. Mickey's fielding leaves you wondering, observed Murray, "but then he steps up to hit and all doubts start to fade."

SENSATIONAL ROOKIE SPRING

No fanfare greeted Mickey Mantle in February 1951 when he reported to the Yankees' instructional camp, preceding spring training. Few sportswriters even knew his name. But the Yankee brass was well tuned in to Mantle and his promise. The organization was keen over the switch-hitting speedster ever since Tom Greenwade signed him out of Commerce, Oklahoma, in 1949. And young Mantle didn't exactly cool the interest in New York with his two outstanding seasons in the minors. Yankee manager Casey Stengel was well aware of Mantle, too, for Mickey had worked out with the Yankees for a few weeks the previous September, although he didn't play in any games.

There were a number of highly regarded minor-league prospects at the instructional camp in Phoenix, Arizona, but Mickey Mantle stole the show. Stengel and his staff couldn't believe his speed: Mantle won all the races, blazed from home to first base in just over three seconds, and exploded out of the box. His power was even more awesome; he made the Phoenix ballpark, hardly a bandbox at 320 feet down the lines and 430 feet to center field, look like a Little League field. His shots sailed well beyond the outfield fence.

Perhaps Arizona's thin air was helping Mantle's drives, but there was no denying that the teenager was hitting the ball farther from both sides of the plate than any switch-hitter in history, moving Stengel to observe, "That kid can hit balls over buildings."

Yet, Mantle was no brute, standing not yet quite 5'11" and weighing between 165 and 175. But he packed power in his shoulders, arms, and back, and his bat was lightning-quick; this combination of strength and bat speed produced his titanic drives. There were some who said he had more power than Babe Ruth, and to add spice to the assertion, he had it from either side of the plate.

Mantle joined the Yankee spring training camp (also in Phoenix this one year), and by mid-March the press was reporting his every move. He became the most publicized rookie phenom in the history of the game. Outstanding rookies such as Clint Hartung, the Giants' answer to Babe Ruth a few years earlier, had been given big buildups, but the pressure on Mantle, who was touted not only as "the next Ruth" but as "the next Cobb," was unparalleled. Branch Rickey, the shrewdest judge of talent of his time, said Mantle was the best prospect he'd ever seen, and White Sox general manager Frank Lane was willing to give the Yankees a quarter of a million for him and "bury him in $1,000 bills" as a bonus.

Still, Mantle's game was flawed. He was a shortstop who wasn't a shortstop. He lacked the necessary finesse, and while his arm was strong, it was also erratic. Besides, the Yankees already had the game's best shortstop—Phil Rizzuto. Third base was open but another rookie, Gil McDougald, who by year's end hit .306 and won the Rookie of the Year honors, gained the upper hand at that position.

Harry Craft, Mantle's minor-league manager, had suggested that the Yankees give Mickey a shot at the outfield. Stengel, too, felt Mantle's powerful throwing arm and his foot speed were better suited for the outfield, so coach Tommy Henrich started giving him a crash course on the fundamentals of outfield play. But there was much to learn and little time to learn it. In one exhibition game, Mantle was struck above the right eye with a line drive because he didn't know how to use his flip-down sunglasses.

To everyone's immense satisfaction, Mickey made fast progress as an outfielder. Against the Indians, he caught a fly ball in right field and fired a perfect strike to the plate, nailing the speedy Bobby Avila by five feet—the best throw Henrich had ever seen. "There isn't any more that I can teach him."

The explosive speed that made Mantle a natural outfielder was displayed spectacularly on the base paths. After Mantle was called out on a bang-bang play at third, Stengel was asked if the umpire had blown the call. "I don't know whether he was out or not," replied Casey thoughtfully, "but I can see why the umpire thought he was. That kid got from first to third so fast they must have thought he ran across the pitcher's box."

On March 16 the Yankees opened a twelve-game barnstorming tour of California, with Pacific Coast League teams providing most of the competition. Joe DiMaggio, a native of San Francisco, was the main attraction, but the Oklahoma hot-shot was the tour's second biggest draw.

Mantle hit majestic home runs in Los Angeles, Sacramento, and San Francisco, and fans and players alike marveled over his wallops in batting practice. Teammates Gil McDougald and Charlie Silvera, natives of the Bay Area, remember well the Mantle homer that left San Francisco's Seals Stadium at a point in right field where few homers had ever cleared. McDougald: "Amazingly, he did it batting right-handed and it cleared the fence by at least 50 feet, right into the heart of a progressive wind that always blew in from right field."

Two high-schoolers came to see Mantle play in the Los Angeles area. One was Johnny James, who will be a Mantle teammate on the Yankees of 1958, 1960, and 1961. James: "Somehow I was fortunate to wangle two great seats behind home plate. . . . On his first trip to the plate, batting left-handed, Mantle hit a line drive over the pitcher's head for a single that was by far the hardest-hit ball I had ever seen. . . . The fans really buzzed after he hit it. To this day that single stands out in my mind.

"What occurred next was equally impressive. The next hitter hit a line-drive single, and Mickey went from first to third with a burst of speed that *really* set the fans to buzzing. My friend and I spent the next several weeks trying to describe those two feats to anyone who would listen."

After winding up their California tour at USC, the Yankees returned to Phoenix for a few days, then broke camp to begin another barnstorming tour, this time of Texas and the Midwest.

No one was sure whether Mantle, who hit Texas-sized homers in El Paso, Beaumont, and Houston, would stick with the big club. Stengel wavered but leaned toward keeping Mickey. General manager George Weiss disagreed. He felt the 19-year-old needed another season in the minors, as originally planned. Virtually all the Yankee players believed the kid belonged with them. With a couple of exhibition games still remaining in Ebbets Field, the brass held off making their decision.

April 15, 1951—Ebbets Field, Brooklyn. After singling, drawing a walk, and nailing a base runner at the plate in his New York City debut the day before, Mickey Mantle on this date shows what he can really do. He singles batting right-handed, singles twice batting left-handed, and caps the day with a left-handed home run off Jim Romano, a Brooklyn native who had a brief big-league career.

Mickey's homer is a tremendous, towering clout, hit high over the 38-foot-high scoreboard in right field; 12,789 chilled patrons become unmindful of the cold and very conscious of the boy from Oklahoma.

The game, won by the Dodgers, 7–6, was the curtain closer on an exhibition season in which Mantle hit .402 and powered nine homers. His great spring performance made it easier for Casey Stengel to convince George Weiss that Mantle was ready for the big show. On this date, in fact, the Yankees picked up Mantle's contract, making him a bona fide Yankee.

Mantle's homer was only "half-hit," asserted sportswriter Tommy Holmes in the *Brooklyn Eagle.* "That's a fact. Fooled on a low inside pitch, Mantle managed to golf the ball after a fashion, hitting it up near his fists. Normally, your rightfielder comes in fast to catch the result of a thing like this, but this fly ball kept traveling up and out until it finally fell in Bedford Avenue. I guess it was the longest handle hit I've ever seen."

Mantle had blown into Brooklyn on the winds of adverse publicity, rejoining the Yankees for the two games at Ebbets Field after a much reported trip to his Oklahoma draft board.

Instant fame had its drawbacks. If Mantle was so physically talented, many Americans wanted to know—and some put the question to the Selective Service—how come he had a 4-F draft classification? The answer was Mickey's history of osteomyelitis, a bone disease he contracted after being kicked in the leg while playing high school football. It was the kind of thing that put the Army at risk of having to pay him a lifetime disability pension. But the decision not to take Mickey caused an uproar and forced a reexamination.

Mantle was relaxed about the second exam, although he wasn't happy about the prospect of being a chronic sufferer of osteomyelitis or a disability case. He was willing to serve and before departing offered a cup of pristine logic: "I'll play baseball for the Army or fight for it, whatever they want me to do. But if I don't go to the Army, I want to play baseball."

Mantle again failed his physical, and even though he did have the support of most people, including influential columnists like Arthur Daley of the *New York Times*, shouts of "draft dodger" fell on Mickey's ears throughout his rookie season. And they had to hurt.

May 1, 1951—Comiskey Park, Chicago. Mickey Mantle was fizzling. The 19-year-old phenom, the Yankees' right fielder since Opening Day, was batting an anemic .222 and had yet to hit a home run. The promise of spring was fading.

On the mound for the White Sox is reliever Randy Gumpert, a physical fitness advocate and pursuer of a notoriously wholesome lifestyle—he gets up with the sun, takes long walks, and drinks gallons of milk. He is a decent journeyman pitcher whose best year was 1946, when he went 11–3 with the Yankees.

Gumpert delivers to Mantle in the sixth with a runner on. Mickey, batting left-handed, swings and connects solidly. A smoking line drive sails over center fielder Jim Busby and into the stands, some 450 feet away.

White Sox pitcher Hal Brown recently recalled that the Mick's blast "was hit so hard that it got there in one second and rattled around in the seats for what seemed like five minutes."

Gumpert still remembers the pitch as "a screwball that evidently didn't screw too much. I was not aware that Mantle had hit his first major-league home run off me until 1956 or 1957. I was sitting in the clubhouse in St. Pete [as a Yankee spring training instructor] and Mantle reminded me that the homer in Comiskey was his first."

The first-homer ball was returned to Mickey, who autographed it nicely and sent it back to Commerce, where his kid twin brothers took it out on the lot and knocked it lopsided.

Given his spectacular spring, Mickey's homer was a long time coming; it had not been an easy time for him. He was scared to death before the opening game against the Red Sox on April 17, aimlessly pacing back and forth, all too aware of the 44,860 Yankee Stadium customers waiting to see his first big-league game. Mickey's face reddened in embarrassment when he was asked to pose for a picture with giants Joe DiMaggio and Ted Williams. As it was, Mickey was a little uneasy playing next to the great DiMaggio. He was only 19, he had come from Class C ball (the first Yankee to make the transition from Class C to the parent club for Opening Day), and he had only 20 outfield games under his belt.

He did manage an RBI single in the opener, and by the end of his first week was hitting .320. Then, for the first time, he slumped. As his hitting slipped, the pressure mounted. He was desperately in need of a big game, and the home run off Gumpert gave it to him.

May 4, 1951—Sportsman's Park, St. Louis. With their 8–1 romp on this day over the Browns, their sixth consecutive win, the Yankees moved into first place. And a ball off Mickey Mantle's bat was one of the hardest hit St. Louis had ever seen.

The Yankees lead 2–1 in the sixth inning and Mantle faces ex-Yankee Duane Pillette with one on. Pillette delivers—"a sinker that I threw too high," Pillette will recall—and the left-handed-hitting Mantle connects. The result is "a fiercesome homer," Joe Trimble of the *New York Daily News* wrote, propelled so hard to right field that it sailed out of the park and "nearly into the Mississippi River." It traveled "more than 450 feet on the fly," according to Trimble's account, but Browns' outfielder Roy Sievers will recall that the ball was three-quarters the height of the light towers when it left the ballpark and still rising—it had to go at least 500 feet, Sievers insists. He says people in St. Louis still talk about this drive.

Sievers was told by fans, who from elevated stands could follow the ball, that it cleared Grand Avenue and banged into a car dealership. Probably the same auto outlet that Ruth's ball struck—the Wells Chevrolet Co., it was called, at least in 1926.

Bob Burns, the veteran St. Louis sportswriter, over three decades later said that the only comparable St. Louis homer "was the one Babe

Ruth hit in the [1926] World Series. The consensus is that these [the Ruth and Mantle drives] are the longest right-field blasts ever hit in Sportsman's Park."

On this freezing night in St. Louis there are 4,545 hardy fans in attendance, including Mickey's mother, his girlfriend, Merlyn Johnson (the future Mrs. Mantle), and Merlyn's mother. After the game, a reporter asked Merlyn about Mickey's homer and she answered, "I expected it. He promised me he'd do it."

May 16, 1951—Yankee Stadium. Mickey Mantle enjoyed one of the best games of his young career, making a couple of fine fielding plays, collecting four RBIs, scoring three runs, hitting safely twice—improving his batting average to .308—and stealing a base. One of the hits was his first home run at Yankee Stadium, hit right-handed.

In the eighth inning, Phil Rizzuto reaches on an error, and Mantle, who earlier hit a two-run single that knocked out Bob Lemon, digs in. Southpaw Dick Rozek, Cleveland's fourth pitcher, remembers: "I threw Mantle a letter-high fastball for strike one, swinging. Then I threw a slightly higher fastball for a swinging strike two. Before the next pitch, I considered throwing another slightly higher fastball—known as 'climbing the ladder'—but changed my mind toward throwing a curve in the dirt. The curve I threw never came close to the dirt and 'hung' nicely—for the hitter—around the letters.

"Mickey handled it in a fashion that was to become frequent: He hit a line drive some 420 feet into the deep left-field stands. I knew when it was hit it was gone, so I didn't watch its entire journey, but our shortstop, Ray Boone, came to the mound and told me the ball literally tore up an empty seat and it was fortunate no one was sitting there."

Mantle's heroics help Vic Raschi and the first-place Yankees trounce the Indians, 11–3. For Rozek, who was tremendously fast in the minors and whose major-league career was shortened by arm troubles, there are, in retrospect, no hard feelings.

But the long ball will fail Mantle. It will take him more than a month to hit his next homer. And for a while in late May and early June he stopped hitting altogether.

Striking out too much was Mantle's biggest problem. This was never more evident than in a Memorial Day doubleheader in Boston, when he fanned five consecutive times and was moved to tears of frustration. The

cagey veteran pitchers around the league quickly learned his weak-
nesses—he couldn't resist high pitches, for one thing—and exploited
them.

The pressure was suffocating and the tension boiling inside him.
When he looked bad at the plate, he tended to get down on himself and
then lose his concentration in the field. Stengel resorted to platooning
him with Jackie Jensen, with the right-handed Jensen playing against
southpaws.

The agony ended on July 13, when Mantle added three strikeouts to
his season total. His average was down to .261, and though he had 45
RBIs, driving in runs at a pace that would give him about 90 for the year,
Stengel informed him that he was going down to the Yanks' top farm
club, the Blues of Kansas City.

"Does this mean that Mantle's through?" reporters asked Stengel.

"You wish you were through like that kid's through," snapped Casey.
He explained that the strikeouts were killing Mantle and he was being
sent to Kansas City to find himself; once he did, he'd be back in the blink
of an eye.

Confused and discouraged, Mantle continued to slump (0 for 22)
with the Blues until he got some good counsel from his father, Mutt.
Feeling sorry for himself, he phoned his father to say he was through in
baseball; he wanted to go home. Mutt was soon in Kansas City, not with
the sympathy soup Mickey expected, but with both barrels blazing. "If
that's the way you're going to take this," Mutt said, "you don't belong in
baseball anyway. If you have no more guts than that, just forget about the
game completely. Come back and work in the mines, like me."

Soon Mickey broke out of his slump and went on a hitting spree. His
best performance with the Blues was a splendid 5-for-5 game at Toledo's
Swayne Field on July 31. He hit two homers—one an enormously high
clout belted into the smog, over a light tower and across Detroit Avenue,
close to 600 feet—and added a triple, double, and ninth-inning bunt
single to complete the hitting cycle.

In 40 games with Kansas City, Mantle batted .361, hit 11 homers,
and had 50 RBIs; he was back with the Yankees in late August. Just as
Stengel promised.

August 25, 1951—Municipal Stadium, Cleveland. The American
League pennant race was in high gear, and a paid crowd of 52,155
watched the Yankees win the rubber game of a three-game series and

move within percentage points of the first-place Indians. The Yanks prevailed, 7–3, on this date because Eddie Lopat pitched smartly, running his lifetime record against the Tribe to 32–8, and because the 1–2–3 men in the batting order—Phil Rizzuto, Mickey Mantle, and Gene Woodling—combined for seven hits, six runs, and five RBIs.

Mantle, in his second game since returning to the Yankees, comes through with a pair of extra-base hits, both batting left-handed against Mike Garcia. He snaps a 1–1 tie in the third by unleashing a two-run home run over the left-center-field fence, and two innings later doubles and scores along with Phil Rizzuto on Gene Woodling's game-breaking single.

Mantle is understandably proud of his roundtripper off the tough Garcia. The Big Bear, trying for his 18th win, will finish the season with 20 victories.

Mantle's overall play is solid as he responds favorably to the pressure of his first pennant race. He wound up hitting .281 (27 for 96), with six homers, from the time he returned from Kansas City to the end of the season.

August 29, 1951—Sportsman's Park, St. Louis. Bombing the Browns, 15–2, the Yankees moved into a first-place tie with the losing Indians, the two teams at 80–47.

Leadoff man Mickey Mantle paces the bombardment with four RBIs and gains the satisfaction of hitting a three-run homer off the legendary—and tough—Satchel Paige. The ninth-inning drive over the right-field barrier traveled perhaps 450 feet.

The ageless Paige, past 45, was a star in the old Negro Leagues before Mantle was even born. A right-hander, he has handled Mantle rather easily this season, giving Mickey a steady diet of rising fastballs, and chuckling at the kid's ineptitude whenever Mickey missed. But today, youth wins the battle and Mantle has the last laugh.

September 19, 1951—Yankee Stadium. The Yankees, outhit 10 to 3, beat Chicago, 5–3, to remain three percentage points ahead of second-place Cleveland. Gil McDougald hit a solo homer and Bob Kuzava was wonderful in long relief, but Mickey Mantle was the brightest star.

It is 2–2 in the fourth inning when White Sox right-hander Lou Kretlow issues two-out walks to Rizzuto and Kuzava. Mantle sends a drive to right and suddenly it's a 5–2 game, the ball falling in the front rows of the right-field stands, just to the right of the Yankee bullpen. It is Mantle's 13th and final homer of 1951. Kretlow allows only two hits before being lifted for a pinch-hitter in the seventh, but both hits are homers and he loses the game.

The Yankees have an important win. They will soon pull away, going on to win the pennant by five games. A World Series with their rivals from across the Harlem River, the New York Giants, winners of a miracle Bobby Thomson pennant in the National League, is in the making. The series will feature two highly publicized rookies, Mantle (13 HRs, 65 RBIs, .267 BA in 96 games) and Willie Mays (20 HRs, 68 RBIs, .274 BA in 121 games). The Yankees win an exciting six-game struggle, but the rookie battle fails to materialize. Mays hits a sickly .182 (4 for 22), while Mantle suffers the first major injury of his career in Game 2. Chasing a fly ball hit by Mays to right center, Mantle steps on a rubber cover of a sprinkler head and sustains serious damage to his right knee. He is carried off the field on a stretcher, his first World Series finished. He headed for an operating table. And it will not be the last time. Not hardly.

1952

May 30, 1952—Yankee Stadium. It was not a good month for either the Yankees or Mickey Mantle. And it ended miserably for the Yankees as they dropped a doubleheader to the Philadelphia A's and at May's end found themselves humbled in fifth place.

The Yankees take a 1–0 lead in the opener with a Mantle homer in the third, but the A's Bobby Shantz blanks the Bombers the rest of the way. The lefty baffles the Yanks with an assortment of curves, knucklers, and change-ups. He strikes out 11, including Mantle twice. However, Mickey goes 3 for 7 in the 14-inning game and has a double to go with his four-bagger.

With the A's up, 2–1, Mantle nearly homers to tie the score in the bottom of the 14th. With one out, he hammers a Shantz delivery some 420 feet to left field, the ball dropping on the ledge atop the auxiliary scoreboard next to the A's bullpen and bouncing into the bleachers for a ground-rule double; had the ball rebounded onto the playing field, Mantle could have had an inside-the-parker or at least a triple, and with skilled bunter Phil Rizzuto up next, he might have been squeezed home. Instead, he dies on second.

Mantle went hitless in the nightcap, and the Yankees almost went scoreless, waiting until the ninth to score a couple of runs.

Finally, the curtain was rung down on a troublesome month. For Mickey Mantle personally, troublesome was hardly the term. On May 6, word arrived that Mickey's father, Mutt, was dead at 40, a victim of Hodgkin's disease. His death wasn't unexpected—he had been seriously ill for months—but the pain for young Mickey was no less acute. After a few days in Oklahoma for the funeral and time with his family, Mickey was back in the Yankee lineup on May 11.

He was still the Yankee right fielder, his gimpy right knee not permitting him to assume the center-field position that was earmarked for him. Indeed, Mantle played right field in both halves of this date's twinbill, with Irv Noren in center. Mantle finished the day hitting .315—he will stay above the .300 mark most of the year—but his homer, the first in exactly one month, gave him only three on the year. His career was in limbo and his personal life in delicate transition.

MUTT MANTLE

In a sense, Mutt is the real hero of the Mickey Mantle story. He groomed Mickey for the major leagues almost from birth. He even named his offspring after a baseballer, Hall of Famer Mickey Cochrane, who was catching for the Philadelphia A's when the younger Mantle joined the family. Mutt wasn't just another frustrated athlete trying to win through his son—he wanted his son to escape the bleak life that was all the local mines could offer. Mutt *knew* that bleak life because that's the life he led.

This was the life spawned by the lead and zinc mines around Spavinaw, Picher, and Commerce, Oklahoma. All week long Mutt clawed at rock far beneath the earth's surface, and only on Sundays, when he played amateur and semipro baseball, could he really enjoy the fresh air and sunshine of the surface world. He loved baseball, and baseball gave him a chance to bask in the warm Oklahoma sun. No matter how tired he may have been, when the weekend came and Mutt had a chance to play baseball, he played baseball.

Life was forever turning against Mutt Mantle. When his own father, Charlie, fell ill with Hodgkin's disease, Mutt traded his house in Commerce for a chance to farm 160 acres along the Neosho River. Mutt wanted his father away from the mines, and for a time all went well. But torrential rains and a bloated Neosho flooded the farm and left Mutt bankrupt. Gritting his teeth, Mutt moved the family into a shack on the edge of Commerce and returned to the mines.

But Mutt wouldn't give up, either on life in general or on his dream of Mickey one day becoming a big leaguer. No sacrifice was too great. He all but matched a paycheck by laying out $22 for a glove for Mickey one Christmas (a Marty Marion model). He had baseball know-how to give to Mickey, too.

Mutt was a baseball expert and a top-notch player himself, with great speed and a fine arm (he pitched and played the outfield). He had to forsake a professional baseball career when he married young and was forced to go to work to support his bride and soon-to-be growing family.

Right from the beginning Mutt schooled Mickey on the art of hitting from both sides of the plate, working with his son countless hours on what was to become Mickey's trademark. Mutt had a way of encouraging and criticizing Mickey without being overbearing—he made practicing fun—and his love of baseball was transferred to his unprotesting son. Not only did Mickey adopt Mutt's love of the game, but he had a burning desire to please his dad, a dad he loved.

Mutt's work paid off. Young Mickey matured into a first-rate ballplayer. He had all the physical gifts. He was an exceptional athlete, great in football and basketball and in every sport he tried (except he couldn't swim a lick). The Yankees signed the 17-year-old right out of high school. The official signing completed, that long, lean, slow-talking Missourian, Yankee scout Tom Greenwade, drawled to Mutt, "I'll tell you this. You know more baseball than the father of any boy I ever signed." Casey Stengel agreed. Not entirely in jest, he was given to say that Mutt should be coaching for him.

Mickey was to learn of his father's grave illness when the pair arrived at a hospital for the repair of the knee Mickey hurt in the World Series. When Mickey climbed out of the cab and pressed his full weight on his dad's shoulder, Mutt crumpled to the ground. Mickey later took Mutt to the Mayo Clinic in Rochester, Minnesota, but nothing could be done. The cancer was too far advanced. Near the end Mutt went to a Denver hospital so his family wouldn't have to see him waste away, the final selfless act in a life of unselfishness.

The loss of Mutt reshaped Mickey's attitude toward baseball. What used to be a game was now the means by which he would support his mother, three younger brothers, a younger sister, and his new wife. Mickey was in a position where he *had* to make it.

June 15, 1952—Municipal Stadium, Cleveland. The Yankees maul Bob Lemon for six runs in the second inning of the opener on the way to an 8–2 victory in today's doubleheader sweep before 69,468. Mantle's three-run homer, his fourth of the year and his first batting left-handed, leads the assault. The homer is Mickey's only hit in nine times at bat (he also walks), dropping his average to .300. But it is a historic time for Mantle watchers—Mickey is now a fixture in center field.

And June was a lot less unmerry than the month of May for Mickey and the Yankees. The day's sweep put the now first-place Yankees' June record at 13–2, with Boston 1½ games back and Cleveland 2½ games.

A CENTER FIELDER IS BORN

The Yankees began grooming Mantle for center field the day Joe DiMaggio said he would retire. Joe made the announcement in the spring of 1951, saying he would quit after the season, and, indeed, on December 11 he made his withdrawal final. "Mantle is green, but he's fast," Stengel said. "He has a remarkable arm. He learns quickly."

But Stengel didn't know that the knee Mickey hurt in the World Series was not healing well. Mickey was unable to run effectively when he reported to spring training in 1952; in fact, he limped around camp like a kid learning to walk.

Mantle fiercely wanted to play center field, but his injury threw the job wide open. Bob Cerv and Jackie Jensen were among those waiting in the wings.

Mantle sat out the early exhibition games, then played right field for more than two weeks. Cerv was in center, and although he displayed great power at the plate, he lacked center-field speed. Mantle got a brief trial in center, but he wasn't ready yet. The knee needed more time.

It was Jensen who opened the regular season in center, with Mantle, still not running well, playing right. Stengel soon soured on Jensen, too. Casey felt Jensen's best position was right field, where he had Mantle positioned. Besides, the right-handed Jensen's long drives to left and left-center were no more than long outs in Yankee Stadium's Death Valley. Stengel decided that Jensen was expendable, and on May 3 the Yankees traded Jensen and pitcher Spec Shea to Washington for an outstanding center fielder, Irv Noren. However, Stengel quickly discovered that Noren was also suffering from knee problems and, under the circumstances, was best deployed in left field. So Mantle became the center fielder again.

But not quite yet. Mutt Mantle's death on May 6 took Mickey away from the club for five days. He played right field when he returned to the lineup, and two days later, for reasons known only to himself, Stengel had him play third base. Mickey made two errors in four chances, then spent several days pulling splinters on the bench. On May 20 he finally made his major-league debut in center field, cracked four hits, and remained in center for three games. Then it was back to the bench for three games before playing right field in the Memorial Day doubleheader, with Noren in center.

On June 3 Mantle played center field and enjoyed another four-hit game. Stengel was now convinced that Mickey's knee was strong enough for center-field duty, and Mantle became the permanent center fielder. It remained his job into the mid-1960s.

Mantle in 1952 was still a raw center fielder—a raw outfielder, period. He led all American League outfielders in errors with 14. But his defensive play was not without a bright, promising side; he also led all the league's fly chasers in turning double plays with five. Just as Mantle was given on-the-job training in outfield play in 1951, so, too, would he have to gain from experience in the playing of center field in 1952.

Mantle still had problems with liners hit straight at him but took some solace in the observation that "they're tough even for a DiMaggio." There's no way of judging how deep they are, he said, "particularly if you lose them—as you usually do—against that grandstand background." (Yankee Stadium, as Mantle's statement correctly implies, presents a bad fielding background for center fielders.)

But he managed the job to Casey Stengel's satisfaction. Young Mickey, as Casey said, "learns quickly."

July 29, 1952—Comiskey Park, Chicago. Mickey Mantle belted a grand slammer that he later described as "the most thrilling homer I ever hit in my life." The Yankees were still in first place but had dropped six of their last seven decisions in a grueling swing through the loop's western cities.

Things didn't start any better tonight, with the White Sox forging to a 7–0 lead. Sox ace Billy Pierce is working on a two-hitter as Hank Bauer leads off the Yankee seventh with a single. Mantle doubles him home and scores on a single by Gil McDougald. The rally produces another run and the score stands at 7–3 until the top of the ninth.

Right-hander Harry Dorish gives a one-out single to Gene Woodling and a walk to Yogi Berra. Johnny Mize singles home Woodling, but Kal Segrist bounces out for the second out and the Yankee threat is about to go by the boards. The third out seems imminent when Jim Brideweser sends a grounder to third baseman Hector Rodriguez, but Rodriguez boots it, allowing Berra to score and Brideweser to reach safety. The unlucky Dorish leaves and Chuck Stobbs takes the hill. Stobbs walks Joe Collins and Irv Noren, who fouls off several full-count pitches, forcing home the third run of the inning and cutting Chicago's advantage to 7–6. The bases are loaded and Stobbs is clearly having control troubles, but

Sox manager Paul Richards elects to have his southpaw work to Mantle. The crowd soon groans as Mickey rocks Stobbs's first pitch into the lower left-center-field stands. Stunningly, the Yankees are now ahead, 10–7.

As usual, the great comeback was a typical Yankee team effort, with reliever Allie Reynolds blanking the Sox in their half of the ninth. But it was Mantle's 16th homer of the campaign that had the 38,967 in attendance muttering to themselves as they solemnly filed out of the ballpark.

Mickey's slam followed by only three days his first in the big leagues. He hit one in a losing cause July 26 in Detroit. The baseball world was already speaking glowingly of this wonderboy on the edge of superstardom, many insisting he was already the American League's most exciting ballplayer. The Yankees weren't missing the retired Joe DiMaggio as much as had been expected, mostly because of Mantle's superb play. At the ripe old age of 20, Mickey Mantle was a member of his league's 1952 All-Star team, although he didn't appear in the game played earlier in the month.

August 11, 1952—Yankee Stadium. A pennant battle between the Yankees and Red Sox is cause enough for excitement in the Bronx, and 51,005 fans turned out to see Boston, winners of the series opener, and the home club go at it. They got to see a 7–0 Yankee win, Mickey Mantle's first two-homer game in the majors, both hit left-handed, and Allie Reynolds's fourth two-hitter of the season.

The third-place Red Sox trailed the front-running Yankees by only four games and had thoughts of pulling up snug. But after being denied by Reynolds and pummeled by the Mick, soon they will fade badly and finish in sixth place.

Boston's starting hurler, 37-year-old Sid Hudson, remembers Mantle's first-inning homer: "Mantle hit a low line drive, barely fair, just inside the right-field foul pole and into the lower stands."

Mantle doubled off Hudson down the right-field line in the fourth, and in the fifth, facing Ralph Brickner, he walloped a two-run homer to give the Yankees a commanding 6–0 lead.

Brickner, who had only one major season, remembers the homer: "I believe the count was one ball and no strikes and, since I was primarily a sinker-ball pitcher, we planned to pitch him low and away, throwing sinkers. I threw what I and catcher Sammy White thought was a good pitch—knee-high, off the plate, and away. The bench even thought it was an excellent pitch.

"What did Mantle do? He hit a line drive by me—head-high—and when I turned around, I saw Dom DiMaggio running back. But the ball kept rising and landed in the right-center-field bleachers. I always thought home runs were hit off pitchers' mistakes, but that was not the case this time. We were all amazed that Mantle could hit a pitch that far away from him for that distance."

September 14, 1952—Municipal Stadium, Cleveland. It was the final meeting of the year between the American League's top two teams. The Yankees (85–57) came into town with a 1 1/2-game lead over the Indians (84–59), but the Indians, winners of nine of their last ten games, had a supposed psychological edge by virtue of their momentum.

A frenzied Sunday throng of 73,609, the largest major-league crowd of the year, swarms into spacious Municipal Stadium and overflows onto the field in the area between the outfield fence and the distant center-field bleachers.

Mike Garcia, on his way to a 22-win season and currently 4–0 against the Yankees, has a string of 28 successive scoreless innings going. The Yankees' Eddie Lopat is injury-ridden but has made a career out of beating the Indians; he brings a 34–9 lifetime mark against the Tribe into the game.

With two down in the first inning, Mantle turns on his explosive speed and legs out a double. He is stranded on second, however. Then in the third, Mantle comes up with one run in and runners on the corners. He tries to score Phil Rizzuto with a two-strike bunt, but Garcia makes a nice play and nails the Scooter at the plate. Berra then delivers a two-run single, another run follows on a groundout, and New York leads, 4–0.

Lou Brissie is doing the Indian pitching when Mantle steps to the plate in the fifth. This time Mickey sends his 20th homer of the season into the crowd beyond the left-field fence, giving the Yankees a 5–0 lead. It is 5–1 when Lopat tires in the sixth. Allie Reynolds comes in and allows only one single the rest of the way, saving another win over Cleveland for Steady Eddie.

An arm-weary Early Wynn allows two more Yankee runs in the ninth for a 7–1 final score. Wynn walks Joe Collins and Mantle; Irv Noren's bouncer forces Mantle at second, and Mickey, in breaking up the potential double play, hurts his knee. He limps off the field as a worried Stengel and Yankee co-owner Dan Topping look on, and Charlie Keller, one of the greats in Yankee history, in one of his last Yankee games goes to the outfield. Lying in the locker room with an ice pack on his knee, Mickey tells the press, "I think it will be all right by Tuesday at Detroit."

Mickey will indeed be in the lineup Tuesday at Detroit.

September 17, 1952—Briggs Stadium, Detroit. Mickey Mantle put on a tremendous hitting performance. The Mick hammered three extra-base hits, two doubles, and a homer, to help the Yanks overwhelm the Tigers, 12–3, for their sixth straight win.

Mantle's four-bagger was swatted to the opposite field and yet struck just below the right-field roof. A year later, Mickey felt it was "the hardest I ever hit." Casey Stengel, impressed particularly with Mantle's opposite-field power, was still talking about this clout the following spring.

At least four Tigers still remembered the homer three and a half decades later. Outfielder Jim Delsing describes the homer as "unbelievably hard hit, like a rifle shot." It was the hardest hit ball he had ever seen at Briggs; it was for pitcher Billy Hoeft as well.

Cliff Mapes remembers a Mantle home run in Detroit, one hit right-handed against a lefty, and while he doesn't recall the exact date, it almost certainly was the blast of September 17, 1952. Mapes, a former Yankee who wore No. 7 in 1951 before Mantle assumed the number (Mickey wore No. 6 as a rookie), was a Tiger in 1952. Recalls Mapes: "The ball started out looking like a cinch double—it went about 10 feet over the head of the second baseman—and then started rising . . . the ball hit the football press box on the roof in right-center field and bounced back almost to second base. Had it not been a home run, Mickey, even with his speed, couldn't have made it to second."

The ball missed leaving the ballpark by just a foot and was still rising when it struck the football press box. Mapes says it compares with Mantle's epic shot at the University of Southern California in March 1951. Mapes witnessed that one, too.

Southpaw Bill Wight, who in 1951 served Mantle his first major-league hit, remembers: "Mickey just exploded on the ball. It was still going up when in an instant it ricocheted all the way back to our second baseman. It's a good thing he didn't hit it through the box because my wife would have been a widow!"

All in all, Mantle's remarkable blast may have been the most ferociously hit opposite-field homer in history.

September 24, 1952—Fenway Park, Boston. Fenway Park is a renowned hitter's paradise. The short distance from home plate to the left-field wall, the so-called Green Monster, makes it so. Yet, to date, Mickey Mantle has been frustrated by this quaint ballpark. Mickey in his first 17 games here batted a feeble .180 and collected only two RBIs.

Mantle turns it around with a sensational performance. In New York's sweep of a doubleheader, he hits a homer, a triple, two doubles, and a single; he scores three runs and knocks in six. Together with Johnny Sain, who wins the opener and saves the nightcap, Mantle's one-man rampage brings the Yankees close to clinching the pennant; New York's lead over Cleveland is two games, with only four games to play.

The Yankees break a scoreless tie in the sixth inning of the opener when Irv Noren and Mantle each hit two-baggers to produce a run. Then Mantle makes a great defensive play in the bottom of the sixth. Dom DiMaggio leads off with a single to center, but when he rounds first base a mite too far, Mantle fires behind DiMaggio, nipping him on his return to first base.

The Bosox fight back and tie the game at 2–2, forcing extra innings. But in the 10th, Noren and Mantle strike again when Noren doubles and scores on Mantle's triple off Dizzy Trout. Sain holds the 3–2 lead in the bottom half, although the final out, a towering fly by Clyde Vollmer with a man on base, is recorded by Noren with his back flush against the left-field wall.

Southpaw Mel Parnell presents Mantle with a unique challenge in the nightcap. Parnell has been a thorn in his side since Mickey came into the league. Mickey so far has gotten only a scratch single off him.

But Parnell can be solved by the Mick on this date. In three confrontations against Parnell, Mickey walks and scores a run, doubles and scores, and smacks a three-run home run.

Mantle's fourth-inning homer gives New York a 7–0 lead and seemingly ices the game. However, Boston battles back and Sain has to come in and put down a ninth-inning uprising, saving an 8–6 victory. Mantle's homer proved decisive.

Afterward, Mantle, cold and tired but elated, told Hy Hurwitz of the *Boston Globe*, "Until today, I thought this was going to be a jinx park. But I believe I got as many hits today as I had in all my previous games here. I think I belong now." Mantle didn't boast about catching up with Parnell, but his big day obviously jacked up his confidence. "I'm sure that I'm going to like it around here now."

The Hub has finally seen the real Mickey Mantle.

September 26, 1952—Shibe Park, Philadelphia. The Yankees ended the pennant race with an exciting 11-inning 5–2 victory over the A's; Casey Stengel joined John McGraw and Joe McCarthy as the only major-league manager to capture four league championships in a row.

Philadelphia's Harry Byrd figures to give the Yankees trouble today and does. Earlier this month, Byrd, a righty who will win the league's Rookie of the Year Award this season, pitched a one-hit shutout against New York, and only five days ago he lost a 1–0 heartbreaker to the Yanks.

Byrd makes only two mistakes today. He allows early-inning solo homers to Irv Noren and Mickey Mantle—it is Mickey's 23rd homer and the final four-bagger of the season. Gus Zernial's two-run homer in the sixth inning ties it, 2–2. When Eddie Lopat, the Yankee starter, gets in a ninth-inning jam, Johnny Sain takes over and puts out the fire.

Mantle opens the 11th with a single to right field. He is forced by Yogi Berra, but Joe Collins delivers his fourth hit of the game and Byrd hits Hank Bauer to load the bases. Then, after the second out is made, Billy Martin comes through with a two-run single. Another run follows when Sain's grounder is booted. Sain sets down the A's in the bottom half, and it's all over.

Champagne flowed at the Hotel Warwick as the Yankees celebrated. This date's win was a total team effort, and so was the garnering of the pennant that nobody thought the Yankees could win without the retired Joe DiMaggio. The key to victory was the emergence of Mantle. Not only did Mickey do a fine job in center field, where others faltered, but he swung a potent stick, batting .311, with 23 home runs, 87 RBIs, and 94 runs scored. He battled back from a serious knee injury and the trauma of his father's death. He excelled down the pennant stretch, hitting .337 in the white-knuckle days of September. He survived the dreaded sophomore jinx, actually raising his average 44 points over his rookie average.

Mantle will receive high honors this season. He will finish third in the voting for the league's Most Valuable Player (Bobby Shantz won), and *The Sporting News*, in selecting its annual Major League All-Star team, will pick an outfield consisting of Stan Musial, Hank Sauer, and Mantle. Not bad for a lightly experienced 20-year-old.

But for the moment, Mickey and the Yankees had a World Series date with the Brooklyn Dodgers.

October 6, 1952—Ebbets Field, Brooklyn. The World Series was moving along nicely for the Brooklyn Dodgers. The Bums had a three-games-to-two lead, and the sixth, and, if necessary, seventh games were scheduled for Ebbets Field, where the Dodgers rarely lost. If the Yankees were to force a Game 7 showdown, however, they had to prevail in this date's do-or-die Game 6.

The Yankees' veteran Vic Raschi, a fierce competitor, and the Dodgers' Billy Loes, a brash bonus kid not too many years removed from Bryant High School in Queens, are the starters. Both are impressive in the early innings. Then Duke Snider hits a sixth-inning solo homer for the Dodgers.

But New York jumps ahead, 2–1, in the seventh, Raschi smashing a single off the pitcher's knee (Loes will say the ball was "lost in the sun"), scoring the go-ahead tally.

Mickey Mantle leads off the eighth. He's having an excellent series with seven hits, including a 450-foot triple at Yankee Stadium, but he has yet to belt one over the fence. The Mick connects. His left-handed drive falls deep in the lower left-center-field stands and puts the Yankees ahead, 3–1.

Mantle's first World Series homer proves to be the winning run. Snider hits another homer in the last of the eighth. But Allie Reynolds records the final four outs, making New York's 3–2 lead stand.

In a story he wrote for the United Press, Mantle stated, "Billy Loes threw me a fastball a little bit above the waist. I think it was a fastball. Half the time I don't know what I hit."

Immediately after the game, there is disagreement among the battery about what pitch was actually thrown, according to Roscoe McGowen of the *New York Times*. Loes, an interesting guy quick with a good quote, speaks in awe of Mantle's homer and says the ball was inside and Mantle was falling away when he hit it. "Where would he have put it if he had really been taking his cut at it?" asks Billy. "It would have gone over the roof—or something." Catcher Roy Campanella, who still gives Loes high marks for his effort, disagrees; Campy insists the pitch to Mantle was "about belt-high and over the plate."

Casey Stengel was worried about finding a starting pitcher for Game 7. He had no choice but to use Reynolds in Game 6. "If I'd held him off for tomorrow, there might never have been a tomorrow," was Casey's snapped explanation. "What would I have been savin' him for then—the junior prom?" Stengel also said this of his dilemma: "I don't think I'll use Reynolds. Don't think I can. I won't say it'll be Lopat. I just don't know who it will be. I'll have to think about it overnight."

Casey could thank Mantle for the chance to make such a decision.

October 7, 1952—Ebbets Field, Brooklyn. Baseball offers no more exciting scene than an exciting seventh game of a World Series. And this Game 7 was a dandy.

Stengel finally decided to start Eddie Lopat, but before it was over, Casey also waved in Allie Reynolds, Vic Raschi, and Bob Kuzava. Brooklyn manager Chuck Dressen put all his hopes on Joe Black, his 28-year-old rookie sensation. Black was a superreliever in 1952 (15–4, 2.15 ERA, 15 saves), but he was a starter in only two of the 56 games in which he pitched. Dressen was asking a lot of him; Black was much used in the series and was being called on again only three days after pitching seven innings.

Thanks to Johnny Mize's RBI-single and Gene Woodling's home run, New York stays even, 2–2, as the late innings approach.

Phil Rizzuto opens the sixth with a screaming line drive that shortstop Pee Wee Reese turns into an out with a great diving catch. Now left-handed Mickey Mantle, who has fanned and grounded out, braces at the plate. Black delivers something hard, perhaps a fastball, maybe a slider—Mickey says later it was a slider—and Mickey lets go, launching the ball over the right-field scoreboard and to the far side of Bedford Avenue. The towering homer, which covers some 450 feet, gives the Yankees a 3–2 lead.

Mantle makes it 4–2 in the seventh with a solid RBI-single to center against Preacher Roe. Then Mickey's buddy, second baseman Billy Martin, saves the game with a sprinting, lunging grab of Jackie Robinson's windblown pop-up near the mound. Martin's alert play is a big one, coming as it does with a 3-and-2 count, two out, and the bases loaded. Had Billy not made the catch—and since no one else was moving on the ball no one else could have—three runs probably would have scored.

Kuzava throttles Brooklyn over the final two innings, and the Yankees have their fourth World Championship in a row, tying the record set by the 1936–39 Yankees. The end came with the big clock above the scoreboard showing 3:55 and the Borough of Brooklyn going into mourning.

In the locker room Mantle was the center of attention. "I don't know just what to say. I'm overjoyed, of course. It's great to be part of this. Believe me, things like this you never forget," Mickey said, and added that he was anxious to return home to Oklahoma, where he expected to spend the winter working in the mines.

Stengel called Mantle, still 13 days shy of his 21st birthday, "the outstanding player of the series." Mickey earned the respect of the Dodgers, too. "Mantle beat us," said Jackie Robinson. "He was the difference between the two clubs. They didn't miss Joe DiMaggio. It was Mickey Mantle who killed us."

Mantle had come through with the clutch hits in the final two games and batted .345 overall. He paced the Yankees with 10 hits, and he tied Gil McDougald for the Yankee lead in runs scored with five.

As promised, Mantle rushed home to Commerce, Oklahoma, where he received a hero's welcome, a sort of a small-town version of a ticker-tape parade. He was a national celebrity, really, a hero everywhere. Everywhere except in Brooklyn.

1953

April 9, 1953—Forbes Field, Pittsburgh. Mantle in warming up for the 1953 season graced Pittsburgh with a memorable dinger, becoming only the third hitter to take one over the right-field roof since the double-deck stands were added to venerable Forbes Field in 1925.

Mantle is up against Bill Macdonald, who went 8–10 with the Pirates in 1950, his only full season in the majors. Macdonald slips a slow curveball past him. "I'd like to see him throw that again," Eddie Lopat tells Allie Reynolds on the bench.

Macdonald tries the same pitch. Mantle crunches it. The ball leaves the playing field some 360 feet from home plate, traveling at an altitude of 100 feet or so as it clears the roof.

One of the two previous roof-clearing homers—all were hit from the left side of the plate—was hit by Babe Ruth. It was the Babe's 714th and final homer, capping a three-homer game he had while finishing up his career with the Boston Braves in 1935.

The other was hit by Pittsburgh's Ted Beard in 1950, one of only six homers he hit in seven big-league seasons. Ruth and Mantle were powerful ballplayers, and Beard may have been strong, too, but he was goatee-sized at 5' 8" and 165 lbs.

Chester L. Smith of the *Pittsburgh Press* reported that "Mickey's was the longest ball ever whacked into the valley behind Forbes Field."

Mantle in his 1985 autobiography, *The Mick*, takes pride in his roof-clearing Pittsburgh shot. "But let's be honest," he writes. "The greater accomplishment was getting to Forbes Field in the first place."

Following an exhibition game the previous day in Cincinnati, Mantle, Whitey Ford, and Billy Martin coveted nearby Covington, Kentucky, and crossed the Ohio River to experience its charms. They wound up missing their train and decided to fly to Pittsburgh the next morning. But no planes were flying the next day because of a snowstorm, so the fun-loving threesome took a $500 taxi ride to Pittsburgh. They arrived late at Forbes Field and missed batting practice, but they hit

27

Casey Stengel's I'm-pissed-off target. Mantle and Martin would play the entire game, vowed Stengel.

So Mantle was not in the best of shape when he unloaded his mighty clout. Babe Ruth, that notorious night owl, would have been proud, but all Casey could muster was "Nice hit, Mickey."

With the scheduled start of the regular season only four days away, Mantle appeared ready. He had an excellent spring with a .412 average, and his Pittsburgh four-bagger, his fourth of the exhibition season, was a precursor of some serious long-ball hitting over the campaign ahead.

April 17, 1953—Griffith Stadium, Washington, D.C. Four games into the season and five days after the birth of Mickey Elven Mantle, the Mick's first son, the Yankees are in Washington and it is the top of the fifth and Chuck Stobbs, the Senator southpaw, retires the first two Yankees, then walks Yogi Berra. Up steps Mantle, whom Stobbs knows all too well, having the previous season served a game-winning grand slammer to the Oklahoman. But he is about to become a victim of a more historic moment. Playing in spite of a charley horse in his left leg, Mantle will usher in the age of the tape measure.

Stobbs delivers a medium-high fastball over the heart of the plate. Mantle, batting right-handed, makes perfect contact. The ball soars and leaves the playing field in left-center at the 391-foot mark, still climbing. It caroms off a 60-foot-high beer sign on the football scoreboard perched atop the last row of bleachers. It eludes the view of the spectators and sails over Fifth Street, coming to rest finally in the backyard of 434 Oakdale Street, several houses removed from Fifth Street.

Some home run! "I shall never forget it as long as I live," says Bill Renna, a 1953 Yankee. A small Griffith Stadium crowd breaks into wild cheers as Mantle circles the bases; silence reigns inside the Yankee dugout as head-shaking players look at one another in utter disbelief.

One eyewitness springs to action. "That one's got to be measured," he says. Arthur "Red" Patterson, the Yankees' publicity director, forsakes the game and bolts from the press box in pursuit of the real story, and he knows a thing or two about real stories, having been a leading sportswriter for the *New York Herald-Tribune* before joining the Yankees several years earlier.

Outside the ballpark, Red finds 10-year-old Donald Dunaway. He examines the ball Donald holds and has the boy take him to the spot where he found it. Then, in exchange for a few favors, the ball is Red's.

Patterson paces off the distance from the landing spot to the ballpark's outer bleacher wall—no tape is used—and arrives at 105 feet. Using the Griffith Stadium dimensions of 391 feet from home plate to the left-center-field fence and an additional 69 feet to the rear wall of the bleachers, he adds the total inside-the-park distance of 460 feet to the outside-the-park distance of 105 feet and finds that Mantle's home run traveled 565 feet!

The 565-foot measurement was accepted by the public. However, Patterson's sportswriting buddy, Joe Trimble, elected not to allow for the three-foot-thick rear wall in figuring the distance (the posted distance from plate to wall was actually 457 feet) and his reports said the homer traveled 562 feet. Whatever the exact length, Mantle's ball was the first to fly over Griffith's left-field bleachers, and the epic clout captured the imagination of the baseball world.

Some were quick to ascribe much of the credit to a favorable wind. The *New York Times* and the *Washington Star* reported that a strong wind was blowing out.

Clark Griffith, the Senators' owner and a baseball pioneer who had seen it all in his 83 years, told the *Star*, "Wind or no wind, nobody ever hit a ball that hard here before."

Looking back on the epic moment, Charlie Silvera, Berra's backup catcher, remembers "some wind," then adds, "But believe me, there was not that much help the way that ball was hit." And while the wind may have helped, the beer sign may have hurt. Les Peden, the Washington catcher, is not alone in believing that Mantle's homer would have gone appreciably farther if it hadn't struck the sign.

Mantle had fired warning shots in batting practice, putting on "an electrifying show," in the words of Louis Effrat of the *Times*. He sent many shots deep into the left-field bleachers. Eddie Lopat, the winning pitcher in the tape-measure game, recalls that one of Mantle's batting-practice drives cleared the bleachers and banged against the scoreboard.

The next day, the Yankees were rained out in Philadelphia, and Stengel used the free time to boast about his prodigy. He rated Mantle as a right-handed power hitter with Jimmie Foxx and said that only Babe Ruth and Lou Gehrig could be compared with Mickey's left-handed power. "And what's more," Casey added, "he's becoming a really good hitter. For the averages, I mean. He has learned to hit breaking stuff, screwballs, knucklers, and sliders."

Mantle's long homer was talked about for days and it is still talked about. It is the standard. Contemporary long shots are always compared with it. These are the Washington Wallop facts.

BAT AND BALL: Mickey's bat was borrowed from Loren Babe, who was with the Yankees only briefly. The ball retrieved by Red Patterson was a battered pellet, knocked lopsided by Mantle's blow and scuffed by the beer sign. Mickey almost literally knocked the cover off the ball.

Patterson wanted to give the ball to Mantle, but Mickey didn't know what to do with it. "If I send the ball home, I know what will happen to it," Mickey joked. "My twin brothers will take it out on the lot, like any 20-cent rocket."

The Yankees took the ball off Mickey's hands and displayed it along with Loren Babe's bat in a trophy case at Yankee Stadium. A few days later, both ball and bat were stolen, but the culprits brought them back after Patterson made a public plea for their return. Following the 1953 campaign, the sacred mementos were turned over to the Baseball Hall of Fame.

THE LEADER OF THE OPPOSITION: Washington manager Bucky Harris was as impressed as anyone who witnessed Mantle's homer. "I just wouldn't have believed a ball could be hit that hard," the dazed Harris said after the game, forgetting for a moment that his team had lost the game, 7–3. "I've never seen anything like it."

But once Harris regained his senses, he became annoyed that Mantle had picked his club to make history against. The Senators, marking the spot where Mantle's homer grazed the beer sign on its way out of the ballpark, had put up a huge baseball as a monument, and for a couple of weeks old Bucky couldn't keep his eyes from roaming toward the landmark. Every time he saw that huge baseball, he was reminded of Mantle and what he had done to his club. Finally, fed up, Harris ordered the baseball painted out.

GRIFFITH STADIUM: Mantle would hit 29 homers at Griffith, but his 565-footer happened to be his first there. This was no easy task because Griffith Stadium was a brutal park for right-handed power hitters; it was more than 400 feet between home plate and most sections of the bleachers running from the left-field line to center. New York sportscaster Warner Wolfe, a native Washingtonian, wrote in his book, *Gimme A Break!*, that "you could go to five straight games and never see a home run into the left field stands." In 1945 you could go to every Senators home game and see only one home-team homer, and that was Joe Kuhel's inside-the-parker.

The 32 rows of left-field bleachers were built in 1924, and for 29 years no one cleared them on a fly, not until Mantle's drive off Stobbs. Joe DiMaggio in 1948 hit a homer that landed two-thirds up the bleachers and bounced out of the ballpark. Reportedly, Harry Heilmann also bounced one out (but lost the homer because he was batting out of turn). Jimmie Foxx in 1938 parked one several rows from the top of the bleachers, and Larry Doby hit a couple up there, too.

Until Griffith Stadium shut down following the 1961 season, Mantle remained the only man to clear the left-field bleachers under game conditions. And right-handed hitters with tremendous strength, men like Foxx, Harmon Killebrew, and Josh Gibson, the great star of the Negro Leagues, all played there.

USHERING IN THE TAPE: The myth says that after Mantle's Washington blast, Red Patterson came armed with a tape measure to every Yankee game. Red liked the concept of measurement but was no metrologist. His storied tape measure simply didn't exist; he paced off home runs. Actually, Red, who left the Yankees in 1954 and went on to great heights in baseball on the West Coast, personally paced off only two Mantle home runs—the one in Washington and a later monster in St. Louis.

But Patterson started the phenomenon known as the tape-measure home run. "Tape-measure job" became part of the baseball vocabulary. Mantle was the greatest practitioner, and for Mickey, any home run traveling in excess of 400 feet was considered a tape-measure job. There was a rush of tape-measure jobs in April 1953, capped by a 475-foot drive by Joe Adcock that was the first home run ever hit into the center-field bleachers at the Polo Grounds in a regular-season game.

LONGEST HOME RUNS: The measurement of Mantle's 565-footer sparked a debate. Was it really the longest in baseball history? No official records have ever been kept on home-run length, but Mickey's 565-footer is "the longest measured home run in a regular-season major league game," according to the 1985 edition of the *Guinness Book of World Records*. *Guinness* cites a 587-footer Babe Ruth hit in a 1919 exhibition game, but makes no mention of a 602-footer Ruth reputedly hit in Detroit in 1926. Immediately following Mantle's 565-footer, however, the Associated

Press reported that this was the second longest homer on record, that Ruth was still the all-time king for distance. (The AP did credit Mantle with the longest right-handed homer, beating by five feet Ralph Kiner's big hit in Pittsburgh in 1950.)

Apparently there is some doubt about the accuracy of the measurement of Ruth's homer in 1926, although H. G. Salsinger, then the sports editor of the *Detroit News*, obtained an affidavit from several witnesses stating that Ruth's homer traveled over 600 feet. But Dan Daniel for one, disputed the distance. "I was there when Ruth hit that homer. The ball went over the fence and was picked up by a kid who rode off with it on his bicycle. No one could figure where it landed," the veteran sportswriter for the *New York World-Telegram and Sun* was once quoted as saying. Daniel wrote in an article in the 1964 *Street and Smith Baseball Yearbook*: "I saw Ruth hit many a powerful and incredibly long ball but he never belted one like that [Washington] wallop of Mickey's."

MANTLE'S REACTION: Some felt the big blast did Mickey more harm than good. That is, Mickey was saddled with the fans' rising expectations. He was now supposed to routinely swat 500-foot home runs. Was the Mick similarly infected? Was he swinging the bat harder than ever?

Mantle did, to be sure, hit some unbelievable drives in 1953—it might have been his most awesome long-ball year—and he did drop 16 points below his 1952 batting average, indications he may have been swinging from the heels. But he wasn't lusting; he was patient, with fewer strikeouts and more walks on the year than his 1952 numbers. He was hurt a lot, too, and this was a major complicator in trying to "read" his performance following the fabulous launching.

THE STOBBS REACTION: Chuck Stobbs wasn't exactly giddy about being the pitcher that allowed Mantle's most famous tape-measure homer. And the taunting melody lingered on. Fifteen years later Morris Siegel in the *Washington Star* described how Stobbs was still haunted by the gopher ball he served to Mantle. Here was a good pitcher, winner of 107 games, mostly with poor clubs, and here were the fans remembering only that Stobbs was the carpenter who built the Mick's launching platform.

Stobbs was sick and tired of being told, "Boy, I'll never forget that home run Mickey Mantle got off you in Griffith Stadium. Will you ever forget it?" How the hell could he? "They expect me to be thrilled about it," Stobbs said of the fans. "To me it was and still is just another home run. Lots of guys hit home runs off me, even Joe DeMaestri one time. Am I supposed to get a bang out of that one, too?"

It seemed Stobbs was reminded of the homer just about every time he left his Maryland home in the suburbs of Washington. Stobbs was selling life insurance in 1968 when he talked with Siegel, and he figured the Mantle homer helped him sell a few policies. But he wanted his 15-year big-league career to be remembered for more than the Mantle homer. "You know," he said, "Mickey didn't get a hit every time he faced me. I got him out a few times, too."

Even Stobbs's wife, Jocelyn, got into the act. "Happy anniversary," she chirped at breakfast one morning. Baffled, Chuck asked what she meant. Mrs. Stobbs swung an imaginary bat and with her hand above her eyes followed the cruelly endless flight of an imaginary ball. "Oh, that thing," muttered Chuck. "Is it another year already?"

April 28, 1953—Busch Stadium, St. Louis. Nineteen days after socking a ball out of Forbes Field and 11 days after clearing everything at Griffith Stadium, Mickey Mantle conquered still another major-league ballpark, driving one completely out of Busch Stadium. (Anheuser-Busch, Inc., purchasers of the St. Louis ballpark, changed the name from Sportsman's Park to Busch Stadium before the 1953 season. They were dissuaded from renaming it Budweiser Stadium.)

St. Louis starter Bob Cain, having already given up a two-run homer to Hank Bauer, flirts with danger in the third inning by walking Vic Raschi and Bauer. With two outs, Mantle, batting right-handed, rips into a Cain pitch—"a bad low pitch," Cain related years later—and Mickey golfs a shot over the back wall in left field. The ball clears the street, lands against a second-floor porch, bounces into a yard on Sullivan Avenue, and gives New York a 5–0 advantage.

Red Patterson years later recalled measuring a Mantle homer in St. Louis, and it is likely this was the one. Red and sportswriter Joe Trimble walked to a nearby house where porch sitters pointed out the ball. Red paced off the distance and 30-some years later will remember its being another long one. He can't recall the exact numbers but remembers it wasn't quite as long as the 565-footer in Washington.

Louis Effrat of the *New York Times* reported that the homer was measured at 494 feet, and Dent McSkimming of the *St. Louis Post-Dispatch* wrote that Browns general manager Rudie Schaffer announced the length as 493 feet. Both distances were to the base of the building that the ball struck, and the ball hit 15 to 18 feet above ground level. Unimpeded, the ball would have gone well over 500 feet.

This home run is sometimes overlooked in recollections of Mantle's tape-measure collection, partly because the one in Washington received so much publicity. What may well have also overshadowed the Mantle shot was an exciting game and one of the most vicious baseball brawls in history.

The Yankees cruise along after Mantle's homer and take a 6–0 lead in the fifth, when Mickey doubles and scores on a Yogi Berra single. But Vic Raschi can't hold the lead and the Brownies tie the score, 6–6. St. Louis actually threatens to capture the game outright in the ninth, loading the bases with only one out, but Allie Reynolds struts in from the bullpen and strikes out Roy Sievers and Bob Elliott, sending the game into extra innings. Then all hell breaks loose.

The 10th inning is one of the wildest on record. With one out and two on, Reynolds taps to pitcher Harry Brecheen, who wheels and fires to Billy Hunter at second base for a force-out. Meanwhile, Gil McDougald attempts to score from second, but Hunter sees him, and his throw home has McDougald by a mile. Gil has only one option and he makes the play perfectly, barreling over Clint "Scrap Iron" Courtney at the plate, jarring the catcher so hard that both the ball and Courtney's glasses are knocked loose. McDougald is safe, and New York leads, 7–6.

Courtney leads off the Browns' 10th. "Scraps was the meanest man I ever met," Satchel Paige once said. "I'm glad I was on his side." The ex-Yankee hates his former club for trading him and is smoking over the McDougald play. "Someone is going to pay," he tells Yogi Berra at the plate. Courtney strokes a shot off the right-field screen that Bauer handles quickly, and with little chance for a double, Courtney, with spikes flying high, slides into diminutive Phil Rizzuto at second base. The Scooter accepts Bauer's perfect peg, slaps the tag on Courtney, and then limps away with two spike wounds.

Several angry Yankees pummel Courtney. The Browns' bench empties and fights erupt all around second base. Umpire John Stevens dislocates his collarbone attempting to restore order. Finally, after relative calm is gained, an effort is made to play ball. But left fielder Gene Woodling is showered with so many bottles thrown from the unruly crowd of 13,463 that several times he makes his way to the infield and demands some kind of protection. With the threat of forfeiture staring him in the face, Browns manager Marty Marion journeys to the bleachers and obtains an armistice.

Play resumes, Reynolds records the final two outs, and the Yankees are 7–6 winners. Many Yankees arm themselves with bats as they leave the field—a brave Marion and other Browns escort them—as bottles rain down.

The whole ugly mess reminds old-timers of the 1922 incident here when Yankee center fielder Whitey Witt was skulled by a bottle thrown from an equally hostile mob. Apparently bottle throwing at Yankee targets is a practiced art on the banks of the mighty Mississippi.

Outside, police disperse those waiting for the Yankees to board their team bus. Meanwhile, the umpires explain why they didn't eject any players from the game—there were simply too many offenders to single anyone out. Umpire Bill Summers: "There was more fist swinging in that mob than I had ever seen in 20 years of umpiring." The league eventually fined Courtney $250 and levied smaller fines on Hunter of the Browns and on Yankees Billy Martin, Joe Collins, Reynolds, and McDougald.

Mantle never brawled as a Yankee ballplayer. Neither did Joe DiMaggio. Lou Gehrig probably didn't either. All these guys did their battling with their bats and gloves. Mantle would not even be implicated, though he was in attendance, in the famous 1957 Copacabana fracas. Mickey had many occasions to be upset when pitchers aimed well-chosen fastballs at his gimpy legs. However, most of Mickey's anger was self-directed. Lucky for the opposition.

Once, in a 1963 brawl at Yankee Stadium in which Joe Pepitone was a lead actor, Mantle took a shove at an Indian player and set off a chain reaction that saw a dozen or so players bite the dust. It was a rare display of aggression on Mantle's part; he was fiercely competitive, yes, but he was not a brawler. He was usually a peacemaker.

It is easy to see why Mantle's 500-foot-plus home run was obscured by other events. But the next day Marty Marion's focus was on Mantle: "I'd say that Mantle today is the greatest player in either league." The Browns manager talked about Mantle's speed rounding first base and his power—so much more than Stan Musial's, said the former teammate of Stan the Man.

But hadn't Mantle a weakness? "Let's see—uh, yes," replied Marty. "There's one thing he can't do very well. He can't throw left-handed. When he goes in for that we'll have the perfect ballplayer."

June 11, 1953—Briggs Stadium, Detroit. With a 6–3 win, the Yankees extended their winning streak to 14 games. While the fine pitching of Jim McDonald and Allie Reynolds and the home-run exploits of Irv Noren and Gene Woodling figured importantly, Mickey Mantle stole the show.

Mantle in the seventh inning, batting left-handed against Art Houtteman, rocketed a shot that crowns the roof in right-center. Only Ted Williams had ever cleared the roof, but the *Detroit Free Press* reported that Mantle's homer would have carried into the next block had the roof been a little lower. Some insist that the ball struck a light tower, maybe the same tower Reggie Jackson hit with his legendary wallop in the 1971 All-Star Game.

The four-bagger extended Mantle's hitting streak to 16 games. He was hitting .571 (16 for 28) this year against the Tigers, and the Yankees were cruising along with a 37–11 record, operating with the biggest league lead of Casey Stengel's Yankee regime, a 6½-game bulge over Cleveland. Mickey was playing the best ball in the game. But things would soon change. Mickey's son is rushed to the hospital with a stomach disorder. Little Mickey is okay, but his dad's performance is about to plummet.

But for the moment, and for a laurel that had not been won since 1947, when Ted Williams achieved the accomplishment, the American League had a legitimate contender for the Triple Crown. Mickey Mantle on June 11 led the league in batting (.353) and RBIs (44) and ranked third in homers (9). He was six homers shy of league-leader Gus Zernial, but there was little doubt that Mickey could catch him.

His 16-game hitting streak would end the next day and soon thereafter the wheels would come off the Mantle wagon. First, Mickey pulled a thigh muscle in his left leg and missed six games. When he returned to the lineup, too quickly perhaps, he aggravated his bothersome right knee, the one he had hurt in the 1951 World Series.

Mantle played through the pain, but his Triple Crown chances were gone. In a big series against Chicago in early August, he would tear ligaments in his right knee in planting his foot while throwing. The tender knee buckled under him and for the rest of the year Mickey would wear a bulky knee brace and would never be completely healthy. In November, a piece of torn cartilage would be removed from the damaged knee.

Mantle's final statistics for 1953 would be disappointing, what with the expectations his June 11 numbers aroused, but considering his injuries, it was a wonder Mickey finished the campaign at all. He would miss 24 games, and when he played, he would not play like a healthy Mickey Mantle. Mantle would hit only .255 after June 11. His Triple Crown totals—.295, 21 home runs, and 92 RBIs—would all be lower than the stats he posted in 1952.

July 6, 1953—Connie Mack Stadium, Philadelphia. The Yankees' road to success was not without its potholes. They found themselves losers in 11 out of their last 15 games as they prepared for a twi-night doubleheader in the park formerly called Shibe. Mantle, whose last homer was on June 23, missed the last six contests because of the pulled thigh muscle, and he was not in the lineup. Irv Noren would play center field.

Thanks mainly to a pair of two-run homers by Billy Martin and Phil Rizzuto, New York scores five runs in the fourth inning of the opener, only to watch the A's rally and close to within 5–4. Casey Stengel squirms uneasily in the Yankee dugout; he knows his team's slide must be halted soon. Now, if possible.

Frank Fanovich, a native of New York City who would join the city's police department after a brief fling in the bigs, was on the mound in relief for the A's. He walks Martin, Rizzuto, and Johnny Sain, loading the bases with one out in the sixth.

It is Noren's turn to bat. But Irv is a left-handed hitter and Fanovich throws left-handed. Stengel plays the percentages and has the switch-hitting Mantle bat for Noren; Mickey steps into the right-handed hitter's box. Fanovich is in a bad jam, and with his control deserting him, he has no choice but to groove his first pitch to Mickey. The ball comes down the middle of the plate, thigh-high, and the next moment soars over the double-deck stands in left-center field, clearing the roof by at least 25 feet according to the Associated Press. The ball probably cleared Somerset Street, where Jimmie Foxx once parked them, but the landing spot was not determined—in fact, the ball would not be found.

Joe DeMaestri, the A's shortstop that day, recalls it was "the hardest ball" he ever saw Mantle hit. He leaped for the ball as it whistled overhead, then watched in surprise and shock as the ball left the park. Both the *New York Times* and the *Philadelphia Inquirer* described the homer as a 500-footer, one of the longest in Philly history. It was Mantle's third career grand slam—and the only grand slam he would hit in a pinch-hitting role. Of more immediate relish to Stengel—and to Mantle—was that it broke open the game and allowed Sain to coast to a

10–5 triumph. This was one long ball Stengel was willing to accept; just the previous week Casey publicly criticized Mickey for going for tape-measure jobs rather than base hits.

Mantle remained in the game and, in spite of his sore thigh, later beat out an infield hit. He sat out the nightcap (returning to the lineup the next day) but he had picked up the club. The Yankees won the second game, too, and would strengthen their hold on first place by going 6 for 8 before the All-Star Break.

The American League had announced the names of its starting eight All-Stars the day before the Philly doubleheader. Among the fans' selections: catcher Yogi Berra, right fielder Hank Bauer, and, of course, Mantle in center. In his first All-Star start, Mickey would go 0 for 2 in a losing cause in Cincinnati.

August 7, 1953—Yankee Stadium. A Mantle homer on this day wasn't close to being another tape-measure job. It didn't even clear the fence, but it was one of the year's most important hits.

The streaking Chicago White Sox invade Yankee Stadium to open a critical four-game series. The second-place White Sox, five games back and the only team within reaching distance of the Yankees, are convinced New York is running scared. Adding fuel to the fire of a bitter rivalry, Chicago manager Paul Richards, whose team has beaten the Yankees nine straight games at Yankee Stadium, announces that he knows a Yankee weakness—he knows how to beat the mighty Yankees. Never mind the Yankees, Casey Stengel says. "If he's so smart, why can't he beat the Philadelphia A's?" Ah, Casey.

Richards gives the starting assignment to right-hander Connie Johnson, who blanked Washington in his only previous start and who takes a 1–0 lead into the bottom of the third inning. Eddie Lopat singles and Joe Collins walks, with one out. Mantle pokes a low liner into left-center that skips past Minnie Minoso. As the ball rolls to the distant wall, first Lopat, then Collins, and finally Mantle, turning on his great speed, cross the plate. Yogi Berra follows the inside-the-parker with another homer, knocking out Johnson, and Billy Martin later adds still another dinger. Lopat hurls seven strong innings, and when his arm stiffens, Allie Reynolds finishes. Everyone does well in the 6–1 win, but the key hit is Mantle's.

The next day Whitey Ford and Bob Kuzava tamed the White Sox with twin shutouts, and the Chicagoans' threat was repulsed. (Chicago would finish third, 11½ games behind New York.) But it was also the day on which Mantle wrenched his right knee. He would sit it out for 10 days and then limp through the rest of the season. He would drive in only 14 more runs the rest of the way.

September 7, 1953—Fenway Park, Boston. On the surface, the doubleheader seemed routine. As if to underscore appearances, the Yanks and Red Sox split. No big sweat for the Yankees, who enjoyed a nine-game lead over Cleveland. But behind the appearances lay a drama, and behind the drama a certain historic animosity.

Nowhere are the Yankees more hated than in Boston. The Red Sox had ruled the American League before the Yankees assumed dominance in the 1920s. That's when the Yankee Dynasty was established through the purchase of a steady stream of excellent players, Red Sox players, among them Babe Ruth. The Rape of the Red Sox, they called it, and Beantowners never forgave the financially strapped Red Sox owner, Harry Frazee, for his talent peddling. Resentment in Boston grew with each new pennant hoisted at Yankee Stadium.

A rabid Red Sox fan had fired off a letter to the Mick in late August. Postmarked "Boston" and received by the Yankee front office, the typewritten letter read in part: "Don't show your face in Boston again or your baseball career will come to an end with a 32.

"Remember I make almost every RED SOX and cheater Yankees game and I'll be sure to be there September 7. I've got a good gang that don't like the Yankees and you'll find out if you play September 7.

"This ain't no joke if you think it is."

The letter was signed, "Yours untruly, a loyal Red Sox fan." Included in a PS were more threats, concluding with this warning to Mickey: "It would be better if you didn't bring your damned team to Boston."

The Boston authorities were notified of the letter. As the train carrying the Yankees neared Boston—the Yanks were in Boston for just the day—two detectives boarded and informed Mantle that they were his bodyguards for the day. They suggested that Mickey not play in Boston, but Mickey wouldn't listen.

The detectives sat behind the Yankee dugout at the doubleheader, and security was beefed up around Fenway Park. There were no incidents, luckily, the threat apparently an empty one. But imagine how Mickey must have felt playing every second of the twinbill.

Mantle was 2 for 7 that afternoon. One of his hits guaranteed that Mel Parnell, who finished 21–8 in 1953, would not blank the Yankees for the third straight time. It sailed over the Green Monster—and Mantle raced around the bases.

September 12, 1953—Yankee Stadium. Mickey hit one of the longest homers in Yankee Stadium history. He has now, in this one short season, astounded ballpark gatherings in Pittsburgh, Washington, St. Louis, Detroit, Philadelphia and New York with his epic home runs.

Leading only 4–3, the Yankees get eight runs in the seventh inning and go on to beat Detroit, 13–4. The big rally's explosive element is Mantle's 20th homer of the season, with two aboard. Mickey, who earlier had hit a towering 420-foot out to left center, is batting right-handed against Billy Hoeft, a good pitcher destined to surrender several Mantle tape-measure homers. Mickey works the count to three and two and then cracks a smoking line drive that is still rising when it arrives high in the left-field upper deck. The ball smashes a seat and rebounds back onto the playing field. Hoeft departs.

Jim McDonald was the winning pitcher. Years later he recalled sitting on the bench listening to coach Bill Dickey say that Babe Ruth and Jimmie Foxx hit balls farther than Mantle. A moment later came Mantle's herculean wallop. Eddie Lopat: "What did you just say, Bill?" Dickey, totally amazed: "I've never seen a ball hit that hard. Forget what I said!"

Observers who saw both Mantle's 565-footer in Washington and the Yankee Stadium drive compared the latter favorably. McDonald, among others, felt this homer was hit harder; this was a rising liner, while the one in Washington was a towering drive. While in awe of the Washington homer, McDonald still had to vote the Stadium shot as the more awesome.

Joseph M. Sheehan pointed out in the *New York Times* that the left-field upper deck at Yankee Stadium had been reached by others, most notably by Foxx in the 1930s, again by Tiger pitcher Zeb Eaton in 1945, and most recently by Walt Dropo this past June 21. But as far as anyone could recall, Mantle's blast was the most ''eye-catching'' hit into this region of seats. Mantle in his career would hit three more homers into the left-field upper deck, but the drive off Hoeft would remain, well, the most eye-catching.

Jim Regan of the Stadium maintenance crew took careful measurements and found that the ball, which struck a seat about six rows above the aisle separating the general-admission section and the box seats, carried 425 feet to the seats, which was 80 feet above ground level. How far would the ball have traveled if unimpeded by the upper deck? 550 feet? 600? 650?

Some observers believed the ball would have actually left Yankee Stadium if only Mantle had hit it a little more toward the bullpen area, just to the right of the grandstand. Casey Stengel was one of these believers.

In a conversation at Yankee Stadium with sportswriter Arthur Daley sometime later, Casey spoke of Mantle's power: "See that last exit in the upper deck in left field. Look. Way up there almost over the bullpen. They say that nobody ever hit one outta the Yankee Stadium. But if the stands didn't get in the way Mantle's would have gone over the wall because it was still climbin' when it smacked the seats."

October 1, 1953—Yankee Stadium. Yesterday's World Series opener, won by the Yanks, wasn't particularly memorable, at least not for the followers of Mickey Mantle. Mickey managed just a single. But a new, sizzling-hot day beckoned for Mantle *and* the Brooklyn Dodgers, and a crowd of 66,786 jammed into Yankee Stadium for Game 2 of a great New York spectacle, a Subway Series.

The Dodgers were fielding what many considered their greatest team ever. Their record was 105–49, and that of the Yankees, 99–52. Three batsmen—Roy Campanella, Duke Snider, and Gil Hodges—all hit more than 30 homers and drove in upwards of 120 runs. Carl Furillo was the batting champ, hitting .344, and Jackie Robinson hit .329. The Dodgers as a team hit higher (.285), cracked more home runs (208), scored more runs (955), and stole more bases (90) than any club in their circuit. The Bums and their fans expected to blast their way past the Yankees, to beat the Bombers at their own game.

Game 2 embodies an interesting confrontation between a pair of veteran left-handers, the Yankees' Eddie Lopat and Preacher Roe, a pair of crafty junkmen. Both go all the way in sterling performances, pitching "more with their brains than their arms," noted the *New York Times'* Arthur Daley.

Lopat, raised on the sidewalks of New York, outslickers the potent Dodgers. He throws screwballs, slow curves, sliders, change-ups, and three knuckleballs.

Roe is equally baffling. The angular one from Arkansas keeps the Yankees off balance. He surrenders a first-inning run when he has trouble harnessing his control but through the first six innings yields only two hits.

Mickey Mantle, still limping on his bad knee, makes a fine catch in the first inning. With Pee Wee Reese on third and two out, he races to deep right-center field to haul in Robinson's long drive.

Brooklyn takes a 2–1 lead in the fourth and Roe sails into the seventh. Billy Martin, who would rap 12 hits in the series, leads off with a fly ball deep to left, not far from the foul line. Robinson runs to the railing, stretches into the seats, and watches helplessly as the ball falls just beyond his reach for a game-tying homer.

The game remains 2–2 heading into the bottom of the eighth. Hank Bauer delivers a one-out single, but Yogi Berra flies out. Mantle, who earlier walked, gets ahead of Roe and sets himself for a 2-and-0 pitch. Roe pulls the string—Mantle later says it was "a change-up of some sort and I think it was a breaking ball"—throwing just the kind of pitch that supposedly seduces Mantle when batting right-handed.

Mickey is caught slightly off stride, but manages to hold his bat back just long enough, and then, though flat-footed, he whips into the pitch and pulls a drive to deep left field. Robinson doesn't bother reaching for this one; the ball drops deep in the lower seats, some 400 feet from the plate. Mantle's first World Series home run at Yankee Stadium puts New York ahead, 4–2, and with Lopat wiggling out of a two-on jam in the ninth, the Yankees have a two-games-to-none lead as the series moves to Ebbets Field.

October 4, 1953—Ebbets Field, Brooklyn. At home the Dodgers turned things around. They won Games 3 and 4. Game 5, now, holds the key, and on a beautiful warm afternoon an overflow crowd of 36,775 gathers in Flatbush.

Mickey Mantle comes into the game mired in a slump. He struck out four consecutive times against Carl Erskine in Game 3, then whiffed twice more in Game 4. Already hobbling on a painful knee, he suffered still another injury before the game even started.

Yankee players had been hustling to get in the cage for one last whack near the end of batting practice. As Irv Noren took his final cut, Mantle turned the corner too soon and caught a line drive on his bare left hand. He was lucky to be alive—lucky that the ball didn't hit him in the head—but he was in pain. Casey Stengel considered scratching Mantle, who insisted on playing after trainer Gus Mauch froze the hand. He played.

Game 5 is all offense. The two teams combine for a total of 25 hits and 47 bases. Six homers fly out of this bandbox, four from bats belonging to the Yankees.

Gene Woodling is an early-inning star. He leads off the game with a home run, and after the Dodgers tie the score, 1–1, on an unearned run in the second, he prevents further damage by cutting down Gil Hodges with a beautiful peg to the plate.

The third inning is the most pivotal round of the fall classic. Hodges opens the door by fumbling what should have been a third-out grounder, allowing the go-ahead Yankee run to score. Rookie Johnny Podres, the Dodger starter, is rattled; he hits Hank Bauer with a pitch and walks Yogi Berra, loading the bases and bringing up Mantle, who had been robbed of a hit by third baseman Billy Cox in his first at bat today. Dodger manager Chuck Dressen removes the left-handed Podres in favor of right-handed Russ Meyer, a 15–5 pitcher this year, forcing Mantle to turn around and bat lefty. Mickey particularly favors his bum knee batting lefty—it often buckles from that side—and he can't take a full swing. Stengel has been urging him to punch the ball instead.

Ignoring Stengel and his bad knee completely, Mickey jumps on Meyer's first offering and drills a tremendous rising drive into the upper tier in left-center field, the opposite field in this case, for a grand-slam home run. Many balls are hit into this sector by right-handed hitters, but it is a rare feat for a lefty swinger. The blow is one of Mickey's biggest baseball thrills and is only the fourth grand-slam homer in World Series history (Elmer Smith, 1920; Tony Lazzeri, 1936; and Gil McDougald, 1951).

Meyer in the locker room afterward felt despondent but bravely talked with the press. "When you throw your best pitch and a guy hits it like that Mantle did, there's just nothing you can do about it," said the Mad Monk. "The pitch was a curveball, on the outside corner and just above Mickey's knees. I remember Carl Erskine had told me that Mantle had been pulling away from almost every pitch. But on this one it was as if somebody had told him where the pitch was going to be, for he stepped in almost before I let the ball go."

The grand slam was Mantle's only hit of the day, Meyer striking him out in the fifth. But the damage was done. Although the Dodgers fought back to make the final score 11–7, Brooklyn could never climb out of the 6–1 hole Mantle put them in.

The Yankees the next day would capture a record-setting fifth consecutive World Championship when Billy Martin singled home Bauer with the winning run in the bottom of the ninth. For Mantle personally, it was a weird series. While hitting .208 (5 for 24) and striking out eight times, he won two games with home runs and garnered seven RBIs, second only to Martin's eight. Mickey's contribution was both valuable and satisfying, coming as it did in spite of his injuries and his decline in the second half of the regular season.

But Martin was the big gun of the series, offensively and defensively, and Stengel seemed as happy about Martin's showing as he was disappointed in Mantle's. Curiously, Casey overlooked Mantle's effort and almost ignored the fact that his center fielder had played hurt.

"They had the kid cold," Stengel said of Mantle, "and we knew it and we kept telling him he had to cut down on his swing and hit down on the ball like we been telling him all year. The kid's got power enough to hit it into the seats just punching like he did for the big one. He can bunt enough with his speed to hit .300, but you try to tell him to stop trying to kill it and he don't do it."

Stengel was looking forward to working with Mantle the following spring. But he said there was one difference between Martin and Mantle. "You tell the fresh kid [Martin] something, and he listens and does it. You tell the other fellow something [Mantle] and he acts like you tell him nothing."

Stengel's exasperation with Mantle aside, the fact remains that Mantle delivered the big hit of the series with his grand slam. "I believe it was the longest and hardest ever hit off me," said Russ Meyer more than 30 years later. "I always liked what [Mickey] said years later in an interview. He was asked what stands out in his mind as one of his big moments in baseball, and he replied that hitting the grand slam in the '53 Series off Russ Meyer—who was a pretty fair country pitcher."

1954

May 22, 1954—Yankee Stadium. Mickey Mantle finally shed his early-season slump in New York's 7–0 triumph today over Boston by going 4 for 5, scoring two runs, and gathering four RBIs as fellow Oklahoman Allie Reynolds pitched a seven-hit shutout to lead the way.

It has been a miserable spring for the Mick. Shortly before spring training camp opened, Mickey had a fluid-filled cyst removed from the back of his right knee. This was the same knee he had submitted to surgeons the previous November for the removal of torn cartilage. He was careless in his rehabilitation, severely aggravating the knee in a basketball game, and thus a second operation was necessary.

As he sat out the spring exhibition games, Stengel fumed. "If he did what he was told after the first operation, he would be playing now," said Casey, who had hoped to work with Mantle to improve his play. "This kid, you can't ever teach him nothing in the spring because he's always hurt. You want to work on him batting left-handed and you can't. You want to do something for him and he don't let you. What's the good of telling him what to do? No matter what you tell him, he'll do what he wants."

Finally, late in the camp, Mantle began running, but he wore a bulky knee brace that prevented him from batting left-handed. He was in the everyday lineup once the regular season got under way. But he wasn't doing well, hitting all of .175 in April. Some were predicting a premature end to his career, recalling the injury-shortened career of Pete Reiser. Mantle was particularly inept batting lefty and sometimes sat against right-handed pitching.

The first three weeks of May did not go well either. But yesterday's game at the Stadium marked a milestone—Mickey hit his first left-handed home run of the campaign. He would really break loose today.

The Mick gets his slump ender going in the third with Truman "Tex" Clevenger, Boston's rookie right-hander, in a jam with one run in and Hank Bauer on third. Mickey, who already singled, bounces to first

45

baseman Harry Agganis and explodes toward first, beating Clevenger to the bag for an RBI single.

He lines a Clevenger delivery into the right-field bleachers for a two-run homer in the sixth. An inning later he faces right-hander Tom Brewer, with Phil Rizzuto on base, and creams an opposite-field RBI triple off the railing in left field. He does all his 4-for-5 damage hitting left-handed.

Can one game turn around a player's season? Mickey in this one game raised his average 37 points, putting himself above the .250 mark. He turned red-hot, knocking in 10 runs in the three-game Boston series. (He came into the series with only seven RBIs.) Through the rest of the month he hit .467 (21 for 45) and by May's end had a robust .311 batting average. His bat was smoking now and his problems with the tender right knee seemed behind him.

Mantle's turnaround game brought delight to Stengel's face. But the Ole Perfesser was now saddled with another concern. The Indians won their ninth in a row on the day of Mantle's slump shedding. The Indians (22–10) were two games in front of the Yankees (20–12). The two clubs were one-two in the American League; the chase for the flag was on!

July 22, 1954—Yankee Stadium. The White Sox have joined the hot pursuit of Cleveland, but the Yankees today pretty much assured a two-team race by sweeping a doubleheader from the Pale Hose, 4–3 and 11–1. Chicago fell 6½ games off the pace, while the Yankees clung to within a half game of the maddening Indians, who took a twinbill from Boston.

The doubleheader's first game is wild. Chicago takes a 3–1 lead into the bottom of the eighth, when Casey Stengel throws no fewer than four pinch-hitters at the enemy. Two of them come through—Eddie Robinson homers and Bill Skowron walks—and Mantle scores Skowron with a two-out single to center. It is a 3–3 game.

The Ole Perfesser is in a pickle. The frantic deployment of pinch-hitters has left his defensive alignment disheveled. So he moves Irv Noren from right field to center, shifts Mantle from center to shortstop, and plays Phil Rizzuto at second base for the first time in the Scooter's long Yankee career.

Mantle made it abundantly clear in the minors that as a shortstop he was no Phil Rizzuto. Still, he had played one inning at short the year before (he would ultimately play seven major-league games at the position), and Stengel contemplated his use there in just such an emergency as now confronted the skipper.

Chicago cannot find the means to test Mantle, who, luckily, does not get a single chance in either the ninth or tenth inning. Perhaps to save himself any possible embarrassment should the game continue, Mickey in the 10th bangs his 20th homer to close the issue.

In the second game, he raps an early two-run single to bust that one open, while Harry Byrd pitches a neat five-hitter. On the doubleheader, Mantle goes 4 for 9, scores three runs, and drives home four. All of a sudden he is a serious candidate for the much-prized Triple Crown. The next morning the papers show the following league leaders in the three Triple Crown categories:

Home Runs

Mickey Mantle	20
Larry Doby, Cleveland	17
Al Rosen, Cleveland	17

Runs Batted In

Mickey Mantle	74
Minnie Minoso, Chicago	74

Batting Average

Irv Noren, New York	.339
Bobby Avila, Cleveland	.330
Mickey Mantle	.323

So his hobbled, impotent beginning notwithstanding, the Mick by midseason was going so well he even had a shot at the elusive Triple Crown. And he showed up well in the recent All-Star Game, too, starting and collecting two hits from the other league's best.

On the league level Mantle was doing great; on the local level he was just another good center fielder. The Big Apple was loaded at the position.

Both Duke Snider, leading the National League at .364, and Willie Mays, his league's home-run leader with 33, were hitting higher and belting homers at a better clip than Mantle. And the Dodgers' Snider and the Giants' Mays will keep right on hammering the ball all season.

August 5, 1954—Municipal Stadium, Cleveland. The Yankees beat the front-running Indians before a Ladies' Day crowd of nearly 50,000 on the strength of Bob Grim's fine pitching, Andy Carey's good defensive work at third, and the long-ball hitting of Mickey Mantle. The win advanced New York (72–35), 1½ games behind the Tribe (72–32) in the tense pennant struggle.

The score was modest, 5–2, but the game was marked by screaming home runs, two by Mantle and one each by Joe Collins and Larry Doby.

Mantle breaks a scoreless game in the fourth with the first of his four-baggers, a solo blast off Early Wynn; and Phil Rizzuto's RBI-single in the seventh makes it 2–0.

Ray Narleski is pitching when the Yankees ice the game in the eighth with their eighth set of back-to-back homers of the year. First, Collins unloads against Narleski, a rookie sensation who will post a 2.22 ERA in 42 games, and sends a tremendous drive into the distant upper deck in right field, a shot of perhaps 475 feet. As Collins crosses the plate, he says to Mantle, the next hitter, "Go chase that."

On Narleski's very next pitch Mantle explodes an even mightier homer. The ball lands in the same right-field upper deck as Collins's but about 25 feet more toward center field and several feet deeper in the upper tier.

Mantle circles the bases, trots into the dugout, where he accepts congratulations, and ambles over to the drinking fountain. Collins is standing there as Mickey casually sips a drink, and, without looking up, asks, "What did you say, Joe?"

"Go shit in your hat," is the best that Collins can muster while Mickey grins from ear to ear.

Mantle's homer tied him with Doby in the home-run derby—but not for long. Doby regained the lead, 24–23, with a two-run shot off Johnny Sain in the bottom of the eighth.

September 2, 1954—Yankee Stadium. Still alive in the pennant race, the Yankees defeated Cleveland, 3–2, to capture the rubber game of a vital three-game set. The Indians (95–38) left town with a modest 3½-game cushion over the Yankees (91–41). For the time being, the league title remains up for grabs.

Casey Stengel won today with Stengel magic. For the first time this season, he has Mickey Mantle batting leadoff, and he announces that Mantle would continue to bat first against righties until he snapped out of his late-season slump. Against lefties, he would bat third as usual.

Today's pitching matchup is a classic, pitting Whitey Ford and his

15–7 record against Bob Lemon (20–5), who puts a personal 11-game winning streak on the line. Not unexpectedly, the two future Hall of Famers control the action—each club manages only three hits.

Mantle's only hit of the game accounts for the only earned run charged to Lemon. The Yankees are losing, 1–0, when Mantle, leading off the sixth, picks out Lemon's first pitch and booms a wondrous wallop that lands halfway up in the right-field upper deck, some 100 feet above the 344-foot mark. Two more runs follow—two errors by first baseman Vic Wertz on tough hard-hit grounders are the key plays—and New York leads, 3–1.

Later in the game Mantle unsuccessfully attempts a two-strike bunt. Afterward, Lemon expresses surprise over this tactic. "I could have kissed him."

Ford protects the lead, barely, in late innings. A Hank Majeski bid for a two-run homer is hauled in by left fielder Irv Noren in the eighth, but Larry Doby puts a ninth-inning homer into the seats, cutting the Yanks' lead to 3–2. Allie Reynolds enters, walks Al Rosen, and then records the final two outs to save Ford's 16th victory.

Rejoicing in his office, Stengel chirped afterward, "We're back in business. But we've got to keep on winning."

The Yankees were not really back in business because they did not keep winning. Not enough anyway. Ten days later, the Yankees would lose a doubleheader in Cleveland and fall a hopeless 8½ games behind.

When the race was over, Stengel blamed Mantle, especially Mickey's long recuperation in the spring, for the second-place finish. Casey was bitter over Mantle's not being ready for spring training and not getting untracked until late May.

"He's gotta change a lot," Stengel said. "He's gotta change his attitude and stop sulking and doing things he's told not to do. He'll have to grow up and become the great player he should be when he reports next spring."

The statistics, however, were in Mantle's favor. Mickey, who hit .300 on the nose and drove in 102 runs, led the league with 129 runs scored, and he finished third in each of four categories: home runs (27), slugging (.525), walks (102), and total bases (285). He also led the league's outfielders with 20 assists. What more did Stengel want? The fulfillment of potential, Casey adherents might respond.

Yet, there is no question that Mantle slumped in the late season. He hit only seven homers after July 22 and didn't hit another after today's No. 27; the league leader, Cleveland's Doby, wound up 1954 with 32. And the fact is that Mantle hit only .265 after that high-water date of July 22. But Mantle didn't cost the Yankees the pennant. Other, more important factors, explained the New Yorkers' failure to repeat.

First of all, the Yankees didn't lose this pennant—the Indians *won* it. Cleveland set a standing American League record for season wins with 111. The Yankees had the highest winning percentage (.669) of any second-place team in league history, and posted the best record (103–51) of any Stengel-managed club. The Yankees played well, but who's going to beat 111 wins?

Cleveland had fabulous pitching. Its stable compiled a phenomenal 2.78 team ERA, almost half a run better than the Yanks' respectable 3.26. The Big Three of Vic Raschi, Allie Reynolds, and Eddie Lopat was now a Downside Two, Raschi having been traded the previous winter after a contract dispute with general manager George Weiss. Reynolds, in his last season, and Lopat had decent 1954s but were no longer big winners. The new ace, Whitey Ford, didn't win another game after today.

Departed standouts of the past were missed. Johnny Mize, who retired following the 1953 World Series, no longer came off the bench with his menacing bat. Bobby Brown was lost to midseason retirement, and Gene Woodling, to an August thumb fracture. And the biggest loss of all came just before the season, when the Army's long arm plucked Stengel's sparkplug, Billy Martin.

For Stengel or anyone else to tag Mantle with the responsibility for the Year the Yankees Didn't Win the Pennant was both ludicrous and unfair.

MANTLE AND STENGEL

Casey Stengel did much for Mickey Mantle's career, especially in 1951. It was, after all, Casey who brought Mantle up a year or so before George Weiss would have. Mickey was grateful because this gave his father, Mutt, the chance to see his boy play in the majors before he died. Stengel also got Weiss to give Mantle $1,000 more than the minimum salary in 1951.

Stengel taught a lot of baseball to Mantle. During Mickey's first couple of years, Casey displayed endless patience with the kid, and while he sometimes snarled at other players, he gently encouraged Mickey. This was standard procedure with Stengel; he handled kids gently and was much gruffer with veterans. When Mickey was still learning the ropes of playing the outfield, he occasionally threw to the wrong base. Stengel corrected his mistakes in a kindly manner. Stengel's tougher stand with Mickey didn't begin in earnest until the 1953 season.

And Mantle enjoyed playing for Stengel.

Yet, there was another, more complex angle to the Mantle-Stengel relationship, and this was embedded in the fact that from the time he first laid eyes on Mantle, Stengel saw a chance to mold the greatest player in the history of baseball. And the player would be a lasting monument to his own managerial skills after he, the elderly Stengel, left the game. Casey was harking back to John McGraw and Mel Ott—Ott, always McGraw's boy. Casey had never produced a great player, at least not from scratch, and he wanted Mickey to be his prodigy and his monument.

Ironically, first Stengel and his constant drumming built Mantle up prematurely, and then, after the young star had indeed achieved greatness, Casey's carping dulled the Mantle luster.

Mantle's seasons usually fell short of Stengel's expectations. For example, take 1958, a year in which Mantle took the homer crown with 42 and hit .304. Casey wasn't satisfied. "I never saw a ballplayer who had greater promise," he said. "He could be the best there ever was. Name me one thing he can't do. You can't. And listen to me. Every year he ought to lead the league in everything."

Stengel kept feeling shortchanged on Mantle. He didn't accept Mantle's many injuries as an excuse either. Mickey's ailments seemed to annoy him, as though Mickey could have ducked them. On occasion the Ole Perfesser had reason to be sore—when Mantle failed to do his rehabilitation exercises, for example, and when he strained himself horsing around.

Mantle's injuries were at the center of the Stengel-Mantle communication failure. Stengel would put Mantle in the lineup as long as Mickey was able to walk, and he left it up to Mantle to scratch himself from a game. Mickey just wasn't the sort to beg out; he felt a responsibility to play under the most painful of circumstances.

There was one pitiful scene in Boston. Mantle was so obviously hobbling on a bum leg that he had to play left field, and finally even Stengel, criticized for risking the Mick's career, saw the cruelty in the situation and gave his star a few days of rest. "He coulda told me he couldn't make it," explained Stengel.

Why didn't Mickey tell him? "He didn't ask me," snapped Mantle. "If he puts me in, I play."

Ralph Houk, who took over as manager in 1961, decided Mantle would play when he, Houk, felt he was able to play. "I think the chief trouble with Mantle is that he tries to play before one injury is completely healed," said Houk. "And, by favoring that injury, he hurts something else." Houk would check Mickey's condition from day to day and Mantle appreciated this.

Stengel felt Mantle wasn't making the most of tremendous natural ability, but he wasn't one to hold it against Mantle for keeping late hours. Casey pretty much let Mantle, Whitey Ford, and Billy Martin have their off-the-field fun. He didn't care about late-night hours or drinking—as a player he had been a reveler, too—as long as it didn't interfere with production on the field. Once in a while he'd scold the trio at team meetings, but then he'd throw them a wink on the way out.

Stengel was annoyed by Mantle's refusal to alter his batting style. Casey wanted Mickey to shorten his lusty swing, to sometimes chop down on the ball and thus take better advantage of his speed; he argued that Mantle was strong enough to hit plenty of home runs with a shorter swing. But Mantle kept swinging from the heels. He wasn't necessarily being wrong-headed; Mickey was suspicious of any suggestions to alter his basic approach to hitting. When the strikeouts mounted, Stengel threw up his arms in frustration. No doubt about it, on hitting, Mantle was stubborn; he was his own man at the plate.

Mantle's explosive temper also irked Stengel, although Casey took some satisfaction from Mickey's caring enough about doing well to get mad at himself. But Casey didn't want Mantle getting hurt in one of his kicking assaults on the water cooler. "Son," he would say, "it ain't the water cooler that's striking you out."

Stengel enjoyed a beautiful marriage with a woman who adored him, but the couple was childless. In some respects, Casey's players were his children, and he had his favorites, like Billy Martin, Yogi Berra, and Mantle. "When my dad died," Mickey once said, "I kinda looked toward Casey. Casey was like my dad."

When one of his favorites let him down, Stengel, feeling the bitterness any wronged father would feel, would express his displeasure openly and publicly. His players would get mad at him, too, but the responses of a fellow like Martin, who would scream back at Stengel, were accepted, even admired, by the crusty old skipper. That fighting spirit, you know. Mantle, however, was quietly defiant; he had been raised to respect authority and he was never a troublemaker. He never considered doing anything that might be construed as showing up Stengel. He just tended to do certain things, like batting, the Mickey Mantle way.

So Mantle and Stengel had their clashes, but the good times outnumbered the bad. They won eight pennants and five World Series fighting on the same side. Mantle finally pleased Stengel in Casey's last season as the Yankees' manager. "At the halfway mark, my most valuable player was Roger Maris," said Casey, summing up the year 1960. "But Mantle has worked hard and hustled hard and now I've got to say he is my most valuable player."

Maris won the 1960 MVP, receiving three more points than Mantle. For once, Stengel had given Mantle more than his share of credit.

Over the years Stengel often endorsed Joe DiMaggio and Yogi Berra, in that order, as the two best players he had on the Yankees. There are those who feel Casey was being disingenuous, that he was purposely trying to light a fire under Mantle to spur him on to even loftier heights. And there were times in retirement when Stengel would blurt out that Mantle was the best he ever managed.

But Casey slighted Mantle in his 1962 autobiography, *Casey at the Bat: The Story of My Life in Baseball*, when he made his all-time all-star selections. The book was written after Stengel had left the Yankees, so it must be assumed that he was free to be perfectly honest. Casey on his all-time all-star squad for the American League, which included all the league's players he had seen from 1912 to 1960, did not have a spot for Mantle. His center fielders were Ty Cobb, Joe DiMaggio, and Tris Speaker. And he wasn't prejudiced against players still in the game— Willie Mays headed his list of the best center fielders in the National League.

In analyzing all his Yankee players, Stengel called DiMaggio "the leading light" and picked Berra as "number two." Mantle came next, and Stengel wrote: "Mantle is third, but he's a man that could still wind up being outstanding in more things than anybody else. Mantle had more ability than any player I ever had on that club."

If Mantle wasn't first on Stengel's list, Casey wasn't first on Mantle's either, or as Mickey often said: "Ralph Houk is the best manager I ever played for."

1955

April 28, 1955—Municipal Stadium, Kansas City. Mickey Mantle may not have been undeniably great yet, but he was getting there. The year 1955 was to be a transition one, during which he chalked up achievements other players only dream about. But there was a general feeling that he should do better.

There were more interrupting injuries, reluctant fan acceptance in the Bronx, and endless comparisons with the great Duke Snider and the greater Willie Mays, co-practitioners of the center-field art in New York. And there was always that detrimental comparison with that loftiest of standards, the Mantle Potential, frequently put forth by manager Casey Stengel.

Mantle today demonstrated that he has yet to attain perfection by passing teammate Andy Carey on the base paths, this on the day of the very first game the Yankees play here against the A's (newly arrived from Philadelphia). But the Yanks mopped up the A's anyway, winning, 11–4, a two-run Mantle homer putting them ahead for good.

Right-hander Charlie Bishop, who won 10 of 32 decisions with the A's from 1952 through 1955, surrendered the Mantle homer. Lack of control was Bishop's problem—he walked better than five men every nine innings. Yet, he was an accomplished athlete, one of the elite to achieve major league status.

Bishop was trying to get the Mick dusty, the way he tells the story. His would-be knock-down pitch, as he recalls it, happened to find the middle of the plate "due to my well-known lack of control." Adds Charlie, "The wind was blowing a gale out to right field; Mickey swung from his heels as usual and hit a high pop fly, which was blown outward to right field at the shortest distance from the plate.

"Mickey's philosophy as a left-handed hitter was to unbutton his shirt and have a good cut. Mine was to throw the ball by him, which I did most of the time. He once commented to me on one of his late-night sojourns in Philadelphia that since he was not able to hit me, he was going to drag-bunt down the first-base line and run up my back. I suggested to him that if I saw any movement of his left foot in the batter's box I might stick the ball in his ear before he was able to bunt, provided I could attain that much control upon a moment's notice."

Mantle this year has adopted a slightly modified stance, standing a little closer to the plate and waiting a little longer to pull the trigger. Once he figured out how to avoid being hit, the adjustment paid off nicely.

Bob Turley helped him, too. Obtained from Baltimore in the off-season, Turley not only gave the Yankees a strong right arm but brought with him an ability to read opposing hurlers' pitches and a willingness to share his readings with Yankee batters. As a fastball hitter, Mickey had a real advantage when he knew a fastball was coming.

But Turley could call all kinds of pitches. Certain pitchers telegraphed their intentions. Just before throwing a curveball, for example, a pitcher might look into his glove. Things like that. Turley would signal Mickey from the dugout—a piercing whistle meant a fastball was coming—and Mantle would act accordingly.

Soon Mantle was able to pick up some telltale giveaways himself; the experience of working with Turley made him a more alert hitter.

May 13, 1955—Yankee Stadium. Mickey Mantle today belted three homers in one game. He went 4 for 4 and drove in all the runs in a 5–2 conquest of Detroit before only 7,177 paid fans, making Friday the 13th his lucky day.

Only three Yankees—Tony Lazzeri in 1927, Ben Chapman in 1932, and Bill Dickey in 1939—had achieved three-homer games at cavernous Yankee Stadium before Mantle's big day. Moreover, Mantle hit the homers from each side of the plate, two left-handed and one right-handed; Johnny Lucadello of the St. Louis Browns was the only player to previously switch-hit home runs in an American League game, in 1940, hitting one run each side of the plate.

Detroit's Steve Gromek, a right-handed 15-year veteran, gets off to a bad start in the first when Andy Carey beats out a bunt and Mantle sends a 2-and-2 offering whistling to right-center. The ball clears the auxiliary scoreboard to the left of the Yankee bullpen and bangs into the bleachers more than 400 feet from home plate.

After singling Hank Bauer home in the third, Mantle takes Gromek deep again in the fifth. This one, hit on a 2-and-0 count, travels well over the 407-foot sign in right-center and lands 430 feet from home plate. Tape-measure job No. 2.

The finishing touches are added in the eighth against southpaw reliever Bob Miller. (The 19-year-old Miller received a $60,000 bonus from the Tigers in 1953, a definite high, and finished with the expansion Mets in 1962, a definite low in anyone's book.) Now Mickey crosses over to the right-handed hitting box and swings at Miller's first delivery. Mickey stings an opposite-field drive along the same line to right-center as the first homer, but this one is hit harder, higher, and farther. It is Mantle's first righty homer of the season. Tape-measure job No. 3 is the best shot of the day.

Reported Joseph M. Sheehan in the *New York Times*: "End to end they would have measured in the neighborhod of 1,300 feet." That's a quarter of a mile. Sheehan believed Mantle was the first player to plant three homers in the distant right-center-field bleachers in the same game.

All three homers were hit off fastballs, the two left-handed homers with a bat left behind by Enos Slaughter, recently dealt to Kansas City, and the right-handed homer with a bat borrowed from Bill Skowron.

The happiest man in the ballpark is Casey Stengel, who is still urging Mantle to cut down on his swing. Whenever he thought Mickey might be listening, he would say, "I've got a feller on my team who thinks he should hit a homer every time and gets mad when the other pitcher won't let him. If he'd just fling his bat at the ball, like this, he'd hit it just as far and maybe wouldn't strike out so much and get so mad."

Sure enough Mantle has been taking Stengel's advice. During this home stand, Mickey has been arriving at the stadium at 10:30 A.M. for extra batting practice with coach Bill Dickey. "Yes, I'm trying to shorten my swing," admitted Mickey after the game. "And I think I'm getting the idea. At least it worked today."

June 5, 1955—Comiskey Park, Chicago. Mickey Mantle had been piling up the base hits, but since his three-homer game of May 13 he cracked only two for the circuit. One of his most memorable tape-measure jobs was hit today.

The second game of a Yankee–White Sox doubleheader is in the fourth inning. Mantle is batting right-handed against Billy Pierce. The air is still. Mantle swings and explodes a savage shot to left; the ball leaves the field midway between the 352- and 365-foot marks and carries over the roof and out of the ballpark.

Most of the New York and Chicago newspapers reported that the ball either landed atop the roof and bounced out, or struck the base of a light tower on its way out. Irving Vaughan in the *Chicago Tribune* wrote that the ball "bounced into 34th Street to shatter the windshield of a parked car."

Two reporters, Til Ferdenzi of the *New York Journal-American* and Jerry Mitchell of the *New York Post*, wrote that Mantle's homer cleared the roof. According to Ferdenzi, "When last seen the ball still had plenty of carry." Ferdenzi felt the ball went at least 500 feet; he added, "The parking lot attendant who recovered the ball talked as though the ball had traveled at least a half-mile."

Mitchell, in his game story, added this important information about the home run: "It left the field at the 360-foot mark, and, since the roof over the upper deck goes back 160 feet, must have traveled well over 500 feet. It was thought by some that the ball hit the base of a light tower back on the roof, but park attendants on the roof came to the Yankee dressing room to tell Mickey it had cleared the roof entirely."

Typically, Mantle low-keyed his latest contribution to long-ball folklore. "I think the one I hit in Washington went further," said Mickey afterward, "higher and further. But then there was a good wind blowing out that day."

The distance of this homer sometimes is given as 550 feet. The White Sox, though they record the number of homers hit over the roof, do not attempt to identify the longest, and Rich Lindberg, a Chisox historian, knows of no roof shot that was ever measured. But Mantle's would have to be compared with one Jimmie Foxx hit on June 16, 1936, the granddaddy of them all at Comiskey.

Actually Foxx in separate games hit two homers over the left-field roof, according to the White Sox, but his second, the longer of the two, either hit the roof or cleared it and cleared 34th Street in its flight of nearly 600 feet, as legend has it. Foxx said it was the longest home run he ever hit.

But Mantle's home run had something Foxx's didn't have—eyewitness verification that the ball cleared the roof on the fly. There happened to be no park personnel on the roof when Foxx homered. Guards *outside* the ballpark claimed it cleared on the fly, but, of course, they were not in a position to say for sure. But give Double X credit for this: He hit two roof shots to Mantle's one.

The White Sox' Dave Nicholson and a strong wind reportedly sent a

573-footer over the left-field roof in May 1964. But John Kuenster, editor of *Baseball Digest*, who at the time covered the White Sox for the *Chicago Daily News*, remembers interviewing upper-deck fans who told him they heard the ball bounce on the roof above them.

Comiskey Park was a pitcher's park from the day it opened in 1910. When the upper deck was built in 1927, dimensions down both lines were fixed at 352 feet and remained so for years, and the center-field distance, which fluctuated, sometimes extended as far as 445 feet. The character of the park changed in 1983.

In the 1982–83 off-season, home plate was moved eight feet closer to the outfield (it was to be moved back again for the 1986 season), and it became 341 feet down the lines and 401 feet to center field. Only 21 homers had ever reached the roof or cleared it before the 1983 season; in the 1983, 1984, and 1985 seasons combined, 19 roof shots were hit.

No doubt the new dimensions were a factor. But there may have been other factors, too. Possibly a livelier ball. Possibly a big breeze. "To me there's a climate, atmosphere difference," White Sox manager Tony LaRussa told the *Chicago Sun-Times* in 1985. "Now you hit the ball well, or decently, and it has a chance to go out." In any case, the recent glut of Comiskey Park roof shots in no way diminishes the mighty clouts of Foxx and Mantle.

The Yankees and White Sox split the doubleheader on this date (June 5), and the Yanks (35–15) held a four-game lead over second-place Cleveland (30–18). In the games between May 11 and the end of May, Mantle had a 16-game hitting streak, batted .433 (29 for 67) and walked 20 times; the Yankees won 16 of 20 games and assumed the lead. It was true: As Mantle goes, so go the Yankees.

June 21, 1955—*Yankee Stadium.* On the heels of record shots in Chicago and Detroit, the latter the first to clear the 440-foot sign in Briggs Stadium's dead center, Mickey Mantle tonight popped the eyes of the home folks. Wrote Louis Effrat in the *New York Times*: "Anything and everything else that happened in the ball game was secondary to what Mickey Mantle did in the first inning."

What Mantle did was author the first home run ever hit to Yankee Stadium's dead-center bleachers. Not once since the Stadium opened in 1923 had a player hit a homer to dead center, which in 1955 measured 461 feet. Not Ruth, not Gehrig, not DiMaggio, not Foxx, not Greenberg—not anyone.

In the first inning, Kansas City's Alex Kellner disposes of the first two Yankee batters. Mantle, batting right-handed and dug in, explodes into a change-up; the ball whizzes past the pitcher, starts to rise, clears the 30-foot-high hitters' backdrop screen in dead center just to the right of the 461-foot sign, and lands in the ninth row of bleachers. The drive is measured at 486 feet.

Mantle would hit into these same bleachers in 1964 with a 502-foot drive, but he would be aided by a stiff wind. Today's drive would remain a bigger thrill for him. Today's homer stands up nicely with Mickey's 565-footer in Washington, D.C., when you consider that he had no wind this time and, in hitting a change-up, he had to provide all the power.

Bobby Shantz, attempting a comeback from injuries with the A's in 1955, recalls, "For sheer force and velocity, I never saw anything like it. It actually sounded like an *explosion*. It went past Kellner's left ear and disappeared into the center-field bleachers."

Jackie Farrell of the Yankees public relations staff wants to get that ball and hightails it out to the bleachers. He is authorized to pay $25 for it, but the ball-possessing bleacherite, one Oscar Alonso, isn't having any of that action. Asserts Alonso, "I've been sitting here since 1927 and I finally got one. This is the first one hit here and the last one. I'm not gonna give it up."

There is a rain delay and Alonso is invited to the Yankee clubhouse—Farrell's doing what he can—where he is reacquainted with Eddie Lopat, his old stickball buddy from the Yorkville section of Manhattan. Some things you'll do for an old buddy; before the TV cameras, Alonso delivers the baseball to Mickey Mantle.

The ball is sent to the Baseball Hall of Fame, to be placed alongside the ball Mantle hit 565 feet in Washington. The bat? Again, Mantle used a borrowed stick, this one belonging to Hank Bauer.

July 12, 1955—County Stadium, Milwaukee. Milwaukee, which only two years ago became a big-league town when the Braves relocated here, hosted the annual All-Star Game. Most of the packed house of 45,643 snoozed through six innings—it was, of course, a partisan National League crowd—as the American League built a 5–0 lead. But the fans came alive with a Nationals comeback.

The Nationals are loaded. On their *bench* are Willie Mays, Hank Aaron, and Stan Musial; arguably the greatest players in the history of the senior circuit, none was elected by the fans as a starter! In addition to their deep bench, the Nationals have the great Robin Roberts on the mound.

But Roberts has first-inning trouble. Harvey Kuenn and Nellie Fox single, Roberts wild-pitches home a run, and Ted Williams walks. Then clean-up man Mickey Mantle, batting left-handed, nails one into the woods beyond the center-field fence. Mantle's three-run homer travels an estimated 430 feet and gives the Americans a 4–0 lead.

Roberts had made a good pitch. Three decades later he recalls that Mickey "was back from the plate and I tried to go away. He hit the ball to dead-center field—and the pitch was away!"

The Americans have a 5–0 lead when Mays turns the tide with a defensive play in the seventh. With one on and two out, Ted Williams rifles a smash to deep right-center. Mays runs to the seven-foot-high fence, times his leap perfectly, and snares the potential game-breaking homer.

Mays isn't through yet. He greets the newly arrived Whitey Ford with a leadoff single in the bottom of the seventh. Mantle temporarily saves Ford by running down two long flies, but the Nationals score two runs. Mays starts a two-out eighth-inning rally with another single off Ford, and before the inning is over, the Nationals put together enough bloopers and bleeders to tie the score at 5–5.

The Americans have a chance to go ahead in the 11th, when Mantle delivers a two-out single that moves Bobby Avila from first to third. Yogi Berra raps one up the middle that has go-ahead RBI written all over it, but Red Schoendienst makes a great stop, fires to first, and nips Berra.

The Americans' Frank Sullivan has pitched scoreless ball since taking the mound in the eighth, striking out Mays to escape a crisis in the ninth. Now he faces Musial in the bottom of the 12th. Stan the Man pulls the first pitch into the right-field bleachers for a 6–5 National League victory.

Although the game was laden with heroics, it boiled down to the feeling that, on this day anyway, Mays's best was able to beat Mantle's best. Willie made a flashy catch and ignited two rallies. Mickey hit a long home run and played solid defense. Essentially, their performances personified the way the public perceived them. And the public saw them as the best their respective leagues had to offer in the 1950s and 1960s.

MANTLE VS. MAYS

The baseball question that bounced around New York City in the 1950s asked, Who is the best all-around center fielder in this town, Mickey Mantle of the Yankees, Willie Mays of the Giants, or Duke Snider of the Dodgers? The answer was a matter of personal choice, which is what made the question good fun. *The Sporting News*, in its annual recognition of the Major League Player of the Year, picked Mays in 1954, Snider in 1955, and Mantle in 1956.

Snider was a great player and is a most deserved Hall of Famer. But he didn't have the physical tools to place him in a class with Mantle and Mays. He was not as fast, as good with the glove, or as strong and true with the throw as were Mantle and Mays. He also played in Ebbets Field, a home-run haven if there ever was one. And even with this advantage, Snider didn't quite post the kind of numbers rung up by Mantle and Mays. The lifetime statistics of the oft-compared trio are as follows:

	G	AB	H	2B	3B	HR	R
Mantle	2,401	8,102	2,415	344	72	536	1,677
Mays	2,992	10,881	3,283	523	140	660	2,062
Snider	2,143	7,161	2,116	358	85	407	1,259

	RBI	BB	SO	SB	BA	SA
Mantle	1,509	1,734	1,710	153	.298	.557
Mays	1,903	1,463	1,526	338	.302	.557
Snider	1,333	971	1,237	99	.295	.540

Note that in slugging average, a statistic many feel is the most relevant barometer of a power hitter's worth, both Mantle and Mays finished at .557. Most of the other edges to Mays are because of Willie's greater number of at bats. What isn't shown is that Mays had ten 100-RBI seasons while Mantle had only four. Part of the reason is that in all the years Mantle was with the Yankees, their great success notwithstanding, the club never had a great leadoff man.

Basically, Mays piled up better stats because he stayed healthier and played longer. Going into the 1965 season, the year Mantle started going downhill, Mickey had one more homer in his column than Mays, and Mickey had batted about 500 fewer times. Willie, who stayed healthy and played 22 seasons, built his statistical edge over Mantle in the years following the 1964 season.

Does the edge Mays has in lifetime statistics mean he was a better player than Mantle? "If you didn't know either one of us and you opened the record book," Mantle told Jane Leavy of the *Washington Post* in 1983, "what would it say? Damn Willie."

Pete Rose has accumulated more hits than Ty Cobb. Does that mean Rose is the better hitter? Hell no! Cobb hit .367 lifetime and Rose is struggling to stay above .300; Rose is in the neighborhood of 14,000 at bats, while Cobb batted 11,429 times.

This is all put in perspective by Bill James in his *Historical Baseball Abstract*. James maintains that Mantle was "clearly a greater player" than Mays when Mickey was in his peak years. "Because even if Mays is given every conceivable break on every unknown—defense, base running, clutch hitting—his performance still would not match Mantle's."

In his best years Mantle created many more runs for his side than Mays. In the 1956, 1957, and 1961 seasons, using James's formula, Mantle created 540 runs, as compared to 466 by Mays in his three best years (1954, 1955, and 1958). And, according to James, Mantle in his best years cost his team 67 fewer outs per year—batting outs, caught stealing, sacrifices, and double-play balls—than Mays.

Comparing the two greats at their peaks, Mantle hit for a higher average, got on base more often, had more power, and was probably faster than Mays. Mays had a reputation for speed and for being a great base runner. But Mantle was better. He was a successful base stealer over 80 percent of the time, while Mays was under 80 percent. Mays hit into 251 double plays, compared to Mantle's 113. Mantle was almost never thrown out in going from first to third either.

Mays was probably better defensively, but, as James points out, the difference in their fielding couldn't possibly make up for the clear offensive advantage resident in Mickey Mantle.

Most of the other newly devised systems rank Mantle ahead of Mays, too. Total average, a system propounded by Thomas Boswell of the *Washington Post*, divides a player's total number of bases by the total number of outs. This method of measuring offensive worth ranks Babe Ruth first at 1.432 (7,972 bases divided by 5,567 outs). It ranks Mantle sixth (1.115), and Mays, thirteenth (1.019).

Comparative evaluations by contemporary players, writers, and experts produced mixed results, but in 1963 one evaluation in particular was notable, that of Gabe Paul, who ran baseball clubs for decades and was an astute judge of talent: "I have to give Mays one edge, durability. Mickey isn't sound and Willie is. Otherwise, if I had a chance to trade for either player, I'd pick Mantle." Mantle was the more "spectacular," Paul felt, alluding to his power and adding, "Power is a big thing in baseball. It can't be cheapened. That is, a fellow has it or hasn't. It isn't a fluke or great accomplishment, like a perfect game. When Mays hits a homer, it is routine. He doesn't hit them any further than anyone else. But that Mantle. When he connects, it's a tape-measure job. Nobody who ever lived has more power than Mantle. I get a kick out of watching him. Everything he does has that extra flourish."

Mantle was spectacular. So was Mays. But Mays, in addition, had a field charm that captivated fans. He had a flair and an infectious joy for the game that he expressed with audacious basket catches, a winning smile, and the famous "Say Hey" that rode on a high-pitched voice. Mantle loved the game, too, but some of the fun was extracted by his string of injuries. Mays was more outgoing, friendlier with fans and the press, although Mantle later in his career would shed some of his reserve.

Mays was perceived as brilliant, as possessing an intuitive genius for making the right play at the right time. Mantle had no such reputation, although the fact is that Mantle was also a smart player. He once made one of the smartest plays in baseball history. In the seventh game of the 1960 World Series, the Yankees, down by a run in the ninth inning of a wild affair, put runners on the corners—Mantle was on first—with one out. Yogi Berra smashed a bouncer to first baseman Rocky Nelson, who stepped on first to retire Yogi. Mantle, realizing that the force was off at second, dove back to first safely under Nelson's tag, allowing the tying run to score. It was the kind of play you see once in a decade or so and it was blotted out by Bill Mazeroski's game-winning homer in the Pirate ninth.

In bad times as well as good, it was always Mantle and Mays measured against each other, as in the 1962 World Series, which drew the two greats into direct competition. Both were struggling, causing one fan to speculate to the top of his leather lungs as to which of the two was the *worse* player. As the story has been told by Mantle, who took the Mays comparisons good-naturedly, all speculation came to an end as the Mick resumed his outfield post after just registering still another out. "Hey, Mantle," boomed the tormentor, "you win. You're the worst."

August 7, 1955—Yankee Stadium. The Yankees suddenly found themselves fighting for their lives. They led the American League by 6½ games on the Fourth of July, but they've frittered that away and then some with a 12–17 July. Now locked in a four-team struggle with Chicago, Cleveland, and Boston for the top rung, the mighty Yankees were imperiled and Mickey Mantle was catching some blame.

Mantle's legs were hurting again, yet he continued to play every day. The fans at Yankee Stadium were subjecting him to fierce booing. The boo-birds even got on Mantle when he hit a home run. Some New York sportswriters believed the abuse of Mantle could ultimately cost the Yankees the pennant, although Mickey said the heckling didn't bother him.

Mantle bangs out a pair of singles in the first of today's two games, but the stumbling Yankees lose again, 4–2, to Detroit. Detroit's second-game pitcher will be 25-year-old right-hander Frank Lary, who has yet to earn his famous moniker—the Yankee Killer.

Mantle gets the Yankees off to a good start with a solo homer in the first. Bob Turley is pitching a whale of a game for the pinstripers but gets into a little trouble in the eighth, when the Tigers tie it up, 2–2. The game moves into extra innings.

Babe Birrer, in relief of Lary, retires the first two Yankees in the bottom of the 10th and has yet to permit a hit in his 2⅔-inning stint. He needs one more out to force another inning. The center-field clock reads 8:28, and the batter is Mantle. Mickey, booed as he bats, responds by cracking a towering home run deep into the third deck in right field, giving New York a critical 3–2 victory—the Yankees just couldn't afford to lose a doubleheader to the second-division Tigers.

"I wish they wouldn't boo the guy," says Tiger outfielder Jim Delsing in the visitors' clubhouse. "It just makes him mad. He's tough enough in a good humor."

At day's end, the frantic first division of the American League looked this way:

Chicago	63–43	—	.594
New York	65–45	—	.591
Cleveland	64–45	½	.587
Boston	63–46	1½	.578

Birrer remembers the Mantle homer: "I got ahead of Mickey on the count, and with two strikes, I attempted to get the ball past him up high.

Mantle was an excellent low fastball hitter batting left-handed, and instead of getting it up, I came in with it down in his power alley. It obviously was gone, so I started to walk off the mound. After taking a few steps I decided to turn around and see how far it went. When I turned around I saw it bounce off the upper deck. It was probably the longest ball I ever threw."

September 2, 1955—Yankee Stadium. Those Three Musketeers of mischief and mayhem—Mickey Mantle, Whitey Ford, and Billy Martin—were reunited with Martin's return from the Army. In Martin's absence, the Yankees finished second to Cleveland in 1954 and were running second to Chicago in the furious 1955 pennant race.

Casey Stengel was delighted to have regained Martin, his sparkplug, and turned Billy loose on the Yankees in a team meeting. Billy's wallet was light and he urged his teammates to bear down harder in the stretch. "I don't know about you guys," said Martin, fire in his eyes, "I don't know how hungry you guys are, but I'm hungry. I need the money. I want to win this pennant real bad."

Stengel is so excited that he decides to play Martin at shortstop in today's game with Washington and bat him third, with Yogi Berra fourth and Mantle dropped down to the fifth slot. Billy comes through with two hits—he will bat an even .300 in 20 games—but his buddies Ford and Mantle have an even bigger day.

Ford pitches no-hit ball over the first six innings. The Mick, after Martin and Berra stroke singles, with Martin yelling encouragement from his perch at third base, gives New York a 3–0 lead by pulling a Bob Porterfield pitch deep into the lower right-field seats. Ford finally gets nicked for a hit in the seventh and it costs two runs, but the Bombers come away with a 4–2 victory.

Meanwhile, the first-place White Sox beat the Indians. Chicago (80–51) now leads New York (80–52) by a half game and Cleveland (79–53) by 1½ games. But the Yankees, on the strength of a 17–6 record in September, will charge into first place by midmonth and go on to win the pennant by three games.

Mantle would experience frustration in September. His game-winning homer today, his 36th, gives him a 10-homer lead over his nearest rivals, Ted Williams and Al Kaline. Mickey has the home-run crown wrapped up, and he looks a cinch to become the first Yankee to hit

40 homers since Joe DiMaggio belted 46 in 1937. With 93 RBIs, Mickey also appears headed for a 110-RBI season.

In two days Mantle would add his 37th home run and a day after that he would drive in his 98th run. Unfortunately, it would be his last homer and next-to-last RBI of the season. Disaster struck on September 16, when he suffered a severe muscle tear in the back of his right thigh while beating out a bunt. He made only two pinch-hit appearances the rest of the way.

But he did win the American League home-run crown for the first time (beating his personal homer record by 10). And he did lead the league in triples (11), slugging (.611) and on-base average (.433). Defensively, he led American League outfielders with a .995 fielding percentage. Still, the muscle tear denied him statistical milestones.

Stengel, meanwhile, had more important matters to contemplate, knowing his team's chances against Brooklyn in the upcoming World Series were less than promising without Mantle at full strength.

September 30, 1955—Ebbets Field, Brooklyn. The World Series shifted to Ebbets Field, with the Yankees holding a two-game-to-zip lead over the Dodgers, an advantage achieved without the services of a badly hobbling Mickey Mantle. The second-game victory had a high price: Reliable Hank Bauer pulled a muscle and would not be available for anything today except pinch-hit duty. Casey Stengel must rely on a pair of backup outfielders, rookie Elston Howard and Bob Cerv.

Stengel isn't planning to start Mantle today, but shortly before game time, Mantle, itchy for action, tells him that his thigh feels better and makes the lineup. In the first inning, Mickey half limps and half gallops into right-center in chase of Carl Furillo's routine fly ball, barely making the catch at the last instant. The next inning Casey moves Mantle to right field, Cerv from left to center, and Howard from right to left.

Brooklyn takes a 2–0 first-inning lead, but the Yankees tie the score in the second. Mantle leads off, making his first plate appearance of the series, and strokes southpaw Johnny Podres's pitch over the 393-foot sign in center. The ball drops into the lower seats for a 400-foot home run. The Yankees score again when Bill Skowron jars the ball loose from Roy Campanella at the plate, but Brooklyn comes alive and puts Bob Turley to rout in their half of the second. The Dodgers, a team that usually destroys left-handers, go on pounding every right-hander Stengel brings in and win easily, 8–3.

Looking ahead, Stengel was unclear as to Mantle's future availability. Mickey had said his thigh felt fine after working out prior to the game. "But the feeling changed after I ran for Furillo's fly," said the Mick, afterward. "It aches right now and I won't be able to tell about tomorrow's game until tomorrow."

Mantle would play in Game 4, limping all the way, but that was about the end of his series. His only other action came in Game 7, when he popped up as a pinch-hitter. He went 2 for 10 in the series.

Podres returned to shut out the Yankees in the seventh game, as the Bums captured their only World Championship in Brooklyn. It was a bitter pill for Stengel to swallow. When it was over, Stengel pointed to Mickey's legs and said, "They were the difference."

The Home Runs of Baseball's Greatest Player

1956

March 11, 1956—Al Lang Field, St. Petersburg, Florida. With the spring training exhibition season barely under way, Mickey Mantle was sending waves of excitement through the Florida Grapefruit League. He literally rippled the waters of Tampa Bay on this date, sending an opposite-field drive, against the wind, over the left-field barrier, the bleachers, and a street beyond, and into the drink.

The Yankees are playing the St. Louis Cardinals and a young right-hander named Bob Mabe, who will not make the Cards until 1958, delivers a fat pitch to Mantle with two on. The Mick unloads the tremendous bay shot with a late swing. And he is running as fast as ever, too. With two out in the ninth, Bill Virdon shoots a bases-loaded liner to deep-center field, an apparent extra-base hit. But Mantle, galloping at racehorse speed, makes a circus catch to save a 4–3 Yankee win.

The next day Mantle hit another one, albeit a one-hopper, into the bay—to "scatter the pelicans," according to Red Marston of the *St. Petersburg Times.*

March 20, 1956—Al Lang Field, St. Petersburg, Florida. Mickey Mantle, who clearly was having his best spring since 1951, collected his fourth Grapefruit homer and it had 'em gaping.

The ball traveled 450 feet, all the New York newspapers said. But eyewitnesses will assert that that distance was just to the fence, and that the ball was high in the sky when it cleared the center-field barrier.

St. Louis Cardinals pitcher Larry Jackson is just glad the damned thing wasn't hit through the box. "Hell, it was 450 feet to the scoreboard," Jackson said some 30 years later. Jackson and Bill Virdon, who was in center field for the Cards, both remember it as the longest shot they ever saw. Both believe the ball went at least 500 feet.

The Mick's homer, one of only five hits by the Yanks, who lost, 3–2, drew an on-the-spot comment from the St. Louis right fielder. "No home run ever cleared my head by so much as long as I can remember," said

71

Stan Musial. "The kid looks different this year. If he hits 60 homers and bats .400, I can't say I'll be surprised."

March 24, 1956—Miami Stadium, Miami, Florida. Facing Carl Erskine, the Brooklyn right hander who once fanned him four times in a World Series game, Mickey Mantle hit another tape-measure job. The ball cleared the 35-foot-high center-field wall at a point 400 feet from the plate, a first at Miami Stadium. Locals called it the longest homer in Miami Stadium history and estimated the length at 450 feet, although the Associated Press reported it as a 500-footer. Al Burt in the *Miami Herald* wrote that "Yankee Publicist Bob Fishel yawned and allowed that Mickey had smote them much farther than that this spring."

Mantle stayed relatively healthy all spring. The pulled thigh muscle that so damaged him late in 1955 was mended, and although in late March he bruised his right leg in a slide, he was as good as new after sitting out a week or so.

Mantle displayed a noticeably cooler head at the plate. He laid off bad pitches and struck out less often. He covered the plate better, adjusting to inside pitches and hitting outside pitches the other way. This new awareness of the strike zone, and ability to handle all types of pitches in the strike zone, made Mickey a better all-round hitter.

There were some important improvements off the field, too. His shyness was wearing off, and he opened up more with the sportswriters, sometimes even volunteering information. He had a new self-confidence, a new maturity as a player and person. He still became angry with himself—he never got over that—but he controlled his rage a little better and resorted less to punching walls and kicking water coolers.

Every spring the experts had been predicting that the season ahead would be the one in which Mantle would attain Ruthian greatness. This spring was no different. Shirley Povich of the *Washington Post* wrote that he had an "inescapable" feeling that 1956 would be Mantle's year: "This is the one when he'll burst into full magnificence, hit more and longer home runs than anybody else, lead the league in batting, perhaps, and certainly get more extra-base hits than anybody else."

It didn't take Mantle long in making a prophet of Povich. He started right away, with a big Opening Day in Povich's Washington.

April 17, 1956—Griffith Stadium, Washington, D.C. Mickey Mantle had the crowd watching goggle-eyed in the Yankees 10–4 Opening Day win over the Senators as he belted two prodigious home runs. Both were hit left-handed off Camilo Pascual and both traveled some 500 feet. The consensus was that the first traveled a little longer, although Mantle said he hit the second harder. But certainly no player before had ever sent a brace of home runs over the 31-foot-high wall in center field.

Mantle also made a pair of scintillating catches, twice hauling the ball in while bouncing off the wall in center field.

The Mick's first homer left the park above the 408-foot mark and landed atop the Carl T. Coleman house at 2014 Fifth Street. The second, which was more of a line drive, cleared the high wall at the 438-foot marker, fell into a clump of trees, and bounced into Fifth Street. The three-run blow gave the Yanks an insurmountable 8–2 lead and drew gasps of admiration from the 27,837. One of the spectators was President Dwight D. Eisenhower.

Yankee coach Bill Dickey in the locker room after the game said, "I only saw one ball hit over that wall before, and that was by the Babe. Do you realize what this boy did—hit two over it in the same game, and both line drives? Mickey's got more power than any hitter I ever saw, including Ruth."

Casey Stengel in talking with Arthur Daley of the *New York Times* made reference to a large tree beyond Griffith's center-field wall, a Washington monument of sorts. "One of those shots Mantle hit in Washington might be traveling yet except it strikes a tree outside the park," Casey told Daley. "They tell me that the only other fella which hit that tree was Ruth. He shook some kids outta the tree when the ball landed. But the tree's gotten bigger in 25 years, and so, I guess, have the kids the Babe shook outta it."

May 5, 1956—Yankee Stadium. The power-packed Yankees, who have now homered in 13 of their first 16 games, collected four on this date and there was not a single cheapie in the bunch. Yogi Berra hit one into the third-tier stands in right field, and Hank Bauer hit another so far to deep-center field that he made it home safely for an inside-the-parker. But the focus was on the red-hot Mickey Mantle.

Mantle hit a pair of titanic left-handed homers, between which he changed the pace with a drag-bunt single past the pitcher. The only out Mantle made in the 5–2 conquest of Kansas City was a fly that Gus Zernial caught in deep left.

Mantle's first homer was hit off a Lou Kretlow change-up and landed high in the upper deck in right. His second, off Moe Burtschy, was a pulled curveball that traveled to a point just inside the right-field foul pole on the front of the upper deck—what almost every New York City newspaper termed the "facade." The facade?

Yes, the facade. Here is the way six of the New York papers described the landing point of the second Mantle homer (the seventh city paper, the *New York World-Telegram and Sun*, didn't publish on Sunday):

- *Times*, Joseph M. Sheehan: "slammed . . . violently against the upper deck facade, near the foul line."
- *Journal-American*, Til Ferdenzi: " . . . off the facade of the top story."
- *Mirror,* Ben Epstein: " . . . just inside the foul pole . . . kicked off the facade of the upper deck."
- *Post*, Leonard Koppett: " . . . Just fair, down the short right field line . . . on a line and up against the facade that fronts the upper deck."
- *Daily News*, Chris Kieran: " . . . off the upper tier facade."
- *Herald-Tribune*, Harold Rosenthal: "ricocheted off the front of the upper deck."

No one has ever determined this by scientific survey, but it is believed that most people reserve the word "facade" for that distinctive green (aged copper) band that hung from the roof of the "old" Yankee Stadium. The Gothic band was decorative and might be better called a frieze; but "facade" it is in baseball vernacular.

At first I thought the New York sportswriters had substituted "facade" for upper-deck facing—the facia at the *bottom* front of the third deck. After all, the old facade was only 16 feet from top to bottom, and a ball striking the facade—quite a story in itself—is a ball that almost leaves the Stadium. And a ball that leaves the Stadium is a first. An incredible near-story! Yet, none of the papers jumped on either the story (the ball's hitting the facade) or the near-story (the ball almost leaving the Stadium). None even bothered to say whether the facade had ever been struck before. This creates an element of doubt.

Did the ball actually hit the facade? Or was it the upper-deck facing? Lou Boudreau, the A's manager at the time, will tell you in no uncertain terms that the ball hit the *facade*, and he was there. Another who was there was Merle Harmon, the A's broadcaster. "I thought it was going completely out of the park," says Harmon. "If not for the roof, it would have hit the subway across the street." Larry Rhea, another A's broadcaster, remembers the ball hitting "the very top of the right-field roof."

So there you have it—his first of three (and there may have been a fourth) shots off the right-field facade. He never did get one completely out of the Stadium, at least not in a regulation game. Batting practice is another story.

Allen Gerbman, a native New Yorker who hawked concessions at the Stadium for many years, says he saw Mantle in batting practice hit a ball out of the Stadium over the right-field bleachers, near the Jerome Avenue subway platform. "I've seen him hit it out of the park over the El," states Gerbman. "How far it went past the El I could not say."

Gerbman is not alone in his assertion. Maury Allen, a veteran New York sportswriter, wrote that Mantle in batting practice "hit a ball out of the Stadium while the other Yankees argued whether it was fair or foul."

Similar experiences are recalled by two former Mantle teammates with the Yankees. Jim McDonald, a Yankee pitcher from 1952 through 1954, remembers seeing a Mantle shot leave the Stadium near the spot where the right-field bleachers meet the bullpen. Willie Miranda, a Yankee infielder in 1953 and 1954, recalls seeing Mantle hit one over the *left-field* roof in a batting practice session.

May 18, 1956—Comiskey Park, Chicago. Dixie Howell, only one out away from nailing down a 7–6 White Sox win, had Mantle to face, and the Mick, besides making several excellent catches in center field, already had a homer, double, single, and a walk to his credit. Howell had the option of pitching around Mantle and facing Yogi Berra. But Berra was hot.

So Howell elects to give Mantle something decent, and Mickey, batting lefty, whacks a dramatic game-tying home run (the Yanks go on to win) into the upper deck in right field. Earlier, batting righty against Billy Pierce, Mantle had unloaded an epic two-run shot 15 to 20 rows deep into the upper-left-field stands.

No one had ever seen such powerful home runs hit from each side of the plate in the same game. It is quite a feat to hit either upper deck at Comiskey Park, and Mickey has switch-hit into both decks.

Mantle and Berra combine for a total of 20 bases. Berra, not known as a spring hitter, is batting .357, and with Yogi going so well in the clean-up spot (collecting a homer and a pair of doubles on this date), Mantle, batting third, is getting sweeter pitches to hit—he's batting .409

to lead the league. (Babe Ruth had a similar advantage with Lou Gehrig batting behind him.) Mantle and Berra are running first and second in the home-run and RBI races, Mantle leading in homers, 15 to 12, and in RBIs, 33 to 32. They are tearing up the league!

THE SWITCHER

The big hits in Chicago marked the third time that Mantle homered, in the same game, from each side of the plate. He would ultimately establish the major-league record in switch-hitting home runs in the same game, accomplishing the trick in a total of 10 games. No one has matched Mickey's unparalleled skill in popping long drives right-handed and left-handed.

Mickey was molded into a switch-hitter at the tender age of 5. Mutt Mantle saw baseball inclining toward platooning and he did not want his son sitting because of a pitcher's delivery direction. He took little Mickey to the yard, and being a right-handed tosser, made Mickey bat left-handed when he pitched to him. Mickey turned around and hit righty, his natural side, when Grandpa Charlie, a left-handed thrower, took the hill.

These three worked hour after hour until, eventually, Mickey, fighting back the initial hatred he had for it because of its unnaturalness, became accustomed to batting left-handed.

Mutt insisted that his son switch-hit, even as early as pee wee baseball. There was one occasion when Mickey, discouraged that he wasn't able to bat more from his natural side—there are many more right-handed pitchers than lefties no matter what league you're in—stepped into the right-handed box against a young righty. Mickey was unaware that his father was watching, and when Mutt saw what his son was doing, he blew up, yelling for Mickey to get on home and never play ball again until he made up his mind to become a switch-hitter. Mickey, determined to please his father, heeded these stinging words, and grew to appreciate his dad's direction. There was a time late in Mantle's career when he was urged to bat right-handed entirely, but, no, Mickey stressed, his dad had worked too hard for him to change now. And he didn't. Besides, Yankee Stadium was built with left-handed pull-hitters in mind.

Mickey had an advantage switch-hitting that outweighed other considerations. Curveballs and sliders broke into him, not away, so he never had to worry about crossfire pitches hitting him. That is, until certain unscrupulous pitchers began aiming balls at his chronically weak knees. Mickey did have a blind spot batting left-handed—fastballs high and tight, which he couldn't resist—but he was never afraid of being hit by a pitch.

So which way was he better? When he first made the Yankees, there were those in the front office who felt he'd go further strictly as a left-handed batter, mainly because of his drag-bunting ability. Later, others, including Yogi Berra, came to feel that the Mick was more lethal right-handed because he didn't strike out as often. In addition, he had more opposite-field power batting righty.

Batting lefty, he had a slight crouch, and righty he stood nearly erect. Just a little difference, maybe, but it created the blind spot for the left-handed Mantle high and tight. Mantle, then, as a left-handed hitter feasted on low pitches, golfing them incredible distances, and as a right-hander hit frozen-rope line drives with a level swing.

There is little doubt that overall Mantle was better hitting right-handed. He hit nearly .350 lifetime from that side and finished with a .298 overall mark. Unfortunately, Mantle was forced to bat left-handed much more often than right-handed, and, in fact, he swatted 373 left-handed homers, compared to 163 right-handed, again, of course, because he batted more often left-handed. Mickey didn't bat as well hitting lefty mainly because of various injuries, most importantly his damaged right knee and the right shoulder injury, which pained him terribly, that stemmed from a 1957 accident.

Casey Stengel thought Mantle was great both ways: "If that kid only hit right-handed he'd be tree-mendous. If he only hit left-handed, he'd be tree-mendous. But since he does his hittin' both ways, he's just tree-mendous."

Robert Ferguson, who began in the majors in 1876, was baseball's first switch-hitter. Until Mantle came along, Frankie Frisch, who broke in with the New York Giants in 1919, was considered the greatest switch-hitter of all time, and Frisch, like Pittsburgh's Max Carey, the man he supplanted as the best, basically was a player who hit for average. The Fordham Flash reached base often and scored lots of runs. But Mantle was the first power-hitting switcher—a pioneer, so to speak. Only switchers Reggie Smith and Eddie Murray have since approached his long-ball prowess.

A quick look at the statistics of Mantle, Frisch, and Carey shows how Mickey changed the art of switch-hitting:

	G	AB	H	2B	3B	HR	R
Mantle	2,401	8,102	2,415	344	72	536	1,677
Frisch	2,311	9,112	2,880	466	138	105	1,532
Carey	2,476	9,363	2,665	419	159	69	1,545

	RBI	BB	SO	SB	BA	SA
Mantle	1,509	1,734	1,710	153	.298	.557
Frisch	1,244	728	272	419	.316	.432
Carey	800	1,040	695	738	.285	.385

May 30, 1956—Yankee Stadium. Mickey Mantle just missed. Batting left-handed against Washington's Pedro Ramos, he powered a home run to the right-field facade. Another 18 inches and Mantle would have been the first player to hit a fair ball out of the Stadium.

In his report for the *Washington Star*, Burton Hawkins wrote, "The ball soared in a majestic arc toward the rightfield roof, certainly one of the most magnificent homers in history." At the apex of the ball's flight, it actually appeared to be higher than the Stadium's roof and heading out. Indeed, the ball might have cleared the roof with any assistance from the wind; but the drive was hit against a quartering breeze. The consensus was that the ball would have traveled at least 600 feet had its flight been unimpeded.

Even Mantle, normally unimpressed by his space shots, was moved to say of this home run: "It was the best I ever hit a ball left-handed." Seven years later, however, a left-handed-hitting Mantle will bang another homer against the same facade and declare this one to have been hit even harder.

For days afterward Stadium customers pointed to the spot that Mantle tapped and shook their heads in wonder. Rival players were also curious. Howard Cosell, a local sportscaster in New York in those days, showed the landmark to Harvey Kuenn of the Tigers. "Did he really hit it up there?" asked an incredulous Kuenn. "Really?"

More important to Casey Stengel, who earlier this season had predicted that if anyone could hit one out of Yankee Stadium it would be Mantle, was the impact of Mantle's three-run homer on the game. It turned around a 1–0 deficit and put the Yankees into a 3–1 lead. New York went on to win, 4–3, in the first game of a doubleheader.

Washington hung tough in the second game. But with the score 3–3 in the fifth, Mantle. batting lefty against Camilo Pascual, boomed a 450-footer halfway up the right-field bleachers, and the Yanks went on to win, 12–5.

When the day ended, Mickey was the major-league leader in batting (.425), homers (20), RBIs (50), runs (45), hits (65), and total bases (135). And he was doing it from both sides of the plate: Seventeen of his homers were hit lefty and he was hitting .472 righty.

Riding the back of Mantle, who set a May homer record with 16, the Yankees had pulled away from the field in the American League pennant race. They now led by six games and would not be significantly threatened.

The facade banger turned Mantle into a hot national celebrity, the cover boy of several prominent news and sports magazines. His 20 homers put him 11 games ahead of the pace set by Babe Ruth in 1927, the year of the Bambino's legendary 60. Babe didn't hit No. 20 until June 11. As usually happens when someone starts hitting a lot of homers, the major leagues as a whole happen to be hitting more homers and the theory spreads that the ball is livelier; as usual, though, it's not proved or disproved.

But the chase was on. Mantle against Ruth, whether Mickey liked it or not. He didn't like it, especially the growing press coverage and what at times seemed an erosion of his privacy.

June 5, 1956—Yankee Stadium. American League baseball has been preoccupied with how to pitch to Mickey Mantle. Today Kansas City manager Lou Boudreau changed the focus from pitching to defensive alignment, introducing the Mantle Shift. Boudreau a decade earlier had devised a shift against Ted Williams, overloading the right side of the field for that notorious pull-hitter.

Boudreau had been pondering the Mantle problem for some time. Suddenly, it came to him; he jotted down some X's on the back of a menu—the Mantle Shift—figuring on using the tactic only when Mantle batted left-handed, and only when the bases were empty (the extreme repositioning of his infielders made the shift impossible with runners aboard).

The Mantle Shift, invoked in the very first inning, makes the Williams Shift look like a trivial defensive adjustment. Only one fielder—the first baseman—is anywhere near his regular position. The second baseman is moved to short right field, the shortstop to the vacated second-base slot, the third baseman to shallow center, the left fielder to deep third, the center fielder to deep left-center, and the right fielder to deep right-center. Thus, there are four outfielders—five if you count the leftfielder at deep third—with only the right-field line and left field exposed, and a ball Mickey pulls into the right-field corner is probably a home run anyway.

The Mantle Shift had holes; it was vulnerable to the bunt, for one thing, and Mantle was one of the best at bunting. Boudreau, who used the Mantle Shift only a few times, says the idea was to get Mantle's attention away from the short porch in right. In other words, to concede Mickey a bunt single rather than risk a homer.

Mantle sees the shift in the first and fourth innings and does the smart thing; he attempts to bunt. But pitcher Lou Kretlow is smart, too; he keeps his fastball high and tight, a tough pitch to bunt. Mickey fouls off his bunts and winds up striking out in both at bats. Mantle does crack a two-run homer off Kretlow in the eighth, but because of the base runner, the shift was not on.

Afterward, Stengel was more concerned about Mantle than the 7–4 licking the A's gave him. He grumbled something about the shift not making sense, but, inwardly, he was worried that it might do injury to his star. General manager George Weiss thought the shift affected Mantle. "It got him thinking," Weiss said, "and that's bad."

The Mantle Shift will be used again in this series, and Mickey will come out of the series in a slump, collecting over the first 13 days of June only one homer and three RBIs.

June 18, 1956—Briggs Stadium, Detroit. With the score tied and a left-handed Mantle up with two on in the eighth, Tiger manager Bucky Harris was worried, although he didn't exactly have the long-ball jitters what with a stiff breeze blowing in Mickey's face.

Harris talks with his pitcher, Paul Foytack, and has barely returned to the dugout when he hears the sickening thwack of bat on ball. Turning, he sees a baseball soar over the roof in right field and onto Trumbull Avenue. Pitcher Virgil Trucks, sitting on the bench, will never forget Harris's dismay-laden comment: "That would bring tears to the eyes of a rocking chair."

Mantle's 25th homer of the season is only the second to clear the right-field roof here (although some reports have it that the ball bounced off the roof). But Mantle's is more impressive than Ted Williams' 1939 dinger, which was hit toward the line. Mantle's wallop leaves the park in right-center, going out between a light standard and the end of the top deck. And because Mantle hit his against a strong wind, some consider it Detroit's most awesome homer.

Foytack remembers the blast not for its majesty but "because it beat me." He was trying to pitch Mickey high and inside. "The pitch was high," he recalls, "but I didn't get it in far enough."

June 20, 1956—Briggs Stadium, Detroit. "There was a time when it was safe to stroll along Trumbull Avenue or sit in the bleachers at Briggs Stadium. No more. Not while Mickey Charles Mantle can swing a bat." That was the lead of Joe Falls's story in the *Detroit Times* on today's Yankees-Tigers game.

Mantle hit a pair of gigantic home runs—"bazooka blasts," in the words of Paul Foytack years later—into the center-field upper-deck bleachers, something no other player had done since the bleachers were built in the late 1930s.

Mickey bounces out and lines out in his first two trips. But in the seventh, batting right-handed against Billy Hoeft, he gets hold of a change-up curve and parks it high above the 400-foot sign in the upper left-center-field bleachers. Hoeft's first pitch to Mantle in the eighth, thrown high and outside, results in a duplicate of the first homer, only this time, Mickey, going with the pitch, sends it into the upper deck in right-center. Even Detroit fans, not by a long shot Yankee boosters, become enthusiastic about Mantle's latest long-ball exploits. About 20 fans, mostly youngsters, climb out of the stands in the ninth and charge to center field for a better look at Mantle and a chance to shake his hand. One kid even falls to his knees and does a salaam. After the final out, when another group tries to touch the Yankee star, umpire Ed Hurley leads interference so that Mickey can reach the safety of the clubhouse.

Mantle is now the greatest drawing card in baseball. American League president Will Harridge at season's end will rate Mantle as a draw with the likes of Babe Ruth and Bob Feller, adding "The reaction this office has received to Mantle's homers—distance homers—is positively stunning. I can't recall anything like it. Everywhere I went, it was Mantle, Mantle, Mantle."

The Mantle challenge to Ruth's 60-homer record, meanwhile, is intensifying. The Mick is now 18 games ahead of Ruth's 1927 home-run pace, a somewhat misleading situation report as knowledgeable fans realize because the Babe had a torrid season finish, belting 17 homers in September.

The Triple Crown picture at this day's end was as follows:

Home Runs

Mantle	27
Yogi Berra, New York	17
Roy Sievers, Washington.	17

Runs Batted In

Mantle	64
Vic Wertz, Cleveland	50

Batting Average

Mantle	.380
Charlie Maxwell, Detroit	.370

July 1, 1956—Yankee Stadium. Mickey Mantle had had no homers to show since his fireworks in Detroit, although he was still getting his share of hits.

Late in the second game of a lusterless Mantle doubleheader against Washington, the Mick breaks out. In his final two at bats he homers from each side of the plate. Both are tape-measure jobs. One ties the game, the second wins it, and the Yanks sweep. The homers put him eight games ahead of Babe Ruth's 1927 home-run pace. Just like that.

Mantle's first homer, off left-handed Dean Stone, reaches the third tier in left field. A rare shot. In the ninth, following Elston Howard's single, Mantle turns around to hit from the left side against Bud Byerly and sends the crowd home with a wallop deep into the Yankee bullpen in right.

July 10, 1956—Griffith Stadium, Washington, D.C. The torch was passing. For years Ted Williams, 37, and Stan Musial, 35, were the brightest stars of the American and National Leagues. Now they were being eclipsed by Mickey Mantle, 24, and Willie Mays, 25. Today, in a moment crystallized in time, Williams, Musial, Mantle, and Mays—all four—hit home runs in an All-Star Game in the nation's capital.

The National League jumps out to a 5–0 lead and wins rather handily, 7–3. The only cause for celebration for the partisan American League crowd, a near-capacity gathering of 28,343, comes in the sixth inning, when the junior circuit musters its lone rally. Nellie Fox opens with a single and Ted Williams and Mantle hit back-to-back homers, knocking out Warren Spahn. But Johnny Antonelli comes in and hurls four scoreless innings thereafter.

Mantle entered the All-Star Game as the player with the most fan votes. He was also the major-league leader in batting (.371), home runs (29), and RBIs (71). In spite of an injured right knee, Mickey wanted to participate. Wearing a cumbersome knee brace and lots of tape, he played the entire game. With the Americans forced to resort to catch-up baseball, manager Casey Stengel couldn't afford to remove his clean-up hitter. Other than the home run, though, Mantle has a poor game at the plate, striking out in his other three at bats.

Mantle had hurt the knee July 4 in an outfield play. It wasn't serious, as the Mick's injuries went, but he had played in only one game since the mishap. He will have to wear the brace a few more weeks, and he will hit only three more homers before July 30.

Mantle would be selected to 20 All-Star squads—two games were played each year from 1959 through 1962—and he would play in 16 games. This date's home run was his second and last, but his All-Star homers were hit against the best the National League had to offer in the 1950s—Robin Roberts and Warren Spahn. Mantle's unimpressive All-Star Game stats are as follows:

G	AB	R	H	2B	3B	HR	RBI	BA
16	43	5	10	0	0	2	4	.233

August 12, 1956—Yankee Stadium. The Yankees swept a double-header from Baltimore with the streaking Mickey Mantle having another big day, reaching base five times and getting Home Run No. 41, his seventh homer in eight days. Mickey was now 13 games ahead of the Ruth pace.

His homer clears the 402-foot sign in left and is hit off Don Ferrarese, a 5'9" southpaw who nearly no-hit the Yankees in May.

When the long day is over, Oriole manager Paul Richards likens the Mick to Ruth as a hitter and to Joe DiMaggio as a fielder. Oriole coach Harry Brecheen chimes in, saying that Mantle is the best slow-ball hitter he's ever seen.

Nearly 30 years later, Ferrarese, the head baseball coach at Victor Valley College in California, says that "Mantle's home run still has me in awe. The situation was this: I had a 3-and-2 count on him and I threw a straight change-up off my fastball. The initial reaction of Mantle was to lunge after the low pitch. . . . My feeling was I had totally fooled him with the slow pitch. With one hand remaining on the bat, he powered the ball into the left-field bullpen in Yankee Stadium, which was approximately 400 feet away."

August 31, 1956—Griffith Stadium, Washington, D.C. President Eisenhower, in a surprise visit, made his first appearance at the ballpark since Opening Day, when he had watched Mickey Mantle blast two tape-measure jobs. Mickey, summoned to the president's box for a handshake before today's game, is told by Ike, "I hope you hit a home run, but I hope Washington wins."

Eisenhower gets half his wish. Mantle indeed hits a homer, his 47th of the year, but the Yankees beat Washington, 6–4. Whitey Ford only has trouble with Jim Lemon, who belts three homers, joining Joe DiMaggio as the only two players to have a three-homer game in Griffith Stadium history.

Mantle snaps a 4–4 tie with a seventh-inning wallop over the high right-field wall. He has five hits this year off Camilo Pascual, and all are home runs.

With this homer, Mantle wound up a great 13-homer August, putting him four games ahead of Ruth. But Ruth's brutal September pace lay ahead.

Mantle appeared to have a more realistic chance at winning the coveted Triple Crown. He led in all three categories by wide margins:

Home Runs

Mantle	47
Jim Lemon, Washington.	26
Roy Sievers, Washington.	26

Runs Batted In

Mantle	118
Al Kaline, Detroit	107

Batting Average

Mantle	.366
Ted Williams, Boston	.346

To make a run at Ruth's record, Mantle needed to get off to a great start in September. But he did just the opposite. In the month's first 10 games, he failed to hit a home run or even drive in a run, going 5 for 33. Pressing too hard, he began swinging at tempting pitches out of the strike zone.

The June dry spell, the twisted knee in July, and the early September slump proved too much in the end. Mickey still had the Triple Crown to shoot for, and he wanted that one badly; but the Ruth challenge was ended.

September 18, 1956—Comiskey Park, Chicago. The Yankees needed just one more victory to clinch their 22nd American League pennant. There was little question that they would eventually clinch it— they had nine games after today—but an element of drama graced this date's game, nevertheless.

Two of the best lefties in baseball, Whitey Ford (18–5) and Billy Pierce (20–7), lock up in a great duel. Ford makes only two mistakes, permitting solo homers to Larry Doby and Walt Dropo. The Yankees get on the board when Mickey Mantle singles home Billy Martin and then tie the score in the ninth when Yogi Berra singles home Martin.

With two out in the 11th and the bases empty, Mantle steps into the right-hander's box. He hammers Pierce's first offering into the left-field upper deck. Ford runs into trouble in the bottom half and Bob Grim relieves him. Gil McDougald starts a honey of a double play from his shortstop position, and Grim strikes out Jim Rivera with the tying run on third. The Yankees win, 3–2, and once again are the American League champions.

Praise was heaped on Mantle in the noisy locker-room celebration that followed. He was both the hero of the game and the star of the season. His game-winning homer was his 50th, exceeding Lou Gehrig's best single-season home-run total. Babe Ruth, Jimmie Foxx, and Hank Greenberg, up to this date, were the only other American Leaguers to have reached 50.

Besides representing a personal landmark, Mantle's home run was the 182nd of the year for the Yankees, tying the league record set by the 1936 Yankees of Gehrig and DiMaggio and friends. This year's Yankees would shatter the record—Mantle's next homer, in fact, broke the old mark—and finish with 190 homers. The club was led, of course, by Mantle (52 HRs) and Berra (30), the most dynamic duo since the heyday of Ruth and Gehrig, but the Bombers had good power up and down the lineup. Hank Bauer (26), Bill Skowron (23), and Gil McDougald (13) all hit double figures in homers.

September 21, 1956—Fenway Park, Boston. Mickey Mantle's 51st home run, a sizzling rocket that cleared the center-field fence and smashed into the rear retaining wall only a foot from leaving the park, was "hit pretty good, all right," Mantle told the *Boston Globe*, which described the tape-measure job as a 480-footer.

The game was meaningless, except that there never is a meaningless Yankee–Red Sox game, and 24,616 watch Boston win, 13–7, and the Yankees set a big-league record by stranding 20 base runners.

But the big story as this three-game series begins is the race between Mantle and Ted Williams for the batting crown. Not long ago, Mantle seemed a shoo-in for the Triple Crown. Now he is in tight races with both Williams and Al Kaline, the latter vying for the RBI lead. Coming into the series, Williams actually leads Mantle, .355 to .350, and even after Mickey goes 3 for 5 with a walk, Williams goes 2 for 4 with a walk and leads, .356 to .352.

But Williams needs at least 400 official at bats to qualify for the title and as of now has only 376. Walks don't count. Ted must get 24 at bats in seven remaining Red Sox games and hold off Mantle at the same time. While Williams would love nothing better than to cop his fifth batting championship, Arthur Daley, for one, believed that Williams would sacrifice the title rather than swing at bad pitches in order to ensure himself of 400 at bats. He is that much of a perfectionist. He would walk rather than hit a pitch a fraction of an inch off the plate.

Which brings up another point that was on people's minds. Would Yankee pitchers, in an effort to help Mickey win the title, walk Williams in their upcoming two series and deny Ted 400 at bats? Yankee pitcher Mickey McDermott, an old teammate of Ted's, tells Clif Keane of the *Boston Globe* on this date that Mantle hasn't asked for assistance. "I know he wants to beat this guy [Williams] on the level," he says.

Mantle will indeed rise to the occasion. He will have a 6-for-9 series and pass Williams, who went 2 for 11 against Yankee pitching, to take the lead, .356 to .350.

September 28, 1956—Yankee Stadium. Mickey Mantle and Ted Williams continued their head-to-head fight for the batting crown, opening a three-game series here that will close the regular season and decide whether Mantle, who has a lock on the homer championship, can add the batting and RBI titles to win the Triple Crown.

Boston pitchers Bob Porterfield and George Susce hold Mantle to a 1-for-4 day, Mickey's one hit, off Porterfield—it will be his last hit of the season—is home run No. 52. Mickey finishes the day at .353.

Williams goes 0 for 3 and walks once. Although he raps three solid grounders, second baseman Billy Martin gobbles each up and turns two of them into double plays. Williams still needs six at bats to reach 400 and qualify for the title, but he has dropped to .348, five points behind Mantle, with only two games left.

Tomorrow Williams will have a golden opportunity to both make ground *and* get his 400 at bats. In an extra-inning affair, he goes to the plate six times, putting him at 400 right on the nose, but he makes only one hit, which just about eliminates him from the batting race. Williams makes a brief appearance in the final game, finishing at .345—with exactly 400 official at bats.

Mantle will be grateful to his Yankee pitchers for their toughness on Williams. Williams ultimately lost the batting crown by eight points because he hit a feeble .196 (11 for 56) against New York. And in the two crucial late-season Yankee–Red Sox series, Ted went a combined 3 for 20, while Mickey went 7 for 14.

Mantle, still bothered by a pulled groin muscle he aggravated running out a double in Boston, pinch-hit in the next-to-last game and walked with the bases loaded. He wanted to play in the final game, but Stengel, perhaps remembering the debacle of the previous World Series, when the Mick was hurt, said that Mickey "isn't right" and sat him down. Stengel, understandably, felt Mantle should be rested for the upcoming World Series.

But Stengel also wanted Mantle to win the Triple Crown, and the only challenger remaining was Al Kaline, whose 126 RBIs placed him three behind Mantle. Stengel received up-to-the-minute reports on Kaline's final-game progress, and when he learned Kaline had knocked in two runs, he sent Mickey in as a pinch-hitter with a man on third base. Mantle drove in his 130th run with a groundout. But the RBI wasn't necessary, since Kaline finished with 128 RBIs.

The Triple Crown, the greatest batting feat since power hitting replaced "inside baseball," was Mickey Mantle's.

The Triple Crown took on importance when its third leg, the RBI, became an official statistic in 1920. A Triple Crown winner demonstrates hitting consistency, power, and ability to hit with men on base. Only the greatest hitters win it and many great hitters—Ruth, DiMaggio, Musial, Aaron, and Mays, to name a few—have never won it.

Mantle happened to lead *both* leagues in all three Triple Crown categories. Since the official birth of the RBI in 1920, only Rogers Hornsby (in 1925), Lou Gehrig (in 1934), and Ted Williams (in 1942) have led both leagues in the three Triple Crown categories; Mantle makes the fourth.

Lou Gehrig was, and is, the only other Yankee to win the American League Triple Crown besides Mantle. Listed below through the 1986 season are the junior circuit's Triple Crown winners, including, for the sake of completeness, retroactive winners (pre-1920):

Player	Year	HR	RBI	BA
Nap Lajoie	1901	14	125	.422
Ty Cobb	1909	9	115	.377
Jimmie Foxx	1933	48	163	.356
Lou Gehrig	1934	49	165	.363
Ted Williams	1942	36	137	.356
Ted Williams	1947	32	114	.343
Mickey Mantle	1956	52	130	.353
Frank Robinson	1966	49	122	.316
Carl Yastrzemski	1967	44	121	.326

Mantle will be the unanimous choice of the Baseball Writers for the league's Most Valuable Player Award and will bring home a whole string of awards. But at the end of September 1956 he had a World Series date with Brooklyn for which to prepare.

October 3, 1956—Ebbets Field, Brooklyn. The World Series opener between those perennial autumn rivals, the Yankees and Dodgers, got off to a ringing start. Mickey Mantle, batting lefty, whacked a first-inning two-run homer high and far over the right-field screen.

Jimmy Powers described Mantle's blow in the *New York Daily News*: "There was a sharp crack and the ball flew in a high arch over the screen, over Bedford Avenue, and into a parking lot filled with pastel-colored cars. An attendant scampered over the tightly jammed autos, stepping callously on shining hoods and fenders as he raced to retrieve his souvenir. In terms of damage to glossy finishes, it was a costly trophy, causing easily $500 worth of destruction."

Apart from the Mantle homer, however, Yankee fans had very little to cheer. Whitey Ford was roughed up, Gil Hodges hit a three-run homer, Sal Maglie hurled a complete game, and Brooklyn won, 6–3.

October 7, 1956—Yankee Stadium. The Yankees, after losing the first two series games, were breathing again. Enos Slaughter gave the club life yesterday with a three-run homer to win Game 3. Now the Yankees turned to their Big Guy, Mickey Mantle, to even matters in Game 4.

Under threatening skies and in front of 69,705 spectators, Game 4 is 1–1 going into the bottom of the fourth inning. Leading off, Mantle sets up a two-run rally when he draws a walk and steals second base as Yogi Berra strikes out. The Dodgers intentionally walk Slaughter, yesterday's hero, but Billy Martin crosses them up with a single, scoring Mantle. A sacrifice fly by Gil McDougald gives New York a 3–1 lead.

Mantle is the leadoff man again in the sixth. On the mound is reliever Ed Roebuck, a right-hander, who retires six of the seven men he faces. But not Mickey. After taking a ball, Mantle booms a towering blast that cuts through a low mist, passes directly over the 407-foot sign in right-center, and drops some 15 rows deep among the scrambling bleacher fans. The home run, a tape-measure job of about 440 feet, puts the Yankees ahead, 4–1, and they go on to win 6–2.

October 8, 1956—Yankee Stadium. Don Larsen assured himself immortality by pitching a no-hitter, a perfect game no less, the first and only one of either kind in World Series history. Twenty-seven Dodgers up, 27 down in order, and 97 pitches in which to do it. When it was over, Larsen had a special hug for Mickey Mantle, who paved the way with his bat and saved the day with his glove.

Sal Maglie of the Dodgers also pitches brilliantly and allows only five hits in a route-going performance. He retires the first 11 Yankees in order. But with two out in the fourth, Maglie comes inside to Mantle, after working the outside corner, and Mickey turns quickly on the ball. He shoots a wicked liner hooking into the lower right-field stands, just inside the foul pole, and the Yankees have a 1–0 lead.

Meanwhile, Larsen is sailing along, though he needs a great defensive play to retire Jackie Robinson in the second. Third baseman

Andy Carey deflects Robinson's hard shot to shortstop Gil McDougald, and Gil's throw from deep in the hole nips Jackie by less than a step.

Now it is the fifth inning. Larsen serves his 51st delivery and Gil Hodges swats a screaming drive on a low but long arc to a point some 430 feet from the plate. The ball splits the left-center-field alley and appears headed toward the wall for an extra-base hit. Taking off from his position in straightaway center, Mantle explodes to his right, covering what seems an Oklahoma mile; then, at the last instant, he extends his left arm to make a spectacular backhanded grab. The crowd of 64,519 lets loose a thunderous roar.

Hodges and the Dodgers not only are robbed by Mantle, but the next man up in the fifth, Sandy Amoros, hits a ball into the right-field seats—but just foul. So Brooklyn is denied two runs by the slimmest of margins.

It is Larsen's day. Hank Bauer gives him a 2–0 lead with a sixth-inning RBI single, and when, with two out in the ninth, pinch-hitter Dale Mitchell takes a called third strike, pandemonium reigns.

The Yankees now have a 3-games-to-2 lead going back to Ebbets Field. But it would take seven games for the Yankees to wrap up the series and avenge last year's disheartening loss to Brooklyn.

Mantle hit only .250 for the series, but four of his six hits were for extra bases—Mickey's three homers actually matched Brooklyn's entire homer output—and he drew six walks. Mantle and Enos Slaughter each scored six runs, tying for the series leadership in that category. All in all, it was a great ending to a great season. For Mantle and the Yankees.

1957

April 10, 1957—Grayson Stadium, Savannah, Georgia. Not all of Mickey Mantle's outstanding home runs were hit in front of big-league crowds in big-league stadiums; some of his best wallops were seen only by tiny crowds in tiny parks as the Yankees barnstormed north each spring. Fans in towns like lovely Savannah jumped at the chance to see Mickey perform.

The Yankees beat a Cincinnati Class A farm team, the Savannah Redlegs, 8–4, before 4,176 enthusiastic fans. Early home runs are hit by Whitey Ford and by Hank Bauer, who smacks a real monster, but the crowd wants Mantle to pole one, although some appreciation is shown for his two singles and his outstanding running catch in left-center field to rob Frosty Kennedy of a hit.

The Mick finally complies. Batting right-handed against a wind and a southpaw named Jimmie Brown, Mickey unloads a tremendous rain-maker over the high barrier at the back of the left-field stands, the ball coming to rest among some southern pines. It is Mantle's sixth homer of the exhibition season, and it's a helluva hit.

A New York sportswriter makes an inquiry of the local press: Had anyone ever cleared the left-field bleachers before? Yes, he is told, and with drives better than Mantle's too. But Judge Julius Fine, who has been watching baseball at Grayson Stadium since 1933, said in 1986, "As far as I'm concerned, Mickey's homer was tops."

The kids of Savannah cared only that they had seen a Mantle homer. When the final out was made, a bunch of autograph-seeking youngsters was in chase of the Mick. Mickey turned it on and reached the dugout just in time to avoid being mobbed.

May 16, 1957—Yankee Stadium. The headlines in the morning papers stared a disbelieving George Weiss right in the face. The stories beneath them told of a brawl at the Copacabana nightclub featuring members of the New York Yankees. The Yankee general manager was more than a little ticked off.

A little birthday party for Billy Martin the previous night turned into a big mess. On hand for the Copa party besides the necessary Martin were Mickey Mantle, Whitey Ford, Yogi Berra, Hank Bauer, Johnny Kucks, and their wives. A good time was being had by all until a group of drunken bowlers started getting obnoxious. Words were exchanged between baseballers and bowlers, and before anyone knew what was happening, one of the bowlers was stretched out cold in the men's room.

Bauer decked him, the bowler later claimed upon filing charges. Bauer strongly denied the allegation and the litigation was eventually terminated because of insufficient evidence. Or as Berra put it, "Nobody did nothin' to nobody" (except maybe a club bouncer).

But the image-conscious Weiss and co-owner Dan Topping go a little nuts, slapping heavy fines on all the Copa Yankees. Casey Stengel is far more restrained, but is upset over his players partying the night before a game without first asking his permission. However, when the party was originally scheduled, the 16th was an open date, but a rained-out game was rescheduled for the night of the 16th. The merrymakers simply went ahead with the party as planned.

Stengel makes some not too subtle lineup changes for this date's game with Kansas City. Ford, the scheduled starter, pitches, but he pitches batting practice. Berra and Martin are also benched. (Billy has recently lost his regular job anyway.) Bauer plays but is dropped to the eighth slot in the batting order. Mantle plays and bats third. "I'm mad at him, too, for being out late," Casey says of Mickey, "but I'm not mad enough to take a chance on losing a ball game and possibly the pennant."

Mantle has a big game. He gives the Yankees a 1–0 lead with a right-handed homer into the left-field seats. He also has a single and walks twice. He has reached base safely six times in a row and 11 times in his last 12 trips. His batting average soars to .364.

Casey's lineup shuffling works to perfection. Elston Howard, playing for Berra, singles home the second run and Bauer singles home the third. There is no better pitcher alive than Bob Turley when his fastball is humming, and tonight it is blazing as Bullet Bob, pitching in Ford's place, throws a four-hit shutout. Turley also starts a triple play. The second-place Yankees (16–8) are 3–0 winners and trail Chicago (16–7) by a half game.

The silly fines aside, the Copa incident left no one scarred—with the exception of Martin. Weiss, who had never liked Martin, blamed him for all the negative publicity resulting from the "brawl." Now, with Stengel's guard weakened, Weiss had his best opportunity to trade Martin. Besides, a fine young second baseman named Bobby Richardson was doing a good job.

Martin was traded to Kansas City in June, breaking up that unique trio of Ford, the streetwise kid from New York; Martin, the graduate of a tough Berkeley, California, neighborhood; and Mantle, the heartland American.

Martin and Ford kept the moody Mantle loose. They could put a bad game behind them, while Mickey would brood in the clubhouse long after the final out. And although Mantle never did acquire the knack of shaking off a bad performance, running around with Martin and Ford took some of the edge off his tenseness.

Mantle was a great friend, too. When Martin's marriage was coming undone in 1953, Mickey was a steadying influence, keeping Billy from cracking up. So close were they that Martin spent the following winter with the Mantles in Commerce, Oklahoma.

Mantle and Martin fed off each other and made good roommates, although George Weiss didn't exactly see it that way. Weiss never credited Mantle with an ability to find his own trouble; to him, Martin was leading Mantle and, to some extent, Ford astray. But as Martin would point out, if he were so bad an influence on Mantle, how come Mickey won the MVP Award and Triple Crown in 1956?

May 23, 1957—Ebbets Field, Brooklyn. Mickey Mantle played his final game here, in the ballpark where he made his New York City debut and where he gave baseball fans so many World Series thrills. The Dodgers will trade Brooklyn for Los Angeles at the season's end; Ebbets Field will evaporate.

Nearly 30,000 pay to see the Mayor's Trophy Game in support of local sandlot baseball. The Yankees win, 10–7. Mantle's 4-for-5 day includes a righty homer, a mighty drive into the upper deck in center field, off Ken Lehman.

As the game's outstanding performer, Mickey wins a handsome watch, which he gives to teammate Al Cicotte, who in six innings allowed only as many hits as he himself made—two. Mickey feels Cicotte is more deserving. It is an act of generosity and fairness completely in character with Mantle's nature, for he was not an ungenerous man.

Mantle looked after his family, helping to support his widowed mother and putting his brother Larry through college. He helped the widowed mother of Fritzie Brickell, who was with the Yankees briefly and who died of cancer at age 30, by lending himself as the big-name draw in a benefit game for Mrs. Brickell. Even though columnist Dick Young had angered him with a piece, Mantle was generous enough to get word to Young that he would cooperate in a magazine article at a time when Young, whose paper was on strike, may have needed the money.

He was good with fellow players, sharing his St. Moritz digs with maritally troubled Joe Pepitone and giving the keys to a vacated house to new Yankee Jerry Lumpe and his family. He continued a tradition of two other big guys on the Yanks, Babe Ruth and Joe DiMaggio, of picking up cab fares and dinner checks when in the company of teammates.

He was good to rookies. "A lot of guys didn't even know my name," Ron Solomini, who never made the big club, told sportswriter Dick Schaap. "He always knew my name." And he was respectful of and sensitive toward all diamond friends and foes. "The thing I really liked about Mickey," says Bill Monbouquette, "was the way he treated everyone the same."

June 12, 1957—Comiskey Park, Chicago. Jack Harshman sat in the clubhouse, talking casually with reporters and listening to the radio description of the waning moments of the Yankee–White Sox game in which he was the starting Chicago pitcher. He had departed in the eighth, leaving a 7–4 lead with reliever Bob Keegan. Harshman had dropped six consecutive decisions to the Yankees and wanted—*really* wanted—this win.

The game is in the ninth inning and Harshman talks easily with the gathered press. Of the three homers hit off him, the lefty says: "Mantle hit a slider for his homer. He did not hit it real good, but it was a home run. You can't argue about that. Skowron's was a screwball and Bauer hit a fastball. I was just fortunate that when homers were hit there was no one on."

Gil McDougald singles with one out. "It might be you're writing this story a little premature, you know," suggests Harshman. "Yeah," answers a reporter, "that big character is up." He meant the Mick. All listen.

Sure enough, Mantle picks out a pitch from the right-handed Keegan and booms it into the center-field bullpen, narrowing Chicago's lead to 7–6.

"They ought to create a new league for that guy," Harshman tells the assembled writers.

White Sox manager Al Lopez takes out Keegan. He brings in a left-hander, who retires Yogi Berra—Yogi is hitting .217 and is one of the reasons the Yanks' attack is sluggish. Then Lopez calls on a right-hander, who fans Hank Bauer to end the game.

This game was a key encounter, or at least was billed as such. A crowd of 40,033 braved a miserable stormy night and several rain delays to exhort the hometown White Sox in what had become the bitterest rivalry in the league. When it was all over, Chicago (33–16) led second-place New York (29–22) by five games.

Mantle was hot as a firecracker, playing ball as well as he did in 1956. Tonight he went 4 for 5, knocking in four runs and hitting homers from each side of the plate for the fifth time in his career. He led the league with 18 homers and was batting .378.

But Mantle took no solace from his big night. He told reporters that he hit a slider and fastball for his homers, then walked away.

June 23, 1957—Yankee Stadium. This big showdown doubleheader between the top teams of the American League attracted 63,787 paid, baseball's largest crowd in two years. The day got off to a classy start with Prime Minister Kishi of Japan, wearing a Yankee cap, throwing out the first ball; before it was over, beered-up fans were cavorting on the playing field.

The Yankees and White Sox split. Chicago wins the afterpiece to salvage one game of the four-game series and snap a 10-game Yankee winning streak. The Yanks (39–23), trailing by six games on June 8, now lead the White Sox (38–23) by a half game. In the recent seven games between the two leaders, Mickey Mantle went 18 for 31—a .581 clip—and New York won five.

Mantle is a scene stealer on this date. Going 6 for 9, he lifts his league-leading batting average to .392 and his league-leading homer total to 21. Included in his safeties are one of the longest homers in Stadium history and a 10-foot topper that becomes a leg hit. He drives in four runs and is only one RBI behind the league-leading Roy Sievers, 52 to 51.

Mantle is taking dead aim at an unprecedented second straight Triple Crown.

In the first inning of the opener, Minnie Minoso drives one into the gap that Mickey somehow reaches but can't hold, and it goes for a double. The White Sox push across a run, then Larry Doby's line drive to deep right-center has "big inning" written all over it until Mantle races after it and picks the ball off the top of the wall.

Thanks to Mantle, a big inning is averted and Bobby Shantz settles down to pitch a six-hitter and win, 9–2. Shantz, making a great comeback after years of arm miseries, is 9–1.

Chicago's Dick Donovan does some fancy pitching of his own in the second game. He is a last-minute starter, despite an aching arm that prevents him from throwing a curveball. He pitches effectively, allowing only three hits through eight innings and looking for all the world like the first man to shut out the Yankees in 1957.

Donovan takes a 4–0 lead into the bottom of the ninth. Bobby Richardson scratches a single, and Gil McDougald bloops a hit. Mantle turns around a Donovan fastball, drilling a monster of a three-run blast that drops in the right-field upper deck; the blow elicits deafening cheers from some and leaves others gasping in disbelief. White Sox manager Al Lopez pulls Donovan—Lopez has nothing but praise for Donovan "but when he got one too high to Mickey in the ninth, I figured he had tired too much"—and brings in Paul LaPalme, who strikes out pinch-hitter Darrell Johnson, with runners on second and third, to end the game.

The fans continued buzzing over Mantle's homer. Reporters were confused, however. The ball had disappeared into a heavy haze and darkness, and no one in the press box saw exactly where it landed. Wherever, it came down purged; manager Lopez said Mantle "hit the shit out of the ball."

It was finally ascertained that the ball dropped in the extreme corner of the upper deck in right, near where the grandstand meets the bullpen. Some newspapers reported that the ball arrived there on the fly, but there were eyewitnesses, among them Chicago sportswriter John Kuenster, who said it first hit the facade hanging from the roof.

Nearly thirty years after the fact, Kuenster is still puzzled that neither the Yankees nor the New York papers had publicized this blast. He said his eyes were riveted on the ball; he saw it hit something solid and bounce back. He isn't so sure anymore that what he saw actually happened—an element of doubt has crept in. But other witnesses have verified his story, including the late Ed Short, long-time publicity director of the White Sox, and veteran Chicago sportswriters Howie Roberts and Edgar Munzel. Roberts, who began covering Chicago baseball in 1924, says the Mantle shot off Donovan and the Jimmie Foxx blast over the roof at Comiskey Park were the two longest homers he's ever seen.

Jim Landis was an outfielder with the White Sox in 1957. Landis: "To me, even after about 30 years, it still isn't hard to remember a wallop of that nature. A pure blast by Mantle that hit the right-field facade, and if it was a couple of feet more to the left, it would have gone clear out of Yankee Stadium. I also feel when it hit the facade it still wasn't on its downward flight."

Donovan was somewhat in awe of Mantle's homer himself. Kuenster remembers being on the train taking the White Sox out of town after the doubleheader. Donovan and catcher Les Moss were late to board. It was obvious Donovan had had a few. They'd be late, too, he said of the assembled, if someone had just hit a ball that hard off them.

July 1, 1957—Memorial Stadium, Baltimore. George Kell Night, honoring the Oriole who recently gathered his 2,000th hit, has drawn the largest night-game crowd—45,276—in the Orioles' four-year history.

The Yankees take a 2–1 lead into the bottom of the ninth. Whitey Ford, who has been sidelined with a strained shoulder tendon since May 21, is pitching in relief. Billy Goodman delivers a two-out run-scoring single, sending the big crowd berserk and the game into extra innings.

Baltimore has a new battery in the 10th—the Z men. Right-hander George Zuverink comes in to pitch, and the catcher now is Frank Zupo, two months shy of his 18th birthday.

Zuverink remembers the fresh-out-of-high-school Zupo as being "very nervous, especially playing against the Yankees." Zuverink retires Gil McDougald. Next is Mantle, and the Oriole pitcher shakes off Zupo a few times because he wants to throw a low inside slider. When he finally delivers, Mantle crunches his 22nd homer, the ball going a mile high and very deep into the bleachers in right-center. Though Bob Maisel in the *Baltimore Sun* reported its length as 425 feet, Zuverink says, "It must have traveled at least 450 feet but was high enough for the fans to scatter to keep from getting hit."

Ford and Bob Grim finish off the Birds in the bottom half, nailing down the 3–2 victory. Whitey has his first win since April 22, his pal Mantle giving him a welcome-back present. And after the game Zuverink kidded Zupo about calling for the wrong pitch.

July 11, 1957—Municipal Stadium, Kansas City. A Mickey Mantle home run won another game for the first-place Yankees and increased their lead over Chicago to 3½ games.

It is a sweltering day and it looks like the Yanks will lose their first game in 12 against the A's this year. They trail, 2–1, in the ninth. But singles by Mantle, Bill "Moose" Skowron, and Harry "Suitcase" Simpson tie the score.

It is still 2–2 when Mantle faces ex-teammate Tom Morgan in the 11th. Batting lefty, Mickey clubs what proves to be the game winner over the left-field wall for his league-leading 23rd homer. It is one of the longest opposite field blasts in the ballpark's history.

At game's end, Mantle was batting a robust .370, 26 points ahead of his nearest rival, Ted Williams.

July 23, 1957—Yankee Stadium. To hit for the cycle (getting a single, double, triple, and home run in the same game) is a feat of hitting versatility. There had been 52 cycles in the 57 seasons of American League history or about one per year, but Mickey Mantle on this date made that number 53.

Mantle also steals a base and gets a fielding assist when he doubles up a base runner in the first game of a key three-game series with the chasing White Sox. The Yanks (60–30) open up a 5½-game lead over Chicago (54–35) with a 10–6 win before 42,422.

Mantle, batting left-handed against Bob Keegan in the third, explodes into a fastball and sends a sky-high homer that finally comes down in the next-to-last row of the bleachers in right field. His 26th homer of the year is his first at home in exactly a month. Stadium superintendent Jim Thomson hastily checks the Stadium blueprints and announces that the ball went about 465 feet.

Keegan, who originally signed with the Yankees out of Bucknell University and who will soon pitch a no-hitter, remembers that the Mick hit the ball "real good"—after Keegan had him out. "Actually, I had him struck out on a 2-and-2 pitch," insists Keegan, "but the umpire called it a ball—Mantle even admitted that to me."

The score is 6–6 in the seventh when Mantle steps to the plate with the sacks full. He clears them with a savage liner into the left-field corner, just out of Minnie Minoso's reach, and winds up on third base. The Yankees never look back.

August 2, 1957—Yankee Stadium. Baseball is beautiful when played beautifully. The Yankees and Indians played one of the best games of the year with one great play following another.

Tom Sturdivant of the Yankees and Don Mossi engage in a splendid pitching struggle. Cleveland assumes a 1–0 third-inning lead but is denied a bigger inning when Sturdivant ends the frame with two bases-loaded strikeouts. Sturdivant escapes further trouble in the fourth; with runners on the corners, Jerry Coleman and Gil McDougald turn a spectacular double play.

Mickey Mantle saves Sturdivant in the sixth. Indian base runners are dancing off first and second when Bobby Avila singles to center. Mantle races in, scoops up the ball, and in one motion fires a perfect strike to the plate, where Yogi Berra makes the tag for the putout.

Cleveland takes a 2–0 lead in the seventh. But Coleman averts further damage by nailing still another runner at the plate.

Mossi, meanwhile, has a no-hitter in the works for 6⅓ innings. Then McDougald slugs a home run and Mantle, the next batter, lines a 1-and-1 roper—the ball never rises more than 15 feet above the ground—cannonading into the left-field seats. It is a 2–2 tie.

The Yankees push across the deciding run in the eighth, and Bob Grim pitches a hitless ninth to preserve a picturesque victory.

August 10, 1957—Memorial Stadium, Baltimore. Mickey Mantle put on one of his patented baseball clinics; it covered hitting, power hitting, bunting, fielding, and speed. He hit a homer and three singles and raised his batting average to .380 in leading the Yankees to a 6–3 win over the Orioles that moved them into a five-game lead over second-place Chicago.

A Maryland tobacco farmer named Ray Moore in the first inning gives up a one-out single to Enos Slaughter, bringing up Mantle. Batting lefty, Mickey sends a 2-and-2 pitch into a tremendous arced flight. Jim Busby runs to the fence, a little to the right of dead center and about 425 feet from the plate, and watches as the ball clears both the fence and a six-foot-high hedge some 30 feet beyond.

Local observers say Mantle's 31st homer is the first ball to clear the center-field hedge. Lou Hatter in the *Baltimore Sun* puts its length, all carry, at 460 feet (an estimate apparently), reporting that "last night's blow is believed the lengthiest ever slammed here."

Mantle, after making the outstanding fielding play of the game in hauling in Bob Nieman's 400-foot bid for extra bases, opens the Yankee third inning by beating out a drag bunt, a daring move on a 1-and-2 count. He steals second and ignites a three-run rally that gives the Yankees a commanding 5–0 lead.

An 18-year-old right-hander, fresh out of a Detroit high school, makes his pro debut for the Orioles in the eighth. His name is Milt Pappas and he will go on to win 209 games in the big leagues. Mantle welcomes the kid to the majors, getting a single off him to complete his four-hit game.

But the evening is best remembered for Mantle's historic homer. In 1986 it no longer stands in Oriole records as the longest Memorial Stadium homer, but it is right up there. The only homer hit out of Memorial Stadium was off Frank Robinson's bat in 1966. Oriole spokesman Rick Vaughn says this ball rolled to a total distance of 540 feet but went 451 on the fly. Memorial's longest on-the-fly homer was a 471-footer in 1965 by Harmon Killebrew. This measured blast didn't beat Mantle's by much—if at all, since Mantle's drive was *estimated* at 460 feet and may have traveled farther.

August 13, 1957—Fenway Park, Boston. The question was, could Mickey Mantle become the first player in history, in either major league, to win back-to-back Triple Crowns? He had a great chance, especially after his fine performance in today's 3–2 win over the Red Sox before 35,647, Fenway's largest crowd of the year.

Mantle and Ted Williams are once again contending for the batting crown. Mickey goes 3 for 3 with a walk, improving his average from .379 to .384. Williams, the only American Leaguer hitting better than Mantle, goes 1 for 2 with two walks, his average climbing one point, to .388.

Mantle leads the league in the other two Triple Crown categories. His home run today gives him 32, two more than Williams and Roy Sievers, and his three RBIs push him past Sievers, 83 to 81.

Tom Sturdivant and Bobby Shantz pitch solidly for the Yankees, and Mantle drives in all three Yankee runs. Mickey gives New York a 1–0 third-inning lead when he singles off the left-field wall, scoring Yogi Berra from second base. But Boston moves ahead, 2–1, and right-hander Frank Sullivan is working with a nice rhythm.

Sullivan loses it for only a flicker in the eighth and it costs him the game. After Gil McDougald opens with a single, Mantle hits a two-run homer into the right-field seats, the game's decisive blow. Mickey has now homered in every league park this season.

The first-place Yankees (73–38) now enjoyed a 5½-game spread between them and the White Sox (67–43). There will be a brief scare when New York stumbles on the road in late August, but the Bombers will go into Chicago and win three in a row, ultimately finishing eight games ahead of the Chisox.

On this date everything was rosy for Mantle and the Yankees. However, about a week later Mantle suffered an ugly gash, as deep as the bone, in his lower left leg. The injury was attributed to shinsplints, and all manner of explanations were offered as to their origin—the hard turf in Kansas City, too much basketball in the off-season, and so forth—but nothing added up. Casey Stengel was told that the leg had been accidentally bumped by the sharp point of a car door. It would be years before the real story came out—Peter Golenbock first reported it in *Dynasty* and Mantle confirmed the account in *The Mick*.

What actually happened was what Stengel had feared would happen all along—that the combination of the temper and competitive fire in Mantle would someday result in his doing something self-destructive. But Casey pictured Mickey harming himself in a water-cooler attack or other such baseball-associated outburst, not, certainly, on the golf course. But that is where it happened.

Mickey and Tom Sturdivant were playing golf at the Englewood Country Club in New Jersey. The fun-loving Sturdivant had a grating, high-pitched laugh that made Mickey's skin crawl. Well, Sturdivant won the golf match, a fact that didn't bother Mantle as much as listening to Tom's screeching laugh. Boiling mad, Mickey swung his putter at a tree limb overhead, and the putter came down and gouged deep into his shinbone. Shinsplints.

The injury ultimately cost Mantle his chance at making history. Too bad, because he stayed right up there for a while in all three Triple Crown categories, but he couldn't overcome shinsplints in September. He couldn't run. After hitting .385 before the game of August 20, he will hit only .268 the rest of the season. For this injury, Mantle had no one to blame but himself. And maybe Sturdivant's unnerving laugh.

August 30, 1957—Yankee Stadium. The Yankees lost to Washington, 4–2, following a long train trip home from their triumphant three-game sweep in Chicago. Mickey Mantle picked up three hits, including a right-handed homer to the right-field seats off Chuck Stobbs, and scored both Yankee tallies.

Even with the recent shinsplints problem, Mantle enjoyed a productive August. He began the month trailing Ted Williams in the batting race by 24 points, .383 to .359, and after this date, which is Williams's 39th birthday, the two are this close:

Williams—150 hits in 398 ABs, .3768.
Mantle—163 hits in 433 ABs, .3764.

Washington's Roy Sievers and Mantle each drive in one run in the Yankee–Senator game and continue to jointly share the league RBI lead with 90. Mantle's 34th homer breaks a three-way tie with Sievers and Williams, giving the Mick the undisputed home-run lead.

On the surface, then, Mantle was in a good position for a drive at winning another Triple Crown. But, in reality, he had hit the wall, and the rest of the year proved to be an absolute waste.

In the Yankees' next seven games, Mantle was used as a pinch-hitter in five games and played center in the other two; over that span, he went 2 for 14, and general manager George Weiss finally stepped in and had him hospitalized.

After an eight-day absence, a taped-up Mantle returned to the lineup on September 13, and miraculously came through with a double and triple in a victory over Chicago. He played nine days, then sat out the final week when the pennant was clinched.

September all too often disappointed. In September, the wear and tear of a season's accumulation of injuries often exacted a toll. In his entire career, Mantle hit 40 homers in April (a partial month in the schedule), 110 in May, 113 in June, 111 in July, 95 in August, and only 67 in September. The injury-plagued Mick often fell into decline as summer fused into fall.

Mantle failed to hit a single home run in September 1957 and collected only three RBIs. With 34 homers and 94 RBIs, he trailed league champion Sievers by 8 and 20, respectively.

Mantle did lead the league with 121 runs scored and 146 walks. His .365 batting average, second only to Ted Williams's .388, was, except for Ted's mark this year, the highest American League average since Williams hit .369 in 1948, and the .365 remains the best ever by a switch-hitter.

Mantle and Williams dominated league hitters in 1957, not only in batting average—Gene Woodling was a distant third at .321—but also in on-base average. Williams led with a .528 on-base average and Mantle followed at .515—Ted and Mickey were on base well over 50 percent of the time! Mantle's figure was the ninth highest on-base average in history (Williams's ranked fifth). Third in 1957 league on-base average was Minnie Minoso, way behind at .413.

The Mick, who had 173 hits and 146 walks, had a great on-base average in 1957 because he had career highs in batting average and walks. As a matter of fact, at the end of July, Mantle, having drawn 114 walks, was walking at a pace that would break Babe Ruth's major-league record of 170 walks, set in 1923.

All in all, the 1957 season was a great one for Mantle, in some respects even better than 1956, and Mickey will capture his second straight MVP Award by one vote over Williams. But how great might the year have been without the golf mishap?

October 5, 1957—County Stadium, Milwaukee. Milwaukee had a bad case of World Series fever. After all, it was the first World Series game in the city's history and Milwaukeeans were wild with anticipation. The Braves and the Yankees had split the series' first two games in New York.

A jam-packed house of 45,804 is in a roaring, festive mood for Game 3. But it turns into a nightmare for the home folks as the Yankees destroy the Braves, 12–3.

An ironic twist for the locals is that one of their own native sons, Tony Kubek, is the Yankee hitting star. The American League Rookie of the Year raps out three hits and scores as many runs. Although he hit a healthy .297 on the season, Kubek hit only three homers in 431 at bats; two of his hits on this date are homers, good for four RBIs.

Braves starter Bob Buhl doesn't survive the first inning when the Yankees jump out to a 3–0 lead. But he does make Mickey Mantle useless for the rest of the series. After Kubek's one-out homer, Buhl seems rattled and he walks both Mantle and Yogi Berra. Mantle, taking a long lead off second base, catches the eye of Buhl, who wheels and attempts a pickoff move. As Mantle dives back to the bag headfirst, Buhl's off-target throw goes into center field. Diving for the errant throw, second baseman Red Schoendienst falls full force on Mantle's right shoulder. Mickey untangles himself and races to third, then scores on Gil McDougald's sacrifice fly.

An inning or so later Mickey's shoulder starts to ache, but he remains in the game, singling in the third and hitting a 410-foot two-run homer off righty Gene Conley in the fourth that gives New York a 7–1 lead.

Mantle's shoulder stiffened overnight. The next morning Mantle could hardly swing a bat or throw a ball. He played Game 4 in pain, but when a situation presented itself in the late innings when he might have to make a critical throw, he came out of the game. He was played sparingly thereafter and was hardly a factor the rest of the series. After going 4 for 10 in the first three games, he went 1 for 9 in the final four. His only series RBIs were the two that rode home on his Game 3 home run.

Just as shinsplints ruined Mantle's Triple Crown prospects, his shoulder injury killed the Yankees in the World Series. Without Mantle at full strength, the Yankees were vulnerable and Milwaukee won the World Championship in seven games.

The shoulder bothered Mantle for years. Other than his numerous knee miseries, in fact, this would be his worst long-term injury. For the next few seasons, Mantle's left-handed hitting would be severely impaired.

1958

April 17, 1958—Fenway Park, Boston. Mickey Mantle hit his first home run of the year and made a tremendous fielding play as the Yankees beat the Red Sox, 3–1.

In Mantle's 11th at bat of the season, following six outs and four walks, he powers a left-handed drive off Tom Brewer over the left-center-field wall. Then, when Pete Daley bangs a hit off the wall in left-center, Mantle handles the rebound perfectly and with a strong peg to second base cuts down Daley with plenty to spare.

His performance on this date notwithstanding, Mickey Mantle did not come out blazing in 1958. By May's end he will have only four homers. The right shoulder that he hurt in last year's World Series was operated on during the winter and was slow to come around. Yogi Berra also started the year slowly, yet the Yankees by May 25 will race to a 25–6 record. Yankee pitching was magnificent and this is what carried the team.

May 9, 1958—Yankee Stadium. After six consecutive home rainouts, the Yankees finally took the field for the first night game of the year in the Bronx. With Mickey Mantle contributing three important hits, including his first Yankee Stadium homer of 1958, the Yankees defeated Washington, 9–5.

The score is 2–2 with two out in the third and Mantle is facing right-hander Pedro Ramos. He crashes a hefty wallop to center field and the fleet Albie Pearson gives chase. Pearson makes a valiant effort to catch the ball, more than 450 feet from the plate, but it tips off his glove and falls safely to the ground, near the monuments to the memories of past Yankee greats Miller Huggins, Lou Gehrig, and Babe Ruth. Mickey circles the bases for an easy inside-the-park homer, and New York has a 3–2 lead.

Later the Yankees break a 4–4 fifth-inning deadlock on a Norm Siebern double, a Mantle single, and a Yogi Berra sacrifice fly. Then they pull away with a three-run seventh, a rally in which Mantle singles, steals third on the front end of a double steal with Berra, and scores a run.

May 20, 1958—Comiskey Park, Chicago. Mickey Mantle legged out another inside-the-park home run. Batting left-handed against Dick Donovan, he hit a line drive into left-center field—earlier he had hit a drive to the same alley that went off left fielder Al Smith's glove for a double—and the ball split Smith and center fielder Jim Rivera. Each apparently thinking it was the other's play, the outfielders suddenly stopped, then watched the ball go to the wall as Mantle wheeled around the bases.

The Yankees licked the White Sox, 5–1, for their seventh win in a row. Believed in the preseason to be New York's principal challenger, Chicago was now 10½ games behind the front-running Yankees and holding up the rest of the league in the cellar. When the Sox finally touched Johnny Kucks for their lone run in the ninth, the unhappy crowd of 36,167 jeered derisively.

June 4, 1958—Yankee Stadium. Mickey Mantle for the first time homered into the distant left-center-field bleachers that run from the visitors' bullpen in left to the hitters' screen in center.

Mantle's homer was reportedly the eighth ball hit into this bleacher area. Previously, only Jimmie Foxx, Hank Greenberg, Joe DiMaggio (twice), Gus Zernial, Andy Carey, and Jim Lemon had reached the distant left-center-field bleachers.

Behind the five-hit pitching of Billy Pierce, the White Sox won, 7–2, also pushing across their first runs in 32 innings in the third. But Mantle's first right-handed home run of the season was the center of attention. The ball carried into the 19th row of the bleachers. Stadium superintendent Jim Thomson measured the drive at 478 feet. Mantle has now drilled homers to all seating areas beyond the Stadium fences.

HITTING AT YANKEE STADIUM

In the 51-year history of the "old" Yankee Stadium, which was closed for renovation following the 1973 season, only 21 homers had been hit into the left-center-field bleachers. Mantle, with four, hit more than anybody, followed by Bill Skowron (three) and Joe DiMaggio (two).

Right-handed power hitters found the Stadium brutal, the toughest park in history. In Mantle's era, the distance was 402 feet to straightaway left field, 457 to left center, 461 to dead center, and 407 to right center. Additionally, the wall went as high as 13 feet 10 inches in some places. The big bulge in left center, the right-handed hitter's power alley known as Death Valley—fly balls went there to die—was not only imposing in terms of distance, but a ball hit in this direction carried poorly, too. A cheap homer could be had down the 301-foot left-field line, but homers down either line are few in any park.

Visiting right-handed power hitters at the Stadium often registered their complaints. Once, in a World Series, after watching a couple of his shots go more than 400 feet and stay within the fences, Hank Aaron told Tony Kubek, "I'm sure glad this isn't my home park." A similarly frustrated Harmon Killebrew once asked Mantle, "How the hell can you play here?"

The late John C. Tattersall researched the home-and-away home-run figures of several power hitters for a piece in the 1976 *Baseball Research Journal* of the Society for American Baseball Research (SABR). Tattersall found that Joe DiMaggio, the greatest right-handed hitter in Yankee history, hit only 41 percent of his 361 career homers at the Stadium (148 at home and 213 on the road). Two other Yankee righties with some power, Elston Howard and Gil McDougald, were even more negatively affected by the Stadium. Howard in his 14-season career, which included 1 1/2 years with the Red Sox, hit only 32 percent of his 167 four-baggers at home, and McDougald, a career Yankee, hit a mere 26 percent of his 112 four-baggers at the Stadium.

As further evidence of the burden the Stadium placed on righty power hitters, look at the home-and-away figures of the three best home-run seasons by Yankee righties:

	Year	HRs	Home	Away
Joe DiMaggio	1937	46	19	27
Joe DiMaggio	1948	39	15	24
Dave Winfield	1982	37	14	23

Righty hitters at the Stadium had it tough, and still have it tough, although the dimensions from left to center have dwindled considerably since the 1974–75 renovation and another reconfiguration of the playing area in 1985. Mantle was obviously at a disadvantage when he batted right-handed at home, but, surprisingly, his career stats don't show any striking disparity between his righty homers at home and on the road. Batting right-handed, Mickey hit 77 homers at the Stadium and 85 on the road. Of course, Mantle might have batted right-handed more at the Stadium than on the road because teams tended to save southpaws for the Stadium.

Still, the slight eight-homer difference in Mantle's right-handed home-and-away homers flies in the face of the estimates that Mantle lost anywhere from 10 to 25 homers a year because of Death Valley. Former Mantle teammate Johnny Blanchard remembers a 1961 doubleheader at the Stadium when Mantle hit several 440-foot outs that would have been homers in any other park. A right-handed Mantle was often pitched to differently at the Stadium, however, with pitchers *coaxing* the Mick to boom 'em to Death Valley; pitchers were willing to play the percentages that Mantle, even with his incredible power, could not consistently beat them with the long ball, not to his power alley anyway. (Yankee southpaws have for decades played the Death Valley game brilliantly, and this is one of the secrets to the club's continuing success, since most teams are top-heavy with right-handed hitting.)

Certainly Mantle would have hit more homers playing in a more favorable park for right-handed hitters, parks such as Ebbets Field, Fenway Park, or Briggs Stadium. Many more homers, perhaps. But the numbers show that he hit 266 homers at home and 270 on the road—not much of a road advantage. And he hit for a .305 average at home as opposed to .291 on the road.

Those who add hundreds of homers to his theoretical total had the Mick played in a different park are probably overstating the case. What denied Mantle more homers than his 536 were injuries and an abbreviated career—his last great year was at the age of 32. Hank Aaron, the all-time home-run leader with 755, got 12,364 at bats, compared to Mantle's 8,102. Give Mantle the same number of at bats as Aaron, and Mickey, projected at his career rate of 15.12 at bats per homer, would have hit 817 homers. On the other hand, applying the same formula, Babe Ruth would have hit 1,051 homers.

The idea that a right-handed Mantle was denied hundreds of homers at the Stadium has a partner in fallacy, and that is the belief that the Stadium was an easy touch for a left-handed Mickey. Left-handed, he hit 189 homers at the Stadium; on the road he hit 185. Four homers over an 18-year career doesn't qualify as an advantage.

As a switch-hitter, Mantle may have been able to neutralize some of the Death Valley difficulty by batting lefty, but he still had to contend with the 461-foot wall in center, and he was a great straightaway hitter. The short porch to right in Mantle's era, running roughly from the 344-foot sign in straightaway right to the 296-foot right-field line, *was* an inviting target. But Tattersall found that Babe Ruth, to cite one well-known Yankee left-handed hitter, in his entire career hit more homers on the road than at home. Few Yankee lefties got unduly fat at the Stadium, in fact. Bill Dickey was an exception: He hit 67 percent of his homers at the Stadium.

Additional arguments that counter the idea that left-handed hitters have it easy at the Stadium:

- Ted Williams, who hit .361 lifetime at home in Fenway Park, hit only .296 at the Stadium.
- Lou Gehrig hit .351 lifetime on the road, compared with .329 at the Stadium.
- Babe Ruth hit 32 of his 60 homers in 1927 on the road and 28 at the Stadium.
- Roger Maris hit 31 of his 61 homers in 1961 on the road and 30 at the Stadium.
- The 1961 Yankees, who set a major-league record with 240 homers, hit 16 more homers on the road than at the Stadium, and the power of that team was predominantly left-handed.

Mantle holds the Stadium record, with 266 home runs, seven more than Babe Ruth. The Babe, however, played at the house that he built six fewer seasons than did Mickey, and although the distances to right field were slightly different in each era, that doesn't account for much.

There is one major difference, though. The short porch in right, originally built for Ruth's benefit, was a single deck in Babe's time. Ruth played his last Yankee season in 1934; the triple-decked grandstand in right wasn't built until 1937. How many balls would Mantle have poled completely out of the Stadium if the single deck in right had remained for him? Probably more than a few. He hit more than 50 homers into the upper deck or off the facade in right—some of his best shots—and some of these would surely have cleared the single deck of Ruth's era. Ruth never hit one out of the Stadium, but he did hit an incredible shot off the scoreboard. The first of three scoreboards at the "old" Stadium, this one stood at the rear wall of the right-center-field bleachers.

Mantle's home runs into the right-field third deck were impossible to measure because the flight of the ball was interrupted so high above ground level. Where they might have come down was left to very uncertain conjecture.

June 5, 1958—Yankee Stadium. Mickey Mantle ran out his third inside-the-park homer in less than a month—half his career total of six inside-the-parkers, which is a Yankee club record.

Mantle, batting left-handed, unloads on Early Wynn. He sends a towering smash to dead-center field, the ball falling beyond the racing Jim Landis and dropping at the base of the 461-foot sign. He legs it across the plate with one of the three runs he scores in a 12–5 rout in the first of two with Chicago.

Mickey doesn't hit a homer in the nightcap—he had homered in all four of the previous games of the series with the White Sox—and Chicago wins, 3–2. But Mickey, who in this series doubled his season home-run output, is hot; he will hit seven homers in seven days and finally climb up among the league leaders.

But the right shoulder is still bothering him. He is batting .295 overall, but his average from the left side is under .250. He will further aggravate his shoulder this month; then, in compensating, he will strain his weak right knee.

July 3, 1958—Griffith Stadium, Washington, D.C. Mickey Mantle kicked off a busy week in the nation's capital, both on and off the field. Just in from Baltimore, where he went 5 for 12 and broke out of a miserable late June slump, the Mick on a blistering hot day popped a pair of long left-handed homers against Russ Kemmerer—"comparable with some of his mightiest blows in the past," according to John Drebinger of the *New York Times*—to lead the Yankees to an 11–3 win over the Senators.

The hitters are aided by a stiff breeze blowing out and what normally is a pitcher's park yields six homers. Kemmerer takes a 2–0 lead into the fifth, then bang-bang, New York is in front, 4–2. Whitey Ford, on his way to his 12th straight win against Washington, singles, Norm Siebern hits a long two-run homer, and Gil McDougald singles. Then Mantle hits a two-run homer.

The ball rockets over the 372-foot mark in right-center field and is still climbing as it clears the 31-foot-high wall with plenty to spare. Burton Hawkins has fun in the *Washington Star*: "Reports drifting back from the suburbs told of Mickey's drive clearing the houses beyond the alley."

Bob Addie was a bit more specific in the *Washington Post*: "The ball landed on a roof across the alley which flanks the right-field wall and then bounced into U Street." It's a shame that this tape-measure job wasn't measured.

Mantle's second homer is boomed about two-thirds of the way into the left-center-field bleachers—wind or no wind, an impressive opposite-field poke. "Mickey wouldn't top that shot often batting right-handed," reported Drebinger. With the two homers (Nos. 17 and 18 of the year), Mickey raises his batting average to .280.

Mantle would return to Washington in six days and along with Casey Stengel and others would testify at a hearing of the Senate Subcommittee on Anti-Trust and Monopoly, which was considering a bill to exempt the major pro sports from antitrust laws. Not surprisingly, a rambling, charming Stengel dialogue was the hearing's highlight, Casey tracing his nearly half century in baseball. Finally it was Mickey's turn, and he was asked what must have seemed to him a rather technical question. The audience roared as he answered, "My views are just about the same as Casey's."

July 5, 1958—Yankee Stadium. This was one of the more bizarre games in the storied Yankee–Red Sox rivalry.

Boston has a 3–2 lead when in the bottom of the ninth Mickey Mantle pulled an enormous home run into the upper deck in right, moving the game into overtime. (Mickey hit seven homers in the first eight games of July.) As the Red Sox load the bases in the 11th, public address announcer Bob Shepherd advises the crowd of 43,821 that "this game must stop at 11:59," as no game started on Saturday night can go into Sunday morning.

When Boston scores twice, the Yankees begin stalling. They argue calls, ever so leisurely change pitchers, and eat up time switching around defenses. It works. At 11:59 P.M., as promised by Shepherd, play stops, and since the home team had not taken its last licks, the score reverts to 3–3. The game would have to be replayed, but all individual records, including Mantle's game-saving 20th homer, go into the record book.

So the Mick was credited with his homer. The right-hander who served it up, Dave Sisler, recalls a moment two years earlier when Mantle was denied a home run, a denial that proved pivotal in the first of 38 big-league wins for Sisler, the son of Hall of Famer George Sisler. On that Fenway Park occasion Mickey had hit a towering shot to center that "looked to me like a home run," according to Sisler. "The umpire at second base ruled that it came down almost vertically on the top of the oval-topped wall and came back in the park. The Yankees were furious."

The 1958 American League's All-Star center fielder was Mickey Mantle and he was flanked by Bob Cerv of the A's and Jackie Jensen of the Red Sox—the three candidates to succeed Joe DiMaggio in 1952 as the Yankee center fielder.

The Yankees waltzed into the All-Star break owning a 48–25 record, good for a commanding 11-game lead over the closest chaser. And after the second half gets under way, they will slowly pull away to an even greater lead.

July 28, 1958—Municipal Stadium, Kansas City. His right shoulder had been aching all year, and by July 18 his batting average had dipped to .270, but Mickey Mantle stubbornly deflected suggestions that he rest. Getting Mickey on the bench for a four-game absence took another injury, a bruised left forearm. Over the seven games since his return, including the game on this date, he batted .556 (15 for 27) and raised his average to .294.

The Mick collects two of the seven home runs hit in a slugfest with the A's. He also singles, draws a free pass, steals a base, and scores four runs. In winning 14–7, New York (64–32) picks up a game and now holds a 15-game advantage over second-place Boston (48–46). No pennant race this year.

Mantle switch-hits his homers. It is the sixth time he does this in the same game, adding to his own major-league record. Batting right-handed, he drives a shot far over the 387-foot mark in right center, and batting left-handed, he sends another well over the 375-foot mark in left center. Not only does Mickey homer from opposite sides of the plate, he knocks both of them out by the opposite-field route.

These were the 13th and 14th Mantle homers of July, which began with Mickey far behind the league's homer leaders. Now he was a contender. The leaders as of the beginning and end of July were as follows:

July 1

Jackie Jensen, Boston.	23
Bob Cerv, Kansas City	20
Roy Sievers, Washington.	18
Gus Triandos, Baltimore	16
Mickey Mantle	14

July 28

Jackie Jensen, Boston.	29
Mickey Mantle	28
Bob Cerv, Kansas City	28
Roy Sievers, Washington.	26
Rocky Colavito, Cleveland	21

September 3, 1958—Yankee Stadium. Mickey Mantle and Yogi Berra may have started the season slowly but by now had reestablished themselves as the heart of the Yankee lineup.

While Yankee Stadium boo-birds took it easy on Berra through his hard times, they hooted Mantle all summer and continued to pick on the Mick even after his bat got hot. Mickey's slumps were accentuated by his strikeouts; on this date, he went down for the 111th time this year, tying his own Yankee record set in 1952. His season total of 120 will both shatter the club mark and lead the league. His bad right shoulder was the main reason for his striking out and for his problems hitting left-handed. The fans, of course, were not fully aware of this and saw only that Mickey wasn't as great as he had been in 1956 and 1957.

The Red Sox lead the Yankees, 5–3, as Mantle steps in to face right-hander Frank Sullivan opening up the Yankee eighth. Mickey, who walked and scored a run earlier, gets some muscle into a Sullivan pitch and creams a third-tier homer to right field. It is home run No. 39 for Mickey, the league leader.

Batting right behind Mantle, Berra shoots a single. Murray Wall relieves Sullivan and Bill Skowron singles. In spite of a play in which Wall picks off Berra at second base, the Yanks do score the tying run in the inning.

Berra atones by homering in the bottom of the ninth with Enos Slaughter and Mantle aboard, and the Yanks have an instant 8–5 victory. As has happened so many times, Mantle and Berra have used the long ball to pull out a Yankee victory. Each has 85 RBIs and they're both among the league leaders.

In their 13 seasons as teammates, from 1951 to 1963, Mantle and Berra homered in the same game 50 times, hitting back-to-back homers on 12 occasions. Overall, the powerful duo swatted 702 homers as teammates, a figure only one other pair of teammates in American League history has topped: Babe Ruth and Lou Gehrig combined for 783 homers in 10 Yankee seasons.

September 17, 1958—Briggs Stadium, Detroit. Excitement swirled around the Yankees. On the train headed here from Kansas City, where the club had nailed down its fourth straight pennant, pitcher Ryne Duren and coach Ralph Houk got into a tussle that made headlines. And after arriving, the players discovered they were being trailed by detectives in the hire of Yankee general manager George Weiss, who wanted to know what might be behind the team's mediocre record since early August. Mickey Mantle, Whitey Ford, and some others picked up on the gumshoe situation early and had some fun with diversionary tactics.

No one expected on-the-field fireworks on this day. The pennant was in the bag and the Tigers were struggling to finish at .500. Only 2,973 pay to see a meaningless game that Detroit will win, 5–2.

However, Mantle in the third inning rewards the few who showed. On the mound is Jim Bunning, one of the toughest pitchers in the league. The tall right-hander would win 224 games and pitch a no-hitter in each major league before returning to his native Kentucky to launch a political career. Bunning delivers and Mantle pulls an explosive drive down the right-field line, fair by about 10 feet. The ball clears the roof and Trumbull Avenue and strikes the second story of a building on the far side of the avenue. Cabbie Bob Gilbert recovers the ball—which must have traveled well in excess of 500 feet.

An amazing aspect of this Mantle homer is that it was "hit into a stiff wind," according to Sam Greene's report in the *Detroit News*. Gus Zernial says the ball was hit into the teeth of a 20- to 25-mph wind. An American Leaguer throughout the 1950s, Zernial, a Tiger in 1958, remembers this homer as the longest he ever saw Mantle hit.

The homer, indeed, drew immediate comparisons with the two previous roof clearers here: Ted Williams's hit in 1939 and Mantle's 1956 shot (which might have bounced off the roof). Wrote Greene: "There is no doubt that Mantle attained greater distance than Williams did 19 years ago. Older park attendants recalled that Williams barely cleared the roof." Greene added that Mantle's homer "deserves comparison with epic homers Mantle hit in Yankee Stadium, Washington and elsewhere."

Yankee pitcher Johnny James still remembers the blast. "I had just been called up from Richmond and was in the bullpen down the right-field line when he hit it. I had never heard such an explosive sound of bat on ball; it was by far the most awesome I'd heard before or since, nor had I ever seen a ball leave a ballpark so quickly. It happened so fast I wasn't sure I actually saw what I thought I had seen."

In his career Mantle hit 42 homers in Detroit, more than in any other road ballpark. And besides his three homers over the right-field roof—in 1956, 1958, and 1960—he hit several more to the roof facade or to the top of the roof. The 1956 and 1958 homers were splendid indeed, but the granddaddy was still ahead.

September 24, 1958—Fenway Park, Boston. The Red Sox closed out their 1958 home schedule the way they began it—by losing to the Yankees. Mickey Mantle hit No. 42 to complete his long-ball season. The Sox's Tom Brewer, who had surrendered No. 1, also gave up No. 42.

Mantle's left-handed drive into the net high above the left-center field wall gave him a three-homer lead over Rocky Colavito—just barely enough of a margin, because Colavito would add two more to his total before the season ended.

In spite of Casey Stengel's disappointment with the Mick in 1958, of the fans' disapproval and the Baseball Writers' skip (they voted Jackie Jensen the MVP; Mickey finished third), the common perception that Mantle had an off year is inaccurate. He remained the best offensive player in the American League in 1958—easily.

Mantle not only won the home-run title but led the league in runs (127) and walks (129). In runs produced (runs scored plus RBIs minus home runs), he led the league with 182, a dozen more than MVP Jensen. He finished second in on-base average (.445) and slugging average (.592), and he batted a more than respectable .304 in a season when the league leader, Ted Williams, hit only .328.

Perhaps the best case for Mantle was made in a revolutionary 1959 article in *Sports Forecast*, a pioneer in recognizing that traditional offensive criteria fall short in determining a player's offensive value. *Sports Forecast* put forth a system it called runner-advancement rating, in which an offensive player—batter or base runner—earned a point every time he advanced a runner, either himself or a teammate. In other words, the system was keyed to total bases—his own and those of members of his team for which he could take credit.

The RAR system had another feature: An offensive player was penalized for hitting into double plays and getting caught stealing.

Sports Forecast finished the article with a table showing a partial application of RAR using the 1958 American League campaign (some stats pertinent to the RAR concept were not kept). But the watered-down table makes clear that Mantle was tops in the American League in 1958.

Top 10 in Runner-Advancement Rating*

Player	TB (+)	BB (+)	RBI (+)	SB (+)	SH (+)
Mantle	307	129	97	18	2
Jensen, Boston	293	99	122	9	1
Colavito, Cleveland	303	84	113	0	0
Sievers, Washington	299	53	108	3	0
Cerv, Kansas City	305	50	104	3	0
Williams, Boston	240	98	85	1	0
Minoso, Cleveland	269	59	80	14	6
Kaline, Detroit	266	54	85	7	3
Power, Kansas City/Cleveland	289	20	80	3	3
Runnels, Boston	249	87	59	1	2

Player	SF (+)	CS (−)	DP (−)	RAR
Mantle	2	3	11	541
Jensen, Boston	4	4	13	511
Colavito, Cleveland	3	2	16	485
Sievers, Washington	7	1	13	456
Cerv, Kansas City	2	3	19	442
Williams, Boston	4	0	19	409
Minoso, Cleveland	2	14	13	403
Kaline, Detroit	5	4	18	398
Power, Kansas City/Cleveland	6	2	13	386
Runnels, Boston	3	2	15	384

NOTE: TB—total bases; BB—bases on balls; RBI—runs batted in; SB—stolen bases; SH—sacrifice hits; SF—sacrifice flies; CS—caught stealing; DP—double plays.

*Without considering bases that runners advanced (exclusive of RBI) or times hit by pitcher.

October 2, 1958—County Stadium, Milwaukee. Mickey Mantle's two homers had little effect on the game's outcome, Milwaukee besting the Yankees, 13–5, in Game 2 of the World Series. The Braves now had a two-games-to-none advantage.

In the very first inning the Braves got to Bob Turley, the Yanks' 21–7 pitcher who will win the Cy Young Award. They scored seven runs in the early rally and continued to bombard a succession of Turley replacements. That the Yankees hadn't been able to win in Milwaukee with their two best pitchers, Whitey Ford and Turley, was most troubling to Yankee followers.

The Mantle home runs were hit off right-hander Lew Burdette, who coasted to his fourth consecutive win over the Yankees in two World Series. The Mick nailed a screwball in the fourth over the center-field fence, and in the ninth he tomahawked a fat fastball high into the left-center-field bleachers.

The second homer made Mantle feel good in that it came down among some Brave fans who had been riding him all game long, mocking him to the tune of the Mickey Mouse Club theme song.

Milwaukee fans dreamed of a four-game sweep, but the Yankees were conceding nothing. Cool and raring to get back home, the Yanks were confident they could win at least two out of three games on their own turf. Casey Stengel spoke for the team when he said, "Sure, we're not in what I would call a rosy position, but this thing is not over by a long shot. Why, only two years ago, we lost the first two to Brooklyn. I seem to remember that we won it at the end, didn't we? There's no law that says we can't do it again. You just never know about those things until they happen. Then you know."

And it happened. The Yankees returned to the Stadium and won two out of three just as they felt they would, then went back to Milwaukee to win two in a row. The highlights of the great comeback: the phenomenal pitching of Turley and Ryne Duren, the clutch fielding of Elston Howard, and the timely hitting of Howard, Hank Bauer, Gil McDougald, Yogi Berra, and Bill Skowron.

Mantle played no notable role in the heroics that brought the World Championship to the 1958 Yankees. But his two homers of this date may have contributed to the Yankee bounce-back in that these blows helped to preserve a semblance of team pride and confidence. At the very least, the Braves were sent a message that the Yankees weren't about to die.

1959

May 12, 1959—Yankee Stadium. Most of the 34,671 who turned out for the season's first night game at the Stadium wondered whether the Yankees would shake their early-season doldrums. They didn't, losing 7–6, to Cleveland. By evening's end, the first-place Indians (16–9) were five games ahead of the sixth-place Yankees (11–14). Mickey Mantle had a big game with three hits in four trips and raised his batting average to .284.

Leading off the third inning, Mantle, batting left-handed against Cal McLish, blasts a drive to the 457-foot sign in left-center field, a tremendous opposite-field poke, and races around the bases for an inside-the-park home run.

Yankee homers are also hit by Elston Howard and Yogi Berra, but Berra, celebrating his 34th birthday, makes an uncharacteristic mistake that sets up the decisive run. It is, in fact, Yogi's first error in a record 149 consecutive games. On a Minnie Minoso steal attempt, Berra throws wildly and Minoso scampers to third and later scores Cleveland's seventh run on a sacrifice fly.

The Yankees trail by a run in the ninth. Tony Kubek delivers a leadoff double against reliever Jim Perry, and home-run hitters Mantle, Berra, and Howard, the 3-4-5 men in the order, are up next. Mantle has yet to be retired and has the minimum task of moving Kubek to third. Steaming mad, Perry slaps his glove, demands the ball from his catcher, and proceeds to strike the Mick out on three fastballs, the last one a knee-high hummer that Mickey misses with a mighty cut. Then Berra pops up. And Howard fans. The tying run dies at second and another not-easy-to-accept loss is handed the Yankee camp.

Mantle's 1959 season had a sour start. He was a one-day holdout in spring training after general manager George Weiss, taking a hard line on contracts and alienating many Yankees in the process, attempted to trim his paycheck by $10,000. Mickey finally negotiated a $2,000 raise, which made him a $72,000 a year ballplayer, but the whole episode left him displeased.

Then he suffered a string of early-season misfortunes. Right away he strained his already tender right shoulder in making an off-balance throw. Then he was hit by a pitch in batting practice and acquired a chipped bone in a finger on his right hand, making it hard to grip the bat tightly. And he was one of several Yankees to come down with the Asian flu.

May 20, 1959—Yankee Stadium. The Basement Bombers—that's what the Yankees were being called. For the first time since May 25, 1940, they were the American League's last-place team. Detroit on this date whipped the defending World Champs, 13–6, on one of the darkest days in Yankee history.

Fittingly, Frank "the Yankee Killer" Lary does the terrible deed. He goes the distance, improving his lifetime record against New York to 18–5. And while Lary kept the Yankee bats under control, the Tigers rocked five Yankee pitchers for 19 hits.

Mickey Mantle's 3-for-5 day didn't spare him from having to absorb, as the most prominent Yankee, the brunt of the home fans' wrath. His home run with two out in the ninth, his sixth of the season, brought him a serenade of boos and hoots as he circled the bases. The fans were holding Mantle hostage; *he* was primarily to blame, in their view, for the Yanks' poor standing.

All the Yankees were booed at Yankee Stadium in the 1959 campaign, but Mantle was singled out for special abuse. He heard the worst booing of his career. Occasionally, spectators threw more than derision his way, and occasionally, Mantle flicked the fans the finger to signal *his* unhappiness with *them*.

Mantle grew testier than usual with the press, and his relationship with some reporters wasn't that good to begin with. It seemed that Mantle was more in battle with the press and fans than he was with the American League opposition.

THE PRESS, THE PEOPLE

Mickey Mantle wasn't exactly schooled in the handling of the press and the fans when he came to New York. He was a shy 19-year-old, proud of his Oklahoma roots but a bit self-conscious about being a country boy. After being ripped off a time or two, he learned to be wary of big-city sharpies. Sportswriters, unfortunately, fell into the sharpie bag. He was reserved with reporters, volunteering little. He was suspicious of them, which was company policy around the Yankees anyway.

Mantle could be surly with reporters who probed too deeply or ripped into him in print. By the same token, he could be open and gregarious with writers he deemed sympathetic.

Players and reporters are often at odds, and an absence of mutual respect is frequently the cause. Some players respect only one ability and that is athletic ability; they look down on the often unathletic reporter. Reporters, on the other hand, tend to see the players as clods who would be swinging picks instead of bats if baseball hadn't been invented. A little bit of this absence of mutual respect may have been at work in the relationship between the Mick and the media.

Mantle got along well with nonprying newsmen, veterans like Ben Epstein and John Drebinger. Old Schoolers. He was less cooperative with some of the New Breeders who were making their mark in journalism in the late 1950s, reporters like Leonard Shecter, who weren't interested in writing box-score stories and who wanted to go beyond runs, hits, and errors.

Shecter, who had a novelty-store face that the company men in the clubhouse would have loved to kick in, was only searching for the truth in the view of Jim Bouton, probably a minority of one in the clubhouse.

Bouton believes that ballplayers tend to isolate themselves from others by reason of their star status. They tend toward a bunker mentality as a team, and nowhere more so than on the Yankees, he says. Bouton liked Mantle as a teammate. Everyone did. And one reason everyone did was that Mantle was in the mainstream of the clubhouse philosophy.

Many reporters hated the Mick's coolness toward them. To unfriendly reporters, Mantle might snarl yes-no answers, give unprintable quotes, or retire to the sanctuary of the trainer's room, off-limits to reporters, and not speak at all.

Another problem was that Mantle was a self-admitted poor loser. He was seldom in a good frame of mind following a Yankee loss—and even the Yankees lost 40 percent of the time—and, unfortunately, most of the press questions came after the game. Clashes were inevitable.

But pushy reporters and photographers were not blameless, either. Some were just plain rude, and Mickey naturally favored those who were considerate. There was the time that a free-lance photographer made an appointment with Mantle, and when the session ran longer than expected, one of a group of nearby newspaper photographers shouted for Mantle to give them a few shots. The free-lancer apologized for taking so long, but Mickey told him not to worry: He had *asked* for Mickey's time, while the others demanded it.

The atmosphere between Mantle and the press improved with the passage of time. The more mature Mantle became, the more tolerant he was of probing questions. He came to the realization that reporters worked under pressure, too. He also accepted criticism better, although it didn't hurt that the stories written about him in the 1960s were by and large a lot friendlier that those of the 1950s.

The boos and catcalls Mantle heard at Yankee Stadium throughout the 1950s continually puzzled him, but Mantle was used to the chorus of disapproval by 1959. He was a Big Guy and all Big Guys hear boos from time to time. Even Babe Ruth heard them. The boos directed at Mantle, though, were unusually mean-spirited and persistent.

It was fashionable to boo Mantle in fashionable New York for whatever reason. Even for no reason. Of course, there was also a contingent of fans who tried to drown out the booing with cheers, but there was no doubt that much of the crowd was hostile to Mickey. Yankee players were annoyed by the Mantle-nagging. Casey Stengel thought it was silly.

How did the booing start? Why was Mantle so picked on? The factors were many.

THE DRAFT DODGER LABEL: Several times in 1950 and 1951 Mantle was examined and rejected by the Army. His osteomyelitis, and later a knee problem, were legitimate disqualifications, but the guy in the street had trouble believing so great an athlete could be physically inadequate for military service. Not a few parents of young men taken by the Army were irate.

"Why ain't you in the Army, you big bum!" self-anointed patriots would yell at Mantle. They called him "draft dodger," or worse, and they didn't let up for a long time.

So right from the start there were people who didn't like Mantle.

THE DiMAGGIO FAN CLUB: When Mantle reached the Yankees in 1951, Yankee fans were in no need of a new hero. They already had the crown prince of baseball, Joe DiMaggio. To many hard-core DiMaggio fans, this new kid Mantle had no right to lay claim to the prince's center-field province. Nobody had that right! These fans scoffed at stories suggesting that Mantle had the potential to be even greater than DiMaggio.

Some DiMaggio fans continued resenting Mantle even after DiMag retired. They never fully accepted Mantle and made him feel unwanted. Many of those who had worshipped DiMaggio sat in the Stadium bleachers. There, in close proximity to Mantle, they could scrutinize and criticize DiMaggio's replacement, the would-be successor to their prince. Mickey didn't mind the booing so much but did become boiling mad when the bleacherites sent tiny missiles his way.

The DiMaggio loyalists weren't the only problem. There were still plenty of Babe Ruth fans around New York who tended to regard as a pretender anyone who had the misfortune of being compared with *their* guy. And Mantle was compared with Ruth as often as he was with DiMaggio.

THOSE WHO FELT LET DOWN: The New York press spared no adjectives in describing the wonderful Mantle they saw in the spring of 1951. Red Patterson remembers returning to New York and having National League president and soon-to-be baseball commissioner Ford Frick ask him, "What are you trying to do? Make another Babe Ruth before he even plays a game?"

The Yankee front office encouraged the Mantle buildup. The raves helped to sell tickets. But the fans became impatient when Mickey took six years to attain the level of greatness they had been led to expect immediately. And so they tended to turn on the kid who was supposed to be the ultimate ballplayer, a combination of Babe Ruth and Ty Cobb. What Mickey was from 1951 through 1955 was a fine All-Star player, but he was not yet a player of Hall of Fame caliber. His most conspicuous statistic in those early years was the strikeout, and the fans certainly weren't wild about that.

Mantle was once again a victim of elevated expectations after having put together fantastic back-to-back seasons in 1956 and 1957. Expecting more of the same year after year, the fans in 1958 and 1959 felt let down again.

Casey Stengel didn't help matters when he kept saying that Mantle should break all the records and lead the league in every category every season. Because Stengel expected more from Mantle, so did the fans. Mantle was supposed to be the greatest ever, right? Maybe "the bum" was overrated.

THE PERSONALITY FACTOR: Mantle didn't play up to the crowds. He was neither showboat nor showman. The Babe Ruth magic wasn't there. The Babe would grin from ear to ear as he circled the bases after a homer, taking his distinctive baby steps, tipping his cap to the crowd, and maybe even throwing in a bow or snapping off a few military salutes. By contrast, Mantle took his home-run trot as though he were embarrassed, rounding the bases with head down, a sheepish expression on his face as though he hoped he hadn't offended the pitcher. There was no acknowledgment of the fans or their cheers.

This was Mantle. His style was to neither play to the crowd nor show up the opposition. It was an acceptable, even admirable style. But fans want their heroes to notice them. To smile. To wave sometimes. Mantle didn't, at least not in the first half of his career. And his detachment from the customers was misread as superjock aloofness—conceit. It was the old shyness-for-arrogance misread, and as he pulled away from the fans, a block of fans pulled away from him.

What emotion the fans did see Mantle express on the field was usually anger. They saw him fling the batting helmet and pound the bat when he struck out, and naturally they concluded that the raw-boned Oklahoman was humorless and full of himself. All the while the Mick *was* having fun playing baseball. But this was a secret kept from the fans.

THE JEALOUSY FACTOR: Doubtless jealousy was part of the picture. Mantle was young, athletic, and handsome. He was paid well to play a game, and he was held up as an idol to millions.

The bald, the meek, and the henpecked wondered why all the cards had been dealt to the Mick. They delighted in booing and mocking him. It was their way of releasing frustrations, of feeling good.

YANKEE HATERS: That Mantle wore pinstripes at the Stadium and "New York" across his chest elsewhere were reasons enough for Yankee haters to boo him. Everywhere there were fans who hated the Yankees for their success; Mantle, who led the Yanks to 12 league championships in his first 14 seasons, was an understandable focal point for their hostility.

A considerable anti-Yankee faction was to be found in New York, especially among National League zealots. When the Giants and Dodgers left New York after the 1957 season, taking Willie Mays and Duke Snider with them, frustrated National League rooters—people embittered by what major-league baseball had done to them—enjoyed nothing more than an afternoon at the Stadium booing the Yankees, especially the Yankee they loved to hate, Mickey Mantle. In their eyes the Mick was a poor facsimile of Mays and Snider.

OFF-THE-FIELD RELATIONS: A reluctant New York celebrity, Mantle was never at ease among the fans. He disliked the notion that the fans owned a piece of him, the notion that it was for their approval, after all, that he displayed his professional wares; it was one aspect of being a professional that Mickey never accepted. Few pros do.

Nick Nicholson, a Washington clubhouse boy in the late 1950s, remembers Mantle, angry after losing, pushing aside a little boy who approached him.

Anne Marie Mueser, a New York writer, remembers having a crush on Mantle as a 13-year-old and being told on asking for an autograph to do the anatomically impossible. "I finally did get Mantle's autograph," she said, "but it wasn't by my own efforts. Each spring, a teacher at the school I attended took a group of boys to visit Yankee spring training in St. Petersburg. Johnny Lahr, one of the students (whose father was best known to most of us as the Cowardly Lion in *The Wizard of Oz*), managed to get Mantle's autograph for me. I don't know how Johnny did it, but several others on the trip remarked that it hadn't been easy."

Mantle had reasons aplenty to be less than accommodating with fans. He suffered verbal and, on occasion, physical abuse at their hands. Kids flipped ink on him or tore off pieces of his clothing. Drunks bothered him in restaurants. Fans threw things at him in the outfield and in 1960 a fan punched him in the jaw as he ran off the field at the Stadium.

Mantle was forced to rent a different house each summer in unsuccessful attempts to avoid crank phone calls and persistent autograph hounds. He couldn't even take his family out without inconsiderate fans ruining things.

Mantle wanted his privacy respected. When he was a kid and his dad took him to St. Louis to see the Cardinals, it was enough just to gawk at the players from up close—his dad wouldn't let him ask for autographs. Maybe Mickey felt the fans should have shown the same respect for *his* privacy as he had shown for Stan Musial's. Whatever, Mickey disappointed his share of autograph seekers.

Mantle tried to sign autographs for everyone at first. He noticed, however, that his time was being monopolized by a gang of kids hanging around Yankee Stadium. Day after day the same kids asked for auto-graphs (which brought a handsome price) and Mickey decided to duck them, a decision made easy by the fact that some of the kids were smart alecks and were quick to call him a bum.

The booing of Mantle peaked in 1959 and 1960. The summit was reached in August 1960, when Mickey failed to run out a ground ball.

A dramatic two-homer game and other field heroics, coupled with sympathetic press treatment and a realization on the fans' part that Mantle had taken their best shots, and, without complaint, survived, suddenly turned things around. The fans began to see another side of Mantle; this guy was not only playing baseball in spite of mounting injuries, but he was too tough-minded to allow their booing to damage him as it might a lesser man.

Ralph Houk helped when he became Yankee manager in 1961 and continually praised Mantle, and as the fans eased up on him, Mickey loosened up with them. After a decade of harsh treatment, of being a "bum," Mickey suddenly—and it was sudden—was the sentimental choice at Yankee Stadium. Anyway, the boo-birds had a nice new target in Roger Maris.

When Mantle and Maris chased Babe Ruth's home-run record in 1961, the fans turned on Maris with no more reason than they had previously booed Mantle. Mickey, in his 11th Yankee season, was an acknowledged great, a lifetime .307 hitter entering 1961, and if Ruth's record was to fall, the fans wanted the ax to be in Mantle's hands. Maris, on the other hand, was a newcomer; worse, he was seen as a usurper who hadn't paid his dues, a man who hadn't in a single season hit as high as .285.

Maris broke Ruth's record, hitting 61 homers, and became a villain. Mantle finished close behind Maris and was loved. He was even seen as an underdog. The fans, as though they were trying to make amends, showered the Mick with affection. In the years that followed, he suffered several serious injuries, and each time he returned, he was more popular than ever.

By the mid-1960s, Mantle was a national institution. He drew great cheers wherever he played, even in the most hostile of cities. The change in the public attitude was spectacular; Mantle had gone from being the most booed player in history to perhaps history's most popular player.

May 23, 1959—Memorial Stadium, Baltimore. Mickey Mantle began a personal turnaround as the last-place Yankees creamed the Orioles, 13–5. Just the previous day, Baltimore's Hoyt Wilhelm had one-hit the New Yorkers in a game in which the hitless Mantle went against his switch-hitting principles and batted right-handed against the right-handed Wilhelm. "I hadn't been hitting Wilhelm's knuckleball anyway," Mantle explained, "so I figured I couldn't do worse, no matter what I tried."

Feeling the heat for the Yanks' poor 1959 start, Mantle will respond by leading the club on a march through the American League standings. On this 3-for-3 date, including a homer, Mantle raised his batting average to a respectable .295 and began a 10-game spurt in which he hit .486. New York will win seven of those 10 games, beginning a gradual climb back into contention, and Mantle at May's end will be hitting .328.

June 17, 1959—Yankee Stadium. On this gloomy, dark day in the Bronx, with temperatures in the 50s, a sparse crowd of 11,078 watched the Yankees beat the White Sox, 7–3.

In the second inning, White Sox righty Ray Moore, laboring, has two on and two out and two runs already in. He goes 3 and 0 to Mantle, who has cooled off a bit since his late May rampage but at day's end is still batting .308. Having gotten the green light, he eyes the crippler intently, then unleashes a mighty swing and sends a majestic rainbow shot deep into the upper deck in right field. "It was the best one I've hit in two years," Mickey said afterward. "I really hit the hell out of it. I knew it when it left the bat."

According to Richard Dozer's game account in the *Chicago Tribune*, Mantle's homer "just missed the facade atop the stratospheric right-field seats before settling halfway into the third deck."

Edgar Munzel reported in the *Chicago Sun-Times* that the ball landed 400 feet from the plate at a height of 70 feet above the playing field. Munzel's perhaps conservative estimate: "If unobstructed the ball probably would have sailed around 470 or 480 feet."

June 18, 1959—Yankee Stadium. New York completed a three-game sweep of the second-place White Sox, winning 5–4 in 10 innings. The fifth-place Yankees (30–29) were now only 3½ games behind the first-place Indians (33–25), and the feeling was that the Yanks were right back in the thick of things.

Leading off the bottom of the 10th inning, with the score 4–4, Mickey Mantle, who earlier had made his 1,300th major-league hit, is batting lefty against Gerry Staley, the workhorse of the league in 1959, with 67 games pitched. Mickey takes a ball, then lashes his 15th homer deep into the lower seats in right field.

June 22, 1959—Municipal Stadium, Kansas City. In the Yankees' 11–6 victory over the A's, Mickey Mantle enjoyed one of his most productive games ever: He hit two left-handed homers and a triple, scored three runs, and drove home six.

Mantle hits a first-inning solo homer and a fifth-inning two-run triple. In the seventh, against reliever and ex-teammate Bob Grim, he hits a three-run homer, a wallop that goes far over the center-field fence, giving the Yankees a safe 10–6 lead. Grim, when asked his estimate of the distance years later, replied, "It went far enough!"

The good news for the Yankees, now only three games from the top rung in the American League, is that the bats of Mantle and Bill Skowron, who hit his fourth homer in four games, are hot. The bad news is the continued slump of Bob Turley, the 1958 Cy Young Award winner who couldn't last long enough to record the victory.

More bad news is ahead. After snugging up to the league leaders, the Yankees will drop three of four games in a crucial showdown at Chicago. Worse, in the second week of July, they will lose five in a row at Boston.

Mantle's season is at its peak, events will prove. On this date, he was sixth in batting (.314), fifth in RBIs (44), and fourth in home runs (17), and moving up the league ladder strongly. Tomorrow he will hit his fifth homer inside a week—then, amazingly, almost inconceivably, he will hit only two more homers through August 3.

The Mantle problem, as usual, centered around injuries. Mantle hurt his right ankle late in June and limped through July. His right shoulder was bedeviling him again; whenever he swung and missed batting left-handed, pain shot through the shoulder. He really shouldn't have been playing, but, with the Yankees struggling to keep in the race, he gave his best.

July 16, 1959—Yankee Stadium. Mickey Mantle was suffering through the most miserable summer of his career. He was an unselfish player who realized his importance to the club; when he pressed to turn the team's fortunes around, he lost his rhythm. His impatience at the plate widened the strike zone and he swung at bad pitches rather than accept a walk— the Yanks needed the big hit. Mantle will wind up striking out 126 times, the most in his career, while drawing only 94 walks, his only dip below 100 walks between 1954 and 1962.

When Mantle struck out, he sometimes reverted to punching dugout walls and kicking water coolers. Though he never stopped trying, his mood darkened and his attitude soured. The fact that he was the villain of the home fans and press didn't help his mood. That Casey Stengel became increasingly irritable only added to the unpleasantness of the summer.

But on this date Mantle enjoys a respite in a doubleheader with Cleveland. In the opener, the Indians take a 5–4 lead in the eighth inning, and a play so characteristic of this Yankee season is chiefly responsible. It is a head-on collision between shortstop Gil McDougald and left fielder Tony Kubek, resulting in injuries to both players—Kubek, the Yanks' leading hitter at .300, leaves on a stretcher—in a dropped ball, and in the tying run scoring.

Mantle has a chance to deliver with two on in the bottom of the eighth. But Mickey, who has only one RBI since June 23, is whiffed for the third out by Gary Bell. Yogi Berra comes through in the ninth, homering, and the game goes into extra innings.

Mantle in the 10th gets another crack at Bell, a good right hander who will win 16 games this season. Bobby Richardson is on base, and two are out, and Mantle wins this battle, whistling a drive into the right-field seats. The Yankees are 7–5 victors.

A dramatic blow like this often meant the end of a Mantle slump. But not this time. Although Mickey added a single and a walk in the nightcap, raising his average to .298, his doldrums were to be prolonged.

The Yankees won the second game, 4–0, behind Bobby Shantz, resulting in a Yankee sweep of the three-game series and knocking the stunned Indians out of first place. And despite all their problems, the fourth-place Yanks, only 5½ games out of first, remained within striking distance. They needed a hot streak, however. But a 12–16 July record would prove catastrophic to their pennant chances.

The Yankees would never get untracked, finishing third with a 79–75 record, 15 games behind the White Sox, the eventual champions. It was a bad year for all concerned. The front office put the players in a poor frame of mind with its tough stance on contracts. Casey Stengel, who turned 69 in July, was losing his grip on the team and, in some cases, the respect of his players. He hurt the psyches of young players, like Norm Siebern and Jerry Lumpe; he rode them hard and both struggled.

The pitching fell apart. Don Larsen and Tom Sturdivant, two pitchers who were counted on heavily, suffered from arm miseries (and Sturdivant was traded away in late May). But the single most puzzling aspect of 1959 was the performance of Bob Turley, who fell to 8–11 after his great 21–7 season in 1958. There was no pop in his fastball, once so alive.

Several key regulars went down. Bill Skowron and Gil McDougald, Stengel's most powerful hitting infielders, both had injury-plagued seasons. Another infielder, Andy Carey, was lost to illness. Right fielder Hank Bauer, a solid if unspectacular player who was a determined winner, turned 37 and hit only .238, with nine homers.

The Yankee lineups of the 1950s were characterized by the tremendous back-to-back punch of Mantle and Berra, with Mantle usually in the third slot. As the Yankees won four straight pennants from 1955 through 1958, the twosome averaged a combined 67 homers per season; they hit only 50 in 1959. The 34-year-old Berra, who might have been baseball's most valuable player for the 1950s—he played catcher, the game's most demanding position, well, besides delivering so much punch offensively—was past his prime and no longer capable of putting the big power numbers on the board. That meant there was less protection for Mantle in the batting order, especially with Skowron hurt. And with Berra's decline (he was still a feared hitter, just not one of the league's most productive), the Yankees were suddenly light in left-handed power.

So, outside of pitching help, the Yankees had three big needs if they were to reestablish themselves in 1960: a new right fielder, a hitter to protect Mantle in the batting order (so that pitchers would be forced to pitch to Mickey), and more left-handed power. All three needs will be satisfied with the off-season acquisition of Roger Maris.

September 7, 1959—Fenway Park, Boston. This was a typical Fenway home-run derby, won by the Red Sox, 12–4. The victory allowed Boston to clinch the season series with the Yankees for the first time since 1948. Casey Stengel was so fed up by it all that he got himself ejected in the eighth inning.

The Red Sox strike for six runs in the second inning, including consecutive home runs by Don Buddin, Jerry Casale, and Pumpsie Green. All three are tremendous blasts, but the longest is whacked by Casale, the pitcher, whose homer "cleared Lansdowne St., the buildings beyond, and disappeared toward the tracks of the Boston & Albany Railroad," according to Roger Birtwell's report in the *Boston Globe.*

The Yankees answer with a pair of third-inning homers, a pinch-hit shot by Andy Carey and a two-run job by Mickey Mantle. Casale, who admits he was "in awe" of Mantle as a rookie, remembers this of the Mick's left-handed homer: "I had a two-strike count on him, and Sammy White called for a low outside waste pitch to set him up for something hard on the knees on the next one. I threw a low pitch about a foot outside and he leaned over and it seemed like he hit it with just one hand—the ball went like a bazooka shot into the screen in left field."

Actually, Mantle's homer hit an upright supporting the screen and bounced back onto the field in left. Mantle stopped at first base, but the third-base umpire, Larry Napp, signaled home run, and Mickey, with Hank Bauer ahead of him, completed the trot.

The funny thing is that Boston's Jackie Jensen had hit a similar blow earlier in the game and got only a double. Hit to center, the ball hit an upright and returned to the field. Umpire Ed Rommel offered no home-run sign and Jensen got only two bases. Several others over the years lost legitimate homers at Fenway the same way, and Mantle once was denied a homer that hit the light tower.

September 13, 1959—Yankee Stadium. The Yankees, long since out of the pennant race, made a big impact on determining the league champion anyway. In a thrilling doubleheader, featuring some of the greatest pitching ever seen, the Yankees swept the second-place Indians, winning, 2–1 and 1–0, and pushed the Tribe 5½ games behind Chicago, winner of a single game.

Bob Turley of the Yankees and Jack Harshman duel in the opener. The game is still scoreless when Turley leaves for a pinch-hitter in the 10th. In the 11th, the Indians reach Ryne Duren and Gary Blaylock for four consecutive singles, the last producing the first run of the game; but when Rocky Colavito is waved home by third-base coach Jo-Jo White, the relay from Mickey to Bobby Richardson to the plate nails Colavito. Eli Grba relieves Blaylock, issues a walk to load the bases, and then strikes out Harshman and Vic Power. The Indians lead only 1–0 after all this, and Indian manager Joe Gordon will later be second-guessed for not pinch-hitting for Harshman.

Leading off the bottom of the 11th, Tony Kubek singles. Then Mantle, hitless in four previous at bats, batting right-handed, connects on Harshman's second pitch and rifles home run No. 29 deep into the left-field stands. The Yankees win, 2–1.

The homer is Mantle's only hit in a 1-for-9 day. He takes the collar in the nightcap against Jim Perry—Mickey went 0 for 8 facing Perry this year—but Duke Maas shut out the Indians in a battle of matching six-hitters. And the people of Cleveland would not soon forget Mantle's one hit. The home run went a long way in sealing the Tribe's fate as a second-place loser.

September 15, 1959—Yankee Stadium. The White Sox, racing to their first American League pennant in 40 years, beat the Yankees, 4–3, and reduced their magic number to clinch first place to four. Mickey Mantle made his final imprint on the glum season with a pair of colossal homers, his 30th and 31st, that drove in all three Yankee runs.

Mantle hits a two-run homer off Billy Pierce in the first inning. Batting righty, Mickey drives the ball deep into the right-field bullpen.

The White Sox and reliever Bob Shaw take a 4–2 lead into the bottom of the ninth. New York gets one run when Mantle, batting lefty this time, unloads a mighty clout landing more than halfway up in the right-field bleachers. It is the seventh time Mantle has switch-hit home runs in the same game.

There was nothing left for the Yankees but to play out the remaining nine games, and then everyone went home. Everyone, that is, except Casey Stengel, who covered the White Sox–Dodgers World Series for *Life* magazine.

For Mantle, it had been the worst season of his peak years. The most glaring disappointment, of course, was the fact that the Yankees didn't win the pennant Mantle was supposed to lead the Yankees to every year. As for individual statistics, there was Mantle's .285 batting average and 75 RBIs, his worst numbers in those categories since his rookie year.

Yet, there were some positive aspects to Mantle's 1959 season:

● The Mick led all American League outfielders in fielding average (.995).

- He was second in the league in stolen bases (21), his career high, and he was caught only three times for the league's highest stolen base proficiency (.875).
- In other categories in the American League, Mantle finished second in runs scored (104), third in slugging (.514) and walks (94), and fourth in homers (31) and total bases (278).
- Mickey won many games with clutch hits in the late innings.

Not bad for an off year.

1960

May 28, 1960—Yankee Stadium. That this season will be any better for Mickey Mantle than the 1959 campaign hasn't been suggested by events to date. He has been slumping terribly, hitting .231, as low an average as he's ever had this far into a season.

Manager Casey Stengel is bedridden with a viral infection. A coach, Ralph Houk, Stengel's heir apparent, is running the Yankees, and his stint at the helm is a preview of things to come. He is faced with his first big decision—to play or bench Mantle—and he keeps Mickey in the lineup. Just as Stengel had been doing this season, Houk has Mickey batting second.

Mantle batting second? It seems sacrilegious, but the power hitters behind Mantle—Roger Maris, Elston Howard, Bob Cerv, Bill Skowron, and Yogi Berra—are off to great season starts. Maris, the new kid obtained from Kansas City, leads the league in home runs and RBIs. If Mantle were to start hitting, and if New York's wretched pitching were to straighten out somehow, look out! For the moment, though, the Yankees are mired in fifth place.

Jim Coates of the Yankees and Washington's Jim Kaat, a young southpaw headed for a long and prosperous career, on this day match zeros through 5½ innings. Mantle, hitless in his last 20 at bats, hears Houk encourage him to "get a hold of one" as he marches to the plate to lead off the Yankee sixth. Kaat slips in two quick strikes. The next pitch is wasted, not by Kaat but by Mantle. Mickey's fifth homer of the season is his second batting right-handed; both right-handed homers have been hit off Kaat to the opposite field, and both have been long, this one carrying over 400 feet to the right-field bleachers.

The second-year pitcher loses his composure and walks three men (one intentionally), hits two batsmen, and gives Gil McDougald a two-run triple, in all allowing three more runs, before retiring Mantle on a called third strike to end the inning. Maris later homers—it is the first time Mantle and Maris homer in the same game as teammates—and Coates breezes to a 5–1 victory, his fifth win without a loss.

Mantle will give further evidence that the prolonged batting slump is behind him by helping the Yankees in their next game to an extra-inning win with three hits, including another homer. But the following day, after catching a fly ball to end a Memorial Day doubleheader at the Stadium, he will be mobbed by fans and punched flush on the jaw. No fracture, but soft food for four days and another apparent setback for the Mick; his June will get under way with a 1-for-13 mini-tailspin.

Even before the batting slump and punching episode, Mantle was in a poor frame of mind. The penny-guarding tactics of general manager George Weiss had finally gotten to him, affecting both his attitude and his play.

THE RIGORS OF RECOMPENSE

Mantle realized his 1959 season took some of the shine off his apple, but he wasn't ready for what Weiss had in mind for 1960, which was a $17,000 pay cut. Noting that the contract he received in January called for a salary of $55,000, Mantle figured it was some kind of mistake and returned the document unsigned. No mistake. No misprint. Weiss told him, "That's what you're worth."

Thus began a test of wills. An angry, resolute Mantle was up against an unyielding Weiss. But with the general manager holding all the cards, there wasn't much that Mickey could do except refuse to play. Spring training camp opened in St. Petersburg, Florida, and Mantle wasn't there. Ten days later he flew to St. Pete and met privately with Weiss. A so-called "compromise" was reached, a humiliating compromise so far as Mantle was concerned. He took a pay cut of $7,000; he would play the 1960 season for $65,000.

Mantle was bitter. He had one "bad" year and Weiss put him through the wringer for it. Now in uniform, he pressed the rest of the spring, trying to show up the general manager, and in doing too much too soon aggravated old injuries.

Mickey was lucky in that this was the last time he'd have to knock heads with Weiss, who at the close of the year will be "retired" along with Stengel. After Weiss's departure, Mickey would never have cause for complaint about Yankee management.

The 1960 salary dispute wasn't the first time Weiss and Mantle had locked horns. They battled on a regular basis, but then again, Weiss battled over money with almost every Yankee ballplayer.

Weiss made players grovel for every cent they negotiated out of him. He dealt man to man—no agent could do a player's negotiating. A few players, tough, sure-of-their-worth types like Yogi Berra, did okay, but if you happened to be lacking in hard-nosed business acumen, if you were, say, a Bill Skowron, advantage was taken of you. Mantle fell somewhere in between the Berras and the Skowrons, becoming a more skilled negotiator as he grew older and wiser.

More often than not Mantle was bitter over the way contract negotiations were handled. Weiss wasn't just tough; he was tawdry. He used insults and threats, once threatening to trade Mantle to Cleveland—baseball's Siberia—for Rocky Colavito and Herb Score. Some believe Weiss *would* have unloaded Mantle had he remained the Yankee general manager beyond 1960.

Weiss wasn't a particularly popular man in baseball circles or with the press. He was seen as something of a cold fish. Heartless. Brilliant but heartless. But in keeping the lid on salary expenditures, Weiss was only doing what Yankee co-owners Dan Topping and Del Webb were paying him to do. Topping and Webb seldom dirtied their hands in filthy lucre matters.

Casey Stengel, however, wasn't always happy with the Weiss way of doing business, and he was especially unhappy over the way Mantle was humiliated in 1960. "Take Mantle," Stengel wrote in his 1962 autobiography. "Since he became a star, he'd never once gone to spring training without some hard feeling over his contract negotiations. And then I'd be told, 'Why don't you make the man mind you?' "

Mantle played his rookie season in 1951 for $7,500 and was happy to get that. His salary increased over the next few years, until he was making $32,500 in 1956, the year he won the Triple Crown. Reportedly, he jumped to $60,000 in 1957, $70,000 in 1958, and $72,000 in 1959. Weiss kicked and groaned for Topping and Webb—and for George Weiss—every dollar of the way.

Once Weiss was out of the picture, Mantle had no contract problems. Reportedly, he made $75,000 in 1961 and $82,000 in 1962; in 1963, he became a $100,000-a-year player. In those days, $100,000 was the pinnacle, the absolute uppermost reaches of the possible.

Mickey was paid $100,000 a year the rest of his career. He was worth every penny, and a whole lot more, not only as a producer but as a performer, as the top drawing card in the American League. Like Babe Ruth in his day and Reggie Jackson in his, Mantle put fannies in the seats.

Mantle is still putting fannies in the seats at Yankee Stadium in the 1980s. He spawned a whole new generation of Yankee fans, the kids of the 1950s and 1960s, now in their thirties and forties, who joined the Yankee camp because of Mantle. These grown-up kids now have kids of their own, and they take the newer, littler kids to the place where they saw Mantle do such wondrous things, Yankee Stadium.

June 1, 1960—Memorial Stadium, Baltimore. Hal "Skinny" Brown, who had an 85–92 big-league record and who in 1960 had his career high of 12 wins, was a journeyman pitcher. He did, however, have great moments. All that separated Brown from a no-hitter on this date was a Mickey Mantle home run.

Brown retires Tony Kubek to start the game. Then after putting Mantle, the second batter, in an 0-and-2 hole, he delivers a high fastball out of the strike zone. But Mickey swings anyway and wallops a homer far over the right-center-field fence, more than 400 feet from the plate. "I've got to give Mickey some credit," Brown, who pitched to only 29 batters, said after the game. "He's got the strength to hit the ball out of any park. And it don't have to be a strike for him to hit it."

Mantle also makes a splendid catch. Turning his back to the plate, he scampers to the fence to spear a Clint Courtney drive with one hand.

Other than the Mantle highlights, the Yankees had a miserable series here. The Orioles won all three games (this date's by a 4–1 score), and when it was all over, the first-place Baby Birds (27–15), as the youngest team in the majors was called, were six games ahead of the fourth-place Bronx Bombers (19–19).

June 8, 1960—Yankee Stadium. The Yankees had long been in a rut, barely playing better than .500 baseball since early August 1958. This extended period of mediocrity led some to believe that the Yankee Dynasty was a thing of the past.

But dynasties and even seasons aside, a game is an event of merit and standing of itself, and this date's was probably New York's finest all-around game so far this season. Bob Turley pitched a three-hit shutout, and his fielders cut down three Go-Go White Sox base runners on the paths. The Bombers also unloaded a quartet of homers, including Nos. 9 and 10 of the year for Mickey Mantle.

Mickey hits both homers into the lower right-field stands, one in the sixth and the other in the eighth. When Roger Maris follows Mantle's second shot with a homer, it marks the first time that Mantle and Maris hit back-to-back homers. It is Roger's 16th homer, matching his entire 1959 output at Kansas City.

The Yankees won, 6–0. They took their recent series with Boston three games to one and were in the process of winning three out of four from the league champion White Sox. There were two very good signs in the Yankee camp. Yankee pitching, which allowed Chicago only seven runs in the series, finally had come around, and so had Mantle. This was Mickey's fourth consecutive two-hit game (leaving out a game in which he walked three times in three trips).

Things were easier for Mantle this year. The red-hot bat of Maris provided great protection behind him in the order—opposing pitchers thought twice before pitching around Mantle—and Bill Skowron, recovered from an injury-plagued 1959 season, was also stinging the ball. So were the other prime power hitters, Yogi Berra and Elston Howard. This also meant that Mantle felt less pressure to carry the offensive load by himself. And Maris was the perfect complement to Mantle, the two of them taking over from the Mantle-Berra duo as the scourge of the league.

June will be a beautiful month for Mantle and the Yankees. Mickey came into the month with only six homers and 15 RBIs and then exploded for 12 homers and 23 RBIs. "I don't know what I was doing wrong at the beginning of the season, and I don't know what I'm doing different now," Mickey told Francis Stann of the *Washington Star* in early July. "I wish I did."

Mantle turned the Yankees around. Every other power hitter on the club was having a good to excellent year, but the Yankees didn't start winning consistently until No. 7 started ripping the ball. The Yankees will be 21–8 in June, making a solid move into pennant contention.

The only negative Mantle news concerned his right knee. The bum knee was beginning to affect his left-handed stroke as much as his bad right shoulder. He limped, actually, because the knee deteriorated with each and every wrenching he gave it in the heat of competitive battle. On June 21 he will hit two homers off Frank Lary in Detroit, then tell newsmen of the problem with the knee: "It hurts worse now than it has all year. It's loose. All the ligaments are torn loose."

June 17, 1960—Comiskey Park, Chicago. White Sox owner Bill

Veeck prided himself on being a regular guy. He didn't take himself seriously and had fun with baseball. However, the Veeck legend was dented on this date when the imperial Yankees, as Veeck saw them, beat him at his own let's-have-fun-with-it game. And Veeck didn't like it.

Veeck had a brand new toy, a $300,000 exploding scoreboard that sent everything but the space shuttle into orbit after a homer—a Soxer homer. But it found nothing to celebrate in a visiting player's homer, and some of the visiting players, Veeck's guests, felt slighted. Pity the fool who draws the wrath of a pro athlete who feels slighted.

Veeck and Bob Fishel of the Yankee front office were good friends, so Fishel apparently felt no qualms about the practical joke he and Casey Stengel had in store for the White Sox in the first game of a key four-game series. When Clete Boyer of the Yanks blasted a second-inning homer, Stengel and Mickey Mantle led the Yankee dugout in a jubilant dance, everyone waving Fourth of July sparklers above their heads in mock compensation for Veeck's one-way scoreboard. In the bullpen, Yogi Berra led another bunch of sparkler-waving Yankees.

Everyone was amused except Veeck, the guy with the sense of humor. George Weiss was not capable of designing such a stunt, but Veeck spotted an element of frugality in it and chose to blame him. "Who's 'bush' now?" asked Veeck after the sparklerworks. "It's typical of George Weiss, who wants to go at a cheaper price."

When Mantle homers in the eighth, Veeck gets another dose of the sparklerworks. The Yanks win, 4–2, and excel throughout the rest of the Windy City series, taking all four games.

July 3, 1960—Yankee Stadium. The Yanks swept a doubleheader with Detroit before 50,556 spectators. The 7–6 opening game was saved in the ninth when right fielder Roger Maris gunned down Casey Wise at the plate and Ryne Duren fanned Charlie Maxwell for the final out with the bases loaded. The second game may have been won because of a pitcher's broken concentration.

The nightcap is in the fifth inning and Detroit leads, 2–1. The Yankees have two men on base and Mickey Mantle batting. All of a sudden, Tiger first baseman Norm Cash, who hasn't stopped protesting a safe call he feels should have been the third out, gives umpire Nestor Chylak a bump. Cash is ejected and a delay ensues as a new Tiger first sacker is brought in.

The delay may have interfered with pitcher Pete Burnside's concentration. When play resumes, Mantle, batting righty, gets to him, parking a wrong-way three-run homer into the right-field stands, and the Yankees take the lead, 4–2, and go on to win their sixth consecutive victory, 6–2. The Yankees have gone 23–5 since June 5 and lead the league by three games.

July 18, 1960—Municipal Stadium, Cleveland. It happened again. Another pitcher—Dick Stigman this time—had his concentration broken while pitching to Mickey Mantle, and, again, it cost plenty.

The Yankees and Indians are knotted at 1–1 in the fourth inning. Elston Howard and Bobby Richardson open with singles, and Whitey Ford loads the bases when Stigman handles his bunt and throws late to third base. Clete Boyer delivers a sacrifice fly, which also moves Richardson to third, and Bobby scores when Stigman doesn't convert Hector Lopez's comebacker into a double play.

The Indians are infuriated when Lopez is called safe on what they feel should have been the third out. When the argument finally subsides, Mantle, whom Stigman had earlier struck out with two on, connects against the distracted rookie and pulls a three-run four-bagger over the left-field fence. The Yankees and the route-going Ford are well on their way to a 9–2 victory.

July 20, 1960—Municipal Stadium, Cleveland. Wherever he played, Mickey Mantle usually hit at least one landmark tape-measure job. On this date he may have unloaded the longest homer in the history of Municipal Stadium, the Cleveland Indians' home since 1932.

Cleveland right-hander Gary Bell in the seventh inning is nursing an 8–2 lead (he will struggle to an 8–6 win) when Mantle launches one over the auxiliary scoreboard and into the distant upper deck in right field. At the time of Mantle's clout, the only other player to have hit one in the same spot was Indian Luke Easter.

Easter sent his big shot into the right-field upper deck on June 23, 1950. It supposedly traveled 477 feet; the Associated Press game story reported that the homer went about 470 feet. The Indians in 1986 still recognize the Easter homer as the longest in their park's history.

Bob DiBiasio, the Indians' current director of public relations, concedes that Cleveland's long-distance homer records are incomplete. For one thing, the Indians didn't make Municipal Stadium their full-time residence until 1947. (The Indians played their big dates here while continuing to use League Park for the bulk of their home schedule from 1932 through 1946.) So for a long time records for such things as long homers just weren't kept. To the best of DiBiasio's knowledge, there have been only a handful of homers hit into the right-field upper deck here. Maybe so, but Mantle alone hit three of them.

Chuck Heaton, veteran Cleveland sportswriter, saw both Easter's wallop and Mantle's shot on this date. "Both blasts were hit into approximately the same area of the upper deck," says Heaton. "Easter's might have been hit a row or two higher, but Easter's arc was coming down whereas Mantle's drive was still on the rise when it crashed into the upper deck. Mantle's was probably the number one hardest and longest ball ever hit here."

Municipal Stadium is a huge oval-shaped park that can hold more than 80,000 fans. The dimensions to the outfield fences have been changed many times over the years. The most radical change was made in 1947, when an inner fence was built and the distance to center, originally 470 feet, became 410. No one has ever reached the center-field bleachers on the fly, but Mantle hit a few homers that either bounced into the bleachers or bounced against the bleacher wall—the old 470-foot fence.

August 15, 1960—Yankee Stadium. The story of this Monday began with the loss of a Sunday doubleheader to Washington that dropped the Yankees from first place to third—*and* with controversy over Mickey Mantle's alleged nonchalance on a groundout.

The play happened in the sixth inning of the second game with the score tied. With Roger Maris on first base and one out, Mantle, homerless in August and showing only two RBIs so far for the month, bounced to third base. Disgusted with himself, he took a few steps, then quit running. Meanwhile, Maris, in trying to break up the double play, barrelled into the pivotman at second. It was a double play in spite of the takeout effort by Maris, who bruised his ribs so badly that he will be sidelined for 12 days.

To the Yankee Stadium assembled, Mantle acted the shirker in his failure to run out the grounder. "Quitter! Quitter!"—the hoots and hollers cascaded upon the Mick as he waited for his glove. But instead of the glove, Mickey got a replacement; Bob Cerv came in to play his position.

Reporters had a pretty good idea of why Mantle was lifted, but they wanted to have it spelled out. Had Mickey, playing with damage to his right knee, hurt himself some more? No, replied Mickey. Was he tired? No. Did he ask out of the game? No. Was his leaving Stengel's idea? "Must have been," said Mickey. "It wasn't mine."

Stengel had a whole lot more to say. He was less than giddy over the double loss, and the Mantle incident left him furious. "Sure I took him out!" Casey shouted. Then he rips Mantle. Then he calms down. Mantle didn't stop running out of laziness or indifference, Casey said, adding, "He gets mad at himself, because he isn't hitting the ball good."

What actually happened was that Mantle had pulled a rock. In the 24 hours following the game, he vigorously maintained that he had not been loafing, that he had lost track of the number of outs. He thought there were two outs. He had been distracted by bench jockeying from the Washington dugout. "I was talking to the catcher and the bench was shouting at me, and I just got all mixed up," Mickey explained to Dick Young of the *New York Daily News*. "I made a mistake, but it wasn't a case of not hustling."

He told Jimmy Cannon of the *New York Journal-American* the same story and he seemed to resent Stengel's overlooking a recent game in which he beat out a one-hop grounder at a critical point. "If I don't hustle on that play, we don't win," he told Cannon. "But Stengel forgets about that."

At the same time, Mantle, who was distressed that Maris was hurt on a play in which he fell asleep, came to an important personal realization. He knew he had lost track of the outs partly because he was focusing too much attention on his own recent lack of productivity (as Stengel suggested). He was so intent on kicking himself that he wasn't always fully alive to the game situation. For the good of the team, he had to get out of himself. He resolved to quit sulking and to remain alert on the field.

As Monday dawned, it wasn't fun being Mickey Mantle. Early rumors had Mantle being either fined or suspended, or both. Dan Topping, the club's co-owner, said he would back whatever action Stengel decided to take against Mantle. Printed reports had it that Mantle's teammates were down on him.

But when a sheepish Mantle entered the clubhouse, he discovered that his teammates were behind him 100 percent. He had made an honest mistake, the players felt—several admitted having pulled the same boner—and some thought Stengel had gone too far in his public rebuke.

The players recognized that Mantle often played hurt, and they assured him that reports about their being down on him didn't reflect the actual attitudes of his teammates.

As Monday's night game approached, no action had been taken against Mantle. In fact, Stengel, who was being curiously elusive about the Mantle matter, had Mickey in the starting lineup. Sitting in the Yankee dugout, Casey fielded questions before the game. "You see his name on the lineup card, don't you?" Casey snapped. "Well, you just watch how he plays tonight."

Mantle may have been in the lineup out of necessity, and with abundant irony. With Maris sidelined because of the injury incurred on the play that put Mantle in the doghouse, Stengel couldn't afford to bench his other big slugger. Casey needed all possible guns because it was the streaking Orioles, now tied with the White Sox for first place, who were in town.

The big game draws 24,233 spectators, many of them there to get on Mantle. As he jogs to center field to start the game, the boo-birds come alive. "Run it out, Mickey" is the least harsh of their yells. Contemptuous, louder-than-usual boos greet him as he steps to the plate in the bottom of the first (though some sympathetic fans applaud), and as Mickey returns to the dugout after grounding out, the boos intensify. But he shuts his ears to the catcalls; tonight he remains alert from first pitch to last.

Baltimore is ahead, 2–0, when Hector Lopez opens the Yankee fourth with an infield hit. Mantle, with another round of raucous boos raining down, faces right-hander Jerry Walker. He gets good wood on Walker's first pitch, a fastball, pulling a two-run homer deep into the right-field bullpen. The ball reaches the second wire fence in the pen— over 400 feet away.

Most of the jeering turns to cheering as Mantle circles the bases. He crosses the plate with the game-tying run, and as he trots toward the dugout, he surprises everyone by tipping his cap to the crowd, a rare Mantle gesture. "You didn't have to run hard on that one, Mick," the Yankees on the bench tell him.

The score remains tied until the eighth, when a Jackie Brandt home run gives the Orioles a 3–2 lead. In the bottom of the eighth, Lopez is walked by Oriole reliever Hoyt Wilhelm. Mantle has had difficulty in the past with Wilhelm's famed knuckleball, and he quickly puts himself in an 0-and-2 hole. He pops a high foul that catcher Clint Courtney gets under—and drops for an error. Courtney is using the oversized catcher's mitt; it is good for handling the elusive Wilhelm knuckler but not for catching pop-ups.

Mantle makes the most of his reprieve. He times a knuckler just right and socks a screaming liner to right. The ball clears the 344-foot sign, landing in the front rows of the lower seats, and as Mickey runs out the home run, the fans are unrestrained in their approval. Mickey shows his appreciation with another tip of his cap. The Yankees lead, 4–3, and that will be the final score.

Mantle's heroics tended to overshadow a fine five-hitter by Art Ditmar and some excellent fielding by infielders Bobby Richardson, Tony Kubek, and Clete Boyer. But it was Mantle, after all, who knocked in all four Yankee runs and, accordingly, was chiefly responsible for putting the Yankees (63–45) back in first place, a half game ahead of Baltimore (65–48) and Chicago (65–48), the latter losers to Detroit.

Reporters and photographers crowded around Mantle in the victorious locker room. "I never wanted to have a good day so badly in my life," said Mickey. "If you have a bad day on top of what happened yesterday, then you're in real trouble."

Mickey felt good. When asked about tipping his cap to the fans, he joked, "I figured I'd better get on their good side while I could, because the next time I strike out they'll be on me again."

This undoubtedly was one of the most dramatic performances in Mantle's career. A turning point in his relations with the fans? No doubt about it—he won over a large body of fans. He might still have to hear a scattering of boos at the Stadium, but never again will he encounter a hostile crowd there. The press may have softened, too; he got nothing but good ink about this comeback effort. And this more mature Mickey Mantle will play absolutely brilliant ball, when not sidelined with injuries, continually from this date through 1964, the last of his prime years.

Stengel was like the cat who ate the canary. He seemed even willing to forget the Sunday episode; there would be no more reprimands, no fine, no suspension. "Now, you ask what I am going to do about Mantle," Casey told reporters. "Well, I'm going to shake his hand. I am very appreciative."

Stengel had a point to make and apparently felt he made it. He was unhappy with Yankee players—and not just Mantle, he added—who failed to run out grounders. He didn't say so, but it appeared that Stengel had drawn the line with Mantle's Sunday incident; in an attempt to end baserunning negligence and nonchalance, Casey decided to make an example of his Big Guy. Or maybe that was why he was so angry to begin with; he expected Mantle, an elder statesman in his 10th Yankee season, to set a good example. Mickey, whether he knew it or not, was looked up to by the younger players. So if one were to believe that Stengel was indeed the master psychologist some credited him as being, he was able, with a single stroke, to stop careless baserunning and to put a jolt in his star player, the model for lesser and younger Yanks.

September 10, 1960—Briggs Stadium, Detroit. The game was over and Mickey Mantle of the New York Yankees sat quietly in the visitors' locker room, eating peanuts and saying matter-of-factly, "He threw me a fastball and I belted it." Mantle spoke of his home run off Paul Foytack, a shot that cleared the right-field roof in Detroit, a shot that got lost, more or less, for 25 years.

Perhaps if Mantle had talked it up a little more, this awesome home run might have drawn more study. But self-promotion was never Mickey's style; he let others talk and write about his extraordinary play and legendary clouts. The "others," for whatever reason, failed to appreciate baseball's longest homer. Perhaps they did appreciate it; perhaps they just couldn't *document* its incredible length.

Then too, the Tigers had no reason to publicize Mantle, the star of the despised Yankees. And the Yankees' own drumbeater, Bob Fishel, wasn't with the club in Detroit. Fishel usually made only one trip per season into each American League city, and this Detroit trip, as he recalls, wasn't the one for 1960. Apparently no one else in the Yankee camp was inclined or able to document the homer's length.

In any case, Fishel, Red Patterson's successor, found the job of determining the length of every Mantle homer too time-consuming in the light of other duties. Once, on returning to the press box after locating the landing spot of one long Mantle homer, Fishel looked up only to see Mantle connecting for another. Still winded from the first homer, he was off and running again.

Actually, by 1960, Mantle's sensational swats had become commonplace. The fans still loved watching them, but one more Mantle boomer wasn't really *news*. Briggs Stadium serves to make the point. A Ted Williams home run in 1939 was the first fair ball hit over the right-field roof, and the feat wasn't duplicated until Mantle's shots in 1956 and

1958. The drive on this date gave Mantle three of the first four homers to clear the right-field roof in Detroit.

The length of Mantle's home run on this date was emphasized by Detroit reporters Sam Greene (*Detroit News*) and Hal Middlesworth (*Detroit Free Press*), but John Drebinger of the *New York Times* had a different focus. The important thing, in the bigger picture back home, was that the Yanks' 5–1 victory over the Tigers, coupled with an Oriole defeat, moved New York into first place by just a half game over the Birds.

The win does not come easy. New York takes a 2–1 lead into the seventh inning, and with two out, Hector Lopez singles and Roger Maris draws a walk. Mantle, batting left-handed against Foytack, a right-hander off whom he struck his first roof-clearing shot back in 1956, takes two balls and then unloads. The ball he crushes to right field climbs higher and higher through a crosswind, leaving the playing field near the 370-foot mark, then clears the 94-foot-high roof. It travels through a light tower, possibly grazing a structural member of the tower, and disappears.

It was during the game or shortly thereafter that several Detroit sportswriters, Edgar Hayes and the late Ed Browalski among them, journeyed to where they believed the ball came back to earth. They discovered that the ball cleared Trumbull Avenue and landed on a fly in the yard of Brooks Lumber across the street.

Paul Borders, a Brooks employee, told them he saw where the ball landed and showed the spot to the writers. Hayes says today that the group believed the ball must have traveled 600 feet, but direct measurement was impossible and the writers didn't know how to handle an indirect measurement situation—a situation in which it was not possible to establish a line from home plate to the landing spot.

Two and a half decades later, in June 1985, the measurement problem was readdressed. In his research for this book, Paul E. Susman became convinced that the staggering force of Mantle's homer was never fully reported. Several eyewitnesses, including Hayes, Browalski, and 1960 Tiger broadcaster George Kell, spoke in breathless tones when Susman interviewed them about the underplayed wallop, although Foytack, while vividly recalling Mantle's taking him out of Briggs Stadium in 1956, didn't remember this one.

Susman returned to the Brooks lumberyard. Hayes, in need of a walker now but still eager to help, met him and identified the general spot where the homer landed. The people at Brooks told Susman that Paul

Borders, the worker who saw the ball come down, was deceased, but they said another lumberyard worker who had been a friend of Borders, a man named Sam Cameron, was still working there and might be of help. Borders and Cameron, longtime Brooks employees, were both depicted as reliable persons.

Cameron was found and was asked if he knew where the Mantle homer landed. Yes—Borders had shown him. Without hesitation, Cameron took Susman to that spot. The ball landed at the base of a shed in which Borders was working. The shed is no longer there—it is the only missing landmark from the 1960 scene—but Cameron recalled *exactly* where it stood.

Accompanying Susman was Robert H. Schiewe, who took charge of the measurements and calculations. A Rolls-Royce dealer and a former semipro baseball player, Schiewe also knows his math and was able to employ the Pythagorean theorem—the answer to the nasty measurement quandary.

Schiewe and Susman measured both legs of the right triangle that is the basis of the theorem; they could calculate the triangle's hypotenuse— the line of Mantle's homer—once the lengths of its legs were established.

They had to be resourceful. They began by determining the thickness of the outfield wall. They next measured a sidewalk just outside the wall, then Trumbull Avenue adjoining, and finally the sidewalk on the other side of Trumbull.

They then measured the distance between the landing spot Cameron had shown them and the second sidewalk, and added this 91 feet to their earlier measurements. Now one leg was completed. Next they needed to determine the distance from the landing spot to the first leg. They knew the first leg's length but they didn't know its location because they couldn't see the foul pole from outside Tiger Stadium (formerly Briggs Stadium) and therefore couldn't align with it. While they couldn't "extend" the foul line, they could get to the foul line itself, and here is what they did: They measured from the landing point to a line intersecting the end of the roof over the right-field stands—from outside the stadium they could see the roof's end. Then they went inside the stadium and picked up where they had left off—at the roof's end—and measured from that point to the right-field foul line.

Now they had both legs: one down the foul line of 565 feet 2 inches, and the other, the leg running perpendicular from the first to the landing point, of 306 feet 8 inches. The theorem says that the hypotenuse is the square root of the sum of the squares of the legs.

The square of the first leg is 319,417.12 and the square of the second is 94,040.35. The sum of the squares is 413,457.47 and the square root of the sum is 643.

Mickey's ball, now established as the longest regular season homer ever *measured*, that is, mathematically determined, traveled 643 feet!

The 1986 edition of the *Guinness Book of Sports Records* states, "The longest measured home run in a regular-season major league game is 565 ft by Mickey Mantle (b Oct 20, 1931) for the NY Yankees vs Washington Senators on Apr 17, 1953, at Griffith Stadium, Wash DC." *Guinness* adds the following passage: "Mantle's homer in Detroit on Sept 10, 1960, which ascended over the right field roof and is said to have landed in a lumberyard, was measured trigonometrically in 1985 to have traveled 643 ft."

The Washington homer invites comparison with the longer Detroit drive. There is at least one striking similarity between the two homers. The landing point for each was set by a single eyewitness. The 565-footer in Washington was based on the statement of a 10-year-old boy who was kind enough to show Patterson where he came into possession of the American League baseball Patterson found him holding. The Detroit eyewitness was Borders, who shared his observation with Cameron. (A second, tenuous similarity: The Washington homer glanced off a beer sign and the Detroit homer may also have hit an object—a piece of the light tower—before reaching the ground.)

The striking difference was that the Washington homer was paced off immediately, while the Detroit homer was measured a quarter century after it was hit, the measurers using a tape and making a nice use of geometry.

Bill Jenkinson, a Pennsylvanian who studies long home runs, was skeptical enough of the 643 figure to go to Detroit and measure it himself. He got a distance in the neighborhood of 643 feet, too, but he remains a nonbeliever. Too much uncertainty, he says, surrounds the actual landing point to make the 643 number—an implausible (to Jenkinson) 78 feet better than the old "record"—credible.

Jenkinson says that Rocky Colavito, in left field for the Tigers when Mantle homered, laughed at the suggestion of 643 feet. Jenkinson guesses that the ball may have traveled 500 feet in the air.

Mantle has said his hardest-hit homer was the one he cracked in a 1963 game at Yankee Stadium against Bill Fischer of the Kansas City A's. This one was still rising when it struck the facade, and a physicist ventured 620 feet as the "lower limit" estimate of its theoretical (unimpeded) length. The estimate was conservatively couched for want of certain information on the homer's trajectory.

The New York shot could have been longer, by theoretical projection, than the 1960 Detroit homer, but we will never know. One thing the physicist's estimate does do, however, is underline the plausibility of the newly measured 643-foot drive in Detroit.

September 17, 1960—Yankee Stadium. The Yankees and Orioles were playing the season's most crucial series, and among the Ladies' Day gathering of 49,055 was 73-year-old Ty Cobb, who prior to the game met with Mickey Mantle and later said, "That boy Mantle is a good one."

Cobb also had some well-intentioned advice for Mantle. "Don't be upset when the fans boo you," said the Georgia Peach, who ought to know. "That has happened to all of us. The good ones survive all boos."

Mantle didn't have to worry about being booed on this date. With two out in the first inning and with Hector Lopez aboard, Mantle, facing Chuck Estrada, the Orioles' rookie right-hander who will tie for the league lead with 18 wins this year, lashes into a 1-and-1 pitch and lifts his 35th home run into the third tier in right field. The Yankees lead, 2–0.

Mantle is out of the picture for the rest of the game. He comes up in the fifth, with two on, to great cheering, but makes the third out on a fly ball. However, Yankee heroes are in abundance. Bob Turley escapes unscathed from a bases-loaded no-out jam, Yogi Berra pops a solo home run, and Roger Maris makes a homer-robbing catch.

Yet, Baltimore clings to a 3–3 tie going into the last of the eighth. Mantle strikes out leading off, but the Yankees load the bases and Bobby Richardson, who had only two RBIs in his last 38 games, delivers a glancing blow off Estrada's glove for a two-run single and a 5–3 Yankee victory.

The Orioles had come into the Bronx tied for first place with the Yankees. But with their second straight defeat, Baltimore (83–60) fell two games behind New York (84–57). The Yanks will complete a four-game sweep, breaking the race wide open, and not lose another game all season; the Yanks were two games into a season-ending 15-game winning streak. The shell-shocked Orioles will finish eight games back.

September 24, 1960—Fenway Park, Boston. Mickey Mantle led the Yankees to a 6–5 10-inning victory over the Red Sox. And with the win, the Yanks, closing in on another American League championship, reduced their magic number to two.

Mantle in the first inning drives in Roger Maris from third base with a surprise drag-bunt single. More than 3½ hours later, with the lights beaming on a chilly late September afternoon, Mantle leads off the 10th against the fifth Boston pitcher, southpaw Ted Wills, a big rookie out of Fresno State. Mickey picks one out and poles his 38th home run; the ball cuts through a stiff wind, clears the left-field wall and strikes high on a light tower. "This would have been a tape measure affair, if it hadn't been for the breezes," wrote Hy Hurwitz in the *Boston Globe*. The Red Sox go down in the bottom half, and the Yankees have their eighth win in a row.

New York will also win the next game here and clinch, and Casey Stengel will nominate Mantle as his club's most valuable player. "It's amazing what he has done for a cripple," said Casey. He talked of Mantle's much improved fielding, his clutch hitting, his great baserunning and his ability to draw walks.

Finally, Casey summed up and made the point he was building to all along. "At the halfway mark, my most valuable player was Roger Maris," Casey said. "But Mantle has worked hard and hustled hard and now I've got to say he is my most valuable player."

The Baseball Writers will disagree. By a vote of 225 to 222, Maris will edge Mantle to win the MVP Award. Neither man hit for high average—Maris batted .283, Mantle .275—but they were easily the top sluggers in the league. Mantle led the league in home runs (40), total bases (294), and runs (119), and Maris was runner-up in all three categories, with 39 homers, 290 total bases, and 98 runs. Mantle was second in the league with 111 walks; Maris had 70. Maris led the league in slugging (.581) and RBIs (112). Mantle was runner-up in slugging, at .558, but he was sixth in RBIs, with 94. His RBI production was hurt by batting second much of the early season.

What might have put Maris over the top, in the minds of the Baseball Writers, was what Roger's addition meant to the Yankees. He wasn't the only factor, of course, but without Maris the Yankees had won 79 games and finished third in 1959, and with Maris the Yanks won 97 games and were pennant winners in 1960. No doubt about it—that's value.

September 28, 1960—Griffith Stadium, Washington, D.C. Mickey Mantle hit Nos. 39 and 40 on this date and the Yankees claimed their 12th consecutive victory, beating the Senators, 6–3. But with the pennant race over, the real drama was Mantle's passing teammate Roger

Maris to win his fourth and, as things turned out, final home-run crown. It capped a year-long chase by Mantle, who since August 15 outhomered Maris, 13 to 4.

Mantle hits both homers off his old pal Chuck Stobbs. The first is a two-run poke. The second, "a shot to be remembered," according to Burton Hawkins in the *Washington Star*, lands three-quarters deep in the left-center-field bleachers—a blast of nearly 450 feet—and Hawkins points out that the center-field flag was limp at the time. (Mantle's famous 1953 homer off Stobbs was aided by a strong wind.) The Mantle homer gave the Yankees 190, tying the American League record set by the 1956 Yankees, and before the season is over the Yanks will set a new league record with 193 homers.

Mickey was taken out late in the game and Jim Pisoni finished in center field. The Yankees had to save the Mick for the upcoming World Series—with the Pirates of Pittsburgh.

October 6, 1960—Forbes Field, Pittsburgh. "It never shoulda stopped raining," mourned a Pirate fan as he and 37,307 others filed out of the ballpark. The rains stopped and the Yankee bats started: The Yanks poured 19 hits on six Pirate pitchers and won the second game of the World Series on this date, 16–3. Now the series was even, the Bucs having won the opener, 6–4.

Mickey Mantle was having trouble batting left-handed. In the series opener, he had gone hitless batting lefty, and he struck out for the third time in the series, again batting lefty, in his first at bat in this game. "Up there lefty I just can't pull the trigger," he said.

Finally, in the fifth inning, Mantle gets his first series chance to bat right-handed. He faces Freddie Green with a man on base, and he doesn't waste the opportunity. He drills a whistling line-drive homer—"a one-iron shot that looked like it was still rising when it hit the seats," recalls Yankee relief ace Ryne Duren—better than 400 feet into the stands in right-center.

Mantle bats righty again in the seventh, this time with two on and Joe Gibbon pitching. Mickey scorches a rising shot that clears the 15-foot-high wall at the 436-foot mark, a bit to the right of dead-center field, and disappears into the trees. After the game, Pirate center fielder Bill Virdon said, "The ball got there more quickly than any ball I've ever seen. As soon as Mantle connected, I took one look and knew I'd never be able to catch it. It looked as though he shot it out of a gun."

The *Chicago Tribune* had an unnamed reporter journey to the back of the ballpark to find out how far the second Mantle homer traveled. There a Pittsburgh policeman named Arthur McBride pointed his nightstick to the spot where he witnessed the landing. Careful calculations by the *Tribune* reporter established that the landing point was 478 feet from home plate.

This homer was the first by a right-handed hitter to clear the center-field wall at the 436-foot mark. It had been done three times previously—by Stan Musial, Duke Snider, and Dale Long—but all three times by left-handed swingers. "I've seen every ball that has been hit over the center-field wall," stated Pirate manager Danny Murtaugh afterward. "Mickey's was the most convincing."

So, although he played only a handful of games in Pittsburgh, Mantle hit two of Forbes's most historic home runs. (The other big Mantle shot was poled in a 1953 exhibition game over the right-field roof of Forbes Field, home of the Pirates from 1909 to 1970.)

Mantle scored three runs and drove in five in Game 2. His five RBIs equaled a World Series record, but that record will soon fall.

October 8, 1960—Yankee Stadium. An outstanding four-hit performance by Mickey Mantle was lost in the shuffle. Bobby Richardson, breaking the World Series record Mantle had tied two days earlier, produced six RBIs on a grand-slam homer and a two-run single, and Whitey Ford pitched a brilliant four-hit shutout. And on this beautiful summerlike afternoon, with 70,001 spectators enjoying it all, the Yankees romped to a 10–0 victory in Game 3 and assumed a two-games-to-one World Series lead over the Pirates.

Mantle's first three hits are made batting right-handed. He helps set up the six-run first-inning explosion (capped by Richardson's grand slam) with a solid ground-ball single up the middle against Vinegar Bend Mizell, the starter who doesn't survive the first. Mantle singles, leading off the second against Freddie Green, and then takes second on a wild pitch and gets nailed attempting to steal third on a peg by catcher Hal Smith.

Mantle faces Green again, with Ford on third and two down, in the fourth. This time Mickey reaches down to lace a knee-high fastball to deep-left field; the ball carries over the 402-foot sign alongside the Pirate bullpen, lands about 10 rows deep, and bounces into the bullpen. Mickey's 14th World Series homer puts him one behind the record holder, Babe Ruth. "I knew I hit it good enough to go out," Mickey said later in the locker room. "In fact, I hit that one harder than I hit the two in Pittsburgh the other day."

Mantle's fourth hit is his first of the series batting left-handed. Fighting off a good George Witt pitch, he bounces a ground-rule double into the right-field seats. However, in his final trip, again batting lefty and with the chance of having the first five-hit game in World Series history, a fooled Mantle takes strike three looking.

The series thus far has shown a noticeable difference between the left-handed Mantle and the right-handed Mantle. Lefty, he is 1 for 7, with five strikeouts, four looking. Righty, he is 5 for 5, with three homers, all of them over 400 feet. A report is afloat that Mantle will abandon switch-hitting in 1961 and become a full-time right-handed hitter.

While denying the report, Mickey admits to having problems batting left-handed. "Let's face it, I just can't hit good from the left side," he says in the victorious locker room. "I haven't been able to do that since I hurt my right shoulder in the 1957 World Series. What I said was that if ever I was traded to Washington or Boston, I might consider hitting right-handed all the time."

After winning Games 2 and 3 so convincingly, the Yankees appeared ready to tear the series apart. But these Pirates were mentally tougher than the Buccaneers the Yankees intimidated and swept long ago in 1927. Despite another massacre, 12–0, the Pirates will win all the close ones and capture the World Championship.

It wasn't easy figuring out how they did it, though. For one thing, Pittsburgh was outscored, 55 to 27. The Pirates' team ERA was a staggering 7.11, as the Bronx Bombers set World Series records for most runs (55), hits (91), extra-base hits (27), and batting average (.338).

Casey Stengel couldn't understand it either. He will be dismissed as Yankee manager in a few days and he knew it was coming—he could smell it in the air. When he was asked if he thought the better team had won, he shot back, "What do you think?"

Mantle had perhaps his greatest fall classic. He batted .400 (10 for 25) and led all players in homers (3) and walks (8), and he tied Richardson for the most runs (8). Richardson set a new record with 12 RBIs, and Mantle was right behind him with 11. And Mickey finished the series playing with a pulled groin muscle.

But despite his great personal performance, Mantle was inconsolable in the losing locker room following the Bill Mazeroski Game 7 homer that turned the world upside down. Mickey sat in front of his locker and cried uncontrollably. He took losing very hard, to begin with, and he especially wanted to win this series because of some pop-off Pirate remarks about the Yankees. His sense of justice was also aroused; he would say many times in the future that this was his only World Series in which the better team had lost.

Mickey was still weeping on the flight home to Dallas. His wife finally turned to him and said, "Mickey, it's only a game." Maybe so. But it was probably the biggest disappointment of Mickey's baseball career.

1961

March 20, 1961—Dodgertown, Vero Beach, Florida. Ralph Houk was facing his first crisis as a rookie manager. His Yankees, losers of eight of nine exhibition games, weren't playing up to the standards befitting the defending league champions, but Houk wasn't worried; he told co-owner Del Webb that things would straighten out.

Mickey Mantle makes a prophet of Houk by leading the Yankees to an 11–8 victory over the Los Angeles Dodgers on this date. He hits a single, a double, and a home run, the last a towering left-handed shot off Roger Craig that clears "everything in sight," according to John Drebinger of the *New York Times*. His performance is another indication that he is headed for a great season.

Houk got Mantle the salary he wanted and Mickey reported to camp a week early. He is in great shape, physically and mentally. He is working hard on the left-handed hitting that was so weak in the previous World Series. He is hitting well and running hard. Except for the chronic pain in his right knee (and that will never ease), he feels good. His attitude is fabulous; he responds positively to the leadership role given to him by Houk, and he appears more self-assured than ever.

Bob Maisel in his *Baltimore Sun* column will write this spring that this more determined Mantle looked better than at any time since 1956. Several players say Mantle is heading for a great year, and one unnamed Oriole, after watching Mickey take batting practice, told Maisel, "I wouldn't be surprised to see him break Babe Ruth's home-run record."

April 17, 1961—Yankee Stadium. Freezing cold weather, a weak Kansas City team, and the fact that it was a makeup game kept the turnout the lowest here in seven seasons. But the 1,947 attendees for New York's third game of the season got to see the beginning of baseball's most fascinating home-run derby. The game was under the control of pitchers Whitey Ford and Jerry Walker. Ford hurled a three-hit shutout. Walker had trouble with only Mickey Mantle, who knocked in all the runs in the 3–0 Yankee win—Roger Maris hasn't yet connected in the infant season.

Mickey comes into the game hitless in his first seven at bats of the season; only once did he even get the ball out of the infield. But in the first frame, following a Yogi Berra walk, he drives Walker's first pitch on a line against the front of the right-field upper deck. The ball strikes the facing so forcefully that it rebounds to the second baseman. Walker recalls that it was "the hardest ball ever hit off me." Mickey drives in Berra again in the third, snapping a line-drive single to right.

Manager Ralph Houk said afterward, "I don't think I've ever seen Mantle more determined to come through with a big year. I could almost feel him burning up inside when he failed to hit in those first two games."

April 26, 1961—Tiger Stadium, Detroit. In one of the wildest games ever played in what was formerly Briggs Stadium, the Yankees beat the Tigers, 13–11, in 10 innings. A crowd of 4,676 huddled in 40-degree weather to watch 31 hits (18 by the Yanks) and seven errors (four by the Yanks). They saw an eight-game Detroit winning streak broken; they could not foresee the telling effect this would have on a Yankees-Tigers pennant struggle carrying into September.

Mickey Mantle whacked two home runs—one from each side of the plate, extending his record for switch-hit homers to eight games—and Roger Maris finally hit his first homer of the season. The red-hot Mantle, batting .342, leads the league in homers (7) and in RBIs (15). Maris is hitting only .200 and in the early season often bats seventh against left-handers.

The Yankees blow a 6–0 advantage and enter the eighth inning down, 11–8. Bobby Richardson singles, takes third on Tony Kubek's double, and scores on right-handed reliever Jim Donohue's wild pitch. Mantle, hitless, works the count to 3 and 2, then propels a game-tying homer into the fifth row of the upper deck in right-center field. "I didn't hit it good," Mantle said later. "It stung my hands."

It is still 11–11 in the 10th. With Hector Lopez on base, Mantle is batting right-handed against southpaw Hank Aguirre and again he works the count to 3 and 2. Aguirre throws his best fastball and Mantle plants a two-run homer about 10 rows deep in the upper deck in left-center. Joe Falls wrote in the *Detroit Free Press* that the ball with "a little more loft would have bounced off the Fisher Building" in downtown Motown. Mantle said the game winner was hit "as good as I can hit a baseball."

"We should have worked on him more carefully," said Detroit manager Bob Scheffing afterward. "Even to the point of walking him, and taken a chance on the next hitter. If the situation comes up again, that's what we'll do."

Were he to be walked in situations like those of the eighth and tenth innings, Mantle would be hollering for the next hitter, Bill Skowron, to knock him around. Leader Mickey Mantle in 1961 was a holler guy.

A FOLLOWER TURNS LEADER

Mickey Mantle slipped into the leadership role Ralph Houk tagged for him with surprising ease. "What a different guy this year," Yankee relief ace Ryne Duren told Doc Greene of the *Detroit News*. "You never used to hear anything out of him in the dugout. Now he's up and down, rooting for the other guys, talking it up. It's great." It was a transformation for which insiders gave Houk the credit.

Mantle was primarily a leader by example. "You hit .350 you're a leader," he told Bob Pille of the *Detroit Free Press*. "You hit .250 and you're not." But Houk wanted more from Mantle than leadership by example. There hadn't been a team captain on the Yanks since Lou Gehrig died in 1941 (that there would never be another Yankee captain was considered precept), but Houk proposed that Mickey serve as unofficial captain. He wanted the Mick to do two things: to lead by example and to keep the team fired up.

Heretofore Mantle hardly projected as leadership material. He minded his own business. He felt uncomfortable passing along advice, although Roger Maris, whom he counseled in Roger's fights with the press and fans, was an exception. Once, when asked why he ran around with Billy Martin, Mantle answered, "There are two kinds of people. There are leaders and there are followers. And I'm a follower."

Houk knew, better than Casey Stengel, how much the Yankee players respected and admired Mantle for his skill, competitive spirit, and courage in playing hurt, as well as his low-key personality. When Houk set up Mantle as the good influence, rather than the bad example Stengel made him out to be, Mickey became more responsible. His temper-tantrum days were just about behind him, too. He had grown into an exemplary, self-controlled leader.

Ralph Houk was good for Mantle. He treated his star center fielder with respect and consideration. He praised Mickey everywhere he went, building up his confidence. Houk knew how Stengel's criticism hurt Mantle. Mantle was the best player alive, Houk would say again and again, and eventually even Mantle had to believe him.

The ability to motivate and to remain eternally optimistic was Houk's managerial strength. He could be tough, yes—the World War II hero (a Ranger, no less) was perhaps the toughest man in baseball—but he didn't put his men down as Stengel could do. Instead, Houk encouraged and praised not just Mantle but all his players.

Houk established a great rapport with his club in the spring of 1961. Everyone's job was clearly defined, Houk doing away with platooning and position shuffling and establishing a regular pitching rotation, all of which won the appreciation of the players who didn't care a whole lot for Stengel's marvelous machinations. Houk, a backup catcher, minor-league manager, and coach for the Yankees since the 1940s, was a company man with the trust of management and the affection of his players. But he antagonized the press and never replaced Stengel in the affections of the public.

Mantle, like the rest of the Yankees, viewed Houk as a player's manager. He respected him and his war record. Mickey already possessed a great sense of obligation to his team and teammates—he played for them, not himself—and his high regard for Houk only enhanced his sense of duty. He didn't want to let Houk down.

So if the Major, as Houk was known, wanted Mantle to be a leader, the Mick wouldn't fail him. He didn't. Mantle was a leader in every sense of the word in the 1960s.

Mantle led through inspiration. He limped when he ran, yet he kept playing. When he swung and missed, he winced in pain, his knees often buckling, yet he kept playing. He had to wrap yards of tape around his legs in getting ready for a game, yet he kept playing. He never stopped playing the game flat out.

The other Yankees saw all this and were inspired to do more or ashamed to do less than contribute a four-square effort. Even Joe Pepitone, a player not noted for being fired up for every game, was jacked up. He told Peter Golenbock, author of *Dynasty*, "There were times when I'd say, 'I don't feel like playing. I'm tired,' and I'd look out in center field, and here's this man, and I'd say, 'Jesus Christ. If he can play, I got to play, too.' "

May 2, 1961—Metropolitan Stadium, Bloomington, Minnesota. The land of 1,000 lakes finally got an up-close and personal look at the legendary power of Mickey Mantle. A king-sized Mantle homer enabled the Yankees to beat the Minnesota Twins, 6–4, in the first game the Yankees ever played here against the transplanted Washington franchise. (Washington was not completely abandoned. The nation's capital this year had an expansion club, also known as the Senators.)

Twins starter Camilo Pascual, working on a lovely extra-inning masterpiece, retires the first two Yankees in the 10th. Then Tony Kubek doubles and Pascual issues two free tickets to load the bases. On a 1-and-1 count, Mantle nails a low fastball—"I didn't mean to put the ball there," said Pascual afterward, fully aware that a lefty Mantle dotes on low fastballs—and sends it easily over the 402-foot mark on the center-field screen. The blast carries at least 430 feet, and, most remarkably, Kubek said afterward, he "just flicked his bat at that pitch."

The Mick's sixth career grand slam was also only the sixth bases-loaded homer hit by a Yankee in extra innings. Mickey joined the likes of Wally Pipp (1923), Babe Ruth (1925), Bob Meusel (1929), Joe DiMaggio (1948), and Tommy Henrich (1948).

Minnesota rallied for two runs in the bottom of the 10th, but Luis Arroyo got the final three outs and the Yankees hung on. The Yankees were 10–5, and seven of their wins could be attributed to Mantle's clutch hitting.

May 4, 1961—Metropolitan Stadium, Bloomington, Minnesota. Again Mickey Mantle played a large role in a New York win as the Yankees beat the Twins, 5–2. In the Yanks' three-game sweep here, Mantle went 6 for 14, extending his hitting streak to 16 games, with four runs and seven RBIs. The Twins didn't walk him once—and paid the price.

New York leads, 3–2, in the sixth inning, and reliever Ted Sadowski is on the mound for Minnesota. Since the second inning, when he relieved Jim Kaat, Sadowski has pitched scoreless ball. Mantle digs in with the bases empty, batting left-handed. Mickey, who singled home the first run off Kaat in a three-run first inning (and scored the third run himself), faces a 25 mph wind besides Sadowski.

Sadowski recalls that the strong wind nearly blew him off the mound. He remembers challenging Mantle, "I bet you can't hit one out against this gale. I bet you a case of beer you won't do it."

"You're on," Mantle shouted back.

On the very next pitch Mantle explodes a tremendous drive into the teeth of the wind. The home-run ball lands better than halfway up in the right-field bleachers; only the wind prevents a tape-measure job of enormous proportions. "I'll take Budweiser!" Mickey yells as he rounds second.

But a tailspin awaited Mickey. He will go hitless in his next four games. Then nagging injuries will accrue: a pulled calf muscle, a groin injury, and a muscle spasm in his right thigh. Maybe this won't be his big year after all.

May 30, 1961—Fenway Park, Boston. This year's Yankees had yet to hit with the fury of the 1960 club. After just dropping a 2–1 decision here, they were starting this holiday only four games above .500; they were in fourth place and they looked like a fourth-place team.

But suddenly it seems more like the Fourth of July than Memorial Day as the Bronx Bombers explode for 17 hits and 38 total bases in a 12–3 pummeling of the Red Sox. It is the first time all year that everybody is hitting—and hitting *long*. The Yankees knock out seven homers.

The Yankee homers—two each by Mickey Mantle, Roger Maris, and Bill Skowron and one by Yogi Berra—are only one shy of the league record set by the 1939 Yankees. Only one of the drives takes advantage of the cozy Green Monster; the others are long shots to center or right field.

The Mick sends a 3-and-2 pitch from Gene Conley against the back of the Yankee bullpen in right for a first-inning three-run homer. Maris homers in the third and Skowron in the fourth (the only cheapie, it barely clears the Monster), and Berra and Skowron blast back-to-back drives in the sixth.

Right-hander Mike Fornieles is mopping up in the eighth without his good curveball, which, against the likes of M & M, spells disaster. Maris hits a three-run 400-foot homer, his 11th of the season, into the right-field grandstand, and Mantle crashes his 13th, a tremendous drive that clears the high wall in almost dead center near the 420-foot mark. It is the first back-to-back shelling by the M & M Boys in 1961.

The bombing will continue all summer—by Mantle, by Maris, by all the Yankee long ballers. Both Mantle and Maris will again clear the fence in the next game here—it will be the fourth homer of the series for Mantle.

June 11, 1961—Yankee Stadium. Mickey Mantle and Roger Maris were playing yo-yo with the American League home-run lead. On this date they combined for three homers in the second game of a double-header the Yankees swept from the Los Angeles Angels, the sweep giving the Yanks 10 wins in their last 11 games.

But it is the M & M defense that steals the show in the opener, in which Ralph Terry pitches a five-hitter and Yogi Berra carries the Yanks to a 2–1 win with a pair of home runs. Mantle makes a miraculous backhand catch of an Eddie Yost smash into the left-center-field gap that seemed destined for extra bases, and Maris takes away two Angel homers, toppling into the right-field seats to rob Ken Hunt and then reaching over the bullpen railing to spear a Ted Kluszewski bid for four bases.

Angel starter Eli Grba is sabotaged in the first inning of the nightcap, when the first two Yankees reach on errors and Mantle plants one upstairs in right field. The home run ties Mantle with Maris for the league lead, but Maris snaps the tie with a pair of solo homers, his 19th and 20th of the year, and the Yankees win, 5–1.

June 21, 1961—Municipal Stadium, Kansas City.

June 21, 1961—Municipal Stadium, Kansas City. Mickey Mantle clouted two of the longest homers in Kansas City history. Tied end to end, the behemoth blasts could have covered a projected distance of 1,000 feet. Both Nos. 21 and 22 for Mickey were hit off right-hander Bob Shaw. They accounted for all the Yankees' runs in their 5–3 victory.

Mantle's first tape-measure job is hit with two aboard. The ball clears the right-center-field barrier and strikes the large scoreboard (which once stood in Boston's Braves Field) located some distance beyond the fence.

The travel distance is something like 425 feet, but that isn't important. Where it hits on the scoreboard—at the very top—is. Some 25 years later, veteran Kansas City reporter Joe McGuff says Boog Powell and Elston Howard also reached the board but their impact points were below where Mantle's ball struck. If Mantle's drive hadn't caught the top of the board, there's no telling how far it might have gone, McGuff says.

Shaw settles down after throwing the first Mantle homer and doesn't permit another run. Until the seventh. Maris triples, then Mantle shoots a towering drive that clears the right-field fence, a grassy slope, and an outer wall and bounces high in the middle of Brooklyn Avenue.

Ernest Mehl of the *Kansas City Times* speculated that the ball might have traveled 500 feet; *The Sporting News* will report the length as 525 feet. Ralph Houk said after the game that it was the longest left-handed homer he had ever seen Mantle hit, and Mickey said, "It felt as good as any I ever did hit."

It was only the fourth ball ever to clear the outer wall in right since the A's moved here in 1955. One was off Mantle's bat (on May 21, 1956), and the other two were hit by Larry Doby and Harry Simpson. Paul O'Boynick in the *Kansas City Times* reported that four American Association players cleared the outer wall (the Kansas City Blues played at Municipal Stadium before the A's), including minor-league slugging legend Joe Hauser, who did it twice and was on this date tied by the Mighty Mick.

June 26, 1961—Wrigley Field, Los Angeles. Mickey Mantle, who hit a memorable distance shot in this old Pacific Coast League park when the Yankees toured the West Coast in the spring of 1951, hit a second-inning solo blast off the ace of the Angels' staff, right-hander Ken McBride, that cleared the deepest part of the park, at the 412-foot mark in center field, tying the score at 1–1.

Reliever Jim Donohue, working with understandable care, walks Maris and Mantle with the Angels ahead by a run and one out in the ninth. Angel manager Bill Rigney summons Art Fowler from the bullpen, a good choice inasmuch as Fowler has allowed only one hit in his last 12⅓ relief innings. Billy Martin's future pitching coach strikes out Yogi Berra for the second out but gives up a 420-foot homer to Bill Skowron, and the Yankees win, 8–6.

The game was a microcosm of the Yankee season. The Yanks battled from behind. The winning pitcher was Whitey Ford (now 13–2) with late-inning relief help from Luis Arroyo. Johnny Blanchard hit a patented pinch-hit homer. Mantle homered. And the scene was set for Skowron to be a hero because the opposition was fearful of M & M, also known as Dial M for Murder.

Neither Mantle's nor Skowron's homer was a gift from the cozy ballpark where the expansion Angels will play for only one year. Both were true major-leaguers. Curiously, Mantle and Maris in nine games in the friendly confines of Wrigley will have only two homers apiece, all of them long shots. It was only 345 feet to both power alleys; in its one year as the majors' softest touch for home-run hitters, Wrigley yielded a record 248 homers.

June 28, 1961—Wrigley Field, Los Angeles. Mickey Mantle knocked in all three Yankee runs on a groundout and two-run homer in a 5–3 Yankee loss to the Angels and Ryne Duren, who made his first start against the Yankees since New York traded him on May 9 and who in eight-plus innings allowed only three hits and struck out 12.

Mantle's opposite-field homer in the ninth carried over the left-center-field light tower. "I thought it was going to be a high fly at first," recalled Duren years later, "but it just kept going up and over the lights. I said to some of my teammates that I didn't think it was going to go out when it was hit." When Duren made this remark in the dugout, Angel pitcher Art Fowler responded that it would have been hit out of an airport.

June 30, 1961—*Yankee Stadium*. Mickey Mantle collected his 25th homer, and although it was one of his longest, it never cleared a fence.

He cracks a towering blast to center field that carries over Washington's Willie Tasby and hits the wall some 455 feet from home plate. The ball rebounds over Tasby's head, and before any Senator can retrieve it, Mantle crosses home plate standing up.

The Yankees win, 5–1, behind the five-hit pitching of Whitey Ford and the three-RBI bat of Roger Maris. Ford (14–2) becomes the first major-league lefty to win eight games in one month since Rube Marquard of the Giants did it 49 years earlier.

The victory capped a 22–10 June for the Yankees. Where did the prosperous month get them? To second place. Detroit (48–26) led New York (45–27) by two games.

July 1, 1961—*Yankee Stadium*. On the day the All-Star voting was announced, Mickey Mantle and Roger Maris showed why they were selected as the only repeat starters from the 1960 American League squad. Three M & M homers and a couple of big hits from a third Yankee All-Star, shortstop Tony Kubek, combined with a great long relief job by Rollie Sheldon, carried the Yankees to a stirring 7–6 victory over Washington.

The Senators give left-handed starter Carl Mathias a quick 3–0 lead. Mantle makes it 3–1 with a blast to left-center-field that clears the wall several feet to the left of the 457-foot sign and lands 10 or 12 rows back. The home run has to travel at least 470 feet. It is only the 11th ball (two by Mantle now) ever hit into the faraway left-field bleachers. It is also Mantle's 1,000th career RBI.

After Washington increases its lead to 5–1, Mantle faces Mathias again following singles by Kubek and Maris. Mickey hits a 400-foot homer that knocks out Mathias, a pitcher who will get into only 11 big-league games and yet give up three Mantle homers.

Mantle is batting left-handed against Joe McClain in the seventh. When the count goes to 2 and 0, the Senators put all four infielders on the right side of second base and left fielder Marty Keough in shallow left. Third baseman Danny O'Connell, who conceived this Mantle Shift, dances on either side of second base until the second-base umpire finally orders him to stay put. Perhaps distracted, McClain walks Mantle. Then, in spite of a pitchout, Mickey steals second and comes home to tie the score on Elston Howard's single.

Dale Long gives Washington a 6–5 lead with a homer in the top of the ninth. But Dave Sisler throws only two pitches in the bottom half and the game is over. Kubek singles on the first pitch and Maris raps the second just inside the right-field foul pole for a homer. Roger's 28th homer, his first in nine days, breaks a tie with Mantle for the league lead.

July 2, 1961—Yankee Stadium. The Senators had seen enough of Mickey Mantle and Roger Maris and the other Yankee musclemen. Completing a weekend sweep, the Yankees hit five home runs in a 13–4 romp. Mantle hit No. 28 and Maris Nos. 29 and 30. For the three-game set the M & M Boys were 13 for 21 (.619), with 7 homers, 12 runs, and 17 RBIs. "Those two beat us by themselves," lamented Washington manager Mickey Vernon.

The two Maris homers put him eight games ahead of the Babe's 60-homer 1927 pace. The first homer hits high off the screen attached to the right-field foul pole, and the second lands in the right-field upper deck.

The Senators work Mantle carefully. Mickey draws four consecutive walks—he comes around to score after two of them—before hitting his two-run homer in the eighth. Hit off right-handed Johnny Klippstein, the ball lands halfway up in the right-field third tier. The homer is Mantle's fifth in four games and extends his soon-to-end hitting streak to 15 games.

Other Yankee sluggers do their part, too. Elston Howard homers into the left-field upper deck, and Bill Skowron whales a homer into the left-field bleachers, becoming the first player in history to reach those distant bleachers three times. Bob Cerv raps a titanic double off the wall in left center at the 457-foot mark.

The Senators are understandably shell-shocked. Rookie Ron Stillwell, who joined the Nats here, was at first impressed by the vastness of the Stadium, until Mantle and Maris came along to "make it look smaller," he said. "What do you do, walk them?" asked Senator infielder Billy Klaus. "Then, that Elston Howard will kill you, and if you walk him, that Skowron will kill you."

July 16, 1961—Memorial Stadium, Baltimore. An electric atmosphere greeted the Yankees as they arrived here for a key series with the Orioles, who were in third place, down by eight games but hoping to fly higher, so gallantly did they battle the Yanks the previous season. But Mickey Mantle sank the locals' hopes in the opener by driving in both Yankee runs in a tense 2–1 victory. However, Detroit (58–31, .652) swept a doubleheader and with a percentage point edge over New York (56–30, .651) took first place.

Baltimore's Steve Barber, a talented 22-year-old left-hander who will win 18 games this year, has one of his better days, allowing only five hits and two walks. But with two out and none on in the fourth, Barber delivers an outside fastball that Mantle socks for his 32nd homer, a tape-measure job to center field that clears the fence 400 feet from the plate, carries an additional 30 feet in the air, bounces on a cinder track, and strikes the scoreboard on one hop. The Yankees lead, 1–0.

Yankee southpaw Bud Daley is even better than Barber. He pitches a four-hitter and the only run he allows, in the sixth, is tainted, as Mantle, who can't get good traction on the rain-soaked turf, lunges and misses by inches a Jackie Brandt pop-up, which scores the tying run.

Barber takes a three-hitter into the ninth. Tony Kubek leads off with a double but can't advance on a fly to shallow right by hitless Roger Maris. With first base open, Orioles manager Paul Richards elects to pitch to Mantle, hitting .326 at day's end, rather than to Elston Howard, the league leader at .373. But Mantle scorches a low-hooking shot that glances off the third-base bag and shoots down the line for a lead-gaining double. He takes third on Howard's 380-foot fly to right, but Bob Cerv grounds out. Still, the one run proves enough for Daley, who escapes trouble in the bottom of the ninth when shortstop Kubek starts a beautiful game-ending double play.

Richards summed up: "Barber pitched good to Mantle. He got the man to hit his down pitch. Mantle hits a two-hopper off the base, and now everybody says we shoulda walked him."

July 17, 1961—Memorial Stadium, Baltimore. The only news in sports, it seemed, was the home-run duel between Roger Maris and Mickey Mantle, both of them running well ahead of Babe Ruth's 1927 pace. On this date, however, baseball commissioner Ford Frick, an old friend of the Babe's, threw a new wrinkle into the chase. Since the 1961 schedule was expanded from 154 to 162 games, Frick said, no one could be credited with breaking Ruth's record unless he did it within the 154 games that made up the 1927 schedule.

Frick's ruling was directed, of course, at Maris, with 35 homers, and Mantle, with 32. Frick said that any player who hit more than 60 homers after the 154th game would get a distinctive mark—the to-become-famous asterisk—beside his name in the record book, showing that the record was set in the longer schedule. In other words, a *tainted* record.

The Yankees then proceeded to just about knock the Orioles out of the pennant race, winning the first game of a twi-night doubleheader, 5–0, to drop the Birds 10 games off the pace. A crowd of 44,332, the largest so far this year here, weathered a stormy evening to see the local club take it in the jugular. The race will now be the exclusive property of the Yankees and Tigers.

Whitey Ford pitches a six-hit shutout, winning his 11th straight game and improving his record to 17–2. The Yanks' final two runs are scored in the sixth, on solo homers by Mantle and Bill Skowron. Mickey, batting lefty against Milt Pappas, hoists No. 33 about 400 feet into the right-field bleachers, and Skowron's is even longer, going about 425 feet into the bleachers in left. The game is played in rain from the third through the sixth.

New York takes a 4–1 lead in the nightcap. Maris hits a first-inning homer off Hal Brown, and Mantle tags Brown for a homer in the fourth. Maris feels good after hitting his home run until he notices a thunderstorm brewing beyond the left-field fence. It is going to be a close call. Finally, with two out in the top of the fifth, the huge thunderstorm strikes and the game is halted. It is already 10 P.M., so the umpires don't have all night to either call the game or continue play.

The umpires waited 65 minutes, and, with the rain continuing, called the game. It had not gone five innings and was not an official game; thus, all the records were washed away along with the game. Maris lost his 36th homer (which would have put him 21 games ahead of Ruth's pace), and Mantle lost his 34th. It was the first homer either had ever lost to rain. (None was washed away for Ruth in 1927.)

Maris was understandably upset over losing his home run but told reporters, "I mind losing the homer, of course, but more important is that game. We're leading, 4–1, with only four outs to go." Mantle cut himself shaving and came out of the shower room with a towel covering his bleeding neck. When asked the inevitable how-do-you-feel-losing-a-homer question, he pulled the towel away and deadpanned, "I cut my throat."

July 18, 1961—Griffith Stadium, Washington, D.C. Mickey Mantle started the long-ball fireworks in a pregame homer-hitting contest that teamed sluggers from the Yankees and Senators with members of Congress. Mickey won the contest, winning a $100 bond for himself and a season pass to Griffith Stadium for his partner, Congressman Eddie Dooley, a Republican from Mamaroneck, New York, with three mighty smashes into the faraway left-field bleachers. One of his clouts landed at the base of a light tower at the top of the left-field bleachers and bounced over the back wall, stirring recollections of his 565-foot homer here in 1953—this ball came as close to duplicating the 565-footer as any hit since, and had the crowd really goggle-eyed.

In the game itself, won by the Yanks, 5–3, Mickey bombs a pair of awesome left-handed homers off rookie Joe McClain. Both make a tremendous exploding sound when hit.

Bobby Richardson leads off the game with a double. Two outs later, Mantle golfs a soaring two-run homer that hits high on the light tower above the right-field wall. It is Mickey's first homer in this park this year; he has now homered in all 10 American League ballparks.

The score is tied in the eighth, when Mantle creams a full-count pitch far over the scoreboard in right-center, putting the Yankees ahead for good, 4–3. McClain recently termed this homer "a tape job," adding, "as best as I can recall, it went out of the park just under the lights and looked as though it was still going up." While the first homer didn't impress him, McClain said of the second, "I believe I was amazed that I could throw hard enough that anyone could hit a ball that far." Joe also remembered, correctly, that Mantle struck out in their other two confrontations in the game.

The two Mantle homers gave him 35 for the season and tied him with Roger Maris for the league lead. The M & M Boys were running 17 games ahead of Babe Ruth's pace of 1927. Afterward, Mantle, who thought that McClain had "good stuff," said he hit a screwball and a fastball for the homers. "I feel better hitting than I ever have," he said. "I don't feel as well running—but up at the plate, I've never felt better."

Mantle in the Yanks' next game will break his tie with Maris. Roger will go hitless in the three games here. Griffith Stadium was a park that gave Maris trouble, but he will hit a home run in Boston and collect four more at Yankee Stadium in a July 25 doubleheader. Mainly because of that big day, Maris will again move ahead of Mantle and by July's end will have a 40 to 39 advantage.

August 6, 1961—Yankee Stadium. Mickey Mantle led the Yankees to a doubleheader sweep of the Twins that gave the Yankees (71–37) a 2½-game lead over Detroit (69–40). The winning edges were thin, so Mantle's standout efforts were the more important; he went 5 for 9, walked three times, scored five runs, collected four RBIs (giving him an even 100), and stole a base. Three of his hits were home runs. The homers gave him a 43-to-41 lead over Roger Maris.

Mantle homers in each of his first two trips against right-hander Pedro Ramos, the second homer, his 361st, pushing him past Joe DiMaggio. Then, with Minnesota leading 5–3 in the fifth inning, Mantle helps tie the score with a double. In the bottom of the 10th, after the Twins score a go-ahead run, Johnny Blanchard hits a homer to tie it at 6–6.

The Yankees in the 15th put runners on second and third, and Mantle draws an intentional pass. Berra hits a grounder that spells inning-ending double play, but he beats the relay to first by an eyelash as the winning run scores.

In the second game, Mantle belts his third left-handed home run of the afternoon to give New York a 1–0 lead against Al Schroll. A four-year major leaguer, Schroll remembers Mantle as one of those rare hitters who "could hit a ball from the trademark to a half inch from the end of the bat and still drive it out of the park." Schroll recalls that on this date Mantle "hit a low, sinking fastball. He did not hit it good—I thought—but it went about 15 rows up in the bleachers. To anyone else, I'm sure, it would have been a routine fly ball. Mantle was awesome with a bat in his hands."

The score is 2–2 in the ninth. Mantle walks, takes second on a single, and goes to third on a groundout. It is 9:22 P.M. when Clete Boyer sends Mickey across the plate with a game-winning single, closing the curtain on 7 hours and 22 minutes of baseball at the ball orchard in the Bronx.

A long day, particularly for Roger Maris, who managed only two singles in 12 at bats. Roger was happy, of course, that his team had won two, but the strain in personally having a bad day, and the increasing pressure exerted by the home-run derby, left him exhausted. He wrote "BAD DAY" on his locker, and when the press came over, he pointed to the words and then to Mantle and said, "He's the one to talk to, not me."

CONTROVERSIES OF 1961

Mickey Mantle and Roger Maris paid a price for monopolizing the spotlight the entire 1961 season. The media attention began getting hectic in August. By September, the M & M Boys couldn't go anywhere without an entourage of reporters and photographers right behind them. Mantle, the established star, had been under the spotlight continually since joining the Yanks as a 19-year-old phenom in 1951 and was used to the glare. Indeed, Mickey in 1956 underwent the pressure and scrutiny associated with the chase of the Ruth record. Now he had the experience to handle pressure, to coolly deal with oft-repeated questions.

Maris didn't have this kind of background. In the end, the price of the fame and celebrity status that Roger never asked for or even wanted nearly left him a nervous wreck. The attention Maris drew in this year of 1961 was foreign to the North Dakotan, who spent his early major-league career in less stressful Cleveland and Kansas City. Even the one New York season under his belt could not prepare him for the intensity and craziness of 1961.

As a very private person, Maris resisted questions about the private Roger Maris. He couldn't understand why his name wasn't confined to the sports pages, why the gossip columnists and news magazines were writing about Roger Maris the person—about *him*. Heck, he was just a ballplayer having a good year, he thought; he became convinced that this chase of Ruth was being blown far out of proportion. He *would* talk *baseball* with reporters, but he grew weary of that, too—of dealing with the same questions.

He had trouble handling the media blitz, but Roger never stopped trying to hit home runs, which, of course, would have been a convenient way to escape the madness. Even after the day-to-day torment became unbearable—maybe about the time a reporter asked, once more, what a .260-hitting humpty-dumpty like you is doing chasing a legend like Ruth—even after losing great gobs of hair, Roger remained great on the field. On reflection: heroic on the field.

Everyone began choosing sides in the home-run derby, and, naturally, Maris ran a poor third behind Ruth and Mantle. Ruth, of course, was revered, as he forever will be. Mantle was the longtime golden boy the fans finally appreciated. Maris was an interloper, in the view of many. To the press, he was a surly so-and-so.

Maris had never batted .300 in the bigs, the press pointed out. Was he worthy to chase the hallowed Ruth? Was he just lucky? Was he a "thrilling freak"? Maris in the spring of 1962 had a disagreement with New York sportswriter Jimmy Cannon, who wrote: "The community of baseball feels Mantle is a great player. They consider Maris a thrilling freak who batted .269." Cannon must have meant the baseball writers were the "community of baseball" because it was the writers who found the most fault with Maris.

Stories began appearing in the summer of 1961 that Maris and Mantle disliked each other and that maybe Roger was jealous of Mickey. Finally, M & M had to blow their cover and explain that they and teammate Bob Cerv were sharing an apartment that summer while their families were back home. They even drove to work together. So any numbskull had to realize that M & M couldn't dislike each other.

That the Mantle and Maris friendship survived the 1961 turbulence is testimony to the maturity and self-assuredness of both men. Mantle and Maris, along with Cerv, would relax at their apartment, watching TV, playing cards, listening to country and western music, or reading the papers and joking about the M & M "feud."

But there *was* a rivalry on the field. Mantle and Maris freely admitted that. However, it was friendly and constructive, each man accepting the challenge the other was offering and bearing down just a little harder. "I hope Roger hits 80 home runs," Mantle told a reporter honestly, "and I hope I hit 81."

But the home-run derby wasn't fair in one respect. Maris batted third and Mantle fourth (Casey Stengel established Mantle as the permanent cleanup hitter late in the 1960 season and Houk left him there), meaning that when Roger batted, the hulking presence of Mickey was on deck, a presence that made pitchers unwilling to "pitch around" Maris. Thus, Maris got more good pitches to hit—all season he wasn't once intentionally walked—although the batters behind Mantle weren't chopped liver either.

The fans began demanding that Ralph Houk give Mantle a fair shake and let him bat ahead of Maris occasionally. You know, equal time. Houk wasn't interested in changing a good lineup, although reportedly the Yankee front office wouldn't have objected had Houk given Mantle the advantage.

The Yankees kept curiously mute when baseball commissioner Frick, considered a Yankee puppet in some circles, issued his asterisk ruling. Why? The front office may have been protecting the Ruth legacy, or perhaps something more relevant—the good rapport the Yankees had with the Babe's widow, who showed up dutifully at special events like Old-Timers' Day. But it was clear that if the choice of Ruth dethroners was between Mantle and Maris, the front office preferred Mantle. That was painfully clear to Maris.

So Maris had a lot going against him. He faced unfriendly fans, a hostile press, a front office that didn't support him, and a commissioner who was protective of the Ruth legacy. He would never really recover from the trauma of 1961.

But Maris did have three things going for him that season. He had the universal support and admiration of his teammates, the sage counsel of a sympathetic Mantle, and an undeniable ability to knock a baseball over the fence. He finally overcame everything and set a new home-run record. Mantle called it "the single greatest feat I ever saw."

On the day Maris hit No. 61, only about 22,000 people were at Yankee Stadium. Would the house have been only one-third filled had Mantle been aiming for No. 61?

Other controversies put the legitimacy of a new home-run record in question no matter who set it. One had to do with the so-called lively ball. As the summer marched on, and the M & M threat to Ruth became clear, Ruth fans and those romanticizing the Ruth legacy searched for reasons why, and the inevitable it-must-be-the-ball-is-livelier talk began. As usual, many a pitcher lent credence to this theory.

Early in August, Howard M. Tuckner wrote a story in the *New York Times* examining the juiced-up ball theory. Baseball commissioner Frick said that both league presidents assured him that the 1961 ball was the same as the one used in 1960. "To the best of my knowledge, the ball has not been hopped up," Frick told Tuckner. "And I know darn well no baseball man has sneaked around the corner and whispered in the manufacturer's ear, 'C'mon, pep up that ball.' "

Several days later the *Times* disclosed its own investigative findings in a front-page story by Tuckner. The *Times* had seven baseballs scientifically tested. The baseballs included a 1927 ball that Ruth had hit for a homer at Yankee Stadium, a 1936 ball autographed by the New York Giants, an official 1960 American League ball, a new 1961 ball donated by the Yankees, and three official American League balls bought at local stores (the purchased balls were the same as those used in the majors according to the manufacturer). The testing of the 1927 ball was circumscribed because the owner of the valuable memento wanted it back in one piece and wouldn't permit it to be cut open for surgical analysis.

In a week of testing, the balls were driven into the air, dissected (except the 1927 ball), measured, and analyzed. While investigator Stephen E. Taub called the study "interesting but inconclusive," *nothing* was found to suggest that it was easier to hit a homer in 1961.

Indeed, a second investigator, Robert W. Battey, said that in performance tests the 1927 ball and 1961 balls "appeared amazingly similar"—exactly what the official major-league ball's manufacturer, A. G. Spalding & Bros., Inc., had been saying to anyone who would listen. Spalding president Edwin L. Parker said that through the years his company had changed the football, basketball, soccer ball, volleyball, tennis ball, and golf ball—but *not* the ball used in major-league baseball. "Today's ball and the one Ruth hit are identical," Parker said.

But the ball is believed to have been enlivened on occasion. The dead-ball era ended, in either 1920 or 1921, when the ball was hopped up in happy response to Ruth's gate magic and perhaps as a result of improved methods of manufacture. A rabbit ball was supposedly introduced in 1930, and by many accounts it remained lively throughout the Depression, when every effort was required to generate excitement and attendance.

Okay. Rabbit balls were introduced from time to time—there is some evidence that the ball is livelier today, too—but not in 1961. Then why so many more home runs? The American League hit more than 1,000 homers in every season from 1956 through 1960, with a league record 1,091 in 1959 and 1,086 in 1960. In 1961 the league would hit 1,534 homers!

The two most obvious reasons for the staggering increase in American League homers in 1961: more teams and more games. Between them, the expansion clubs, the Angels and Senators, hit 308 homers in 1961. The expanded schedule, with the eight original clubs playing 64 more games, contributed to the increased home-run total as well.

The best argument for detracting from the M & M homer blitz

(besides the obvious one of a longer schedule) was the dilution-of-pitching-talent theory. Ted Williams had brought it up in the first Tuckner piece. "I don't want to take anything away from Roger Maris and Mickey Mantle," Williams was quoted as saying. "They're both great hitters but they're batting against guys they never would have seen in previous years." M & M were sometimes batting against pitchers who wouldn't have been in the league but for expansion. Expansion had created twenty new pitching jobs and supposedly those who filled the jobs, one-fifth of the league's pitching positions, were either too green, too gray, or too inept.

But there were a few inconsistencies in this argument. For one thing, in 1961 there would be more homers hit in the not-as-yet-expanded National League than in any season since 1956. For another, in 1961 the ERA of the National League actually increased more than the ERA of the American League: The ERA in the National jumped from 3.76 in 1960 to 4.03 in 1961, while the Americans' ERA went from 3.87 to 4.02.

Another inconsistency: In 1961 only six American League players hit more than 30 home runs, and only Maris and Mantle hit more than 46. When the American League expanded again in 1969 and 1977, admittedly with a lesser impact than in 1961, the league home-run leaders, respectively, were Harmon Killebrew, with 49, and Jim Rice, with 39.

Did the M & M Boys feast on lambs in 1961? It doesn't appear so at a glance. Each player hit a few homers off rookies, journeymen, and graybeards (not necessarily to a degree greater than in any other season), but the bulk of the Mantle and Maris homers, considering that they hit 115 between them, were hit against major-league pitchers of some renown.

September 3, 1961—Yankee Stadium. A hot streak in mid-August put Roger Maris in control of the home-run derby: Maris had 53; Mickey Mantle, 48. But for once the derby was taking a backseat to pennant-race excitement.

The first-place Yankees and second-place Tigers concluded the most important series of the season. The Yanks had already won the first two games. They won the second game with Mantle on a bunting spree. After tying the game with a squeeze bunt, Mickey in swinging away pulled a muscle in his left forearm. He was left in the game for defensive purposes. He couldn't swing the bat, however, and had to bunt in his final at bat, beating it out for the base hit. It looked like the Yankees might lose Mantle for three or four days.

When Mantle awoke on this date, he told roommates Roger Maris and Bob Cerv that his arm felt better and that maybe he'd be able to play. Maris and Cerv, knowing the severity of the injury, were doubtful. But at the Stadium, Mickey got heat treatment, taped up his arm, and took the field for batting practice. After tattooing a few off batting-practice pitcher Spud Murray, Mickey told Ralph Houk that he wanted to play, and the manager wrote his name in the lineup.

Detroit takes a 1–0 lead in the top of the first inning. After Tiger right-hander Jim Bunning gets the first two Yankees out in the bottom half, Maris singles, and Mantle, on a full-count pitch, swings and connects, grimacing in pain as he does, sending home run No. 49 deep into the lower right-field seats. The Bombers go up 3–1 when Yogi Berra follows with a homer into the Yankee bullpen.

Mantle takes an extra-base hit away from Bunning in the fifth when he sprints deep into Death Valley to make a great running catch. But the Tigers fight back and score two runs in the ninth to go ahead, 5–4.

Mantle, who had struck out twice since homering, leads off the Yankee ninth. On the mound is a fourth Tiger pitcher, right-hander Gerry Staley, a low-baller who is tough to take downtown. But Mickey wastes no time, blasting Staley's first pitch some 450 feet into the right-center-field bleachers. Home run No. 50 ties it up and sends a throng of 55,676 into a roaring tribute.

The Yankees quickly wrap it up. With two men on base, Elston Howard sends both runners and himself home on a drive into the left-field stands. Detroit (86–50) leaves town limping, demoralized, and 4½ games behind the Yankees (90–45).

Mantle's two homers give him 370 lifetime, moving the Mick into eighth place on the all-time list, one ahead of Ralph Kiner. It also means that Mantle and Maris have become the first teammates in history to hit 50 homers apiece in a single season. Mantle is back in the Babe Ruth chase, too. He is three games ahead of Ruth's 1927 pace, while Maris, who managed only a single in four at bats, is eight games ahead of Ruth.

But when a new day dawns, Mantle wakes up with his arm hurting worse than ever, forcing him to sit out a Labor Day doubleheader.

September 5, 1961—Yankee Stadium. His aching arm having undergone whirlpool therapy, ultrasonic treatment, and massage, Mickey Mantle returned to the starting lineup to hit home run No. 51. He then added a single and scored in a four-run Yankee rally that iced a 6–1 victory over Washington, the Senators' 20th defeat in their last 21 games. New York's win, coupled with Detroit's doubleheader loss, gave the Yankees (93–45) a commanding 7½-game lead.

Mantle leads off the second inning and knocks right-hander Joe McClain's first offering into the third tier in right field, tying the score at 1–1. Roger Maris still has 53 homers and is mired in a 9-for-64 slump. He went 0 for 4 after going 0 for 8 in the Labor Day doubleheader. However, he will hit No. 54 the next day and No. 55 the day after that.

September 8, 1961—Yankee Stadium. The Tigers, losers of eight straight games, have fallen by the wayside. The Yankees with a 9–1 rout of Cleveland on this date, making their ninth straight win, opened up an insurmountable 10-game lead. Detroit will win 101 games on the season and yet finish eight games behind New York.

The focus now is solely on the home-run derby. Roger Maris goes hitless, but with 55 home runs, he is seven games ahead of the Babe's pace. Mickey Mantle hits his 52nd homer, batting left-handed off Gary Bell. He also scores a run in the first inning after being intentionally walked—in the first inning! He walks again in the eighth, then leaves for a pinch-runner after having fouled a pitch off his foot.

Mantle's fifth-inning homer comes on the heels of a two-run homer by Tony Kubek and sets off a spontaneous demonstration by the 41,762 in attendance. The fans were letting Mickey know that they were behind him in what now seemed a very difficult task of keeping up with Maris and catching Babe Ruth. He was the underdog now. "I've never heard so much cheering for me in all my years with the Yankees." a moved Mantle said. "They 've never been so good to me."

With the home run Mantle tied his previous career high of 52 homers in 1956. Mantle and Maris now had a combined total of 107 homers, tying the teammate record set by Ruth and Lou Gehrig in 1927. A Maris homer in the next game (No. 56) will break the record, and the M & M Boys won't stop until they push the new mark to 115 homers.

September 10, 1961—Yankee Stadium. The Yankees beat Cleveland twice, 7–6 and 9–3, sweeping the five-game series, concluding a profitable 12–0 home stand and improving their overall home record to 61–15.

The main attraction for the 57,824 fans, of course, is the home-run derby. Mantle gets No. 53 in the nightcap. Roger Maris doesn't reach the seats and still has 56 homers; for the day he has two singles in six official at bats. Mantle goes a combined 2 for 5, with three walks. His other hit is a key triple in the opener. But time is running out; only 10 games remain before baseball commissioner Frick's 154-game cutoff (18 games remain overall).

Cleveland right-hander Jim Perry draws the hoots of the crowd when he walks Maris and Mantle in the first inning of the nightcap. In the third, however, Perry gives Mantle a pitch he can handle and the ball ends up deep in the lower right-field stands.

The latest home-run developments are almost overshadowed by a couple of wild incidents. The opener is interrupted when two teenagers jump the fence and advance menacingly on Indian center fielder Jimmy Piersall. Piersall doesn't wait to see what the kids have in mind; he punches one, then chases the other and barely misses with a hard kick aimed at the seat of the pants.

The other incident happens in the second game when Clete Boyer is apparently robbed of a three-run homer by an umpire who doesn't see the ball go in the stands—he only saw the ball on the field after it rebounded off the seats—enraging the home fans.

The Yankees will soon open a road trip in Chicago, with stops to follow in Detroit, Baltimore, and Boston, and with Mantle deteriorating physically. Not only does his arm still hurt and his legs ache, but when he reaches Baltimore he has developed a bad head cold/virus infection.

Burning up with fever, he receives a penicillin shot and will make only one pinch-hit appearance in the entire four-game Baltimore series in which the Yankees clinch the pennant and Maris, who hit Nos. 57 and 58 in Detroit, hits No. 59. But the 154-game cutoff point will pass before Roger can chalk up No. 60.

September 23, 1961—Fenway Park, Boston. For the first time in six days Mickey Mantle was in the Yankee starting lineup. Mickey blasted home run No. 54, Whitey Ford improved his record to 25–4, and Luis Arroyo set a new club record with his 61st relief appearance as the Yankees beat the Red Sox, 8–3.

Mantle, still weak, comes to the plate in the first inning with two on and one out, facing right-hander Don Schwall, who will be voted Rookie of the Year. The Mick unloads a solid smash into the right-field bullpen for a three-run homer.

The home run puts Mantle five behind Roger Maris, who walks twice and singles, with only six games left in the season. Mickey's chance of catching Maris is outside at best, and he is still very weak. When Mantle singles in the seventh, young Tom Tresh comes in to run for him.

Mantle's shot off Schwall proved to be the final Mantle homer of the year. Mickey will play in the next game in Boston but after that will not have an official at bat the rest of the season. Still feeling weak when the Yankees return home, Mantle, on the advice of a friend, sees a doctor who turns out to be a quack. He gets a shot of something that only makes his condition worse, and, because the injection was applied too high on the right hip, on September 28 he goes into a New York hospital, where an abscess is drained surgically. Maris will hit Nos. 60 and 61 at Yankee Stadium, Mantle witnessing the breaking of Ruth's record on TV from his hospital bed.

The hip abscess ruined Mantle for the World Series with Cincinnati. He was pale and sick and had a golf-ball-sized cavity in his hip when released from the hospital. Hardly able to walk, let alone run, he sat out the first two series games at the Stadium, watching the Yanks and Reds split.

In the Yankee workout at Crosley Field before Game 3, Mantle, still limping and hurting, put on a show. He took eight swings and knocked every ball in every outfield direction, either up against the wall or over it. He still couldn't run, but he played Game 3 and went 0 for 4, two of the outs long fly balls to center. Maris won it with a ninth-inning homer.

Game 4 was 0–0 in the fourth when Maris drew a leadoff walk. Mickey, whose wound had already opened and was beginning to bleed, laced a wicked shot off the scoreboard in left-center and Maris moved to third. Under normal circumstances, Mickey would have had a cinch double, but he could barely make it to first. Mickey stood on the bag, gritting his teeth, his face sweating and blood rolling down his leg. Ralph Houk sent in a pinch-runner, and Mickey was through for the series.

Mickey sat on the bench until the blood began to seep through his uniform, and then he was helped to the clubhouse, where some of his horrified teammates saw yards of bloody gauze pulled from the wound. The Mick was still on the rubbing table after the game. Tony Kubek once described the scene this way: "Most of the guys took one look and left.

They couldn't take it. I don't know why, but I stayed and watched while they treated it. It was awful. You could see the bone. I knew then what kind of guy Mantle was."

Mantle had made only one hit in six at bats in the series, but it seemed to get the Yanks hitting. They won Game 4 handily and kept on hitting to take Game 5 and the World Championship.

The World Series was won with Mantle playing little and with Maris hitting only .105 (2 for 19), proving the tremendous balance and depth of the club. Game 5, in fact, was won through the heroics of second-line players Hector Lopez, Johnny Blanchard, and Buddy Daley. This club, winner of 109 regular-season games and one of the best ever, had great pitching, great fielding, great depth, and, especially, great power. It set a standing major-league record with 240 home runs, led by Maris (61), Mantle (54), Bill Skowron (28), Yogi Berra (22), and Elston Howard and Blanchard (both 21). The only department the 1961 Yankees came up short in was speed. The Yanks stole just 28 bases—Mantle had 12 of them—but then, again, this team didn't need to steal many.

The heart of these Yankees was Mantle and Maris. Maris will win the MVP Award, and it is hard to argue with his selection. But Mantle had perhaps his greatest season. Statistically, 1956 may have been better, but sage baseball men said that Mantle was a more complete ballplayer in 1961. He was a smarter player. He was a leader. He stole bases when it counted. He grounded into only two double plays. He was a better fielder.

Mantle was outdone by Maris in the home-run derby, and yet Mickey, with 54 homers, hit more than anyone in major-league history who did not win the home-run crown, and he hit the most ever for a switch-hitter. His home-run ratio of 10.5 homers per 100 at bats is the fourth best in history—Ruth owns the top three—better even than Maris's 10.3, which ranks sixth. To Roger's credit, he hit 61 homers with only 67 strikeouts, while Mantle struck out 112 times. Yet, Mantle, the guy who didn't make contact as often, outhit Maris, .317 to .269.

Mantle was the 1961 league leader in runs (132), walks (126), and slugging (.687), while Maris led in homers, runs (132—a tie with Mantle), and RBIs (142). Mantle displayed a little more versatility, finishing one-two with Norm Cash in both slugging and on-base average. Cash finished second in slugging, at .662, but he beat Mantle in on-base average, .488 to .452.

Cash led the league in hitting (.361) and had a great year. But 1961 belonged to Maris and Mantle—and Babe Ruth. The 1961 statistics of M & M and the 1927 stats of Ruth are as follows:

	G	AB	H	2B	3B	HR	R
Mantle	153	514	163	16	6	54	132
Maris	161	590	159	16	4	61	132
Ruth	151	540	192	29	8	60	158

	RBI	BB	SO	SB	BA	SA
Mantle	128	126	112	12	.317	.687
Maris	142	94	67	0	.269	.620
Ruth	164	138	89	7	.356	.772

He was No. 6, aged 19, and a rookie. Mantle didn't move into his famous No. 7 until his second Yankee season. (Photoworld)

Yankee coach Tommy Henrich, who helped Mantle with his outfielding, joins his pupil at the batting cage in April 1951. (Photoworld)

Superstar and super prospect—Joe DiMaggio and Mantle—at San Antonio's Mission Stadium, where Mickey doubled and scored a run in an exhibition game with the Missions on April 5, 1951.

Bovard Field, the old University of Southern California baseball plant where on March 26, 1951, the Mick hit two mighty homers. The arrow at top traces a 500-foot-plus shot; the lower arrow represents a wallop that cleared the baseball field and then the width of the practice football field, traveling 654 to 660 feet. (Photo courtesy of Bob Schiewe)

One of Mantle's most important hits was this solo homer at Ebbets Field in Game 7 of the 1952 World Series. It snapped a 2-2 tie, and New York went on to beat Brooklyn, 4-2.

A grand slam homer at Ebbets Field in the 1953 World Series gave the Mick one of his greatest thrills. Yogi Berra (8), Joe Collins (15), and Hank Bauer (9) share in his moment. (National Baseball Library)

From left, homer hitters Mantle, Gil McDougald, Eddie Robinson (2 HRs) and Billy Hunter, celebrating New York's 7-6 win at Detroit on June 6, 1955. Mickey got the longest-drive award for a clout that cleared the 440-foot marker in dead center.

Billy Martin and Mantle had lots to smile about in 1956, the year Mantle won the Triple Crown, Martin was a league All-Star, and the Yankees won the World Championship.

Don Larsen sweated this one out. His perfect game, at Yankee Stadium in the 1956 World Series, was in jeopardy when Mantle exploded into deepest Death Valley and robbed Brooklyn's Gil Hodges of an extra-base hit.

Mantle never shed his shyness completely but he looks pretty sure of himself here.

Left: Number 7 waits his turn at the Yankee Stadium batting cage. In the distance is old Yankee Stadium's crown—the facade—that Mickey hit in at least three, maybe four, games.

Right: Mickey strikes out—something he did often.

Opposite page, above: Thank goodness Mickey didn't listen to that chop-down-on-the-ball stuff—the Casey Stengel formula for Mantle's hitting .400.

Opposite page, below: From left, Tony Kubek, Don Larsen, and Mantle—the stars of the Yankees' Game 3 victory in the 1957 World Series. Mantle's smile masked a shoulder injury, suffered in the win, that rendered him useless for the rest of the Series, won by the Braves.

From left, Yankee sluggers Bill Skowron, Yogi Berra, and Mantle, the most menacing trio in late-1950s baseball.

Mantle creams one left-handed—you can tell by his eyes that it's gone—at Yankee Stadium circa 1960, when Mickey was winning his fourth league home-run title in six seasons.

Mantle awaits his turn at bat on May 2, 1961, in the first major league game the Yankees ever played in Minnesota. Mickey won the game with a 10th-inning grand slam homer. (Minneapolis Star and Tribune)

Mantle, on June 30, 1961, records his sixth, and final, career inside-the-park homer on a blast that carried to Yankee Stadium's center-field wall. No need to slide, Yogi Berra (8) and Roger Maris (9) signal Mickey. (National Baseball Library)

When Mantle hit his 39th homer of the 1961 season, it gave him and Roger Maris a total of 79 homers. The final count would be 115.

From left, the greatest players of the early 1960s: Roger Maris, San Francisco's Willie Mays, and Mantle. Maris, for a few years anyway, was in the same class as Mantle and Mays.

The injury that more than any other ruined a Mantle season was the broken foot he suffered in June 1963. Mickey manages a smile, but the two-month lay-off had him pondering retirement. (National Baseball Library)

A dramatic Mantle return. After two months on the sidelines, Mickey on August 4, 1963, stroked a late-inning pinch-hit homer against Baltimore, tying a game that the Yankees won in extra innings. The homer answered one of the greatest ovations in Yankee Stadium history, awarded Mickey as he came to bat.

Youthful Bobby Murcer, a Yankee rookie in 1965, sandwiched between Mantle and Roger Maris, clearly his idols. Murcer conjured up memories of young Mantle—both were highly touted Oklahomans who came up playing shortstop.

Whitey Ford, winner of 236 Yankee games—still the club record—waves goodbye to Yankee Stadium and his career in 1967 as Mantle watches. (National Baseball Library)

Blessed with explosive speed, when Mantle dragged a bunt left-handed, it was almost a certain hit if he got it past the pitcher. Even after his legs failed him, he would on occasion try to beat one out. (National Baseball Library)

Mantle and Tiger pitcher Denny McLain follow the flight of career home run No. 535, hit at Tiger Stadium late in the 1968 season. McLain gave Mickey a gift pitch, "one for the road," so to speak.

1962

April 10, 1962—Yankee Stadium. It was Opening Day and it was as if 1961 had never ended. It was, all over again, Roger Maris, Mickey Mantle, and Babe Ruth, the latter's memory evoked by the presence of Mrs. Babe Ruth, who threw out the first ball. Maris and Mantle both homered in the first game of 1962. And Luis Arroyo, who picked up his 1961 Fireman of the Year Award before the game (when Maris received his 1961 MVP), escaped a threat in the ninth to save a 7–6 Yankee victory over Baltimore.

Incredibly, Moose Skowron, who combined with M & M in 1961 for a threesome record of 143 home runs, also homers. The Moose creams a two-run inside-the-parker off the center-field wall near the 461-foot sign. Maris sends a three-run homer into the lower right-field seats. And in the bottom of the eighth, with the Orioles ahead, 6–5, Mantle, leading off batting lefty against reliever Hal Brown, slams a screaming line-drive homer into the right-center-field bleachers beyond the auxiliary scoreboard, a shot of about 425 feet. The drive "in point of time elapsed might well have set a new record," according to Bob Maisel of the *Baltimore Sun.*

Elston Howard is up next after Mantle's game-tying homer and he doubles. Skowron singles off Hoyt Wilhelm, scoring Howard with the decisive run. "Boys," said Baltimore manager Paul Richards afterward, "It's pretty tough to beat this outside baseball that these Yankee animals play."

May 6, 1962—Yankee Stadium. In this Yankees-Senators double-header split, Mickey Mantle and Roger Maris showed again why they were the most feared hitters in the league. Combined, the M & M Boys gathered seven of the Yanks' 12 hits. Mantle hit three homers on this day. Maris hit one homer and made a great catch to rob Ken Retzer of a homer. And the Yankees, off to a fine 14–7 start, owned first place by 1½ games.

The opener belongs to Dave Stenhouse, the Senator right-hander who in his first big-league start pitches seven strong innings, keeping the ball low and on the hitters' fists. He wins, 4–2, making only one mistake, and that mistake results in a memorable tape-measure job by Mantle.

Following a Maris double in the fourth, Stenhouse goes 3 and 0 to Mantle. The Mick has been walking with incredible frequency—29 walks in his first 19 games of 1962—and he isn't looking for a walk this time. Instead, he jumps on the crippler and sends a two-run homer to the farthest portion of the right-field bleachers. The *New York Times* reported the next day that the ball landed in the 32nd row of bleachers (there were only 32 rows, I believe) and the *Washington Star* cited the 28th row. Whichever, the clout is better than 460 feet. "I didn't think he'd go for the 3–0 count," said Stenhouse in the locker room.

Jim Bouton of the Yankees, in *his* first major-league start, mixes up his pitches beautifully and allows only seven hits, all singles, to win the second game, 8–0. He is aided by three fine Hector Lopez catches and the slugging of M & M.

Maris and Mantle nail back-to-back first-inning homers off Pete Burnside, both into the same area of the lower right-field seats. But while Roger pulls his, Mantle, batting right-handed, slices an opposite-field homer. Then, in the seventh, with Maris aboard, Mantle reaches the right-field seats batting lefty against Jim Hannan. For the ninth time Mickey has homered from both sides of the plate. This feat has been accomplished only 10 times up to this date in the history of the American League, and Mickey Mantle owns nine of those times!

Mantle's bat was sizzling. With his 4-for-8 day, he improved his batting average to .367 (22 for 60), the third best average in the league, and with so many walks, he was reaching base at an astounding rate. He had six homers—on the same date the previous year he had nine—three behind league leader Leon Wagner. Everything he had accomplished in 1961 seemed within his reach in 1962.

But Mantle will experience a slump over the next 12 days, making only six hits, one of which is a home run. He will be denied the chance to break out of it; on May 18, straining to beat out an infield grounder that proved to be the final out in a New York defeat, he collapsed along the first-base line. He had severely torn the muscle on the inside part of his right thigh, and when he pounded against the ground, he bruised ligaments and tore cartilage in his other knee.

For the first time since 1953, in spite of all his injuries in the interim, Mickey will play in fewer than 144 games in a season and will need an extended period of recovery.

June 16, 1962—Municipal Stadium, Cleveland. Back with the Yankees after his May 18 muscle tear, Mickey Mantle has taken batting practice for several days but has yet to get into a game, although manager Ralph Houk indicates that he will use him as a pinch-hitter should "a desperate situation" arise.

A desperate situation arises in the eighth inning. With Cleveland ahead, 7–6, the Yankees have two men on base and pitcher Marshall Bridges due up. Houk casts a glance down the dugout. "Mick," he says simply. When Mantle steps out of the dugout and limps to the plate, the crowd, putting aside its partisan feelings for the moment, roars a loud and sincere tribute to the Mick.

Cleveland manager Mel McGaha goes to the mound and brings in his ace reliever, right-hander Gary Bell, destined to give up eight Mantle homers. Mickey is determined not to strike out or hit the ball on the ground so he'd have to run hard. His reflexes are slow, his timing off— he's vulnerable to a good fastball.

Bell throws a fastball. Mickey misses it. Another fastball. Mickey catches this one. He sends it some 450 feet over the right-center-field fence, and the Yankees lead, 9–7. The fans, recognizing the event for all that it signifies, stand and cheer with unrestrained joy as Mickey gimps around the bases. The cheering continues long after Mickey ducks into the dugout—he isn't just a Yankee hero any more, he is a *baseball* hero— and he is so overcome with emotion that all he can do is manage a sheepish grin as his teammates congratulate him.

Unfortunately for the Yankees, the Tribe rallied for a 10–9 win on a ninth-inning two-run homer by Jerry Kindall, his fourth hit of the game.

It was a big win for the first-place Indians (34–24), who now lead the third-place Yankees (32–24) by one game. Though Cleveland will sweep the four-game set, it was a confident Yankee club that departed the Mistake on the Lake now that Mantle was back. Not all the way back, however. Mickey will make two more pinch-hit appearances before playing in the field on June 22—in right field. It will be a while before he regains his speed and quickness in the outfield; he will not take up his regular job in center until July 17. Even then, he often left games in the late innings, and Jack Reed finished up in center.

*   *   *

In Mantle's absence, opposing pitchers worked carefully to Roger Maris, not giving him good pitches to hit, and Maris struggled. The Yankees had another problem in the 25-game period since the Mantle injury; also sidelined were their pitching stars of 1961, Whitey Ford and Luis Arroyo, both out with sore arms.

The Yankees were two different clubs in 1962. With Mantle in the everyday lineup—he appeared in 123 games but as a pinch-hitter in six— the Yankees' record was 75–42. Without Mantle they were 21–24 (including the six losses when Mantle was used as a pinch-hitter). Now, that's value.

Chiefly because his value to the Yankees was so graphically apparent, Mantle won his third Most Valuable Player Award. Some thought Bobby Richardson was more deserving, and Mickey was one of them; the Mantles' 1962 Christmas card to the Richardsons was addressed to the Most Valuable Player. Bobby hit .302, with a league-leading 209 hits, and he played a dynamite second base. But the Yankees revolved around Mantle, who had been nosed out in the MVP voting several times in the past.

Mantle hit 30 home runs in 1962, drove in 89 runs, and hit a strong .321. He led the league in slugging (.605) and on-base average (.488), and, in spite of having played in only 123 games, he walked 122 times to lead the league in that category for the fifth time. His string of nine consecutive 100-plus-runs-scored seasons was broken, but he still scored 96 runs in limited action. And to top everything off, Mickey this year won his one and only Gold Glove Award (it became a league award in 1959) for his fielding excellence. Most important, however, the Yankees just weren't the Yankees without him.

July 4, 1962—Yankee Stadium. Mickey Mantle closed out a breathtaking four-game series with Kansas City with two home runs, giving him five for the series, and for the third day in a row reached the right-field upper deck. The Yankees and Athletics split a holiday doubleheader, the A's winning the opener, 11–1—New York made five errors in their worst effort of the year—and the Yanks winning the second game, 7–3.

The Yankees are losing the afterpiece, 2–0, when Mantle, who went 0 for 2 with a walk in the first game, comes to bat with a man on base in the fifth. On the mound is Dan Pfister, a right-hander out of Plainfield, New Jersey. Mickey unloads a two-run homer into the right-center-field bleachers, and it's tied, 2–2.

Pfister will recount years later that this was no ordinary home run. As he tells the story, he had walked Mantle twice earlier, and, with the count 2 and 0 on high fastballs, he decided, what the hell, I'll try an overhand curveball. When Mickey connected—not very solidly, Pfister remembers, Mantle cracking his bat at home plate—it looked like a routine fly ball. Instead, the ball kept carrying and carrying until it sailed well over the 407-foot sign. As Mantle rounded third base in his home-run trot, he looked over to Pfister with an expression that seemed to say, "Sorry about that, buddy."

The Yankees won it with a five-run sixth that included another Mantle homer, a towering upper-deck shot to right field (off John Wyatt). It was Mickey's 389th career homer, moving him past the still active Duke Snider and into seventh place on the all-time list.

July 6, 1962—Metropolitan Stadium, Bloomington, Minnesota. Mickey Mantle and Roger Maris both hit a pair of homers in the Yankees' 7–5 win over the Twins.

Now seeing pitching more to his liking, with Mantle back in the lineup and hot, Maris has hit nine homers in his last 11 games. Mantle, incredibly, has hit seven homers in his last 12 official at bats!

Twin pitcher Camilo Pascual is no ordinary right-hander. He is an All-Star who comes into the game with a 12–4 record and who is on his way to a 20-win season. But he falls behind, 4–0, before retiring a batter. After opening singles by Tom Tresh and Bobby Richardson, Maris and Mantle hit back-to-back homers for the third time in four games.

Mantle hits another homer in the third, and Maris wallops his second in the fifth. Mickey's shot gives him home runs in four consecutive at bats (including his last game), tying an American League record accomplished previously by eight others. He now has 17 homers; Maris has 21.

With the M & M Boys hitting lights out, the whole Yankee attack was rejuvenated. On this date, Cleveland (46–34) owned first place, with New York (44-33) half a game behind. But the Yankees will make July their best month of the season, going 23–8, and establish a tight grip on the top rung. The Indians will fade out of the picture, and two surprising clubs, the Angels and Twins, will be left to challenge the Yankees.

August 28, 1962—Yankee Stadium. It was a critical point of the season. The Angels and Twins are hanging doggedly 3½ games behind the first-place Yankees. The Yanks have just broken a six-game losing streak, but concern in the Bronx continues.

Inclement weather jeopardizes the game, but the Yankees and Indians begin playing in a light drizzle anyway. Bill Stafford retires the first 10 Indians before surrendering a homer to Al Luplow, and Cleveland leads, 1–0.

The drizzle turns to rain and the wind begins to gust as the Yankees bat in the bottom of the fourth. After Roger Maris walks, Mickey Mantle faces Indian pitcher Jim "Mudcat" Grant, who throws his best pitch, a fastball, figuring Mantle will never see the ball through the wind and water. But he figures wrong: Mantle drives the ball right through the gale and into the bullpen.

The winds and the rain intensify even more in the fifth. With two out in the bottom half of the inning, umpire Frank Umont stops the game. The umpires wait almost an hour and a half before calling it, but the game is official, and the Yankees are 2–1 winners.

Mantle on the previous date, when the club snapped the losing streak, was 4 for 5. From August 27 through the end of the year, he will hit at a .438 clip (35 for 80).

September 10, 1962—*Tiger Stadium, Detroit.* On this date Mickey Mantle became only the seventh major leaguer to hit 400 career home runs, joining 400-club immortals Babe Ruth (714), Jimmie Foxx (534), Ted Williams (521), Mel Ott (511), Lou Gehrig (493), and Stan Musial (460), the last the only active player ahead of Mantle in homers.

Southpaw Hank Aguirre, the Detroit starter, is having his best season in a 16-year big-league career. (He will finish with a 16–8 log and a league-leading 2.21 ERA.) He comes into this game with a 1962 record of 3–0 against New York. He leads, 1–0, in the fifth. Then Mantle booms a home run into the lower deck in center field. No. 400 is a tape-measure job of close to 450 feet.

The score is still 1–1 in the ninth. Bobby Richardson is on second with one out. Tiger manager Bob Scheffing confers with Aguirre. When Scheffing returns to the Tiger dugout, Aguirre gives Mantle, who had singled in the seventh, an intentional pass. Hector Lopez, breaking an 0-for-22 collar, plates one run with a single, Mantle scores on an infield out, and Ralph Terry has a 3–1 win, his 21st of the campaign.

It was a big victory because second-place Minnesota lost. The Yankees (86–61) now lead the Twins (82–64) by 3½ games, and the Angels (81–64), by 4.

Mantle's homer was not only a milestone but marked his return to the lineup after a week's absence because of a pulled abdominal muscle. His return seemed to pick up the Yanks, who had split six decisions with the Mick sidelined.

September 18, 1962—D.C. Stadium, Washington. Before the game a reporter asked Yankee manager Ralph Houk what Mickey Mantle meant to the Yanks. "He lights us up," replied Houk. "Maybe it's because our players feel that in him we've got a fellow who can do more things better than anybody in the game. Watch him," Houk added pointedly. "If he gets us three quick runs, we'll score six or seven." So what happened? Mantle hit a first-inning three-run homer and the Yankees beat the Senators, 7–1.

In fact, Mantle belts two homers, both batting left-handed against Tom Cheney, who just last week struck out 21 Orioles in a 16-inning game. Not only that, he makes a beautiful leaping catch in deep center to rob Chuck Hinton, all to the benefit of Ralph Terry, who wins his 22nd game, the most by a Yankee right-hander since 1928.

Mantle's first-inning homer follows a pair of walks. It is his first in the new ballpark, and it is long, the ball striking a spot over the "ball" (part of the ball-strike count) on the huge right-center-field scoreboard, about 410 feet from the plate and 25 feet above the ground. Center fielder Jimmy Piersall amuses the crowd by catching the rebound and firing the ball into the empty seats in the upper deck. Mantle's third-inning homer, hit on a line over the right-field fence, is off a 3-and-0 pitch that Cheney is just trying to throw for a strike.

The first-place Yankees (90–63) are closing in on another American League championship. It hasn't been a classic pennant race by any means, but pesky Minnesota (86–67) and Los Angeles (82–70) have won enough to keep the pressure on a New York club that is not nearly as devastating as it was in 1961. Minnesota's loss on this date pushes the second-place Twins four games back with only nine games left to play.

The Yankees will finish with a record of 96–66, five games ahead of the Twins, and play an exciting seven-game World Series against the San Francisco Giants. The series was supposed to be a matchup of two superstars, Mantle and Willie Mays, but as had happened in 1951,

---

*Washington's new ballpark was renamed Robert F. Kennedy Stadium in 1969.

Mantle and Mays were hardly factors in the outcome. Mays hit .250 (7 for 28), with two extra-base hits, and Mantle hit .120 (3 for 25), with one extra-base hit. It would be Mantle's worst World Series at the plate, yet it would be satisfying all the same; the Yankees emerged victorious, the seventh, and final, World Championship for Mickey Mantle.

1963

April 10, 1963—Municipal Stadium, Kansas City. The Yankees looked bad in spring training, their injury list including such key players as Mickey Mantle, Roger Maris, Whitey Ford, Tony Kubek, Tom Tresh, Joe Pepitone, and Clete Boyer. But as 8–2 victors on Opening Day here yesterday, and as the winners on this date by a 5–3 margin, the banged-up Yankees weren't looking too shabby.

A crowd of only 3,855 turns out for the second game in numbing 45-degree weather. The miserable playing conditions victimize Yankee starter Bill Stafford, who, with a shutout going in the seventh inning, makes a pitch, feels a twinge in his elbow, comes out of the game, and never regains the form that made him one of baseball's most promising young pitchers.

Mantle helps Stafford to an early 3–0 lead with a third-inning, two-run home run. It comes batting right-handed off sinkerballer Ted Bowsfield, who will have a 37–39 lifetime major-league record but has enjoyed success against the Yankees. In his rookie season of 1958, three of his four wins were at the Yankees' expense. Years later Bowsfield noted with undisguised pride that Mantle once named him to a list of the toughest pitchers he ever faced. But Bowsfield made no bones about the fact that Mantle—"a frightening sight to pitchers and that included me!"—reached him for a "titanic blast" to left field on this date, recalling, "In the old [Kansas City] ballpark, there was a huge Butternut clock half way up the light standard, and the outfielder that day was Chuck Essegian. He informed me later that the ball was just going up as it went past the Butternut clock sign."

But Mantle can't escape injury. In his final at bat, he pulls a muscle in his left side, an injury that nearly steals him from the home opener in New York the next day. (He will play in the New York opener and even hit a homer, however.) But then on April 13, while slamming a double-play grounder, he will re-pull the side muscle—a muscle tear along his rib cage actually—forcing him to sit on the sidelines for two weeks. Upon

187

returning, he is unable to bat righty and has to sit against southpaws, and when he goes 3 for 22, he encourages speculation that his career is on the downslope. His legs will ache, too, Jack Reed sometimes taking over for him in center field in the late innings. But on May 6 he will begin a three-week stretch in which he hits .357 (20 for 56) and pops seven homers.

May 22, 1963—Yankee Stadium. Mickey Mantle was angry. Thinking long ball and swinging viciously, he was fooled by a slow curve from Kansas City's Bill Fischer—fooled so badly that his weak knees nearly buckled under him.

The A's dugout enjoys the spectacle and lets Mantle know it. None too happy to begin with when he took the batter's box to lead off the 11th, the Yankees having frittered away a 7–0 lead, the Mick turns crimson. He's definitely thinking long ball now, while Fischer and catcher Haywood Sullivan, according to what Sullivan said later, are thinking deception; they want to keep the slugger off balance. The count is 2 and 2, and they'll try to sneak a fastball by him.

Fischer lets go and Mickey swings with fierce power and perfect timing. He connects so solidly that the sound of bat on ball resembles a cannon shot, and there is no doubt that the Yanks are 8–7 winners. The ball heads for the right-field roof. Yogi Berra is not alone in at first believing it is about to leave the park—"My God! That's it!" Yogi shouts—before realizing that it might not clear the top of the Stadium. It doesn't; it hits the facade atop the right-field grandstand.

Had the ball not met an obstacle, there's no telling how far it would have gone. "It was the hardest ball I ever hit," Mantle has said. It was the hardest-hit homer *anyone* ever hit in the opinion of many experts, and everyone who saw both this shot and the famous May 30, 1956, ball that Mantle bounced off the facade agreed that the latter was made to look puny by comparison. It was the closest anyone has come to hitting a fair ball out of the old ball orchard in the Bronx.

The ball struck the facade a few feet from its top. The key difference between this blast and Mickey's Memorial Day drive seven years earlier was that this time, by all accounts, the ball was *still rising* when the kiss occurred.

Which gave rise to speculation. How far would the homer have traveled had not the "old" Stadium's Gothic green crown intervened? A physicist at the University of Arizona gave the answer: a minimum of 620 feet.

Dr. James E. McDonald, the physicist, made studies of long-ball trajectories and found that multiplying the distance between a drive's beginning and its summit by 1.70 gave a result that matched its actual length. A summit of 250 feet from the plate spelled a 425-foot drive (250 × 1.70). If an impeded drive's summit were known, its theoretical distance could be determined, in other words.

In a May 24 Associated Press report, McDonald said Mantle's homer, assuming it was at its peak as it struck the facade, would have carried 620 feet. But, he said, if Mantle's ball had not reached its summit—as all the onlookers asserted—the projected distance would have been greater, possibly much greater.

McDonald could have determined the probable summit were he supplied certain information. In a May 29 letter to the Yankees, he asked the club for information about the "inclination of the ball's line of flight" as it met the facade, ferreting, "Did anyone familiar with making angular estimates make any statements about the angle at which the ball was rising at impact?"

The professor was working a dry hole. It would be tough to estimate the angles, William J. Guilfoile of the Yankee front office said in a June 4 reply. So McDonald was forced to assume that the ball was at its summit at the point of impact. Taking the distance from this point (which, incidentally, was 108 feet from the ground) to home plate, a distance of 367 feet,* and applying the 1.70 multiplier, McDonald settled on the conservative and rounded-off projected distance of 620 feet.

On June 6, McDonald again wrote to Guilfoile. He was sorry that there wasn't any "quantitative estimates of the angle of impact," he said, adding, "but if there's no doubt among competent observers about the fact that the ball was still rising, then 620 feet is a rather reliable *lower* limit to the distance the ball would have traveled had there been no obstacle."

Whatever its theoretical length, it was a homer that excited even Mantle, who normally was not all that impressed with his long-distance shots. "That was the only homer I ever hit that the bat actually bent in my hands," he told reserve first baseman Dale Long. "I watched it," he

---

*The actual distance subsequently measured by the Yankee Stadium grounds personnel was 374 feet, but since McDonald was rounding off at the conservative 620-foot mark to compensate for uncertainty, he seemed to ignore the seven-foot disparity between the measured distance and that first supplied him for his calculations (374 feet x 1.70 is actually 636 or, more exactly, 635.8 feet).

related to Joe Donnelly a few years later for a *Sport* article about his greatest thrills. "I thought it would go out; I really did."

Mantle had borrowed the bat from Long, who believes that had it not been for the facade the blast would have gone 700 feet. The bat's length and weight of 35 inches and 33 ounces matched Mantle's own bat but was styled a little differently, Guilfoile told McDonald, who was also studying batting and throwing mechanics. In Long's memory, however, it was 36 inches and 35 ounces—a bat today's players "don't even attempt to swing," Dale points out.

Mantle's game winner left the players of both teams dumbfounded. None could really put into words the unbelievable sight he was witness to. Two coaches, Jimmy Dykes of the A's and Frank Crosetti of the Yankees, contemporaries of Ruth, Gehrig, Foxx, and Greenberg, agreed that the Mantle homer had never been topped, or in the words of Dykes, it "was the hardest hit ball any man ever hit." And fewer than 10,000 spectators were there to see it, and anyone among the assembled who may have blinked missed it, so fast did the ball bang against the facade and bounce back to second base.

Fischer, much improved over the journeyman hurler he used to be, pitched 84⅓ straight walkless innings in 1962 to break a record held by Christy Mathewson. Having this year learned a slow curve from A's manager Eddie Lopat, Fischer came into this game with a hot 6–0 record. He took his first loss, and the Mantle blast, philosophically. "He gets $100,000 a year," he was quoted as saying. "I get $10,000. He has to be making it for some reason."

But over 600 feet? Ten years prior to this date Bob Feller was quoted as saying following Mantle's cyclopean 565–footer in Washington, "There isn't a man that ever played baseball who could hit a ball 600 feet under his own power" (that is, without the help of a friendly wind). But apparently that is what Mantle did, in a projected sense, at least. Try to find someone to refute it.

For his part, Mantle feels he pulled the pitch too much to get it out. He talks about a spot a little to the left of the right-field roof where the ball might have cleared the Stadium over the bullpen. (Indeed, if a home run is ever hit out, it most likely will be there.) Manager Ralph Houk concurs. "A little more toward center field and it goes out of the park," Houk says. "No question about it."

*　　*　　*

So Mantle looks like he is on his way to another big year. That is, until June 5 in Baltimore, when he will all but get to a Brooks Robinson drive in right-center only to run out of outfield and into a chain-link fence, twisting his spikes and ending up with a broken bone in his left foot, as well as cartilage and ligament damage to his left knee. He will be carried off the field and will not see action again for a good two months. Some will think his season is over; others believe his *career* might be over.

The long-term Mantle inactivity will mean more to attendance figures than to the outcome of the pennant race. With the league's top drawing card sidelined most of the summer, Yankee Stadium's 1963 attendance will be the lowest since 1945, and the American League will slump to its worst overall gate in five years.

The Yankees will play June, July, August, and most of September without starting their eight regulars in the same game; Mantle and Roger Maris, who will have a combined 484 at bats, will be in the same starting lineup only about 30 times all year. Yet, this incredible 1963 Yankee team will win 104 games and make a mockery of the pennant race, finishing 10½ games ahead of the second-place White Sox.

How did they do it? With Elston Howard leading the way and winning the MVP Award (.313 batting average, 28 home runs, 85 RBIs). With great bench strength. And with four fine starting pitchers—Whitey Ford (24–7), Jim Bouton (21–7), Ralph Terry (17–15), and Al Downing (13–5).

August 4, 1963—Yankee Stadium. He had not played since he broke his foot on June 5. Rumors had it that his retirement was nearing. Truthfully, Mickey Mantle was down; thoughts of retiring had indeed crossed his mind.

Mantle, who according to doctors, would be lucky to play again in 1963, rejoined the club several days ago because manager Ralph Houk needed his leadership—if he couldn't have his bat—and because Houk thought it might pick up Mickey's spirits, too. Mickey soon grew restless waiting on the bench and hearing the same question day after day: When would he play? He still couldn't play in the field, but finally, he might be ready for pinch-hit duty.

The Orioles, 7–2 winners of the first game of a doubleheader on this date, are winning the second game, 10–9, going into the bottom of the seventh. The scheduled Yankee hitter is pitcher Steve Hamilton, but the fans sitting on the third-base side see Mantle at the bat rack and they begin clapping. The rest of the crowd picks up the cheering in anticipation, and when Mantle takes his first step out of the dugout, the crowd of 38,555 rises as one in a thunderous standing ovation, one of the loudest ever heard at the Stadium.

It *is* a moment not soon to be forgotten, and it isn't confined to the Stadium. On this warm Sunday afternoon, New York area residents are enjoying the day at parks, pools, beaches, and backyards, and many are listening to the Yankees on the radio. It is about 7:30 when Mantle is announced. Fun seekers in the twilight of their weekends gather around their radios.

Mickey walks stiff-legged to the plate with instructions from Houk not to run hard on a grounder. He prays that he won't strike out and let down all the fans cheering for him. On the mound is George Brunet. Batting right-handed, Mickey takes Brunet's first pitch for a strike. The second pitch comes toward him. Mickey swings, and ropes a line drive. It reaches the left-field seats. The score is now 10–10.

Mantle had hit tons of balls harder and farther, but this might have been the sweetest home run of his career. The fans were screaming wildly as Mickey rounded the bases. Goosebumps appeared on his arms and tears welled up in his eyes. Mickey had only one regret and that was that his father, Mutt, wasn't alive to share the magic moment.

The Yankees went on to win, 11–10. In the locker room afterward, the press crowded around Mantle. Of the first ovation, Mickey said it "actually chilled me. I was shaking. I could feel the bumps rising on my arms. I told myself, I'll settle for a single." Of the homer, he said, "I didn't think it would go. I didn't think I had pulled it enough. I didn't see it go into the seats, but I saw the umpire signal and I told myself, I'm a lucky stiff. Gee, but I'm a lucky stiff."

Mantle also admitted that the home run might have been tainted because someone interfered with left fielder Jackie Brandt. Brandt was furious. "I could have caught that ball," he said. "But just as I was about to, some soldier just laid down on me—I couldn't get up. Why don't they put a screen on top of those short fences out there, and keep those fans out of the game? That was a heck of a way to lose a game."

The Orioles may have been upset, but everyone else felt great for Mantle. His popularity soared higher than ever. Bill Gallo, the outstanding sports cartoonist/journalist of the *New York Daily News*, captured the historic event in a "Two Kids Talkin' Sports" cartoon. One kid, looking at

Mantle hitting his pinch-hit homer, asks another, "Wadda you wanna be when you grow up?" The second answers, "Right now, a pinch-hitter!"

September 1, 1963—Memorial Stadium, Baltimore. Mickey Mantle was being used strictly as a pinch-hitter, and even that role was denied him the past week. Fans home and away called his name whenever a pinch-hit situation came up, but Mickey pinch-hit only seven times, going 0 for 4, with three walks, since his dramatic homer on August 4. The August 4 homer was for the fans; the homer he hit on this date was an inside story that delighted the players.

Legend has it that Babe Ruth hit many a home run on days when he was nursing a bad hangover. Mantle's homer awakened the legend; his teammates found the same amusement in his homer that Ruth's teammates enjoyed when an overpartied Bambino popped them out in the 1920s and 1930s.

Teammates Mantle, Whitey Ford, and Dale Long had partied far into the previous night on the Maryland farm of friends of Mickey's. Mickey was in no condition to play ball when he got to the ballpark, but then he didn't expect to play anyway.

Baltimore leads, 4–1, as the Yankees come up in the eighth. Mickey is half asleep in the dugout corner when Ralph Houk asks him to bat for the pitcher. The Mick, feeling ornery, straightens himself up, uncrushes his cap—Ford had been sitting on it—and goes up to face left-hander Mike McCormick after a one-out Clete Boyer single. Ford's final words of advice: Swing at the first fastball.

Now, the Orioles are fully aware of the situation. Hank Bauer, an Oriole coach, had seen how Mantle looked when he arrived at the park, and the Birds feel there's no way Mantle can play.

Mantle, remembering Ford's advice, jumps on McCormick's high fastball—the first pitch—and sends a long homer over the left-field fence, cutting Baltimore's lead to 4–3. He laughs all the way around the bases, not at McCormick but at himself. Bob Maisel of the *Baltimore Sun* wrote in his column the next day that the Yankees acted "as if they were celebrating New Year's Eve." Ford, he wrote, "raised his hands over his head, then lowered them to the ground as though he might be worshipping some god."

Mickey finally finishes his home-run loop, exhausted. He trots into the dugout, looks at the cheering crowd, and tells his incredulous teammates, "Those people don't know how tough that really was."

There are two out in the same inning when Richardson singles. Dick Hall relieves McCormick, and Tom Tresh, who earlier had hit a right-handed homer off McCormick, wallops a two-run homer batting left-handed—becoming only the third American Leaguer to switch-hit homers in the same game—and New York takes a 5–4 lead, the final score.

Maisel later told Houk, "It's all like a bad TV script. Mantle comes out of the dugout, kneels in the on-deck circle and gets an ovation. Then, he goes to the plate and gets an even bigger one. The expectation grows as the opposing manager comes out to talk to his pitcher, everybody in the park looks at the guy next to him and says, 'Watch him hit a home run,' and he promptly hits the first pitch nine miles out into the great beyond. The guy has two hits since he broke his foot here and both are home runs against Baltimore."

The next day Mantle plays his first game in the outfield, in center field, too, since the June 5 accident. He will begin gingerly, with occasional pinch-hit appearances and abbreviated games in center, but all timed so as to have him ready for the World Series between the Yankees and the Los Angeles Dodgers. Mickey will hit .333 in September, raising his overall average to .314 for the year. His 15 home runs, his fewest since 1951, came in only 172 at bats.

October 6, 1963—Dodger Stadium, Los Angeles. The Yankees were in a deep hole in the World Series. In succession, they had fallen victim to great pitching performances by the Dodgers' Sandy Koufax, Johnny Podres, and Don Drysdale. With New York on the verge of a humiliating four-game elimination, Whitey Ford took the mound to oppose Koufax. The two greatest pitchers of their time put on a show worthy of their reputations.

Ford pitches seven innings—he left for a pinch-hitter in the top of the eighth—allowing only two hits, both by Frank Howard. The gigantic 6'7" Howard, who in the opener at the Stadium touched Ford for a mighty double off the 457-foot sign, opens the scoring with an enormous fifth-inning home run into the eighth row of the left-field upper deck; it is the first fair ball hit into the top deck in the ballpark's two-year history.

Koufax is not as overpowering as he was in the opener, when he struck out 15, but he is nonetheless in command. In the seventh, Mantle, hitless against him in five series at bats, gets hold of a first-pitch, letter-high fastball—Koufax has the best fastball in baseball—and smokes a vicious home run into the left-center-field pavilion, well beyond the 380-foot mark. The homer gives Mantle 15 in World Series competition and ties him with Babe Ruth for the record. It also ties the game.

Los Angeles takes a 2–1 lead in the bottom of the seventh and Koufax makes the one-run lead hold up, although he has a scare in the ninth. After Bobby Richardson gets a leadoff single, and Tom Tresh and Mantle are both called out on strikes, Elston Howard reaches on an error, pushing the tying run into scoring position. But Hector Lopez grounds out, and the Dodgers have a stunning four-game sweep. Koufax has chalked up a six-hitter, striking out eight and walking none.

The Dodgers achieved the sweep with pitching—the Yanks scored only four runs in the entire series! While the Yanks hit only .171, the Dodgers were almost as feeble at .214. Mantle, heading for another knee operation in the off-season, showed only a bunt single to go with his homer in 15 series at bats. Roger Maris was injured in Game 2 and got only five at bats, but it is doubtful that he could have made much of a difference against the outstanding Dodger pitching.

The Yankees were disappointed, but they knew they had been soundly beaten. "I hate to lose this series, of course," said Mantle, "but it was a good pitching series and that's about all. Losing the seventh game to the Pirates in 1960 was much tougher to take." While he was a big-spirited loser, Mantle all the same had this observation, reported Leonard Koppett of the *New York Times:* "I don't care if the Dodgers beat us 10 straight games. I still think we have a better team."

1964

June 13, 1964—Yankee Stadium. The hurtin' Yankees, with a new field boss this season in Yogi Berra (Ralph Houk having been moved up to general manager), were doing their best to keep up with first-place Chicago, in town for a five-game set.

Berra, like Houk in 1963, was faced with injuries galore. Early in the season he lost his entire outfield—Mickey Mantle, Roger Maris, and Tom Tresh—to pulled hamstring muscles. When he started his eight regulars on May 23, it was only their second game together this season.

Mantle, who underwent off-season surgery on his left knee, didn't hit his first home run until May 6, the latest date so far in his career. He hobbled through the early season with muscle pulls and then on May 26 pulled a muscle in his left thigh, which, except for a few pinch-hitting appearances, kept him out of action for two weeks.

Mantle returned to the starting lineup on June 9 in Boston, where two days later he hit a pair of homers. The Yankees were managing to keep their heads above water in spite of the long casualty list, and they were home now for the key series with the front-running White Sox.

They beat the White Sox, 6–3, on this date, for the third time in 24 hours. The third-place Yankees (30–21) were now within two games of the Chisox (31–18), thanks to great relief pitching by Bill Stafford and Pete Mikkelsen, a couple of key hits from Tony Kubek, and a big game from Mantle.

Mickey gives the Yankees a 1–0 lead in the first inning with a single up the middle that scores Bobby Richardson. In the fourth, with the White Sox ahead, 3–1, Mickey, batting righty against Frank Kreutzer, reaches for an outside pitch that he drives into the right-field seats for a solo homer. In the seventh, Hector Lopez runs for Mantle, whose 3-for-3 day elevates his average to .331 and whose homer gives him a club-leading 11 on the year.

In this five-game series, the first critical showdown of the year,

Mickey will go 7 for 16, with three walks, and New York will win all five games.

June 17, 1964—Yankee Stadium. Dick Radatz was known as the Monster. A husky 6'6", he was a hard-throwing relief specialist who can be viewed as the Goose Gossage of his day. It was with the Red Sox from 1962 through 1965 that he was at his terrifying best. His 181 strikeouts this year (in 157 innings) set a standing reliever record.

Radatz has a 3–1 lead in the eighth and Mickey Mantle leads off for the Yankees. Batting left-handed, Mantle skies to right and tosses his bat in anger. But the ball carries . . . and carries . . . It carries into the bleachers for a home run! The Monster, of course, helped supply the power on this one; he also helped by getting the ball too low, having had good success with the Mick on previous occasions with fastballs at higher locations.

Years later Radatz remembered the fly ball Mantle homer. He also recalled what Mantle said to him. "When he reached home plate, he looked out to me and said, 'I finally got you!' "

The Yankees tied the score in the ninth, but Boston scored in the 12th to win, 4–3. It was Radatz's fourth straight win over New York.

June 21, 1964—Comiskey Park, Chicago. The Yankees won a pair of excellent pitching duels, 2–0 and 2–1, on this date, and for the first time this year moved into first place. New York (37–23, .617) was eight percentage points ahead of Baltimore (39–25, .609) and 2½ games ahead of Chicago (34–25).

Great Yankee pitching performances are turned in by Jim Bouton and Pete Mikkelsen in the first game and by Al Downing and Bill Stafford in the 17-inning second game. Downing strikes out 13 men in 12 innings but allows Chicago's only run in 41 innings against the Yankees.

The two Yankee runs in the opener are the result of home runs by Elston Howard and Mickey Mantle. Both are hit against Juan Pizarro, who this year will go 19–9. Mantle's seventh-inning blast, batting right-handed, goes deep into the left-field upper deck. Mickey departs the first game early and is an unsuccessful pinch-hitter in the nightcap, which the Yankees win in the 17th when White Sox shortstop Al Weiss bobbles a bases-loaded grounder.

The Yankees' ability to beat up on the White Sox was the most important factor in their rise to first place. They will complete a four-game sweep here, giving them nine wins in nine games between the two contenders in a span of 11 days and running their season record against Chicago to 10–0. Without this domination over the Chisox, in fact, the Yanks would be well back. Mantle certainly did his part; in the 10 games with the Sox (he played in eight and pinch-hit in one), he hit .429, with five of his 12 hits going for extra bases. He also drew five walks.

The Yankees are headed for Baltimore to see if they can hold first place against manager Hank Bauer's Birds.

June 23, 1964—Memorial Stadium, Baltimore. The Yankees and Orioles opened a big series before 31,860 fans, the largest crowd here since Opening Day. The home team treated their roaring rooters to a spectacular come-from-behind victory that nudged the Orioles into first place by two percentage points and snapped New York's five-game winning streak. Worse, the Yanks will also drop the final two games of the three-game set.

The Yankees jump on Oriole starter Wally Bunker, knocking him out early, and take a commanding 7–2 lead in the seventh inning on a three-run Mickey Mantle homer. His 14th of the year, Mantle's blast into the right-field bleachers is hit off right-hander Chuck Estrada. Meanwhile, Yankee starter Rollie Sheldon is sailing, allowing only a pair of Boog Powell homers.

In the eighth the Yankees have two men on base and two out. Manager Yogi Berra, who must have thought Sheldon was tiring, has Johnny Blanchard bat for the pitcher. The Orioles give Blanchard an intentional pass, the next man pops up, and the Yanks miss a chance to put the game away.

Berra's lifting of Sheldon—it will later be perceived as an unfortunate gamble—backfires in the Oriole half of the eighth. Sheldon's replacements, most notably Pete Mikkelsen, are shelled for seven runs—all seven scoring after two are out. The Birds lead, 9–7.

Stu Miller is pitching for Baltimore in the ninth. Bobby Richardson pops out. Mantle takes a called third strike, and he is so unhappy with the call that he hurls his batting helmet and draws a rare ejection. Roger Maris follows with a homer, but Tom Tresh strikes out to end the game.

Berra is second-guessed by some of his players, setting the pattern for the summer. Most of the grumbling is done in private with general manager Ralph Houk, and Berra soon loses the confidence of the front office, too. In the eyes of many, he is guilty of several sins on this date.

First, the lifting of Sheldon proved unwise. (But *was* Rollie tiring?) Second, with shortstop Tony Kubek injured, Yogi moved his slick-fielding third baseman, Clete Boyer, over to short and played supersub Phil Linz, not a proficient third sacker, at third. So it appeared that Berra had weakened two positions instead of settling for one (in having Linz play shortstop), and several of Baltimore's hits in the seven-run eighth squirted through the revamped left side; a couple got past Linz that Boyer might have handled. Finally, Mikkelsen, the pitcher roughed up the most—Pete was a Berra "find" and some members of the bullpen thought that Yogi was giving the rookie too much work, and at their expense—was a sinkerball pitcher who depended on a good fielding infield to gobble up the preponderance of ground balls he induced.

There were those who felt right off that Berra, or anyone in his shoes, would have a hard time managing a team that he had played for the previous year. Yogi had been with the Yankees a long time, had built friendships with guys over whom he was now the boss. But senior Yankees Whitey Ford and Mantle had no problem with the revised relationship. Ford, in fact, doubled as Berra's pitching coach, and Mantle gave his old pal a 100-percent effort, but then again Mickey played all-out regardless of who was manager.

August 12, 1964—Yankee Stadium. The Yankees went 19–10 in July to hang in the pennant race. Their games from August 7 to 20 were confined to the Orioles and White Sox, the other two contenders. The first series, against Baltimore here, wasn't good for either the Yankees, losers of three of four games, or Mickey Mantle, hitless in the first two games and then the victim of a pulled groin muscle. After an open date, Chicago came in and partially avenged their 0–10 record against the Yanks by sweeping a doubleheader. Mantle was back in the lineup, going 3 for 8, breaking an 0-for-17 collar, and hitting a ninth-inning home run in the discouraging 8–2 second-game defeat.

The third game is critical for the Yankees, who began this date 3½ games behind Baltimore and 2½ behind Chicago. The Yanks had lost seven of their last nine games, five of six against the teams ahead of them in the standings. Into the gloom steps Mel Stottlemyre, a right-hander just recalled from Richmond, where he had gone 13–3 with a 1.43 ERA. Manager Yogi Berra gives him the ball.

Stottlemyre falls behind, 2–1, in the fourth inning. Mantle leads off the bottom half batting left-handed against Ray Herbert. The count goes to 3 and 1. Then Mickey gets under a fastball and sends the ball high, very high, into the sky—so high, in fact, that Mantle believes he has flied out. But high in the sky is good, because a strong wind is blowing out to center field. Center fielder Gene Stephens goes back, and back, and back—years later Mantle's teammate Stan Williams recalls that "it seemed like the ball was in the air a full five minutes"—until his back is flush against the 461-foot sign in dead center. He looks up in amazement (the scene will be captured on the front page of the next day's *New York Daily News*) as the ball clears the hitters' background screen and lands 15 rows deep in the bleachers.

This area of the dead-center-field bleachers had been reached only once before—by Mantle on June 21, 1955. Danny Sullivan, the assistant stadium superintendent, announced that the ball had traveled just over 500 feet, and what became known as a 502-footer remains the longest *measured* home run in Yankee Stadium history. Of course, the facade shots hit by Mantle and probably several of his upper-deck jobs *would* have gone farther if no obstacle had intruded. While the wind did help it, there was all the same a certain majesty about this high fly ball.

It is now a 2–2 game, and the slumbering Yankees are seemingly awakened. In the sixth, Roger Maris hits a two-run homer, the third Yankee long ball of the game. (Clete Boyer had hit one earlier.) Mantle lines a single. He turns on the afterburners and slides into third base on Joe Pepitone's single to center, then slides home on a popfly that second baseman Don Buford drops in shallow center.

It is 5–3 when Mantle leads off the eighth. Batting right-handed this time, against Frank Baumann, Mickey pushes a solid line-drive homer, his 25th of the season, about 350 feet into the lower right-field seats. It is Mickey's third homer in his last five at bats. And it marks the 10th—and final—time that Mantle switch-hits homers in the same game, a standing big-league record.

Stottlemyre finishes his major-league debut with a strong seven-hitter and a 7–3 victory. He walks only one man, his sinkerball induces 21 ground balls—19 are outs and two are muffed for Yankee errors—and he gives the Yankees a badly needed shot in the arm.

But it is the Mantle performance that really picks up the club. The euphoric spirit around the club will help carry the Yankees past the White Sox the next day and then to a two-out-of-three series advantage in Baltimore. But in Baltimore, Mantle will bang his sore left knee on the ground diving into first base, jamming it badly; he will be bothered by the knee the rest of the year.

The Yankees will go to Chicago and, with Mantle limited to making only one pinch-hit appearance, lose four in a row. And on board the team bus on getaway day, Phil Linz will play a poor rendition of "Mary Had a Little Lamb" on his harmonica and have his famous altercation with Berra. The team seemed in shambles as it headed for Boston, where the local citizenry would like nothing better than to finish off the Yankees and lay them to rest.

August 22, 1964—Fenway Park, Boston. The Yankees' season hit a new low, the Yanks dropping the first two games here to extend their losing streak to six. The second Red Sox win was an afternoon game on this date, the front end of a day-night doubleheader played in chilly, rainy, foggy—and most of all, gloomy—Boston.

The Yankees have a 3–2 lead in the afternoon game, but the Red Sox strike for three runs in the eighth, Dick Radatz is unhittable in the late innings, and Boston has a 5–3 victory. Yogi Berra spends the long rest period between games trying to lift the spirits of his players. "No sense getting down," he keeps saying. "Let's just go out there as if we'd just had a big party."

Right-hander Jack Lamabe is the Boston starting pitcher in the evening game. Bobby Richardson singles in the first inning and Mickey Mantle comes up with two out. Mickey had returned to the starting lineup the previous day after a six-day absence. He has gone 0 for 7 in the first two games here. He is playing in great pain, hobbling around the best he can on his bad knee, and playing left field to cut down on his running. But he nails home run No. 26 into the right-field bullpen, and New York has a 2–0 lead.

With Mickey showing the way, the rest of the game is, well, the big party that Berra wanted. Mantle adds an RBI double, Roger Maris drives in three runs, Johnny Blanchard hits a homer, Mel Stottlemyre pitches a six-hit shutout for his third consecutive win since his recall from Richmond, and the Yankees snap their six-game losing streak, 8–0. Late in the game, his work done, Mantle surrenders left field to Hector Lopez.

At day's end, the first-place Orioles (76–47) are 1½ games ahead of the White Sox (75–49) and 5½ games in front of the Yankees (70–52). It is announced that Baltimore Mayor Theodore R. McKeldin and Chicago Mayor Richard Daley have a dinner bet on the outcome of the American

League pennant race. If the Orioles don't win, McKeldin will owe Daley a dinner of Chesapeake Bay steamed crabs; if the White Sox don't win, Daley will owe McKeldin a dinner of Chicago steak. Nothing is said about the Yankees; most people think they are dead.

The next day Mantle will breathe more life into the club. He will hit another two-run homer to give the Yankees a 2–0 lead, and New York beats Boston, 4–3. The two wins over Boston start something; the Yankees will roll on to 26 wins in their next 33 games. Mantle got it going.

September 4, 1964—Municipal Stadium, Kansas City. Charles O. Finley might have gone to war with anybody, or with anything. This year he was at war with the short right-field porch at Yankee Stadium. He complained about the 296-foot distance down the line and about the low fence in right. The Yankees win so much, argued the maverick A's owner, because the short porch gives them an unfair advantage. "I'm tired of Yankee domination because of a 296-foot fence in right field," he snapped.

Finley figured all he needed to do to win some pennants, or to win some attention, was to duplicate the Yankees' porch at his ballpark. In the spring of 1964, he had a strange-looking fence built curving to a point 296 feet from the plate but just a few feet off the right-field line to conform to the league rules on mandatory foul-line distances. The fence ran straight back to 325 feet at the foul pole. "K-C Pennant Porch" was written on the new fence. It was clearly a way to skirt the rules, but baseball commissioner Ford Frick and American League president Joe Cronin were not fooled; Finley was ordered to take down the new fence or face fines and forfeitures of A's games after the regular season started. He moved the fence back some and renamed it the "K-C One-half Pennant Porch."

Finley put chalk lines in the right- and left-field corners of his ballpark, and when a ball was caught beyond these lines, his public address announcer told the crowd, "That would have been a home run in Yankee Stadium."

Surviving a scare or two on this date, the Yankees beat the A's, 9–7, in 10 innings. The first-place Orioles were also beaten, and Baltimore (81–54) and Chicago (82–55) fell into a virtual tie for first, with New York (77–56) three games behind. But the Yanks were in better shape in the loss column.

The Yankees trail, 2–0, in the fourth, when Roger Maris singles and Mickey Mantle and Elston Howard hit back-to-back homers to give the Bombers a 3–2 lead. Mantle, playing left field and moving with a pronounced limp, singles in the eighth and leaves the game for pinch-runner Mel Stottlemyre, with the Yankees ahead, 5–4. But with two out in the ninth, Ken Harrelson hits his second homer of the game, and the 5–5 tie goes into extra innings. The Yanks outscore the A's, 4–2, in the 10th to win; batting in Mantle's place, Hector Lopez draws a key walk.

Mantle's big homer was laced about 330 feet into the "K-C One-half Pennant Porch." It would have been a homer into the short porch at Yankee Stadium, true, but Howard's homer over the 410-foot fence would have been an out at the Stadium.

The whole porch thing was crazy. The Yankees took advantage of the short right-field porch because they had the left-handed hitters— Ruth, Gehrig, Dickey, Keller, Berra, and Maris, among others—to do so, and they had the pitchers to keep the opposing hitters from tattooing the porch too often. If Finley had been allowed to keep his "Pennant Porch," *his* pitchers probably would have yielded more homers in that direction than the visiting pitchers.

What Finley didn't say was that in the previous nine years the Yankees had hit more home runs on the road than at the Stadium. Death Valley, the huge expanse from left field to right center, more than compensates for the porch. Back in May, in a game against the A's, Mantle slammed a 440-foot blast that was caught in deep-center field, and Bob Fishel, the Yanks' public relations man, took the press-box mike and announced, "That would have been a homer in Kansas City."

Mantle, in games against the A's this year, hit three homers at Municipal Stadium and four at Yankee Stadium. Of the three here, two probably would have been outs to left and left-center in the Bronx. And at least three of the four at the Stadium—one over the 402-foot sign in left, one into the right-field bleachers, and one deep into the right-field bullpen—would have been easy homers in Kansas City.

September 17, 1964—Yankee Stadium. The front-page headline of the *New York Times* said it all: YANKS, ONCE "DEAD," REGAIN FIRST PLACE. The Yankees had posted a 17–7 record since the second game of August 22 while Baltimore went 12–14, and Chicago, 13–12. The

Yankees (86–59, .593) now led the Orioles and White Sox (both 88–61, .591) by two percentage points.

The Yankees, in whipping Los Angeles, 6–2, on this date, are led by the Big Guy, Mickey Mantle, who has one of his best games of this season and one of the most thrilling games of his career. Mel Stottlemyre and Rollie Sheldon pitch splendidly and the New York defense turns five double plays, but still it all comes back to Mantle.

The game is scoreless in the fourth when Roger Maris beats out a bunt for one of his three hits. Batting left-handed against Fred Newman, Mantle promptly breaks a 2-for-28 dry spell with a line-drive ground-rule double to left, sending Maris to third. Both score on a Tom Tresh single. Tresh then scores to complete a three-run rally.

Mantle in the sixth lines a single to center, his 2,000th hit in the majors, thus joining the other 2,000-hit Yankees—Babe Ruth, Lou Gehrig, Joe DiMaggio, and Yogi Berra. The crowd gives Mantle a standing ovation and the Mick eventually scores, making it 4–0.

In the seventh, Mantle follows a Maris single with a left-handed homer off Bob Duliba, and the Yankees go up, 6–2. It is the 31st of his season and the 450th of his career, and a second wave of cheering greets the milestone. Mickey departs late in the game, and Roger Repoz replaces him in right field.

This is the Yankees' second win in a streak that will run 11 games. The Yanks will protect first place for the remainder of the schedule; the final standings will show New York (99–63) one game ahead of Chicago (98–64) and two ahead of Baltimore (97–65). Mantle will hit .346 (18 for 52) from this date on.

The team is finally intact, the injured having returned, Yogi Berra points out, and finally there has been some clutch hitting. Berra deserves some credit, for he kept cool when others would have panicked. The bringing up of Mel Stottlemyre (9–3, 2.06 ERA) in August and the acquisition of Pedro Ramos (eight saves and one win) in September didn't hurt, either.

But many believed that this was a pennant Mantle just wouldn't let slip by the Yankees.

When the exciting pennant race is over, the Yankees will be making their way to St. Louis to play a Cardinal team that also had to come from behind to get to the World Series.

October 10, 1964—Yankee Stadium. This was a memorable home run, this homer by Mickey Mantle in Game 3 of the World Series with St. Louis. It won the game in the bottom of the ninth, 2–1, and it set a new record of 16 home runs in World Series competition, Mickey besting the longstanding record of Babe Ruth.

It was a dramatic, decisively stroked conclusion to a sparkling struggle. But beyond all that, it was, for Mantle, a uniquely satisfying moment.

He is playing in right field, Roger Maris having taken over in center in the later part of the season, in a switch designed to save Mantle's legs. But the Mick still feels strange in right; with one error already under his belt—leading to an unearned St. Louis run in this 1–1 game—Mantle almost misses a Curt Flood drive with two on and two out in the ninth.

When Mantle enters the dugout, he throws his glove in anger. First up in the bottom of the inning, he reportedly tells Elston Howard he will hit the first pitch out of the ballpark. Twenty years later Tony Kubek still remembered the moment well. Everyone in the Yankee dugout knew what was coming, Kubek said—Mantle just looked so determined to win it when he went to the plate—and Mickey does indeed hit the first pitch for a game-winning home run.

Veteran knuckleballer Barney Schultz had just come into the game in relief of Curt Simmons, who had been lifted for a pinch-hitter. The story of Schultz's 1964 season was a warm one; the Cardinals picked the 20-year veteran of 18 professional teams out of the minors and he led them to the pennant over the final two months of the season. He was well liked, had a good sense of humor, and had everyone rooting for him. The downside of the dramatic Mantle homer was that it was off Schultz; he had thrown as his first World Series pitch, in his words, "a knuckler that didn't knuckle," and he buried himself in tears in the locker room.

Mantle drove the ball into the third deck of the right-field stands. He thought it might go foul but it stayed fair by 40 feet.

The game is memorable, too, as a great pitchers' duel between the winning Jim Bouton and Simmons. The 67,101 fans hang on every pitch, the tension mounting throughout the afternoon, building for Mantle's climactic clout.

St. Louis has the go-ahead run on third base in the sixth, seventh, and ninth innings but can't score. Bouton is getting the Cardinals to hit the ball where he wants them to hit it. Simmons, meanwhile, is keeping the Yankees off stride with off-speed pitches. Elston Howard, a Yankee for

10 years and nine World Series, felt it was the most exciting World Series game he'd ever seen.

When Mantle brought sudden-death victory to the Yankees, normally restrained third-base coach Frank Crosetti joined him in his home-run trot from third to home, while the pinstriped professionals in the Yankee dugout went a little nuts. The huge crowd went a little nuts, too, on this gray autumn day in New York.

October 14, 1964—Busch Stadium, St. Louis. Another Bouton-Simmons pitching duel? It was shaping up that way, Curt Simmons breezing into the fifth inning with St. Louis leading, 1–0, in Game 6, which the Yankees had to win to stay alive in the series.

But Tom Tresh gets a leadoff double and scores on Jim Bouton's two-out single. Then in the sixth, Roger Maris and Mickey Mantle hit home runs on successive pitches, and New York has a 3–1 lead. Maris hits a change-up onto Grand Avenue, and Mantle's right-handed opposite-field homer finds lodging in a screen atop the right-field roof.

Barney Schultz takes the mound for the Cardinals in the eighth and runs into immediate trouble. Phil Linz gets a leadoff single, takes second on Bobby Richardson's sacrifice bunt, and goes to third on Maris's grounder to the right side. Mantle is walked intentionally, and Elston Howard singles Linz home. Tresh walks to load the bases. Gordie Richardson comes in to pitch and surrenders a grand-slam home run to Joe Pepitone. The Yanks are ahead, 8–1.

Bouton, after getting out of serious trouble in the first inning, blanks the Cards until the eighth, although Dal Maxvill gives the crowd a thrill and Mantle a surprise in the fifth. The slight second baseman lines one over Mantle's head; Mantle, playing shallow right field, barely has time to get back to make a fingertip catch. The Cards add two more meaningless runs, the Yankees win, 8–3, and the series is tied at three games apiece.

Mantle's homer was his 17th in World Series play and added to his record. "I'm very careful with Mantle," Simmons said after the game. "I really put some speed on that pitch. It was away from Mantle but he was going with me."

October 15, 1964—Busch Stadium, St. Louis. The Yankees got licked in Game 7 of the World Series, and with the painfully long drought that lay ahead, it is the last World Series they will see for a dozen years. Mickey Mantle will never see another.

With St. Louis ahead, 6–0, in the sixth, a left-handed-hitting Mantle nails a Bob Gibson pitch for a three-run homer. The homer bothers Gibson, who later said in the clubhouse, "He hit a fastball away from the plate and rode it to left. That man has power."

The Yankees score twice more and the Cards once more before the final out is recorded and 30,346 fans celebrate a 7–5 win and the bringing of the World Championship to heartland America.

Mantle's opposite-field homer to the left-center-field bleachers was one of three homers Gibson yielded. Phil Linz and Clete Boyer both had solo homers in the ninth. The series ended on Bobby Richardson's pop-up, with Gibson still on the mound and Roger Maris and Mantle due up next.

Mantle had hit the ball hard in the eighth. It was, Bob Broeg wrote in the *St. Louis Post-Dispatch*, "the kind of towering drive Babe Ruth used to hit, a soaring fly that fortunately had much more height than distance." Curt Flood got under it.

Even in a losing cause, this was a sterling World Series for Mantle. He hit .333 and led all series performers in homers (3), runs (8), RBIs (8), and slugging (.792). And Mickey established lifetime World Series records for homers (18), RBIs (40), runs (42), walks (43), extra-base hits (26), and total bases (123).

So the 1964 campaign was over. It was the last real Mantle-like season for the Mick. He was just about to turn 33, but he seemed much older, and he was physically drained. He should have been able to look forward to several more prime years, but his career had peaked. It was about to tumble downhill.

For one thing, Mickey was no longer a great center fielder. He didn't get to drives like he used to. Late in the 1964 season, for the good of both his legs and the team, Mantle played right field at home and left field on the road, wherever there was less ground to cover. In the World Series, critics pointed out that Cardinal base runners took liberties with the Mick's once strong throwing arm; his shoulder was unsound and his fragile knees prevented him from planting himself. As any good team would do, the Cards exploited the weakness.

Mantle, in fact, played the 1964 season hobbled. He started with only one leg; he was vulnerable and he did, indeed, sustain an assortment of injuries—to the knee, to the groin, to the hamstring . . . everywhere. But he got into 143 games, and he played better than anyone had a right to expect.

Wait a minute: He had MVP credentials. He led the league in on-base average (.426). He was second in slugging (.591). He was third in home runs (35) and RBIs (111). He was fourth in batting (.303). (Mickey hit .424 righty and .241 lefty, but he hit 20 of his 35 homers lefty.) He *led* the Yankees to the pennant.

Somehow, Brooks Robinson of the Orioles, who hit .317, drove in a league-leading 118 runs, and played a great third base, but who didn't come close to Mantle's other stats and who didn't pick his team out of the rubble to win the pennant, got the MVP Award. It wasn't a bad choice; it just wasn't the correct one.

It was over. Mantle would never again be the complete player that he was in his glory days—glory days that lasted nearly a decade. He wasn't up to it physically. Now and again he would show a glimmer of his former self—a long home run, a great catch, a daring move on the base paths—but it was only a glimmer. And the Yankees wouldn't be the Yankees for a long, long time.

The Home Runs of Baseball's Most Popular Player

1965

April 9, 1965—Astrodome, Houston. The first indoor ballpark in history, the $31.6 million Astrodome, opened its doors for a game between the Houston Astros and the New York Yankees. Perhaps no exhibition game ever attracted so much national interest.

The crowd of 47,876 included visitors from 38 states; reportedly, 40 percent of the tickets were bought by out-of-staters. Texas Governor John Connally threw out the first ball, and President Lyndon B. Johnson and the First Lady, en route to their Texas ranch, decided to pay a visit and arrived during the second inning.

The Taj Mahal of Baseball was said to be the last word in sports stadiums. The upholstered, temperature-controlled dome transformed the playing field into a great stage. Its luxurious private suites and Galaxie Gift Shop, where a Lady Hamilton wristwatch sold for $325, wowed fans and players alike. It was Texas-style big with a space age shine. It was also sterile.

Johnny Keane, who replaced Yogi Berra as Yankee manager following the 1964 World Series, puts Mantle in the leadoff position so that Mickey can be the first batter in the history of the Dome. On the second pitch thrown to him by right-hander Dick Farrell, Mantle singles to center for the first hit in the Eighth Wonder.

The game is still scoreless when Mantle faces Farrell again in the sixth. This time Mickey sends up a space shot in astro country, launching one over the center-field fence just to the right of the 406-foot marker; the sphere strikes the rail in front of the cushioned pavilion, rebounding onto the field where Jimmy Wynn retrieves it and flips the souvenir to a lucky fan. It is the first home run in the new park and the highlight of the game, for the Yankees anyway, who go down, 2–1, when pinch-hitter Nellie Fox singles home the winning run in the 12th inning.

The home run was also the highlight of a Mantle spring that was anything but encouraging. "My legs feel better than ever," Mickey had said in February on signing his 1965 contract. After a winter of isometric exercises, he expected—maybe even tried to will—good wheels. But in spring training the truth soon emerged. After 14 seasons of brutal punishment, after numerous operations, the legs of Mickey Mantle were failing the test.

They hurt Mickey at the plate and in the field. He couldn't swing the bat with his old, powerful, fluid motion, nor could he cover the ground necessary to play center field. An anxious Johnny Keane made a move that would last for the duration of 1965, shifting the Mick to left field, and Tom Tresh from left to center.

Then late in spring training Mantle showed signs of regaining his old form at the plate, and the memorable Astrodome clout further fueled hopes of another big Mantle season. Indeed, Mickey began the regular season batting .308 in April (12 for 39), with four homers.

May 10, 1965—Fenway Park, Boston. The injury-riddled Yanks—and among the riddled were such key players as Mickey Mantle, Roger Maris, and Elston Howard—lost again and are in ninth place with a 9–14 record.

Mantle makes his first appearance in the starting lineup since manager Johnny Keane eight days ago allowed him to play both ends of a doubleheader loss to Baltimore. Mickey has been limping around on his aching legs ever since, unable to play except for pinch-hit duty. An hour before the game he goes to Keane and asks to be put in the lineup. He has a three-hit game, but his big day is trumped by Carl Yastrzemski, who drives in all three Boston runs with a sacrifice fly and a pair of homers.

On this day, rookie right-hander Jim Lonborg, who will eventually win more than 150 big-league games and a Cy Young Award, is still searching for his first win, and he gets it, 3–2. Lonborg will recall nearly two decades later the trouble Mantle gave him in his quest for his first major-league victory.

Mantle strikes out in the second inning on what Lonborg recalls was "my best curveball ever." In the fourth, Mickey pulls a line-drive single to right field, knocking in a run and tying the score at 1–1. In the seventh he ties it at 2–2 with a home run into the right-field seats.

Boston leads, 3–2, with two out in the ninth. Mantle doubles high off the left-center-field wall and leaves the game to a standing ovation as a pinch-runner comes in. The ball "barely stayed in the park," Lonborg recalls. "It hit the wall just two feet from the top. Dick Radatz came in to get the last out and save my first victory."

Leonard Koppett wrote a column in the *New York Times* in which he favorably compared the job Yogi Berra did in 1964 with that turned in so far by Keane. Koppett said that Mantle's physical shape in 1964, following his knee surgery, was supposed to be worse than this spring, or so the Yankees claimed. However, Berra removed Mantle in the late innings, sat him down in second games of doubleheaders, and rested him in day games after night games. By contrast, Keane foolishly played Mantle 18 innings on May 2, and Mickey wasn't right for more than a week. It will take Keane some time to realize what Berra knew from the start—that Mantle needs periodic resting.

May 11, 1965—Fenway Park, Boston. The Yanks' Mel Stottlemyre had a good sinker and went all the way to beat the Red Sox, 5–3. But the game belonged again to Mickey Mantle, who, although badly hobbled, homered and reached on two walks and an error, giving him seven successive times on base in this series.

Mantle's home run, his sixth of the year, put him one behind the league leaders. Will McDonough of the *Boston Globe* subsequently made use of the clout for a fascinating anatomy-of-a-Mantle-homer piece fleshed by the locker-room comments of impressed Red Sox players.

Mickey hit the homer batting righty against Arnie Earley on a 3-and-2 count. "I wanted to give him that good hard sinker away," said Earley. "He hit the one before off the end of the bat and it hurt so much he yelped." The sting was so intense, Mantle had to get some resin to relieve it.

"The fingers on his hand turned white, they hurt so much," said catcher Bob Tillman. "At the plate he doesn't say anything. Usually he just grimaces once in a while when he swings and the leg hurts. But this time he yelled when he hurt his hand."

Pitcher Earley: "Before I threw the 3-and-2 pitch, I waited to see how he'd set himself up. As he got set, I watched him scraping the dirt in the back of the box and from the arc of his practice swing I could see his bat missed covering the outside corner of the plate by about three inches."

So Earley aimed for the outside portion of the plate. "It was a little wide and low," he said. "But I didn't care because I wouldn't have minded walking him." He liked his pitch.

But Mantle didn't try to pull it, or let it go by either. Instead, he went with the pitch and sent it flying about 430 feet from home plate; the ball landed in the right-center-field seats several rows beyond the Red Sox bullpen.

June 5, 1965—Yankee Stadium. The physical equipment of Mickey Mantle was wearing out but the greatness was still there; even on a so-so day such as this one he could help lift the Yankees to victory. The real Yankee hero, however, in a 4–3 win over Chicago, was Mel Stottlemyre, who went the full 10 innings (on 153 pitches) and hit his first big-league homer.

The White Sox take a 2–0 first-inning lead, the second run scoring when left fielder Mantle allows a single to go past him. However, Mickey does prevent further damage with a fine running catch of a long drive by Tom McCraw.

The Stottlemyre homer comes in the third—the Yanks' first run in 24 innings—and Mantle in the sixth ties the score with a homer into the right-field bleachers off lefty Gary Peters.

The score is 3–3 in the ninth when manager Johnny Keane makes his standard late-inning defensive change, removing Mantle from the game, shifting Tom Tresh from center field to left, and putting Ross Moschitto in center. The strategy pays off when Tresh makes two sprinting catches of balls Mantle probably couldn't have run down.

The Yankees load the bases in the bottom of the 10th. Elston Howard bats for Moschitto and lines a game-winning single to left field. It is an emotional comeback for Howard, who one month ago underwent elbow surgery.

June 18, 1965—Yankee Stadium. The Yankees routed the first-place Twins, 10–2. However, Minnesota (36–22) still held a 10-game lead over the seventh-place Yankees (27–33).

Mel Nelson, the Minnesota starting pitcher, is a well-traveled 29-year-old who has played for 10 minor-league teams and is getting his third chance to stick in the majors. In this, his Yankee Stadium debut, he will last only two-thirds of an inning.

Mickey Mantle, batting right-handed in the first inning with the bases loaded and one out, hits a fastball away and arches a grand slam into the front rows of the lower right-field seats. Three more Yankee home runs follow in the game, including a roundtripper by Ross Moschitto, batting in Mantle's slot. It is the first, and only, major-league homer for Mantle's defensive caddy.

Years later, Nelson recalled, "That evening Mantle told our third-base coach Billy Martin that he was just trying to make contact and hit a fly ball to drive in a run. As it turned out, it was far enough to drop over the fence for a grand slam."

June 22, 1965—Yankee Stadium. In the first game of a doubleheader, Kansas City's John O'Donoghue cruised into the bottom of the eighth with a 6–0 lead only to have the smooth sailing disturbed by the home runs of Ray Barker and Mickey Mantle. Mantle's drive, hit right-handed, carries over the 457-foot sign and travels at least 475 feet into the left-center-field bleachers. It is only the 18th homer ever hit into these bleachers. Mickey limps around the bases with No. 11 under his belt and O'Donoghue departs. But the A's go on to win, 6–2.

The Yankees trail, 2–1, in the fourth inning of the second game. Mantle is on second base when A's pitcher Fred Talbot uncorks a wild pitch. Though his legs are killing him, Mickey will still try for the extra base if the situation suggests the gamble. Now, representing the tying run, Mickey turns the corner at third and breaks for home. He is only a few strides from the plate when the upper hamstring muscle in his left leg snaps. He slides, in pain, into home. Talbot tags him out. Grimacing, the Mick struggles to his feet. He leaves the game, and he will be out of the lineup for three weeks.

The Yankees rally to win, 4–2, but their situation is bleak. Hopeless, really, with Mantle out. He will not even so much as pinch-hit until July 1, and it will be 10 days more before he returns to the everyday lineup. The Yankees (29–36) are in seventh place, 10½ games behind first-place Minnesota (38–24). The June 21 cover of *Sports Illustrated* showed a weary Mantle wiping his brow; accompanying it were these words: NEW YORK YANKEES: END OF AN ERA. *Sports Illustrated* was right on the money.

The Yankees will limp home in sixth place with a 77–85 record and then do worse in 1966 and 1967. A major reason was the decline in Mantle's production—Mickey finished 1965 hitting .255, with 19 homers and 46 RBIs—but almost everyone on the team except Mel Stottlemyre and Tom Tresh fell off from their peak years. Injuries, age, or both caught up with four regulars—Mantle, Roger Maris, Elston Howard, and Tony Kubek.

Look at just one aspect of the Yanks' run production: Maris missed

116 games and Mantle missed 40—and of the games Mantle did play, he made 15 pinch-hit appearances and gave way to Ross Moschitto late in many others—and together Mantle and Maris hit only 27 homers. Compare that with the 115 combined homers they hit in 1961 and it doesn't take a genius to see that the difference showed up in the won-loss columns.

Tresh and Joe Pepitone, both young and talented, might have filled the void caused by the M & M decline. Neither did; Tresh perhaps tried too hard (and later injuries caught up with him, too), and Pepitone probably didn't try hard enough. Except for Roy White and Bobby Murcer, both of whom got just a peek with the big club in 1965, the farm system wasn't producing. And patchwork trading didn't cut it either.

The pitching staff consisted of three top-notch pitchers—Stottlemyre (20–9), Whitey Ford (16–13), and Pedro Ramos (19 saves)—and two others—Al Downing and Steve Hamilton—who did creditable work. After them, there was nothing. Many of the quality young pitchers who had arrived in the early 1960s had been traded away, didn't develop, or, in the cases of Jim Bouton and Bill Stafford, suffered irreversible arm damage. And again, there was no immediate help from a farm system that had dried up.

In 1965, for the first time, Mantle felt that his baseball career was winding down. He still was arguably the most exciting American League ballplayer—the fans still stirred in anticipation whenever he stepped into the batter's box—but his legs were shot. His locker-room routine consisted of rubdowns and diathermy before games and whirlpool soaks afterward. He played with his legs wrapped in seven-foot-long elastic foam bandages—the often-used comparison was with an Egyptian mummy—and his legs after a game would be pinched ash white from mummification.

Little or no cartilage, necessary for cushioning, was left in either knee. Running was painful, especially when he changed direction or stopped suddenly. When he ran hard to beat out a hit, he would have to run well past the bag in order to gradually stop. His knees would often stiffen up, especially when the weather was cold and wet, and when it happened during a game, he'd have to come out. In addition, his thigh, groin, and hamstring muscles were permanently weakened by numerous miseries.

Mantle's right leg bothered him so much batting left-handed—sometimes it even buckled under him—that beginning in 1965 he was forced to exaggerate his uppercut swing, hurting his batting average. Once he had been able to work himself out of slumps with drag bunts, but that was no longer possible.

But Mantle's physical problems weren't confined to his legs. In throwing, a piercing pain shot through his right shoulder, the one he originally hurt in the 1957 World Series. In effect, his throwing arm was dead; sometimes he would toss the ball to center fielder Tresh to return it to the infield. Unable to charge a ball, or change direction, or make sudden stops, and unable to make a strong throw, Mantle, it could be said, was handicapped in the outfield.

PLAYING HURT

The question over the first half of Mickey Mantle's career was, how good will he be once he fulfills his potential? The question over the second half was, how good would he be if it weren't for all those injuries?

Fact: Mantle absorbed more punishment than any Hall of Famer in history. Red Sox star Carl Yastrzemski talked in May 1965 to Will McDonough of the *Boston Globe* about Mantle. "The guy is the greatest," said Yaz. "I don't see how he does it. Every time he takes a step you can see the pain flash across his face. I could see a guy playing with a bad back or a sore arm or something else. But your legs—they're everything in this game. Why if that guy were healthy he'd hit 80 home runs."

"It was truly remarkable that Mickey Mantle could play as long as he did on those legs of his," Dr. Sidney S. Gaynor, the Yankee team physician in the Mantle years, once said, "and it took a remarkable amount of determination to do it. He had two operations on his right knee and finally developed arthritis in it. He had operations on his left knee, right hip, and shoulder. He had a broken foot and several broken fingers. He had at least six painfully pulled hamstring muscles in his career and numerous muscle tears in his thighs and groin."

In the July 1966 issue of *Sport*, Joe Donnelly wrote of watching Mantle put on his uniform: "As Mantle strips down it seems as if vandals have hacked at a marble statue. There's a chunk of flesh missing from his right buttock, a memory of the abscess that blood-soaked his uniform in the 1961 World Series. His knees are hatched with the scar tissue of three operations. The shoulder has the rawest and ugliest cut of all. It starts out almost needle thin on the blade, runs along it and down into the bicep.

As it broadens out, you can see where the doctors ran into more damage than had been anticipated. To some the scar resembles a question mark; to others, a 7."

Baseball gave Mickey Mantle everything he had in life, but it extracted quite a bit, too. Whitey Ford recalls times when it was a long hard struggle for the Mick to get out of his chair to leave a restaurant. One story has it that Mickey's knees locked up so badly that, on at least one occasion, he had to be carried out of a restaurant.

With little or no cartilage left in either knee, making for a bone-on-bone situation, Mantle, by the mid-1960s was permanently crippled, and he walked with a trace of a limp once his career ended. In 1983 Jane Leavy of the *Washington Post* followed Mantle on the golf course. He rode in a cart. "I don't walk," he told her. "I can't walk."

Mantle never complained about the pain he endured, although there probably wasn't a day he was with the Yankees that he didn't feel some degree of pain. He didn't want sympathy. "Sometimes I think the fans feel sorry for me," he said late in his career, "sorry that I've been hurt, sorry that I won't be playing for too much longer. But I don't want sympathy."

Mantle correctly felt that, considering everything, he hadn't had "too bad a career." Yet, it was easy to dream about the kinds of numbers he might have posted had he been healthier. How many more homers would he have hit? How much farther would he have hit the ball? But pause and consider these *real* numbers: Mantle played in more games (2,401) and had more at bats (8,102) than any Yankee in history.

There can be only one explanation for Mantle's enduring 18 seasons of almost constant pain—intense drive. Yes, he loved the game, and, yes, he was courageous. But there was something else; baseball was his life. In the August 1965 *Sport* article "The Twilight of a Hero," Arnold Hano asked Mantle if *he* thought he was a courageous man. Mickey shook his head. "No," he insisted. "The only thing I can do is play baseball. I *have* to play ball. It's the only thing I know. So it doesn't matter if my legs hurt. I've got to play. What else would I do?"

Mantle grew up loving the game, the fun of playing it, and the competition it provided; above all else, Mantle was a great competitor. And then there was his father, Mutt Mantle, a baseball fanatic, who loved to see young Mickey do well in the game; nothing pleased Mickey more than to please his father. So Mickey had a burning desire to excel in the game, to be great.

When injuries began dismantling him, it was his determination that made him carry on. Sure he had courage, but what he really had was a tremendous mind-over-matter willpower. He surrendered no more than his enjoyment of the game to injuries. "I always loved the game," he once said, "but when my legs weren't hurting, it was a lot easier to love." Retirement, something Mantle dreaded, finally became a definite if unattractive alternative.

Mantle's endless string of muscle pulls and tears, a doctor once told him, was attributable in part to his great strength in certain driving muscles. When he exploded all this main-muscle strength in throwing, batting, or running, he put great stress on ligaments, cartilages, and smaller muscles. Inevitably, these lesser body parts were damaged. Explosions cause damage.

A number of the Mick's injuries can be singled out as having the worst impact on his career.

HIGH SCHOOL: After being kicked in the left shin in football practice, Mantle developed osteomyelitis, an infection of the bone marrow that can be deadly. The disease, affecting his left leg from the ankle to the knee along the line of the shinbone, was controlled and eventually arrested with penicillin, but in Mickey's early years with the Yankees his future was in grave doubt. Any jar or bruise to the shin risked an osteomyelitis flare-up. Fortunately, it never happened, but the disease might have contributed to Mantle's being a slow healer.

1951 WORLD SERIES: This injury to Mantle's right knee (now neither leg was sound) was Mickey's first serious Yankee injury, and the one that laid the groundwork for all his subsequent knee troubles. He hooked his spikes on an outfield sprinkler cover, and it took five months for the knee to mend; it was never really right thereafter. Mantle was partly to blame because he didn't do his rehabilitation exercises, and the following spring he was unable, as planned, to immediately succeed the retired Joe DiMaggio in center field. Of more lasting consequence, Mickey had trouble rounding the bases and going back on balls hit directly over his head because he could run well only in a straight line. His knee forced him to become a tape artist, too.

AUGUST 1953: Both Mantle's legs had betrayed him all year. The capper came when Mickey, planting his right foot in making a throw, had his right knee buckle and ligaments tear. Sidelined for 10 days, he returned to play the rest of the year wearing a knee brace. But this was a *major* injury. And he made it worse by playing off-season basketball after undergoing an operation in November in which a piece of torn cartilage was removed. The postoperative activity produced a large fluid-filled cyst behind his right knee. Mickey had the cyst removed in February and limped to a slow start in 1954.

SEPTEMBER 1955: In beating out a bunt, Mantle severely tore a muscle in the back of his right thigh. He hardly played in the Yanks' last nine games, costing him a 100-RBI season (he had 99), and then he missed most of the World Series (won by Brooklyn). Not a long-term injury—just an ill-timed one to Mantle and the Yankees and the fortunes and legacy of both.

AUGUST 1957: Mantle's infamous shinsplints—a self-inflicted wound caused when he thrust his golf putter deep into his lower left leg—cost him a chance at winning a second consecutive Triple Crown, and he landed in the hospital for several days in September. The wonder is that his osteomyelitis didn't kick up from the trauma of such a deep gash.

1957 WORLD SERIES: The worst long-term injury of Mantle's career, other than the knee injuries, happened when Milwaukee's Red Schoendienst fell on Mickey's right shoulder in a play at second base. The Mick was of little use the rest of the series, the Yankees lost in seven games, and the shoulder never fully healed. He reported to camp in 1958, saying the shoulder felt okay, but his throws told another story and he soon had to admit the truth. He got off to a poor 1958 start, and the season ended with his left-handed batting average at .288, following a .342 lefty mark in 1957. This injury hampered Mantle's left-handed hitting the rest of his career, not to mention his throwing: In 1960 he hit .349 righty and .247 lefty, and in 1964, .424 righty and .241 lefty.

1959: A succession of bothersome ailments led to an unsatisfactory season. Mickey further damaged his right shoulder in making a throw, suffered a chipped bone in his right index finger when hit by a batting-practice pitch, caught the Asian flu, and hurt his right ankle—all before the season was even half over.

SEPTEMBER 1961: Mantle fell by the wayside in his home-run duel with Roger Maris because of a succession of last-month maladies. It started with a pulled muscle in his left arm and was followed by a virus and an abscess deep inside his hip, resulting in another trip to the hospital. Mickey made a brave but futile attempt to contribute in the World Series, which New York won in five games over Cincinnati.

MAY 1962: Mantle sustained the worst muscle pull of his career when he tried to beat out a grounder. He fell with a severely torn muscle high on the inside of his right thigh and suffered damage to his left knee when he hit the ground. It was more than a month before he could return to the starting lineup; without this injury, his 1962 statistics could have been among the best of his career.

JUNE 1963: An injury that cost Mantle more playing time than any other in one season was incurred when he ran into a chain-link fence in center field, breaking a bone in his left foot and doing cartilage and ligament damage to his left knee—his "good" knee. The broken foot kept Mantle out of the everyday lineup for three months; the knee injury meant another operation following the World Series. The knee still bothered Mickey in 1964 and he had to move out of center field. Now, neither of his knees was working the way knees are supposed to.

JUNE 1965: This Mantle hamstring tear required a three-week recovery period. By now, his hamstring and other leg muscles were chronically weakened. Mickey missed 40 games in 1965, mainly because of leg ailments.

NOVEMBER 1965: The right shoulder that in the last two months of 1965 pained Mantle so much that he could barely throw was further abused in a touch football game with his son and his brothers Roy and Ray. His shoulder was so badly wrenched that Mantle told Yankee general manager Ralph Houk it looked like he had reached the end of the line. Houk turned back the retirement talk and had Mickey go to the Mayo Clinic in January. There, in a four-hour operation, bone chips and calcium deposits were removed from his shoulder. One chip was sawing at tendons that had to be tied together. After five weeks at the Mayo Clinic, Mantle reported to spring training, although no one really knew whether he'd be able to throw a baseball. At first he couldn't rear back to throw; for the longest time he did little more than lob the ball. His left-handed hitting was slow to come around, too. He was discouraged, but he never gave up. Finally, four days before the season opened, though he couldn't throw a ball any harder than a 12-year-old, Mickey cracked the starting lineup. He was also in the lineup Opening Day, beating all the odds, and came through with a pair of hits—one a long double.

Though more injuries lay ahead, especially in 1966, Mantle miraculously got into 144 games in both 1967 and 1968, his final two years. By then, however, the cumulative effect of the hurts had badly deteriorated his skills.

The summary of Mantle injuries shows that, on occasion, Mickey did damage to himself off the field, whether playing basketball, golf, or touch football. The competitive urge, if you will, was often his own worst enemy. But he was a risk taker, especially on the baseball field. The only concession he made to the preservation of Mickey Mantle was in not diving for a ball hit to the outfield; he knew that one bad spill on his vulnerable knees could be a career ender.

Mantle was occasionally reckless off the field, staying out too late and more than once coming to the ballpark hung over. His drinking, by his own admission, probably shortened his career. Or at least hurt the quality of the career he did have.

Judging from Mantle's actions when he was in his twenties and thirties, he had a live-for-today attitude. After all, his father and his father's two brothers died of Hodgkin's disease before they were 40, leaving Mickey with the grim feeling that a short life might be in store for him as well. But was it true, as legend has it, that Mantle believed he wouldn't live to see 40? "That's been overplayed," he said late in his career. "I don't believe that at all."

The implication was that Mantle was obsessed with early death, a story that probably *was* overplayed. Death wasn't an obsession with Mickey; it was more like an awareness, an awareness hanging over him that was seldom verbalized. He might mention it as a joke, as when he told Yankee player representative Jerry Coleman not to worry about a pension plan for him because he wouldn't be around long enough to collect on it. Or blurt out something revealing to Joe Pepitone while under the influence of alcohol. Or tell Hank Bauer, who scolded him for arriving at the park hung over, "My father died young. I'm not going to be cheated."

His playing days long ended, Mickey Mantle, alive and well, has expressed some regret over the abuse to which he subjected his body. His story exemplifies that old lament, "If I had known I was going to live this long, I'd have taken better care of myself."

September 4, 1965—Yankee Stadium. The Yankees, losers of a doubleheader to Boston, 1–0 and 7–2, gave their fans another poor day. Mickey Mantle, who didn't play the opener, made the only Yankee noise—and the crowd delivered its loudest noise—when he unloaded his 19th home run in the second game.

Mickey, batting right-handed, hits a mighty drive into the opposite-field bleachers, a homer of at least 420 feet. With all the troubles he's had this year, Mantle, incredibly, is only eight homers behind the league leader, Willie Horton.

The victim of the Mantle homer, Dennis Bennett, who pitched in both major leagues, years later recalled this Mantle homer with admiration. "I remember I had worked the count to 3 and 2," he said. "I then threw a curveball, low and on the outside corner. I said to myself, Strike three. But the ball landed in the right-center-field bleachers. I wanted to call time and shake his hand; he had hit one of the best pitches I think I threw in the big leagues."

But this was Mantle's last home run of 1965. Mickey had been red-hot in the first 18 days of August, hitting .396 (21 for 53) and improving his average to a team high of .274. But after August 18 he batted an anemic .169 (11 for 65).

Some thought he would retire. He was given a Mickey Mantle Day at the Stadium on September 18, a farewell gesture in case he did decide to hang it up. A huge crowd turned out, Mantle played in his 2,000th Yankee game, and more than $32,000 was raised in Mantle's name and contributed for research in the fight against Hodgkin's disease.

1966

May 9, 1966—Metropolitan Stadium, Bloomington, Minnesota. Inspiring as it was, Mickey Mantle's readiness for the 1966 campaign, following major surgery on his right shoulder in January, was overshadowed by a miserable early season for the Yankees. When the won-lost record sank to 4–16, manager Johnny Keane was fired, and Ralph Houk stepped down as general manager to replace him. Of the Keane firing, Mantle said, "We let him down." Mickey made a personal apology.

But Mantle and Keane were never close. Mickey and his teammates were used to managers who didn't mind off-the-field shenanigans as long as a player's performance between the lines wasn't handicapped. Keane, however, was different from Casey Stengel, Houk, and Yogi Berra, his predecessors. He crusaded to save the souls of the wayward Yankees; the players collectively resisted salvation. Mantle, as was his nature, didn't make waves. He quietly did his job, but, like his teammates, he harbored a resentment toward Keane and his regimentation.

There were moments when Mantle bristled in anger over his treatment by Keane. Like the time in spring training when Keane, knowing Mickey had a hangover and eager to make an example of him in front of the team, tried to wear him out shagging fly balls. Once, okay, but when Keane pulled the same stunt again, a hard Mantle throw nearly decapitated the slight manager.

Keane should have been smart enough to realize that he would come in a very poor second in any popularity contest with Mantle. Joe McCarthy was faced with a similar situation with Babe Ruth when he became Yankee manager in 1931, only McCarthy had the good sense not to draw a line with the popular Ruth, to look the other way when Ruth wandered astray. Keane, a Bible Belter and by most accounts a nice enough guy, could be nastily unsubtle in humiliating Mantle. Or maybe he was just inept in his assessment of the slugger, like when he would have him taking 3-and-0 pitches.

Keane *did* move Mantle back to center field in 1966. But Mickey started slowly at the plate: He didn't drive in his first run of the year until his 10th game, and Keane was long gone when he got his next RBI.

With Houk back in the dugout, the Yankees rode a euphoric high. They won their first two games under Houk. Then, on this cold 43-degree night, they won again, beating the Twins, 3–2. Mantle nailed his first home run of the season over the left-center-field fence batting lefty against Jim Perry—it was the latest date of his career for his first homer, coming in New York's 23rd game. Roger Maris also homered (the first time M & M homered in the same game in over a year), and Joe Pepitone rifled a ninth-inning homer off the right-field foul pole for the victory margin.

The Yankees will keep rolling, winning 13 of their first 17 games under Houk. Then the roll will come to an end and more realistic times will prevail.

June 28, 1966—Fenway Park, Boston. The winning spree that began when Ralph Houk took over as manager was long a thing of the past, and the Yankees, beaten 5–3 by the last-place Red Sox, now found themselves with a 30–38 record. With first-place Baltimore 15½ games ahead, seventh-place New York was now hopelessly out of the pennant picture.

Boston right-hander Jose Santiago pitches a shutout except for the slugging of Mickey Mantle. The Mick knocks in all three Yankee runs with a first-inning two-run homer, a blast hit deep into the right-center-field bleachers, and an eighth-inning opposite-field homer stroked into the left-field screen. The crowd of 14,922 gives Mickey a standing ovation following the second blow.

Five Yankee errors lead to three gift runs, and, ultimately, to defeat.

June 29, 1966—Fenway Park, Boston. The resurgent Mickey Mantle again walloped two home runs and this time the Yankees beat the Red Sox, 6–5. Both Mantle homers were hit left-handed, like the two of the previous night. Both were at the expense of ex-Yankee Rollie Sheldon.

Tom Tresh and Bobby Richardson open the game with back-to-back singles. Then Mantle whacks Sheldon's first pitch into the screen in deep left-center.

Richardson, who goes 5 for 5, leads off the third with a home run. Mantle knocks out Sheldon by waiting just long enough on a change-up, then ripping it into the seats down the right-field line. Joe Pepitone, connecting against Lee Stange, makes it three homers in a row. It is the first time the Yankees have hit three successive homers since Charlie Keller, Joe DiMaggio, and Johnny Lindell did it in 1947.

With his homer in his last at bat the previous night, Mantle had hit three consecutive homers. The next time up, batting right-handed against Dick Stigman, Mickey disdained a chance for a record-tying fourth consecutive homer, going with an outside pitch instead and punching a single to right field.

The next day Mantle will go 0 for 2 and draw three walks from the smartened-up Red Sox, and Boston wins the rubber game of the series, 3–2. Then the Yankees head south to open a three-game set in the nation's capital.

July 1, 1966—D.C. Stadium, Washington. Mickey Mantle, as red-hot at the plate as he's ever been, led the Yankees to an 8–6 triumph over the Senators, thrilling an appreciative crowd of 16,104, who gave him three standing ovations.

Batting left-handed against Phil Ortega, Mantle opens the scoring with a first-inning solo homer that clears the scoreboard in right-center. Later Mickey singles and scores on Joe Pepitone's homer. Then he delivers an RBI-single, and in his final at bat, he draws a walk. He leaves the game in the sixth inning with his club leading, 8–2.

Mantle is having great results with a slight adjustment he made recently. Realizing that batting left-handed he was having trouble pulling fastballs and recognizing that right-handed pitchers were throwing the ball past him, Mickey swallowed his pride and began choking up on the bat an inch or two. At 34, he had become adaptable.

July 2, 1966—D.C. Stadium, Washington. It was another day of standing ovations for Mickey Mantle. He started the steamy afternoon slowly, hitting into a first-inning double play and then, in the third, sending center fielder Don Lock to the fence with a towering fly ball.

Washington is ahead, 3–2, with southpaw Mike McCormick on the hill and Mantle batting right-handed. Mickey is still getting around well from the right side and, with no need to choke up, is swinging from the end of the bat in his normal style. He precipitates a mild argument when he calls time as McCormick delivers his first pitch, but he is plenty ready on a 3-and-1 offering and pumps a 450-foot homer off the facing of the mezzanine in dead-center field, tying the score.

Mickey's buddy, Whitey Ford, is not enjoying the same success as the Mick. The Senators explode for seven runs in the bottom of the sixth with consecutive homers by Frank Howard, Lock, and Ken McMullen.

The winless Ford, in his first start since May 24 because of an elbow injury, said afterward that his elbow felt good; he just couldn't keep the ball low.

Mantle is often out of a game by the ninth inning, but since New York is behind by seven runs, Ralph Houk gives Mickey his final at bat in the ninth. Not wasting the opportunity, Mickey slices a full-count pitch off the scoreboard beyond the right-field fence. But McCormick finishes with a five-hitter and a 10–4 win, seven of the Senators' runs unearned.

In less than a week's time, Mantle has doubled his home-run output for the year, to 14. At first it was reported that his seven homers in five games tied a major-league record held by Babe Ruth, Jim Bottomley, and Vic Wertz. However, Mickey's streak does not qualify because he didn't homer in *each* of the five games; he was homerless in the final game at Boston.

July 3, 1966—D.C. Stadium, Washington. The Yankees and Senators scrapped in 100-degree heat, and once again it was a Mickey Mantle day. Joseph Durso in the *New York Times* observed that "the eyes, the attention, the cheers of the crowd . . . were for Mantle, as they had been in Boston last week," and that he was "lionized like a conquering hero in both cities." The heroics of Mantle had transcended hostile attitudes in two hotbeds of anti-Yankee sentiment.

Batting right-handed in the first inning, Mantle lines Pete Richert's first pitch into the opposite-field seats, the ball landing just inside the right-field foul pole, and the Yankees lead, 1–0. Since Mickey homered in his final two at bats yesterday, he has three straight homers for the second time within a week.

Mickey is retired in each of his final three at bats. He is replaced late in the game by Lu Clinton, which costs him an at bat because the Senators, down 5–0 in the eighth, rally to tie the game in the ninth on a three-run homer by light-hitting Eddie Brinkman.

Bobby Richardson hits an 11th-inning homer, giving the Yankees a 6–5 lead, and Pedro Ramos closes the door in the bottom half. But not before the Nats throw a scare into the Yanks on a weird play that goes something like this: Paul Casanova moves from first base to second on a Brinkman sacrifice bunt, but when he overruns the bag, he continues on to third, knocks the ball loose from the waiting Tom Tresh, and then dashes home, only to be thrown out at the plate—by a mile—by Ramos, who had been backing up third. "He was a wild man," third-base coach

Eddie Yost said of Casanova afterward. "The only way I could have stopped him was to have tackled him."

And so the Mantle homers had brought a touch of class to the now-concluded series, sloppily played by two lusterless second-division teams. Mickey was hitting homers at the greatest rate in American League history—he now had hit eight in six games—and, record or no record, it was the best power spree since Roger Maris hit seven homers in six games in 1961.

All the more remarkable were the circumstances in which Mantle was hitting the homers. Many thought he was washed up; certainly until this comeback, he had done nothing spectacular to prove the doubters wrong. Only five months ago he was a patient at the Mayo Clinic. When he reported to spring training, he threw the ball as though he had just decided to take up the game, and he grimaced in pain when he swung the bat left-handed.

So he had come a long way; his 15 homers put him within range of Frank Robinson, the league leader with 20.

Thanks to the six-game span in which he hit eight homers, made three singles, and drew five walks for an 11-for-20 streak, Mickey pulled his batting average up to a respectable .282, tops among Yankee regulars.

A temporary lull awaited Mantle on his return home. He will go 1 for 14 in the Yanks' first five games back at Yankee Stadium, and the Yanks will lose four of them.

July 7, 1966—Yankee Stadium. Rollie Sheldon had been pitching a great game for Boston. Then he was thrown out at the plate in the top of the ninth, and when he carried his 2–0 lead into the bottom half, it seemed like he had left something on the base paths. He walked the first two Yankees and was lifted in favor of Don McMahon. The Yankees soon tied the game on Jake Gibbs's pinch-hit RBI-single and Tom Tresh's sacrifice fly.

Now there are two out and two on and Mickey Mantle at the plate batting left-handed. Mantle hammers a 2-and-1 inside fastball into the lower deck in right field. The three-run liner breaks a 1-for-17 slump for Mantle and gives New York a stunning 5–2 victory.

"I knew he'd come through for us," said manager Ralph Houk afterward. "Give me Mick in the clutch any time."

July 8, 1966—Yankee Stadium. Mickey Mantle hit two huge home runs in a doubleheader against Washington, giving him 11 homers in 14 games. The Mick had a big day all around, going 5 for 8, including a bunt single, a rarity for him these days, and making a great catch to rob Fred Valentine of an extra-base hit. Then, one of the greatest streaks of Mickey's career came to a screeching halt as he tore a muscle in his left leg.

In the opener, batting left-handed, Mantle belts a long opposite-field homer off Dick Bosman. With right-hander Ron Kline pitching for Washington, leading 7–6 in the ninth, and with two down and Bobby Richardson on base, Mantle, bringing gasps from the crowd and scaring the hell out of the Senators, sends a 400-foot-plus drive to left-center that is grabbed by center fielder Don Lock for the game's final out.

The Yankees overcome an early 4–0 deficit to win the nightcap, 7–5, with Ray Barker's two-run single putting them ahead for good. The highlight, however, was a tremendous Mantle homer, struck batting lefty against Jim Hannan; the ball landed in the center-field bleachers for his third and least famous shot to this area. "Mickey skied it almost straightaway over the monuments, just to the left of the 461-foot sign," Hannan recalled some 20 years later. "They replayed it on TV about eight times. It looked like it took one hop to the back wall."

Mantle gets his third consecutive hit of the second game in the fifth inning, popping one down the left-field line that neither left fielder Frank Howard nor shortstop Eddie Brinkman can reach. It's a sure extra-base hit, but Mickey winces as he rounds first base and has to retreat. "He could have made third easily," Washington manager Gil Hodges said afterward. "When I saw him on first I thought this is our lucky day."

It wasn't Mantle's lucky day. He had torn a hamstring muscle in his left thigh. He limped off the field, and it will be 10 days before Mickey is able to pinch-hit and 12 days before he's back in the starting lineup.

Mantle sat at his locker cubicle and slowly began unwinding his leg bandages. Disgusted, he threw a bandage across the room and pounded his fist into his palm. "Why is it," he asked the gathered reporters, "this happens every time things are going well?"

No one could say why the injury jinx had struck again. Mickey touched his hamstring. "This will take two weeks, I imagine, from the way they've reacted before," he explained (and he was right, too). "It's not sore yet, but it'll be very sore tomorrow."

To add insult to injury, Mantle on this date was snubbed by Sam Mele, the American League's All-Star manager, who passed Mickey over in filling out his roster. In fact, Mele somehow passed over both Mantle, the league's hottest hitter and biggest name, and Boog Powell, tied for the league lead in RBIs. It was the only year between 1952 and 1968 that Mantle wasn't an All-Star. Mele could have used the two sluggers; the Americans will lose, 2–1, in 10 innings.

August 26, 1966—Yankee Stadium. "Throw away the script, fellas, you can't beat Mt. Olympus," is the way George Cantor led off his game story in the *Detroit Free Press*. "Mickey Mantle, last of the genuine thunderbolts, limped off the bench to crash a two-run ninth-inning homer and crush the Tigers."

Up until Mantle's last-minute heroics, it looks like Detroit starting pitcher Earl Wilson will be the game's star with his seventh straight win. When Wilson pokes a long eighth-inning homer into the left-field upper deck, giving Detroit two runs and a 5–3 lead, the Tigers appear to be in good shape. And Wilson's relief, Hank Aguirre, pitches a scoreless frame in the bottom of the eighth.

Aguirre is still pitching in the ninth. Elston Howard starts things off with a double. As Clete Boyer steps in, a great cheer goes up. The crowd is excited because Mantle, who hasn't played in 11 days after yet another pulled leg muscle, has stepped into the on-deck circle.

Boyer rifles an RBI-single, making it 5–4, and the crowd rises as one to greet Mantle, who is hitting for pitcher Hal Reniff. Mickey, batting right-handed, swings and misses Aguirre's first pitch. Groans. But he connects on the second pitch and sends a drive on a high arc toward the lower right-field seats. Right fielder Al Kaline goes to the barrier, leaps desperately, but comes down empty as the ball clears his glove by several feet. Mickey's fifth career pinch-hit homer wins the game, 6–5, and the fans go nuts as he circles the bases.

Yankee fans haven't had much to cheer about lately. Since the day Mantle was injured in Detroit, the Yanks have been playing .300 baseball. At day's end, eighth-place New York (57–72) is 26 games behind first-place Baltimore (82–45).

And things got worse still. The Yankees struggled through an 8–15 September and finished dead last, at 70–89, 26½ games behind the league champions, the Orioles. Mantle, who had hit .333 (24 for 72), with 10 homers, in July, slipped to .309 (17 for 55), with two homers, in August. After this date, he did not hit another homer; he drove in only one run and scored only two. The problem was that Mantle hardly played—he got only 18 at bats after this date—because of injuries to his legs, his right big toe, a finger that was jammed, and a hand that was wrenched, the latter making it impossible for him to grip the bat.

So a season that had begun with Mantle's unexpected return, reason enough for celebration, and peaked with his torrid home-run spell in midseason, ended on a downer. Yet, while Mickey played in only 108 games and got only 333 at bats in 1966, when he played, he played remarkably well. His limited playing time hurt his accumulated stats, like homers (23), RBIs (56), and runs (40), the last also hurt by the fact that he often left for a pinch-runner and didn't get credit for the run that he set up, but he did very well in the percentages.

Though Mantle didn't play enough to qualify for any percentage titles, he did accomplish the following:

- Hit .288, easily the best on the Yankees among those players batting at least 100 times; it was 53 points higher than the team's average.
- Slugged at a .538 clip, the level of Harmon Killebrew, who finished second in the league in slugging average.
- Hit homers at a 6.9 home-run percentage, identical to the percentages of Killebrew and Boog Powell, who finished second and third in homers, with 39 and 34, respectively.
- Played in 97 games in the outfield without making a single error for a perfect fielding percentage of 1.000.

All things considered, Mantle had a very good 1966 season. Still, it would not have shocked anyone if Mickey had decided to hang it up. Since his decline in 1965, however, three baseball goals had kept him playing and though one, winning the MVP Award for the fourth time, seemed out of range, the other two were getting close: He wanted to hit 500 homers and he wanted to pass Lou Gehrig and play more games than anyone in a Yankee uniform—big factors in his decision to come back in 1967. Another factor was Ralph Houk's plan to shift Mickey to first base to save wear and tear on his fragile legs.

1967

April 29, 1967—Yankee Stadium. Mickey Mantle was doing fine as a first baseman; he was errorless in 10 games at his new position (he missed three games after pulling a hamstring on Opening Day).

Perhaps it was because he was concentrating on his fielding that he was not hitting with his accustomed power. He came into this date's game against the Angels, on a beautiful, sunny day with temperatures in the 60s, still looking for his first extra-base hit of 1967.

The Yankees and Angels are in a 1–1 tie in the bottom of the third inning, with two out, Fred Talbot on first base, and Mantle batting left-handed against veteran Jack Sanford. Mickey connects, sending a towering blast into a good breeze. The ball still manages to go way beyond the 407-foot sign in right-center. The Yanks are up, 3–1, and the fans continue cheering long after Mickey is settled in the dugout. "People are happy to see me hit a home run because they're always afraid it might be my last," he said later.

Mantle adds a run-scoring single (Ray Barker replaces him at first base late in the game), Talbot tames California on two hits, and the Yankees have a 5–2 victory. For the moment, the Yankees and Red Sox are tied for first place with matching 8-5 records.

"It's good to see the Big Guy get going," manager Ralph Houk said afterward. "He's fielding at first base better than we ever expected. Now that he's hitting, he could pick up the club. He's still the leader."

DEFENSIVELY SPEAKING

Ralph Houk, desperate to keep Mickey in his everyday lineup, yet recognizing that Mantle was no longer an everyday outfielder, decided that he would play the Mick at first base in 1967. "I've never played first base before," said Mantle in December 1966, "but I'll do anything to help."

The official announcement was made late in January, when Mantle signed his 1967 contract. The plan was for Mantle and incumbent first

232

baseman Joe Pepitone, a player uniquely gifted at either first or center, to exchange positions. Mickey would no longer have to make those long outfield runs that imposed so great a toll on his legs. The Yanks would gain a great hitter at first and, on paper, at least, a tremendous defensive outfield made up of Tom Tresh in left, Pepitone, and Bill Robinson, who had a great gun.

Ironically, first base was the only position Mantle had never before played. His defensive background was as follows.

CATCHER: Mickey was a catcher when he began playing peewee ball at the age of 10. He was, after all, named after Mickey Cochrane, one of the greatest catchers of all time.

SECOND BASEMAN: A smart coach saw that the 11-year-old Mickey's great speed was being wasted behind the plate and moved him to second.

PITCHER: When he wasn't playing in the infield for Commerce High School, Mickey pitched, although he never considered pitching as a career—he wanted to play every day. With the Yankees, Mickey perfected a knuckleball that was said to flutter so outrageously that even Yogi Berra couldn't handle it. Mickey loved to horse around with the knuckler, springing it on unsuspecting newcomers in a friendly game of catch. Jake Gibbs picked up a broken nose trying to catch a Mantle knuckler.

SHORTSTOP: In 1948, Mickey, 16, was tacked to the shortstop position by Barney Barnett, his semipro coach, in order to take better advantage of his strong arm. He broke into pro ball as a shortstop the following year. The problem was that his arm was undisciplined and his hands weren't quick enough to adjust to bad hops.

RIGHT FIELDER: Casey Stengel moved Mantle to right field in 1951 because he wanted the rookie's bat in the lineup and there wasn't a ghost of a chance of the kid's unseating Phil Rizzuto at shortstop.

CENTER FIELDER: Mickey, overcoming a bad knee, finally replaced the retired Joe DiMaggio in center late in the spring of 1952. And he became a fixture.

THIRD BASEMAN: Mickey was suddenly thrust into a 1952 game at third in a hare-brained Stengel scheme and made two errors in four chances. The display may have dissuaded Casey from carrying out a plan to install Mickey permanently at third in order to lessen the strain on the Mick's bad knee. In any case, Mickey never again played at third base.

LEFT FIELDER: In the latter part of 1964 Mickey was forced from center to left field because of his ailing legs. Johnny Keane continued to play him in left in 1965. But playing left field in the old Yankee Stadium was no picnic! It was the toughest "sun field" in the majors; the circular wall made a hit the left fielder was trying to retrieve do some unpredictable things; and it was huge, resulting in a lot of ground needing to be covered.

So in 1967 Mantle was back in the same learning mode that he was in as a rookie 16 years earlier. He was learning a new position under an instructional program that began with spring training. He would do well to learn his lessons as thoroughly as he did in becoming an outstanding out fielder.

And learning to play the outfield wasn't easy. He had to get the feel of getting a good jump on a ball, to judge fly balls, and to deal with the drives hit right at him. Picking out balls was no easy task at Yankee Stadium, with its smoky daytime haze and murky late-afternoon shadows (and from Mickey's perspective in center it was even tougher, with the pitcher's mound cutting off the batter and making the ball seemingly rise out of the ground). He learned to open it up in the outfield, run like hell, throw all out—be a factor. To take advantage of all his physical assets.

Mickey mastered it all. If he did misjudge a fly ball, he usually ran it down with his blazing speed. But he didn't misjudge many.

Mantle harnessed all the strength in his powerful throwing arm and made low, crisp, accurate throws, whether to the cutoff man or to the proper base. He also developed a trick or two, such as throwing *behind* a base runner to catch him napping. When his legs were sound, he covered great gobs of ground.

Tris Speaker was considered the all-time premier defensive center fielder, the top of the line, the standard by which to judge center fielders. Speaker, who played from 1907 to 1928, was a contemporary of Stengel, establishing his reputation in the dead-ball era that ended in the early 1920s. "They say Tris Speaker used to outrun the ball, which I guess he did," Casey said early in Mantle's career. "But Speaker was outrunning the dead ball. This kid Mantle outruns the live ball."

Stengel made sense, and what he said about Mantle could be applied to other great fly chasers since Speaker's time, players such as Joe DiMaggio, Willie Mays, Jimmy Piersall, and Paul Blair. These players had it tougher than Speaker; they were trying to catch up with a more spirited sphere that traveled to its destination much quicker than the old dead ball. The lively ball may have helped hitters, but it made playing center field more difficult than in Speaker's heyday.

Mantle could, and did, make the spectacular play. He once teamed up with right fielder Hank Bauer in a stunning catch. It was at Yankee Stadium in 1958, and a drive split Mantle and Bauer and headed toward the auxiliary scoreboard. Bauer couldn't quite reach the ball with his gloved hand but did bat it in the air, keeping it alive and allowing Mantle to race under it and make the catch for the out.

His power and speed overshadowed his fielding, but Mantle was indeed a great center fielder. Now, in 1967, his lack of mobility—he could move well sideways but that was all—forced him out of the outfield. If there had been a designated hitter in 1967 (the DH didn't come along until six years later), Mantle would have been perfectly suited for the job and would probably have played a few more years. (What better argument for the DH than the Mantle example, giving an aging lion a chance to play a little longer. The other argument—that a player should have to field a position, be a complete player—somehow seems trivial when given the Mantle test.) Ralph Houk had to find a position for Mantle. First base was the only choice. Maybe Mantle's only chance to keep playing.

There were skeptics galore. Still fresh in some observers' memories was the distasteful experience that Joe DiMaggio suffered late in his career when Stengel suddenly played Joe at first one day, making the Yankee Clipper never more ill at ease on a ball field. Other aging sluggers had been moved to first in the past, and with the exception of Tommy Henrich, who adapted to the position marvelously, few distinguished themselves around the bag. Some sportswriters even felt that playing first, given all the sudden starts and stops, would be just as taxing on Mantle's legs as playing the outfield. Others said he would be seriously hurt if, for instance, a bad throw were to take him into the path of a speeding runner.

Mantle refused to be intimidated or swayed in his willingness to give first base a try. And Houk was willing to move Mantle back to center field if the experiment fizzled, although Houk was convinced that the reduced running demands of the first-base position would make Mickey's legs stronger and allow him to play more.

Outfielder Mantle's conversion to first baseman was baseball's biggest story in the spring training of 1967. It was 1951 all over again for Mantle—another crash course learning to play a new position. He had to learn how to cover the bag and handle throws, how to play bunts, when to cut off throws—the whole nine yards. Essentially, the 35-year-old superstar was a rookie again, and he had to eliminate rookie mistakes. Joe Pepitone helped him with his footwork around the bag and called Mickey "a natural." "I wasn't great, just adequate," admitted Mantle. True. He was adequate in 1967. He improved only through hard work and played the position better in 1968.

But he accomplished what many felt he wouldn't be able to: He played first base and he played it for a whole season. When the 1967 campaign ended, Mickey had a right to feel self-satisfied, even if he would have liked to be a better first baseman. He made eight errors, but five American League first basemen made more. "First base still has some problems," Mickey said, "like bunts and pop fouls. I have trouble getting to them with these knees of mine. But last spring training I had doubts about playing first base. Now I've done it."

April 30, 1967—Yankee Stadium. A second big day in a row for Mickey Mantle, who doubled and homered in the first game of a doubleheader and got a pinch-hit double in the second game. He finished the day with 2,215 hits, one more than Joe DiMaggio, and now only Lou Gehrig and Babe Ruth were ahead of him on the Yankees' list of all-time most hits. The Cap Day crowd of 47,980 spent most of the day cheering Mickey.

The opener is 1–1 in the bottom of the 10th. California starter George Brunet gets the first out. Then Dick Howser beats out a bunt and Tom Tresh singles. Angel manager Bill Rigney brings in right-hander Minnie Rojas, who goes 1 and 1 to Mantle. Mickey then parks the third pitch into the right-field third deck for a game-winning three-run homer. Mickey, who had jarred himself in a slide two innings earlier, trots around the bases to a great ovation, a big grin on his face—and heads straight to the clubhouse for a whirlpool bath.

California leads in the second game, 4–2, when Mantle delivers his ninth-inning pinch-hit double to pass DiMaggio in total hits. Mickey leaves for pinch-runner Ruben Amaro, who is stranded. The 4–2 defeat knocks the Yankees (9–6) out of first place, half a game behind Detroit (10–6).

May 14, 1967—Yankee Stadium. A player to hit 500 home runs in a major-league career would have to average 30 homers per season and be in his 17th season on the occasion of his 500th homer. Mickey Mantle, playing his 17th season, came into this date with 499 career homers. Five hundred home runs would put him in an exclusive club with only five other members: Babe Ruth (714 homers), Willie Mays (546, still active), Jimmie Foxx (534), Ted Williams (521), and Mel Ott (511). Ever since Mickey hit No. 499, the fans have been screaming for No. 500. No. 499 was hit 11 days ago and the fans were impatient and Mickey was pressing and the Yankees were playing poorly.

A crowd of 18,872 turns out on a dreary, overcast day. The Baltimore Orioles are the stagehands in the Mantle drama. In the first inning, batting against Steve Barber, Mickey sends a potential double-play grounder to third baseman Brooks Robinson, but the hard shot handcuffs Robinson for an error, a key play in a three-run rally. Against Wally Bunker, Mickey singles in the third and fouls out in the fifth.

He is still looking for No. 500 as he bats in the seventh. Joe Pepitone has hit a two-run pinch-hit homer, his first homer of the year, giving New York a 5–4 lead. Even Mark Belanger has homered, the *first of his career.* But Mickey is still looking. He can't like whom he sees on the mound; it is Stu Miller, a slow-balling junk artist, off whom Mantle has never hit a regular-season homer and off whom, Mickey recalls later, he can't even remember getting a single.

So, with two out and none on in the bottom of the seventh, with New York ahead, 5–4, it is Mantle against Miller. Mickey takes a ball, a called strike, two more balls, swings and misses to run the count full, and fouls off a pitch. But the next pitch he catches, pulling a line drive deep into the lower right-field stands. Home run No. 500. Mickey circles the bases, as usual, with his head down. As he approaches third base, Robinson tells him, "Nice going." Third-base coach Frank Crosetti rarely shakes hands on a homer, but he breaks tradition and pumps Mickey's hand. Mickey crosses the plate, shakes hands with Elston Howard, the bat boy, and Tom Tresh and, escorted by police, walks into the dugout. "He was pale as a ghost," said Whitey Ford later.

The crowd is still standing and cheering through Howard's turn at bat and chanting, "We want Mickey!" But Mickey, never a hot dog, stays inside the dugout. The crowd is still cheering when Mickey takes his position in the top of the eighth. There will be plenty of time for celebration and interviews later, but first there is a game to finish and, unfortunately, Mantle is "in a fog," as he says later.

The Orioles in the eighth put runners on first and second with one out. Brooks Robinson bounces to shortstop, a potential double play, but Mantle drops the relay from second baseman Horace Clarke. Frank Robinson stops at third, and Mickey, anticipating more daring from the fleet Robinson, picks up the ball and fires it home—wildly. Frank jogs home on the Mantle error (no error was charged on the dropped throw), and the Yankee lead is cut to 6–5.

What could have been an embarrassing situation if the Yankees had lost is remedied by Dooley Womack, who retires the final four Orioles in order for the win in relief, a victory that because of Mantle's 500th homer, said Womack over a decade later, was his greatest moment as a Yankee.

No. 500 had come just the way Mickey had wanted it to; all week he had been saying No. 500 wouldn't mean anything to him if it didn't help the Yankees win a game.

The home-run ball was retrieved by 18-year-old Louis DeFillippo of Mount Vernon, New York, who presented the ball to Mantle outside the Yankee clubhouse in exchange for a season pass and some Mantle souvenirs. DeFillippo said he had moved from center field to first base in amateur ball after Mantle made the switch.

Mantle got to keep the 500th ball, but the bat Mickey used went to the Baseball Hall of Fame. Actually, the bat belonged to Pepitone. Mickey was always switching around and this time used Pepitone's bat. Joe kidded about wanting his light 30-ouncer returned.

"I wasn't really tense about hitting it, but about everybody writing about it," Mantle told broadcaster Phil Rizzuto on TV after the game. "We weren't doing well and everywhere you'd see 'when is Mantle going to hit 500' instead of about the team winning or losing. Now maybe we can get back to getting straightened out."

Mantle himself *did* get straightened out, hitting eight home runs in a span of 13 games. But the Yankees (12–13), tied for fifth place and six games out of first, were headed for oblivion; their initial early spurt proved short-lived and out of character.

Mantle didn't really know what kind of pitch Miller had thrown. "I think he took a little off his change-up," he joked to reporters. But Miller said he threw a good pitch, a change-up down and away. "I'm embarrassed I threw a homer," Miller said. "If he had let it go by, it would have been a ball, I'm sure of that. It was definitely outside. . . . I know it was low." Years later Miller said that "the pitch that Mantle hit was my best pitch" and that "Mantle knew I was going to throw that pitch. That was the only home run Mantle hit off me in five years."

Two days after hitting No. 500, Mantle was honored at Yankee Stadium in pregame ceremonies on "500 Night." In the bottom of the 11th inning, Mickey's bases-loaded single beat Cleveland, 4–3. Thus concluded a three-day celebration, easily the season's highlight.

June 5, 1967—Yankee Stadium. A strange game, won by the replacement of the recently retired Whitey Ford, Thad Tillotson. In his second big-league start, Tillotson won, 4–2, on a six-hitter. The two Senator runs scored on a weird 200-foot inside-the-park homer by Bronxite Mike Epstein, whose looper down the left-field line escaped into the corner untouched. It was the strapping Epstein's first game for the Senators, who doubtless had in mind a little more long ball than 200 feet.

The score is 2–2 when Mickey Mantle leads off the Yanks' eighth. Mickey, having gone 0 for 3, is batting righty against southpaw Darold Knowles. Mickey takes a golf swing at the second pitch and slices it into the lower right-field stands. It is the first homer of the season allowed by Knowles.

Knowles, a very able reliever, years later would remember he "had just lost two games in three days at Baltimore," and he "was not going to let Mickey beat me. I threw a sinker a foot outside and ankle-high, and he swung. I remember saying to myself, Thanks, Mick, for chasing one. I thought it was a little fly ball to right, but it went deep in the right-field stands for No. 508 and my third loss in four days."

June 24, 1967—Yankee Stadium. Mickey Mantle used to hit home runs to help keep the Yankees in first place. Now he was hitting homers to keep them out of last place. Without a 4–3 win over Detroit on this date, the ninth-place Yankees (30–35) would have fallen below Washington (31–38). New York will finish in ninth place, with a record of 72–90.

Fred Gladding, owner of a 1.49 ERA, takes over the Detroit pitching in the bottom of the ninth with the score tied 3–3. Mantle leads off batting left-handed. The count goes to 2 and 1 and the Mick turns the next pitch around, sending a beaut about halfway into the right-center-field bleachers, a drive of at least 440 feet. His 14th homer of the year is his eighth game-winning hit—seven on home runs. And it is a big defeat for second-place Detroit; tomorrow the Yankees will beat the Tigers again, completing a three-game sweep.

Mantle, hitting only .239 on the season, has been having an up and down season. He batted only .207 (18 for 87) in May, but he hit nine homers, including his memorable 500th. He will hit .264 (19 for 72) in June, but collect only three homers. Earlier in the month he reached another milestone, breaking Lou Gehrig's record for most games played by a Yankee, thus realizing his final realistic baseball goal.

July 25, 1967—Yankee Stadium. Jim Kaat will pitch in the major leagues for four decades (the 1950s, 1960s, 1970s, and 1980s), winning a total of 283 games. The outstanding southpaw won 25 games in 1966, his best season, and this year will claim another 16. In his career he will be touched by seven Mickey Mantle home runs, but to him the one on this date stands out most clearly.

Recalls Kaat: "I'm leading 1–0 with two out in the ninth inning and no one on base. On a 3-and-1 count, I tried to throw an inside fastball and Mickey hit it over the 457-foot sign to tie the game. The game was rained out with the score 1–1. It was replayed later and we lost, 1–0. We lost the pennant in 1967 by one game."

The "we" were the Minnesota Twins, who will indeed fall one game short of the league champions, the Red Sox.

This is a great pitching duel between Kaat and Al Downing. Minnesota's Harmon Killebrew, the league leader in home runs, hits No. 29 in the first inning to give the Twins a 1–0 lead. There is no more scoring until the bottom of the ninth.

The weather has been threatening all evening. In fact, a brief but heavy downpour has delayed the start of the game, besides flooding the outfield and dugouts. Now, with two out in the ninth and Mantle, 0 for 3 so far, up, another storm is moving into the Bronx, and lightning is flickering across the sky. Billy Martin, coaching for the Twins, runs out to talk with Kaat, only one out away from a shutout. The umpires break up the meeting, anxious to finish the game before the rains hit. And it starts to drizzle.

On the 3-and-1 pitch, Mantle blasts the ball into the left-center-field bleachers, his fourth and final shot to this distant area, for a game-tying 460-foot-plus homer.

Soon thereafter a heavy rain begins falling and the infield is covered. Twelve minutes later the tarpaulin is removed when the storm stops. Then it begins raining again, and the infield is covered again. Finally, at 11 P.M., with the rain still falling, the umpires call the game. However, all individual records count. The game will be replayed as part of an August 18 doubleheader, and, again, the Yankees will win, 1–0.

The Yankees were really suffering from a power shortage. The club had hit only 62 home runs, and of these, Mantle had 19. And Mickey will hit only three more homers the rest of the year.

September 2, 1967—Yankee Stadium. New York beat Washington, 2–1, in only one hour and 51 minutes. The game started at 7 P.M. and the fans were out of there before 9. Mel Stottlemyre, who allowed only six hits and walked none, threw only 90 pitches. If you dozed off for a moment after a hard day at the shop, you missed this one.

Washington's Bob Priddy has a two-hit shutout through seven innings and takes a 1–0 lead into the bottom of the eighth. Bill Robinson leads off with a single, and with one out, Mickey Mantle bats for Ruben Amaro. Mickey takes two balls, swings and misses, takes strike two looking, and watches ball three. Full count. Priddy throws a fastball, outside the plate, and Mantle, widening the strike zone as he must, flicks his wrists and pulls the ball deep into the lower right-field seats, the ball bending around the foul pole, the two-run homer fair by about 10 feet.

This is the kind of moment that the Stadium crowd is paying to see. The crowd numbers only 8,645 but they make a lot of noise when Mantle trots around the bases.

Mickey was not in the starting lineup because of a jammed knee, suffered in the opening game of this home stand five days earlier. He took batting practice this evening but favored his right knee and was scratched. Then came his pinch-hit, his 14th game-winning hit of the season— eight by homers. This amid speculation that he may be retiring to become a broadcaster.

Mantle in the next Yankee game will hit his final 1967 homer. He will add one more game-winning hit. Told later that he had 15 game-winning hits in 1967, Mickey cracked, "I didn't think we won that many games."

He finished with 22 homers, the only Yankee to top the 20-mark. His 55 RBIs placed him second behind Joe Pepitone, who had 64. His .245 average was well ahead of the team average of .225. The American

League as a whole hit .236, so Mantle actually hit better than the average American Leaguer by nine points.

Perhaps the most amazing stat for Mantle in 1967 was his club leadership in games played. Gimpy legs and all, he got into 144 games, more than any other pinstriper.

1968

May 6, 1968—Yankee Stadium. Mickey Mantle was batting only .232, but against Cleveland on this date he banged his 522nd homer, breaking a tie with Ted Williams and putting him alone in fourth place on the all-time homer list.

Roy White singles with one out in the first inning. Then Mantle, batting righty against Sam McDowell, slices the home run beyond outfielder Leon Wagner and into the lower deck in right, and the Yankees have a 2–0 lead. The ball will be going to the Baseball Hall of Fame.

McDowell settled down and didn't permit another run. He struck out 14 Yankees (Mantle once), giving him 30 strikeouts over two straight outings to break Bob Feller's 1938 American League record of 28 strikeouts in back-to-back games. McDowell also got the game's biggest hit, a two-run single, and he held on for a 3–2 victory when he escaped a bases-loaded, one-out jam in the ninth inning.

McDowell, who five times led the American League in strikeouts, recently recalled the two homers Mantle hit off him. The one on this date "was a change-up in which I *knew* that I had him fooled. Yet, he hit it out to the opposite field. To this day that still astonishes me!

"I have pitched against many of the 'greats'—players like Mays, McCovey, Aaron, Stargell, Clemente, Kaline, and on and on—and to me there was no greater player than Mantle. I concentrated and bore down on him more than any player in baseball. I personally believe every pitcher did, and this is why his accomplishments are so astounding.

"What I remember most about my pitches to Mantle that he hit out of the park was the fact that neither pitch was a mistake. This is quite significant, as many real good players will hit your mistakes and not too many can hit the perfect pitches. In fact, I can only remember one other time I threw a pitch where I wanted it and a player hit it out. That was hit by Kaline."

May 30, 1968—Yankee Stadium. Mickey Mantle, going 5 for 5 with three runs and five RBIs in the first game of a doubleheader, injected some drama into an otherwise humdrum holiday split between the Yankees and Senators. Leonard Koppett in the *New York Times* saw Mantle as "a fading star flared up to peak luminosity for one game."

In the first inning of the opener, following a Roy White walk, Mantle faces right-hander Joe Coleman, who recently struck him out four straight times. Not this time though. The Mick rockets a tremendous two-run home run that lands in the top tier in right field. The next time Mantle faces Coleman, in the third, he singles and scores on Joe Pepitone's double, dashing all the way home from first base.

Mantle leads off the fifth with a homer off right-hander Bob Humphreys, a journeyman relief pitcher. "It was a slider that didn't do anything," Humphreys said years later. "He really didn't hit it very well. It was kind of a high fly ball that fell into the lower stands in right field." Mantle bats against Humphreys a second time in the sixth and smokes a hard grounder past first base for a run-producing double.

The crowd is on its feet urging Mantle to get his fifth straight hit when he steps in against right-hander Jim Hannan in the eighth. Mickey comes through, drilling a run-scoring single over the shortstop's head. He leaves for a pinch-runner amid a roaring tribute from the 28,197 paid.

It could be said that this was Mantle's most productive game. It was Mickey's fourth, and final, five-hit game and his third 5-for-5 game. The three 5-for-5 efforts:

● July 9, 1955: 1 double and 4 singles
● May 24, 1956: 1 homer, 4 singles and 1 walk
● May 30, 1968: 2 homers, 1 double and 2 singles

Mantle began the day batting only .223, but his 5-for-5 effort boosted his batting average 31 points, to .254. The Senators this season must have thought they were seeing a young Mantle. Mickey will hit .455 (20 for 44) against Washington and draw 13 walks, and the Yankees will make the Nats their biggest patsies, going 14–4 against them. They beat them in the first game of this doubleheader, 13–4.

Mantle sat out the afterpiece, won by Washington, 6–2. Mickey was in the on-deck circle with two out in the ninth, with intentions of pinch-hitting, and what was left of the crowd pleaded for Gene Michael to keep things alive and give Mickey another at bat. Alas, Michael struck out, ending the game.

Afterward, Yankee manager Ralph Houk agreed that it was a shame Mantle didn't play in the second game. However, Houk explained, he and Mantle had an agreement that Mickey doesn't start the second game of doubleheaders or a day game after a night game. Houk was asked why he didn't lift Mantle early in the first game, when the Yankees had a big lead, and save him for the second game. "It doesn't work out that way," Houk said. "He can play through a long game and be okay, but if he is taken out and rested an hour or more, then he stiffens up."

The big Mantle performance upstaged the league's hottest hitter, Frank Howard of the Senators, the leader in all three Triple Crown categories. Big Hondo came into the twinbill with 19 homers—15 this month—but he failed to clear the fences in a 1-for-9 day. He did hit five fly-ball outs—two going very deep—but Death Valley gobbled them up, proving once again that Yankee Stadium is murder for right-handed power hitters.

June 7, 1968—Yankee Stadium. New York, in eighth place (24–30) and a distant 10½ games behind the first-place Tigers (34–19), split a doubleheader with California. Mickey Mantle didn't play in the opener, but in the nightcap, won by the Angels, 8–4, he hit a first-inning two-run homer, his seventh of the year, and made a thrilling defensive play.

The defensive play went like this. Jim Fregosi is on third base and Roger Repoz is on first with nobody out in the eighth inning. Don Mincher bounces to Mantle, wide of first base, and Mickey, who starts to throw home, sees that Fregosi has stopped down the line. Mickey runs right at Fregosi, who is forced to retreat toward third. Mickey makes the perfect play. He chases Fregosi just the right amount and then gives the ball to third baseman Bobby Cox, who tags the runner out going home. The alert Mantle continues on to third base and accepts a return throw from Cox. He tags out Repoz, sliding in for a spectacular double play.

The next day's game was cancelled because New York City was observing a memorial for the slain New York senator Robert F. Kennedy.

June 29, 1968—Yankee Stadium. Mickey Mantle was fading and Reggie Jackson of the Oakland A's was coming on. Both homered in the first game of a doubleheader, won by the A's, 5–2, Mantle tying the score at 2–2 in the sixth with a two-run homer, his 11th of the year and No. 529 of his career, and Jackson breaking the tie in the eighth with a 425-foot shot, his ninth homer of the year and No. 10 of his career. Jackson will go ahead of Mantle later in the season and finish with 29 homers; 18 years later he will surpass Mickey in career homers, too.

Mickey will not hit another home run until he hits two on August 10, a long dry spell, and five days later he and Jackson will hit homers in the same game again. Mantle, a much better all-around player than Jackson, nonetheless shared similarities with Reggie. Both were strong, both unleashed huge cuts at the plate, and both hit the ball great distances.

Mickey doesn't start the second game. Oakland leads, 4–3, in the eighth when Tom Tresh triples and Andy Kosco walks. Mickey comes to the plate as a pinch-hitter for Charley Smith and receives the obligatory standing ovation, and Oakland pitching coach Bill Posedel goes out to the mound for a chat with right-hander Diego Segui. Mantle takes a ball and then connects, sending a solid drive that heads straight for the monuments in deepest center field. The ball lands about 10 feet in front of the monuments and Mantle limps into second base with a two-run double. He rubs his aching left leg and departs in favor of pinch-runner Gene Michael, the crowd of nearly 25,000 standing and cheering, savoring one of the last great Mantle moments at the Stadium. The Yankees hang on to win, 5–4.

The Yankees (32–39) are in eighth place and 14½ games behind the first-place Tigers (48–26). They are out of contention, but they will play decent ball in the season's second half and finish fifth (83–79).

Mantle will limp home with a season's average of .237. As dismal as that seems, it was still seven points above the league average. The final few months were a countdown to the inevitable end of Mantle's career. Although no announcement to this effect was made, it was becoming obvious that this will be Mantle's last campaign.

Mantle did put two pretty good stats on the board for a player in his last season. He led the Yankees with 18 homers. In the history of the game only four players had hit more in their final seasons: Ted Williams, with 29 in 1960; Hank Greenberg, 25 in 1947; Roy Cullenbine, 24 in 1947; and Joe Gordon, 19 in 1950. And Mantle drew 106 walks, second in the league behind Carl Yastrzemski's 119, a fair enough indication that American League pitchers still respected the Switcher.

WHERE, OH WHERE IN HISTORY?

In summarizing Mickey Mantle's place in baseball history, the following points come to the fore.

HOME RUNS: When Mantle retired with 536 home runs, he placed third on the all-time list. Only Babe Ruth and Willie Mays were in front of him. But Hank Aaron, Frank Robinson, and Harmon Killebrew would soon pass him. Then, in 1986, Reggie Jackson passed him, Mickey falling to seventh. An outstanding ranking, nonetheless.

Mike Schmidt, and possibly Dave Kingman, are the only current threats to Mantle's position, and even they are still a good piece down the road.

TAPE-MEASURE HOMERS: It has been established that Mantle hit baseballs a long way. But did he hit them the farthest? The vast majority of those connected with baseball in the Mantle era who in recent years were interviewed by Paul Susman—and he talked with a bunch!—say he did; Mantle consistently hit the longest balls they'd ever seen, they insisted.

Susman's survey respondents ranged from old-timers like Frank Crosetti, a teammate of Ruth, Gehrig, and DiMaggio and a coach of Mantle, who said Mantle's "consistent power" was tops, to a guy like Frank Bolling, who played on the Braves with Aaron, Adcock, and Mathews and who said that none of those long-ball hitters could touch Mantle.

However, Bill Jenkinson, a fellow member of the Society for American Baseball Research, who feels he has done more research on tape-measure homers in general than anyone alive, honestly disagrees. Jenkinson fully appreciates Mantle's monstrous 1963 shot off Bill Fischer that nearly left Yankee Stadium, and he is impressed by the number of tape-measure jobs that Mantle hit when past his prime (the prime age, in power terms, being in the mid-20s, says Jenkinson). But he rates Mantle no better than third among players who consistently hit the longest home runs. Jenkinson rates Ruth first and Jimmie Foxx second, and has Mantle tied with Frank Howard for third.

Ruth's wallops really impress Jenkinson. He realizes that the mythical 602-footer Ruth was said to have hit in Detroit in 1926 was a fabrication, but he insists that this one has been confused with another homer Babe hit in Detroit that really did travel 600 feet. Another thing, he says, most of Ruth's longest homers were hit in the early 1920s, before the arrival in the majors of Crosetti, Bill Dickey, and others who said Mantle's was longer. A legitimate point.

Jenkinson was 12 in 1959 when he saw Mantle hit an eye-opening shot over the roof at Philadelphia's Connie Mack Stadium (previously Shibe Park) in an exhibition game; Mantle had done this once before, against Frank Fanovich of the A's in a 1953 game. Jenkinson has determined that Foxx, who played for the A's from 1925 through 1935, hit 27 homers over the roof at Shibe in left field.

The question is how many of Mantle's 50-some right-field upper-deck shots at Yankee Stadium, turned around to left field, would have left the lower-roofed Shibe Park? Some of Mantle's best shots were impeded by the upper deck at Yankee Stadium.

Some credence must be given to Jenkinson's long-baller rankings because, after all, he has studied the homers of Ruth and Foxx; Susman and I have not.

STRENGTH: Ruth and Frank Howard were very large men, and *The Baseball Encyclopedia* lists Foxx at 6', 195 lbs., although his pictures make him look much bigger. When Mantle came up to the Yankees in 1951, he wasn't quite 5'11" and he weighed about 170 pounds, and he could still nail the ball farther than anyone in the game. Though he never matured beyond about 195 pounds or so, he was probably the strongest man in the game, especially in the upper body and arms. And he hit with the whole body.

But Mantle was more than just a strong man. It was easy for a huge guy like Frank Howard to send a long one flying occasionally; Mickey's distance, and consistency, came just as much from the fact that he was so coordinated. His timing was perfect.

SPEED: Before his legs disintegrated, Mantle was baseball's fastest runner. He was clocked once from the lefty batter's box to first base at 3.1 seconds. He rarely grounded into double plays, moved in a flash from first to third, broke up double plays with bruising force, and was a great percentage base stealer, enjoying a success rate of upwards of 80 percent through most of his career. He stole only when absolutely necessary, too. On a running club, he might have stolen 100 bases a season when healthy.

Jimmie Foxx certainly whaled many a long ball, but did he win ball games on the base paths the way Mantle did? Hell, no.

SWITCH-HITTING: Mantle resurrected a dying art in becoming the greatest switch-hitter in history. Switcher Pete Rose has since tabulated more hits than anyone else, but his switch-hitting will be a historical footnote; it isn't Rose's switch-hitting that captures the public's imagination, not like Mantle's anyway; it is Rose's grit, persistence, and overachieving persona.

Eddie Murray has been a very good, consistent, power-hitting switcher for a decade, and, if he remains healthy, he has a chance of outdoing Mantle's power stats. But Murray hasn't been as spectacular as Mantle, who still stands supreme as the greatest switch-hitter.

MVP VOTING: Mantle not only won three MVPs but probably deserved at least three more. He finished first, second, or third in the balloting nine times in a 13-season period between 1952 and 1964.

BUNTING: Only Phil Rizzuto was in Mantle's class as a bunter, and the Scooter himself has said that Mickey was the game's greatest drag bunter, another lost art the Mick returned to the game. A great two-strike bunter, Mantle in 1957 bunted safely something like 12 times with two strikes against him.

DRAWING WALKS: Like Babe Ruth and Ted Williams, Mantle was walked often by cautious pitchers. When he retired, Mickey was third on the all-time list, behind Ruth and Williams (Carl Yastrzemski and Joe Morgan have since passed him).

Mantle led the league in walks five times and the Yankees 14 times. He drew over 100 walks in 10 seasons, even in his final, fade-away season.

BATTING AVERAGE: Mantle hit better than .300 in 10 of 18 major league seasons. Contemporary sluggers of the Mick fared less well. Harmon Killebrew hit .300 only once, and that was in a 4-for-13 season, and Frank Howard never hit .300 in any kind of season. Other "pure" hitters of Mantle's era couldn't quite match Mickey's .298 lifetime batting average either; Al Kaline hit .297, Duke Snider .295, and Frank Robinson .294. Even Willie Mays—and there are probably as many people who feel Mays was the greatest player ever as there are boosters of

Ty Cobb, Babe Ruth, or Joe DiMaggio—hit only four points higher than Mantle.

Mantle entered 1968 batting .302—the final mark for Mays—but his .237 season lowered him below .300, the bitterest pill Mantle ever had to swallow. One reason he hit only .254 over his last four seasons was that he often had to widen the strike zone to keep from being pitched around.

Part of the answer to why Mantle didn't hit for a higher lifetime batting average is found in the fact that in swinging from the heels he sacrificed his average for home runs; yet the main reason Mickey and the other great sluggers of his era didn't have higher lifetime averages is that the times conspired against them. Everything is relative, and in the 1960s and, to a lesser extent, the 1950s, pitching dominated the game.

The pitchers of the 1960s held the upper hand. Through a long, evolutionary process, big-league pitchers now had in their arsenal a vast repertoire of pitches (and the universal use of the slider was the key here). They had the advantage of pitching from a high mound (since lowered) and throwing to a large strike zone (since reduced). When a starter faltered, a strong reliever was ready in the days when having strength in the bullpen was no longer novel.

It was just a hell of a lot tougher to be a hitter in the 1950s and 1960s than it was in the free-hitting 1920s and 1930s. Trick pitches like the spitball were banned in the 1920s and prevalent but ignored in the 1960s. In addition, in the American League, new parks in Baltimore, California, and Oakland were pitchers' parks.

John Thorn and Pete Palmer raised another interesting point in *The Hidden Game of Baseball*, quoting a 1981 letter from George "Specs" Toporcer to sportswriter Red Smith. Toporcer, a big leaguer in the 1920s who stayed in the game in a number of capacities thereafter, was quoted as saying that "anyone who does not think the game and the number of worthwhile players have improved from decade to decade—with the exception of the war and immediate postwar years—does not know whereof he speaks. Yes, outstanding stars of yesteryear would star today, but most people who try to rate them are misled by statistical evidence, which makes the old ones appear far greater than they actually were."

The reason, says Toporcer, that sensational stats like Ty Cobb's .367 lifetime batting average were made was because they were "achieved only because the rank and file players were far inferior to those of today, thus enabling the stars to stick out like a sore thumb." (*Note:* One reason the talent pool was thinner was that there were no blacks and few Latins playing in the majors.)

Toporcer, in an earlier magazine article, ranked the 12 greatest hitters as he saw them, placing Ruth first and Mantle 11th, just ahead of Frank Robinson. Cobb didn't make the list. Toporcer may have been right, too. Look at it this way: Though Cobb outhit Mantle by 69 points in batting average, in slugging average, perhaps a better yardstick of a great hitter, Mantle was clearly superior, .557 to .513 for Cobb.

RUN PRODUCTION: Mantle has been faulted for not piling up bigger numbers in the RBI department. His ranking was barely in the all-time top 30 going into the 1986 season. Injuries were a big factor, as, for example, in 1962, when he missed about one-quarter of the games and collected only 89 RBIs. And in his last few seasons he hardly ever got a good pitch to hit, especially with men on base. In addition, considering the overall weakness of the Yankee lineup, RBI opportunities weren't that many.

The Yankees lacked little when they were winning 12 pennants in Mantle's first 14 Yankee years, but they never really had an exceptional leadoff man. Not like an Earle Combs, who set the table so brilliantly for Ruth and Gehrig, or a Rickey Henderson. No telling how many more RBIs Mantle might have garnered had he batted behind a guy like Henderson.

Mickey made up for any RBI deficiency with an ability to score runs. In nine consecutive seasons (1953–61), he scored more than 100 runs and led the league in runs scored six times. He actually scored more runs (1,677) than he drove in (1,509), a rarity among the great power hitters.

STRIKEOUTS: Mantle broke the career strikeout record held by Ruth, who whiffed 1,330 times, and extended the new mark to 1,710. Willie Stargell in 1978 broke Mantle's record. Also surpassing Mantle have been Lou Brock, Bobby Bonds, Tony Perez, and Reggie Jackson. Reggie, the current strikeout king, is on his way to setting what may be an unreachable record; he was approaching 2,400 strikeouts going into 1986.

Ruth, Mantle, and Jackson all struck out a lot because they took big cuts. Mantle was accused of being fooled too often, but his strikeouts were more attributable to the nature of his swing. And Mantle was a lot harder to strike out from his natural side, the right-handed side. In computing figures available from 1957 through 1968, Mantle struck out once per 4.1 at bats left-handed and once per 5.9 at bats right-handed.

INJURIES: Lingering in the memory of many fans is a picture of Mantle batting left-handed, pulling away from a low inside pitch and having his knees buckle. Two points: It took unparalleled determination for Mantle to play as long and as well as he did, and his career stats were badly damaged by the injuries.

FIELDING: Mantle wasn't the best center fielder of all time, but he was among the elite. His range was taken for granted because the spacious center field at the Stadium limited the wall-crashing catches that make a center fielder look spectacular. And before his 1957 shoulder injury he could throw with the best of them.

THE LEGACY: Players with the tag "the next Mickey Mantle" have had a great burden placed on them. Two Yankees of the 1960s, Tom Tresh and Bobby Murcer, never shed the tag, and though both had outstanding careers, their stats were often unfairly compared with Mantle's. Yet they never resented Mickey, but instead idolized him. Tresh even named a son Mickey. Baseball men who should have known better pinned "the next Mickey Mantle" label on kids outside the Yankee organization, too. Like Clint Hurdle, a disappointment, and Kirk Gibson, who took a long time to grow out of the tag.

Detroit's Al Kaline was a great player, a Hall of Famer and probably the second best player in the American League, after Mantle, when they were in their prime. "You're not half as good as Mickey Mantle," a kid once told Kaline in the early 1960s. "Son," replied Kaline with a smile, "*nobody* is half as good as Mickey Mantle."

September 19, 1968—Tiger Stadium, Detroit. Mickey Mantle was stuck in a tie with Jimmie Foxx for third place on the all-time home-run list, and time was running out. The season, which almost everyone felt would be Mickey's last, was nearly over.

Detroit's Denny McLain recently became the first major-league pitcher to win 30 games since Dizzy Dean did it in 1934. Now, with the help of two homers by Norm Cash, McLain has a 6–1 lead and a bead on win No. 31 in a game that doesn't matter to the Tigers, who already have been crowned the American League champions.

So the pennant is in the bag and McLain on this cool, gray, September day is coasting when Mantle, who already has a single and two walks, comes up with one out and the bases empty in the eighth. The Detroit fans rise in a standing ovation, anticipating Mickey's final plate appearance in their city. He hasn't had a home run since No. 534 nearly a month ago.

McLain waits for the cheering to die down and then shouts something to catcher Bill Freehan. He throws two juicy-looking fastballs on the inside portion of the plate that Mickey takes for called strikes. After chatting with Freehan, who tells him to be ready for another fat pitch, Mickey motions where he wants the ball.

McLain accommodates. His next pitch is a medium-speed fastball that is over the plate and knee-high—the kind of groove pitch that is the specialty of batting practice pitchers. Mickey whips his bat and crushes a home run into the upper deck in right field, just inside the foul pole. "Thanks!" he yells to McLain as he takes his home-run trot, and as he nears home plate, McLain salutes him. "McLain has made a fan of me for life," Mickey later said.

Home run No. 535, besides closing the scoring in a 6–2 Detroit victory, breaks Mantle's tie with Foxx and moves Mickey into undisputed possession of third place. There is no one else within his reach now, no more targets to shoot for. Babe Ruth, the home-run leader, is way ahead with 714. Willie Mays, the runner-up, has 585 and is still going strong.

"I got a feeling he wanted me to hit it," said Mantle of McLain after the game. "I think it was just a straight fastball." Over in the other locker room, McLain feigned innocence. "I think you guys think I gave it up on purpose," he told the press, smiling. Mantle was, and is, his idol, he noted. "Baseball is going to be sad when he leaves," said Denny. "None of them other gopher balls are special. This one I'll remember a little bit more."

Did McLain groove the pitch? "You don't think I'd deliberately throw him a home-run ball, do you?" he protested. "There would be a scandal and an immediate investigation of baseball." And everyone broke up laughing.

A bit of controversy ensued, however. Some felt McLain's generosity had been misdirected, that he had betrayed the principles of the game. Several days later Red Smith addressed the question in his column. He said that under the circumstances—the pennant clinched, the big lead—McLain did nothing wrong. And, besides, wrote Smith, "there was no assurance Mantle would hit it. It simply is not possible to pitch a home run on purpose. Lob up a cantaloupe and tell the batter it is coming, it is still a playable 5 to 1 he will pop it up, beat it into the dirt or miss it altogether."

Smith agreed with Harry Markson, director of boxing for Madison Square Garden. "When a guy has bought 534 drinks in the same saloon, he's entitled to one on the house," said Markson.

September 20, 1968—Yankee Stadium. New York, in a struggle for third place with Cleveland and Boston, suffered a big blow on this date, losing to the Red Sox, 4–3. In the end the Indians will take third place; the difference between third and fifth, where the Yankees ended up: $1,000 per man, not an inconsiderable sum, and a little pride.

Boston's Jim Lonborg pitches only his third complete game of the year; he had hurt his knee in an off-season skiing accident and struggled most of 1968. Carl Yastrzemski contributes two singles and a homer in raising his batting average to .306; he will lead the league this year with a .301 average.

Lonborg leads, 1–0, in the third inning when Mantle, batting left-handed, lines home run No. 536 into the right-field seats to tie the score. Those fortunate enough to be among the 15,737 spectators watch Mantle circle the bases for the last time. Mantle's final two homers were hit off the league's Cy Young Award winners of 1967 (Lonborg) and 1968 (Denny McLain). And this "legit" home run will erase any doubts about the Mick's passing Jimmie Foxx.

Mantle over the next week will slump, going 1 for 17. Finally, on September 28 in Boston, Mickey played his final game, one day before the end of the season, receiving a great ovation on his first trip to the plate. Boston right fielder Ken "Hawk" Harrelson had tears streaming down his face, he recalled years later.

Mickey made an out and went into the dugout for the final time. Ralph Houk replaced him at first base with Andy Kosco, who would end up hitting the game-winning homer. Mickey sat in the dugout for a while, then went into the locker room and changed clothes. It was all over.

But all winter long the speculation was hot and heavy as to whether Mantle would quit the game. Mickey, at the urging of the Yankees, waited until spring training to settle the issue. On March 1, 1969, he arrived at Fort Lauderdale and disclosed that he was indeed retiring.

"I don't hit the ball when I need to," Mantle told a packed press conference, "I can't steal when I need to, I can't score from second when I need to."

It wasn't that the Mick quit the game; it was that the physical paraphernalia necessary to play the game quit him. The spirit—the sizzling fuse—was still there, but the powder was inert; he needed to get a hit or steal or score, but it just wasn't in the arsenal. The explosive start for a ball or a base, and the explosive whip of his bat at a pitched ball, were no more.

To many Mantle fans it would be a long time before baseball was baseball again. Even today, nearly two decades after Mantle played his final game, many would say there never has been an all-around great like Mickey Mantle, before or since.

Mickey Mantle's 536 Regular-Season Home Runs

- The table entries lacking narrative comment are for those home runs that are more fully described in the text. The in-text descriptions can be located easily by date.
- In some instances only one game of a doubleheader is alluded to in the table.
- The symbols used are ordinary. Those that may need explanation are BB, base on balls; SB, stolen base; RH, a right-handed Mantle homer; and LH, a left-handed homer.

1951

1 DATE: May 1, 1951   PLACE, OPP.: Comiskey Park, Chicago White Sox   SCORE: NY 8, CH 3   SWING, POS. IN ORDER: LH, 1st   PITCHER: Randy Gumpert   MEN ON: 1   STATS: 1 for 4, 1 run, 3 RBIs   POSITION: RF

2 DATE: May 4, 1951   PLACE, OPP.: Sportsman's Park, St. Louis Browns   SCORE: NY 8, SL 1   SWING, POS. IN ORDER: LH, 1st   PITCHER: Duane Pillette   MEN ON: 1   STATS: 2 for 6, 1 run, 2 RBIs   POSITION: RF

3

DATE: May 13, 1951
PLACE, OPP.: Shibe Park,
  Philadelphia, A's
SCORE: PH 5, NY 4
SWING, POS. IN ORDER:
  RH, 2nd
PITCHER: Alex Kellner
MEN ON: 1
STATS: 2 for 4, 1 BB, 2 runs, 2
  RBIs
POSITION: RF

In the first game of a double-header, Mickey Mantle hits his first right-handed homer in the bigs. In trying to bunt he popped out to end the opening game with the tying run on third base. And in the second game, which the A's also won, he missed second base.

4

DATE: May 16, 1951   PLACE, OPP.: Yankee Stadium, Cleveland Indians   SCORE: NY 11, CL 3   SWING, POS. IN ORDER: RH, 2nd   PITCHER: Dick Rozek   MEN ON: 1   STATS: 2 for 4, 1 BB, 3 runs, 4 RBIs, 1 SB   POSITION: RF

5

DATE: June 19, 1951
PLACE, OPP.: Yankee
  Stadium, Chicago White Sox
SCORE: NY 11, CH 9
SWING, POS. IN ORDER:
  LH, 1st
PITCHER: Lou Kretlow
MEN ON: 2
STATS: 3 for 4, 1 BB, 2 runs, 4
  RBIs, 1 SB
POSITION: RF

A big day with the bat. Mantle's homer into the right-center-field bleachers broke a 6–6 tie in the first game. But he failed on two makable catches that went for extra-base hits.

6

DATE: June 19, 1951
PLACE, OPP.: Yankee
  Stadium, Chicago White Sox
SCORE: CH 5, NY 4
SWING, POS. IN ORDER:
  LH, 1st
PITCHER: Joe Dobson
MEN ON: 0

Mantle homered again, into the lower right-field stands, his first two-homer day in the majors.

STATS: 1 for 4, 1 run, 1 RBI
POSITION: RF

---

7 DATE: July 7, 1951
PLACE, OPP.: Fenway Park,
  Boston Red Sox
SCORE: BO 10, NY 4
SWING, POS. IN ORDER:
  LH Defensive replacement
PITCHER: Ellis Kinder
MEN ON: 0
STATS: 1 for 1, 1 run, 1 RBI
POSITION: Substitute RF

Mantle, a late-inning sub, was
the Yanks' only bright spot,
sending a ninth-inning homer
into the right-field bleachers.

---

8 DATE: August 25, 1951   PLACE, OPP.: Municipal Stadium,
Cleveland Indians   SCORE: NY 7, CL 3   SWING, POS. IN
ORDER: LH, 2nd   PITCHER: Mike Garcia   MEN ON: 1
STATS: 2 for 5, 2 runs, 2 RBIs   POSITION: RF

---

9 DATE: August 29, 1951   PLACE, OPP.: Sportsman's Park, St.
Louis Browns   SCORE: NY 15, SL 2   SWING, POS. IN
ORDER: LH, 1st   PITCHER: Satchel Paige   MEN ON: 2
STATS: 2 for 6, 1 run, 4 RBIs   POSITION: RF

---

10 DATE: September 8, 1951
PLACE, OPP.: Yankee
  Stadium, Washington
  Senators
SCORE: NY 4 WA 0
SWING, POS. IN ORDER:
  LH, 1st
PITCHER: Bob Porterfield
MEN ON: 2
STATS: 1 for 4, 1 run, 3 RBIs
POSITION: RF

The youngster Mantle stole the
show on an Old-Timers' Day
honoring former manager Joe
McCarthy. With Eddie Lopat
and Porterfield locked in a
scoreless duel in the seventh,
Mantle hit a shot into the very
last rows of the right-field
bleachers near the railing alongside the Yankee bullpen, 450 to
465 feet.

11

DATE: September 9, 1951
PLACE, OPP.: Yankee
 Stadium, Washington
 Senators
SCORE: NY 7, WA 5
SWING, POS. IN ORDER:
 LH, 1st
PITCHER: Dick Starr
MEN ON: 0
STATS: 2 for 4, 1 run, 1 RBI
POSITION: RF

Mantle's was one of five Yankee homers, four of them served up by Starr.

12

DATE: September 12, 1951
PLACE, OPP.: Yankee
 Stadium, Detroit Tigers
SCORE: DE 9, NY 2
SWING, POS. IN ORDER:
 LH, 1st
PITCHER: Virgil Trucks
MEN ON: 0
STATS: 1 for 5, 1 run, 1 RBI
POSITION: RF

Mantle turned Trucks's first pitch of the game into a tremendous homer deep into the right-field upper deck, then went 0 for 4 with three strikeouts. Mantle's hit might have traveled 600 feet and left Yankee Stadium had it been hit more toward the Yankee bullpen, according to eyewitnesses.

13

DATE: September 19, 1951   PLACE, OPP.: Yankee Stadium,
Chicago White Sox   SCORE: NY 5, CH 3   SWING, POS. IN
ORDER: LH, 1st   PITCHER: Lou Kretlow   MEN ON: 2
STATS: 1 for 4, 2 runs, 3 RBIs   POSITION: RF

1952

14

DATE: April 21, 1952
PLACE, OPP.: Yankee
 Stadium, Philadelphia A's
SCORE: NY 5, PH 1
SWING, POS. IN ORDER:
 RH, 3rd

Mantle gave New York a 1–0 lead when he clipped Shantz for a first-inning homer that barely cleared the left-field fence.

PITCHER: Bobby Shantz
MEN ON: 0
STATS: 1 for 4, 1 run, 1 RBI
POSITION: RF

---

15   DATE: April 30, 1952   Mantle's sixth-inning blast
PLACE, OPP.: Yankee   traveled some 420 feet.
  Stadium, St. Louis Browns
SCORE: SL 9, NY 4
SWING, POS. IN ORDER:
  RH, 8th
PITCHER: Bob Cain
MEN ON: 1
STATS: 3 for 4, 2 runs, 2 RBIs
POSITION: RF

---

16   DATE: May 30, 1952   PLACE, OPP.: Yankee Stadium,
Philadelphia A's   SCORE: PH 2, NY 1   SWING, POS. IN
ORDER: RH, 1st   PITCHER: Bobby Shantz   MEN ON: 0
STATS: 3 for 7, 1 run, 1 RBI   POSITION: RF

---

17   DATE: June 15, 1952   PLACE, OPP.: Municipal Stadium,
Cleveland Indians   SCORE: NY 8, CL 2   SWING, POS. IN
ORDER: LH, 2nd   PITCHER: Bob Lemon   MEN ON: 2
STATS: 1 for 5, 1 run, 3 RBIs   POSITION: CF

---

18   DATE: June 17, 1952   The Yankees overcame an early
PLACE, OPP.: Briggs Stadium,   6–1 deficit in a comeback
  Detroit Tigers   capped by a game-tying Mantle
SCORE: DE 7, NY 6   homer to the upper deck in left-
SWING, POS. IN ORDER: center—the first one ever hit up
  RH, 6th   there according to the *Detroit*
PITCHER: Billy Hoeft   *News*, and one of the longest
MEN ON: 0   homers of early Mantle vintage.
STATS: 2 for 5, 2 runs, 2 RBIs
POSITION: CF

---

19 DATE: June 22, 1952
PLACE, OPP.: Comiskey Park,
   Chicago White Sox
SCORE: CH 2, NY 1
SWING, POS. IN ORDER:
   LH, 5th
PITCHER: Marv Grissom
MEN ON: 0
STATS: 2 for 3, 1 BB, 1 run, 1
   RBI, 1 SB
POSITION: CF

A game-tying seventh-inning Mantle homer was Grissom's only mistake.

---

20 DATE: June 27, 1952
PLACE, OPP.: Yankee
   Stadium, Philadelphia A's
SCORE: NY 10, PH 0
SWING, POS. IN ORDER:
   LH, 5th
PITCHER: Bob Hooper
MEN ON: 1
STATS: 1 for 3, 2 BBs, 2 runs, 2
   RBIs
POSITION: CF

Mantle got the Yankees off and running with a two-run homer in the fourth inning.

---

21 DATE: July 5, 1952
PLACE, OPP.: Shibe Park,
   Philadelphia A's
SCORE: NY 3, PH 1
SWING, POS. IN ORDER:
   RH, 5th
PITCHER: Alex Kellner
MEN ON: 0
STATS: 1 for 3, 1 BB, 2 runs, 1
   RBI
POSITION: CF

With two out in the sixth, Mantle crunched a towering shot into the upper deck in left field to tie the score at 1–1. He helped preserve the win with a fine grab in the ninth.

22

DATE: July 6, 1952
PLACE, OPP.: Shibe Park,
 Philadelphia A's
SCORE: NY 5, PH 2
SWING, POS. IN ORDER:
 RH, 5th
PITCHER: Bobby Shantz
MEN ON: 0
STATS: 2 for 4, 2 runs, 1 RBI
POSITION: CF

Mantle and Gil McDougald had big games in the opener of a doubleheader, both homering and doubling (Gil also singled) to lead the Yanks to a win. For Mantle it was No. 3 for the season off Shantz, who posted a 24–7 record and won the league's MVP Award for 1952.

23

DATE: July 13, 1952
PLACE, OPP.: Yankee
 Stadium, Detroit Tigers
SCORE: NY 11, DE 1
SWING, POS. IN ORDER:
 LH, 5th
PITCHER: Marlin Stuart
MEN ON: 2
STATS: 4 for 5, 2 runs, 4 RBIs
POSITION: CF

Mantle broke an 0-for-15 collar in the opener of a doublebill, contributing a single to the Yankees' five-run third inning. He followed with two more singles and a homer into the right-field bleachers.

24

DATE: July 13, 1952
PLACE, OPP.: Yankee
 Stadium, Detroit Tigers
SCORE: NY 12, DE 1
SWING, POS. IN ORDER:
 RH, 5th
PITCHER: Hal Newhouser
MEN ON: 1
STATS: 1 for 4, 1 BB, 2 runs, 2
 RBIs
POSITION: CF

Mantle homered into the left-field seats for his fifth consecutive hit of the doubleheader, a streak that ended in his next at bat. Mantle has hit homers from both sides of the plate on the same day, if not in the same game.

25

DATE: July 15, 1952
PLACE, OPP.: Yankee
    Stadium, Cleveland Indians
SCORE: CL 7, NY 3
SWING, POS. IN ORDER:
    LH, 5th
PITCHER: Early Wynn
MEN ON: 0
STATS: 2 for 3, 1 BB, 1 run, 1
    RBI
POSITION: CF

Mantle's was one of several solo homers Wynn allowed in the late innings. His landed deep in the right-center-field bleachers, one of his best shots yet.

26

DATE: July 17, 1952
PLACE, OPP.: Yankee
    Stadium, Cleveland Indians
SCORE: CL 11, NY 6
SWING, POS. IN ORDER:
    LH, 5th
PITCHER: Steve Gromek
MEN ON: 0
STATS: 1 for 5, 1 run, 1 RBI
POSITION: CF

Mantle's second-inning homer is of little consequence because the Tribe had already taken Chief Allie Reynolds's scalp and a 6–0 lead in the first of two games.

27

DATE: July 25, 1952
PLACE, OPP.: Briggs Stadium,
    Detroit Tigers
SCORE: DE 2, NY 1
SWING, POS. IN ORDER:
    LH, 5th
PITCHER: Art Houtteman
MEN ON: 0
STATS: 3 for 4, 1 run, 1 RBI
POSITION: CF

Mantle was the Yankee offense, but he also made a costly base-running mistake. Mickey's blast into the upper tier in right field gave New York a 1–0 lead in the fourth inning. In the sixth, Yogi Berra raced to third on Mantle's third consecutive hit, but there he died when the Yanks ran out of outs, one of which was registered by Mickey when he got trapped between first and second.

28

DATE: July 26, 1952
PLACE, OPP.: Briggs Stadium,
Detroit Tigers
SCORE: DE 10, NY 6
SWING, POS. IN ORDER:
RH, 5th
PITCHER: Ted Gray
MEN ON: 3
STATS: 2 for 5, 1 run, 4 RBIs
POSITION: CF

Mantle hit his first grand-slam homer in the first inning. He swatted an 0-and-2 pitch into Section 3 of the left-center-field upper deck, amazing those observers who happened to see him reach the upper deck in successive games from each side of the plate.

29

DATE: July 29, 1952   PLACE, OPP.: Comiskey Park, Chicago
White Sox   SCORE: NY 10, CH 7   SWING, POS. IN
ORDER: RH, 4th   PITCHER: Chuck Stobbs   MEN ON: 3
STATS: 2 for 5, 2 runs, 5 RBIs   POSITION: CF

30

DATE: August 11, 1952   PLACE, OPP.: Yankee Stadium, Boston

31

Red Sox   SCORE: NY 7, BO 0   SWING, POS. IN ORDER:
LH, LH; 3rd   PITCHERS: Sid Hudson, Ralph Brickner   MEN
ON: 0, 1   STATS: 3 for 4, 3 runs, 3 RBIs   POSITION: CF

32

DATE: August 30, 1952
PLACE, OPP.: Yankee
Stadium, Washington
Senators
SCORE: NY 6, WA 4
SWING, POS. IN ORDER:
LH, 1st
PITCHER: Randy Gumpert
MEN ON: 0
STATS: 2 for 3, 2 BBs, 2 runs, 1
RBI
POSITION: CF

Mickey homered in the third into the right-field seats, breaking a 1–1 tie and putting the Yankees in front for good.

33   DATE: September 14, 1952   PLACE, OPP.: Municipal Stadium, Cleveland Indians   SCORE: NY 7, CL 1   SWING, POS. IN ORDER: RH, 3rd   PITCHER: Lou Brissie   MEN ON: 0 STATS: 2 for 4, 1 BB, 2 runs, 1 RBI   POSITION: CF

---

34   DATE: September 17, 1952   PLACE, OPP.: Briggs Stadium, Detroit Tigers   SCORE: NY 12, DE 3   SWING, POS. IN ORDER: RH, 3rd   PITCHER: Bill Wight   MEN ON: 0 STATS: 3 for 5, 1 run, 3 RBIs   POSITION: CF

---

35   DATE: September 24, 1952   PLACE, OPP.: Fenway Park, Boston Red Sox   SCORE: NY 8, BO 6   SWING, POS. IN ORDER: RH, 3rd   PITCHER: Mel Parnell   MEN ON: 2   STATS: 3 for 4, 3 runs, 4 RBIs   POSITION: CF

---

36   DATE: September 26, 1952   PLACE, OPP.: Shibe Park, Philadelphia A's   SCORE: NY 5, PH 2   SWING, POS. IN ORDER: LH, 3rd   PITCHER: Harry Byrd   MEN ON: 0 STATS: 2 for 5, 1 run, 1 RBI   POSITION: CF

1953

---

37   DATE: April 17, 1953   PLACE, OPP.: Griffith Stadium, Washington Senators   SCORE: NY 7, WA 3   SWING, POS. IN ORDER: RH, 4th   PITCHER: Chuck Stobbs   MEN ON: 1 STATS: 2 for 3, 2 BBs, 1 run, 2 RBIs, 1 SB   POSITION: CF

---

38   DATE: April 23, 1953
PLACE, OPP.: Yankee
    Stadium, Boston Red Sox
SCORE: NY 6, BO 3
SWING, POS. IN ORDER:
    LH, 4th
PITCHER: Ellis Kinder

With two out in the ninth, Mantle hit a game-winning homer off Kinder, the league's best reliever. The ball traveled about 420 feet and landed 10 rows deep in the right-field bleachers.

MEN ON: 2
STATS: 3 for 4, 1 BB, 3 runs, 3
   RBIs
POSITION: CF

---

39   DATE: April 28, 1953   PLACE, OPP.: Busch Stadium, St. Louis
Browns   SCORE: NY 7, SL 6   SWING, POS. IN ORDER:
RH, 4th   PITCHER: Bob Cain   MEN ON: 2   STATS: 2 for
5, 2 runs, 3 RBIs   POSITION: CF

---

40   DATE: April 30, 1953
PLACE, OPP.: Comiskey Park,
   Chicago White Sox
SCORE: NY 6, CH 1
SWING, POS. IN ORDER:
   RH, 4th
PITCHER: Gene Bearden
MEN ON: 0
STATS: 1 for 4, 1 run, 1 RBI
POSITION: CF

For the first time, Mantle homered in support of his buddy
Whitey Ford, the shot to left
center breaking a scoreless tie.
The ball didn't actually clear the
fence; a fan reached out and
touched the ball and the White
Sox argued that it should have
been a double.

---

41   DATE: May 9, 1953
PLACE, OPP.: Fenway Park,
   Boston Red Sox
SCORE: NY 6, BO 4
SWING, POS. IN ORDER:
   RH, 4th
PITCHER: Bill Werle
MEN ON: 0
STATS: 2 for 5, 1 run, 2 RBIs
POSITION: CF

With the score 3–1 in the Yanks'
favor, Mantle led off the third
with a mighty blast that hit a
light tower above the netting in
left field. With two on and two
out in the fifth, Mickey skied a
drive to deep center field.
Jimmy Piersall sped toward the
left edge of the bullpen, near
the 420-foot mark, to make a
sensational backhanded catch.

42

DATE: May 25, 1953
PLACE, OPP.: Yankee
   Stadium, Boston Red Sox
SCORE: BO 14, NY 10
SWING, POS. IN ORDER:
   LH, 4th
PITCHER: Ellis Kinder
MEN ON: 0
STATS: 3 for 4, 2 BBs, 1 run, 3
   RBIs
POSITION: CF

Mantle's contributions to a slug-fest of nearly four hours included a 400-foot-plus homer into the right-field bleachers.

43

DATE: June 4, 1953
PLACE, OPP.: Comiskey Park,
   Chicago White Sox
SCORE: NY 9, CH 5
SWING, POS. IN ORDER:
   RH, 4th
PITCHER: Billy Pierce
MEN ON: 2
STATS: 3 for 5, 2 runs, 4 RBIs
POSITION: CF

In the third inning, Pierce, who won 18 games and pitched seven shutouts in 1953, tried to throw a fastball past Mantle, who drilled a 420-foot homer into the Yankee bullpen to give the Yanks a 5–0 lead. Chicago rallied to tie the score, then Mantle in the tenth got a leadoff single to ignite a four-run game-winning rally.

44

DATE: June 5, 1953
PLACE, OPP.: Busch Stadium,
   St. Louis Browns
SCORE: NY 5, SL 0
SWING, POS. IN ORDER:
   LH, 4th
PITCHER: Bobo Holloman
MEN ON: 1
STATS: 2 for 5, 2 runs, 2 RBIs
POSITION: CF

Mantle extended his hitting streak to 10 games with a single in the third, and in the fifth he drove a ball into the right-center-field seats.

45   DATE: June 11, 1953   PLACE, OPP.: Briggs Stadium, Detroit
Tigers   SCORE: NY 6, DE 3   SWING, POS. IN ORDER:
LH, 4th   PITCHER: Art Houtteman   MEN ON: 1   STATS:
1 for 2, 3 BBs, 2 runs, 2 RBIs   POSITION: CF

---

46   DATE: June 18, 1953
PLACE, OPP.: Yankee
   Stadium, St. Louis Browns
SCORE: NY 5, SL 0
SWING, POS. IN ORDER:
   RH, 4th
PITCHER: Dick Littlefield
MEN ON: 1
STATS: 1 for 3, 1 BB, 1 run, 2
   RBIs
POSITION: CF

The Mick's middle-inning, two-run dinger to left was more than Eddie Lopat needed in the first game of a doubleheader; the Yanks won both ends by shutouts.

---

47   DATE: June 21, 1953
PLACE, OPP.: Yankee
   Stadium, Detroit Tigers
SCORE: NY 6, DE 3
SWING, POS. IN ORDER:
   RH, 4th
PITCHER: Hal Newhouser
MEN ON: 1
STATS: 3 for 4, 3 runs, 2 RBIs
POSITION: CF

Mantle in doubleheader action collected a single, double, triple, and home run, and New York's defense, led by Gil McDougald, turned seven double plays. Mickey's homer in the opener was hit the opposite way deep into the Yankee bullpen, measured by a Yankee emissary at 425 feet.

---

48   DATE: June 23, 1953
PLACE, OPP.: Yankee
   Stadium, Chicago White Sox
SCORE: CH 11, NY 3
SWING, POS. IN ORDER:
   LH, 4th

Mantle in the seventh inning, with New York down 10–2, hit a homer deep into the lower right-field seats.

PITCHER: Virgil Trucks
MEN ON: 0
STATS: 2 for 4, 1 BB, 1 run, 1
    RBI
POSITION: CF

---

49 DATE: July 6, 1953   PLACE, OPP.: Connie Mack Stadium,
Philadelphia A's   SCORE: NY 10, PH 5   SWING, POS. IN
ORDER: RH, Pinch-hitter   PITCHER: Frank Fanovich   MEN
ON: 3   STATS: 2 for 2, 1 run, 4 RBIs   POSITION: PH-CF

---

50 DATE: July 26, 1953
PLACE, OPP.: Briggs Stadium,
    Detroit Tigers
SCORE: DE 5, NY 3
SWING, POS. IN ORDER:
    RH, 3rd
PITCHER: Al Aber
MEN ON: 1
STATS: 2 for 5, 1 run, 2 RBIs
POSITION: CF

Mantle gave the Yankees the lead in the first game of a twin-bill with a third-inning shot deep into the upper deck in left-center field. It was his first homer in nearly three weeks but his 100th hit of the season.

51 DATE: July 26, 1953
PLACE, OPP.: Briggs Stadium,
    Detroit Tigers
SCORE: NY 14, DE 4
SWING, POS. IN ORDER:
    LH, 3rd
PITCHER: Dick Weik
MEN ON: 1
STATS: 1 for 5, 1 run, 2 RBIs
POSITION: RF

Mantle was one of four Yankees to homer in a 19-hit attack. In spite of bothersome injuries—he played right field, with Irv Noren in center—he hit homers from each side of the plate in a doubleheader. And for the second time this year, Mantle hit a ball here that reached the top of the right-field roof.

52   DATE: August 7, 1953   PLACE, OPP.: Yankee Stadium, Chicago White Sox   SCORE: NY 6, CH 1   SWING, POS. IN ORDER: LH, 3rd   PITCHER: Connie Johnson   MEN ON: 2   STATS: 1 for 4, 1 run, 3 RBIs   POSITION: CF

---

53   DATE: September 1, 1953
PLACE, OPP.: Comiskey Park,
  Chicago White Sox
SCORE: NY 3, CH 2
SWING, POS. IN ORDER:
  LH, 3rd
PITCHER: Virgil Trucks
MEN ON: 0
STATS: 1 for 2, 2 BBs, 1 run, 1
  RBI
POSITION: CF

Mantle provided the winning margin in a tightly contested game before 45,000 plus. His seventh-inning homer into the lower right-field stands made it 3–1.

---

54   DATE: September 7, 1953   PLACE, OPP.: Fenway Park, Boston Red Sox   SCORE: BO 7, NY 4   SWING, POS. IN ORDER: RH, 5th   PITCHER: Mel Parnell   MEN ON: 1   STATS: 1 for 3, 1 BB, 1 run, 2 RBIs   POSITION: CF

---

55   DATE: September 9, 1953
PLACE, OPP.: Yankee
  Stadium, Chicago White Sox
SCORE: NY 9, CH 3
SWING, POS. IN ORDER:
  RH, 5th
PITCHER: Billy Pierce
MEN ON: 1
STATS: 1 for 4, 1 BB, 1 run, 2
  RBIs
POSITION: CF

This was the Bubblegum Game. The Mick, after putting the finishing touches to a seven-run rally in the fifth with a two-run shot deep into the left-field seats, was photographed out in center field blowing a huge bubble with his wad of bubblegum. Stengel, displeased, publicly rebuked Mantle for his unprofessional behavior. Mickey apologized and said it wouldn't happen again, although he did get a nice endorsement fee from the Bowman Bubble Gum Company.

---

56 DATE: September 12, 1953   PLACE, OPP.: Yankee Stadium, Detroit Tigers   SCORE: NY 13, DE 4   SWING, POS. IN ORDER: RH, 5th   PITCHER: Billy Hoeft   MEN ON: 2 STATS: 2 for 4, 2 runs, 3 RBIs   POSITION: CF

---

57 DATE: September 20, 1953
PLACE, OPP.: Fenway Park,
 Boston Red Sox
SCORE: NY 10, BO 8
SWING, POS. IN ORDER:
 RH, 3rd
PITCHER: Mickey McDermott
MEN ON: 1
STATS: 2 for 4, 2 BBs, 2 runs, 2
 RBIs
POSITION: CF

A Mantle homer helped World Series–bound New York to a three-run first inning.

1954

---

58 DATE: April 19, 1954
PLACE, OPP.: Fenway Park,
 Boston Red Sox
SCORE: NY 5, BO 0
SWING, POS. IN ORDER:
 RH, 3rd
PITCHER: Mel Parnell
MEN ON: 0
STATS: 2 for 5, 1 run, 1 RBI
POSITION: CF

Boston won the morning game, 2–1, as Mantle struck out four times—Ellis Kinder fanned Mickey on three pitches with two out and the bases loaded in the ninth. But, in the afternoon game on this Patriot's Day, Mantle belted home run No. 1 of six-game-old 1954.

---

59 DATE: April 21, 1954
PLACE, OPP.: Yankee
   Stadium, Boston Red Sox
SCORE: NY 5, BO 1
SWING, POS. IN ORDER:
   RH, 3rd
PITCHER: Leo Kiely
MEN ON: 0
STATS: 1 for 3, 1 BB, 1 run, 1
   RBI
POSITION: CF

Solo homers by Mantle, Gil McDougald, and Yogi Berra led the way. McDougald's barely cleared the 301-foot sign down the left-field line, and Berra's just went over the 296-foot mark down the right-field line, but Mantle's clout went into the right-field bleachers.

---

60 DATE: May 7, 1954
PLACE, OPP.: Yankee
   Stadium, Philadelphia A's
SCORE: NY 2, PH 0
SWING, POS. IN ORDER:
   RH, 3rd
PITCHER: Morrie Martin
MEN ON: 0
STATS: 1 for 3, 1 run, 1 RBI
POSITION: CF

Martin had a great game going until Mantle led off the seventh with a towering home run over the 402-foot sign in left field that landed beyond the double row of boxes, a drive of at least 425 feet.

---

61 DATE: May 21, 1954
PLACE, OPP.: Yankee
   Stadium, Boston Red Sox
SCORE: BO 6, NY 3
SWING, POS. IN ORDER:
   LH, 3rd
PITCHER: Frank Sullivan
MEN ON: 1
STATS: 1 for 4, 1 run, 2 RBIs
POSITION: CF

With Boston up 6–1 after erupting for six runs in the sixth, Mantle, who struck out three straight times, got his fourth chance against Sullivan in the eighth, this time driving a two-run shot over the auxiliary scoreboard in right field and into the bleachers.

62

DATE: May 22, 1954   PLACE, OPP.: Yankee Stadium, Boston Red Sox   SCORE: NY 7, BO 0   SWING, POS. IN ORDER: LH, 3rd   PITCHER: Tex Clevenger   MEN ON: 1   STATS: 4 for 5, 2 runs, 4 RBIs, 1 SB   POSITION: CF

63

DATE: May 23, 1954
PLACE, OPP.: Yankee
  Stadium, Boston Red Sox
SCORE: BO 10, NY 9
SWING, POS. IN ORDER:
  RH, 3rd
PITCHER: Bill Henry
MEN ON: 2
STATS: 2 for 5, 1 BB, 1 run, 4
  RBIs
POSITION: CF

The Red Sox took a 3–0 first-inning lead, but Mantle tied the score in the third with a tremendous three-run homer into the left-field stands. He added a run-scoring single, but struck out to end the game.

64

DATE: May 25, 1954
PLACE, OPP.: Griffith
  Stadium, Washington
  Senators
SCORE: NY 9, WA 3
SWING, POS. IN ORDER:
  LH, 3rd
PITCHER: Sonny Dixon
MEN ON: 0
STATS: 3 for 5, 1 BB, 2 runs, 1
  RBI
POSITION: CF

Mantle beat out two infield hits, drew a walk, struck out twice, and then, in the one time he hit the ball out of the infield, homered in the eighth over the right-field wall.

65

DATE: May 29, 1954
PLACE, OPP.: Fenway Park,
Boston Red Sox
SCORE: NY 10, BO 2
SWING, POS. IN ORDER:
LH, 3rd
PITCHER: Sid Hudson
MEN ON: 0
STATS: 3 for 4, 1 BB, 3 runs, 2
RBIs
POSITION: CF

Mantle singled, homered into the netting above the Green Monster in left, and doubled in his first three trips, extending his hitting streak to 10 games and pulling his batting average above .300.

66

DATE: May 30, 1954
PLACE, OPP.: Fenway Park,
Boston Red Sox
SCORE: BO 3, NY 1
SWING, POS. IN ORDER:
LH, 3rd
PITCHER: Willard Nixon
MEN ON: 0
STATS: 1 for 3, 1 BB, 1 run, 1
RBI
POSITION: CF

Nixon made only one bad pitch along the way—a slow curve that Mantle planted in the right-field bullpen, extending his hitting streak to 11 games and tying the game at 1–1.

67

DATE: June 6, 1954
PLACE, OPP.: Yankee
Stadium, Baltimore Orioles
SCORE: NY 5, BA 2
SWING, POS. IN ORDER:
LH, 3rd
PITCHER: Don Larsen
MEN ON: 1
STATS: 2 for 4, 2 runs, 2 RBIs
POSITION: CF

Larsen, on his way to a 3–21 season, gave up a Mantle homer into the right-field stands, Mickey's first against the first-year Orioles, the former St. Louis Browns franchise.

68

DATE: June 10, 1954
PLACE, OPP.: Yankee
   Stadium, Detroit Tigers
SCORE: NY 9, DE 5
SWING, POS. IN ORDER:
   LH, 3rd
PITCHER: Ralph Branca
MEN ON: 0
STATS: 2 for 5, 2 runs, 2 RBIs
POSITION: CF

The Yankees went long ball on Branca, breaking open a 3–3 game with middle-inning homers by Yogi Berra, Bobby Brown, and Mantle.

69

DATE: June 20, 1954
PLACE, OPP.: Comiskey Park,
   Chicago White Sox
SCORE: NY 16, CH 6
SWING, POS. IN ORDER:
   LH, 3rd
PITCHER: Don Johnson
MEN ON: 1
STATS: 2 for 3, 3 BBs, 4 runs, 2
   RBIs
POSITION: CF

Mantle was one of four Yankees to homer, and he reached base five times.

70

DATE: June 26, 1954
PLACE, OPP.: Municipal
   Stadium, Cleveland Indians
SCORE: NY 11, CL 9
SWING, POS. IN ORDER:
   LH, 3rd
PITCHER: Bob Hooper
MEN ON: 0
STATS: 2 for 5, 1 run, 2 RBIs
POSITION: CF

Mantle made a bad throw, helping the Indians take a 2–1 lead in a wild one. He made amends, however, with an RBI double and a homer off Hooper, putting the Yanks in front, 7–5.

71

DATE: June 30, 1954
PLACE, OPP.: Fenway Park,
　Boston Red Sox
SCORE: BO 6, NY 1
SWING, POS. IN ORDER:
　LH, 3rd
PITCHER: Willard Nixon
MEN ON: 0
STATS: 1 for 3, 1 BB, 1 run, 1
　RBI
POSITION: CF

Mantle averted a Yankee shutout with a fifth-inning opposite-
field homer into the left-field
net.

72

DATE: July 1, 1954
PLACE, OPP.: Fenway Park,
　Boston Red Sox
SCORE: NY 8, BO 7
SWING, POS. IN ORDER:
　LH, 3rd
PITCHER: Frank Sullivan
MEN ON: 1
STATS: 2 for 5, 1 run, 3 RBIs
POSITION: CF

The Yanks scored five runs in
the third on homers by Mantle,
Hank Bauer, and Andy Carey.
Mantle and Bauer later made
spectacular catches at key moments.

73

DATE: July 3, 1954
PLACE, OPP.: Yankee
　Stadium, Washington
　Senators
SCORE: NY 3, WA 2
SWING, POS. IN ORDER:
　LH, 3rd
PITCHER: Bob Porterfield
MEN ON: 0
STATS: 2 for 4, 1 run, 3 RBIs
POSITION: CF

Mantle knocked in all three
Yankee runs, extended his hitting streak to 12 games, and
raised his batting average to
.320. One of his hits, an opposite-field homer, traveled nearly
400 feet into the left-field seats.

74

DATE: July 5, 1954
PLACE, OPP.: Connie Mack
   Stadium, Philadelphia A's
SCORE: NY 7, PH 4
SWING, POS. IN ORDER:
   LH, 3rd
PITCHER: Arnie Portocarrero
MEN ON: 0
STATS: 1 for 5, 1 run, 1 RBI
POSITION: CF

After splitting every one of their 10 doubleheaders so far this season, the Yankees finally swept one, beating the A's 7–4 and 11–2. Joe Collins and Mantle hit back-to-back homers off Portocarrero.

75

DATE: July 7, 1954
PLACE, OPP.: Yankee
   Stadium, Boston Red Sox
SCORE: NY 17, BO 9
SWING, POS. IN ORDER:
   LH, 3rd
PITCHER: Tom Brewer
MEN ON: 0
STATS: 3 for 4, 1 BB, 4 runs, 2
   RBIs
POSITION: CF

Mantle hit his 12th left-handed homer in a row in a slugfest that included a mighty Ted Williams wallop into the right-field upper deck.

76

DATE: July 19, 1954
PLACE, OPP.: Yankee
   Stadium, Detroit Tigers
SCORE: NY 8, DE 0
SWING, POS. IN ORDER:
   RH, 3rd
PITCHER: Ted Gray
MEN ON: 0
STATS: 1 for 3, 1 BB, 2 runs, 1
   RBI
POSITION: CF

The Yankees led, 1–0, in the third inning when Mantle arced a high homer deep into the lower seats in left field, his first right-handed homer since May 23.

77   DATE: July 22, 1954   PLACE, OPP.: Yankee Stadium, Chicago
White Sox   SCORE: NY 4, CH 3   SWING, POS. IN ORDER:
LH, 3rd   PITCHER: Don Johnson   MEN ON: 0   STATS: 2
for 5, 1 run, 2 RBIs   POSITION: CF, SS

---

78   DATE: July 28, 1954
PLACE, OPP.: Comiskey Park,
    Chicago White Sox
SCORE: NY 7, CH 5
SWING, POS. IN ORDER:
    RH, 3rd
PITCHER: Jack Harshman
MEN ON: 2
STATS: 3 for 5, 3 runs, 3 RBIs
POSITION: CF

Chicago was leading, 5–4,
when rain halted play for more
than an hour. When the umpires ordered play resumed,
Mantle belted a ninth-inning
homer, with two on, to win the
game, the ball landing in the
lower stands in left-center.

79
80   DATE: August 5, 1954   PLACE, OPP.: Municipal Stadium,
Cleveland Indians   SCORE: NY 5, CL 2   SWING, POS. IN
ORDER: LH, LH; 3rd   PITCHERS: Early Wynn, Ray
Narleski   MEN ON: 0, 0   STATS: 2 for 3, 2 BBs, 2 runs, 2
RBIs   POSITION: CF

---

81   DATE: August 8, 1954
PLACE, OPP.: Briggs Stadium,
    Detroit Tigers
SCORE: DE 10, NY 8
SWING, POS. IN ORDER:
    RH, 3rd
PITCHER: Billy Hoeft
MEN ON: 1
STATS: 2 for 6, 2 runs, 2 RBIs
POSITION: CF

Detroit took an early 4–0 lead,
but the Yankees fought their way
to an 8–8 tie. Late in the game,
against right-hander Steve Gromek, Mantle, who had already
homered, just missed a titanic
565-foot three-run homer as the
ball cleared the right-field roof
but hooked foul just before
reaching homer territory. Detroit won in the tenth.

82   DATE: August 12, 1954   The game was tied, 4–4, when
PLACE, OPP.: Yankee   Mantle's eighth-inning homer
  Stadium, Philadelphia A's   settled the issue.
SCORE: NY 5, PH 4
SWING, POS. IN ORDER:
  LH, 3rd
PITCHER: Arnie Portocarrero
MEN ON: 0
STATS: 2 for 3, 1 BB, 2 runs, 2
  RBIs
POSITION: CF

---

83   DATE: August 15, 1954   Mantle's home run was his 11th
PLACE, OPP.: Yankee   against Boston this year. In 22
  Stadium, Boston Red Sox   games with the Bosox in 1954,
SCORE: NY 14, BO 9   he hit .376 (32 for 85), with 26
SWING, POS. IN ORDER: runs and 28 RBIs.
  LH, 3rd
PITCHER: Hal Brown
MEN ON: 0
STATS: 2 for 3, 3 BBs, 3 runs, 2
  RBIs
POSITION: CF

---

84   DATE: September 2, 1954   PLACE, OPP.: Yankee Stadium,
Cleveland Indians   SCORE: NY 3, CL 2   SWING, POS. IN
ORDER: LH, 1st   PITCHER: Bob Lemon   MEN ON: 0
STATS: 1 for 4, 1 run, 1 RBI   POSITION: CF

1955

85   DATE: April 13, 1955
PLACE, OPP.: Yankee
   Stadium, Washington
   Senators
SCORE: NY 19, WA 1
SWING, POS. IN ORDER:
   LH, 3rd
PITCHER: Ted Abernathy
MEN ON: 2
STATS: 3 for 5, 3 runs, 4 RBIs
POSITION: CF

Mantle's fourth-inning homer, a long drive into the right-field bleachers, gave Whitey Ford, who stroked three singles himself, a 7–0 cushion on Opening Day. Also, for the first time in his career, Mickey was hit by a pitched ball.

86   DATE: April 18, 1955
PLACE, OPP.: Memorial
   Stadium, Baltimore Orioles
SCORE: NY 6, BA 0
SWING, POS. IN ORDER:
   LH, 3rd
PITCHER: Harry Byrd
MEN ON: 1
STATS: 1 for 3, 1 BB, 1 run, 2
   RBIs
POSITION: CF

Whitey Ford and Mantle teamed up again. Ford pitched a three-hitter and Mantle closed the scoring with a screaming two-run drive well up into the right-field bleachers.

87   DATE: April 28, 1955   PLACE, OPP.: Municipal Stadium,
Kansas City A's   SCORE: NY 11, KC 4   SWING, POS. IN
ORDER: LH, 3rd   PITCHER: Charlie Bishop   MEN ON: 1
STATS: 2 for 3, 2 BBs, 3 runs, 2 RBIs   POSITION: CF

88   DATE: May 3, 1955
PLACE, OPP.: Municipal
   Stadium, Cleveland Indians
SCORE: CL 7, NY 4

The Yankees temporarily went ahead, 4–3, in the sixth inning on Mantle's homer.

SWING, POS. IN ORDER:
  LH, 3rd
PITCHER: Mike Garcia
MEN ON: 2
STATS: 1 for 4, 1 run, 3 RBIs
POSITION: CF

---

89   DATE: May 6, 1955
PLACE, OPP.: Fenway Park,
  Boston Red Sox
SCORE: NY 6, BO 0
SWING, POS. IN ORDER:
  LH, 3rd
PITCHER: Frank Sullivan
MEN ON: 0
STATS: 1 for 4, 1 BB, 1 run, 1
  RBI
POSITION: CF

Mantle, who finished the game batting only .257 (18 for 70), gave Bob Turley the only run he needed with a first-inning shot that cut against a whistling wind and landed in the Yankee bullpen.

---

90   DATE: May 7, 1955
PLACE, OPP.: Fenway Park,
  Boston Red Sox
SCORE: NY 9, BO 6
SWING, POS. IN ORDER:
  LH, 3rd
PITCHER: Ike Delock
MEN ON: 0
STATS: 2 for 5, 1 BB, 2 runs, 1
  RBI
POSITION: CF

One of the day's big hits was rookie Elston Howard's first big-league home run. In the eighth, Mantle put New York ahead, 6–5, with a towering home run to dead-center field.

---

91   DATE: May 11, 1955
PLACE, OPP.: Yankee
  Stadium, Cleveland Indians
SCORE: CL 4, NY 3

Solo home runs by Andy Carey in the fourth and Mantle in the eighth weren't enough to catch Wynn.

SWING, POS. IN ORDER:
  LH, 3rd
PITCHER: Early Wynn
MEN ON: 0
STATS: 2 for 4, 1 run, 2 RBIs
POSITION: CF

92
93
94
DATE: May 13, 1955   PLACE, OPP.: Yankee Stadium, Detroit
Tigers   SCORE: NY 5, DE 2   SWING, POS. IN ORDER:
LH, LH, RH; 3rd   PITCHERS: Steve Gromek (2), Bob Miller
MEN ON: 1, 0, 0   STATS: 4 for 4, 3 runs, 5 RBIs   POSITION:
CF

95
DATE: May 18, 1955
PLACE, OPP.: Yankee
  Stadium, Chicago White Sox
SCORE: NY 11, CH 6
SWING, POS. IN ORDER:
  LH, 3rd
PITCHER: Mike Fornieles
MEN ON: 3
STATS: 1 for 2, 3 BBs, 2 runs, 4
  RBIs
POSITION: CF

Ahead, 7–6, the Bombers in the seventh had the sacks filled for Mantle. But the Mick first had to wait for a rhubarb to be settled. "What's all the fuss about?" Mantle asked catcher Clint Courtney. "I'm going to hit one out of here." And he did, too, for a 400-foot grand-slam homer.

96
DATE: June 3, 1955
PLACE, OPP.: Comiskey Park,
  Chicago White Sox
SCORE: CH 3, NY 2
SWING, POS. IN ORDER:
  RH, 4th
PITCHER: Jack Harshman
MEN ON: 0
STATS: 1 for 4, 1 run, 1 RBI
POSITION: CF

Mantle's sixth-inning homer off the upper deck in left-center tied it at 2–2, but with the bases loaded in the seventh, Mantle bounced out gently to Harshman.

97   DATE: June 5, 1955   PLACE, OPP.: Comiskey Park, Chicago
White Sox   SCORE: NY 3, CH 2   SWING, POS. IN ORDER:
RH, 4th   PITCHER: Billy Pierce   MEN ON: 0   STATS: 1
for 4, 1 run, 1 RBI   POSITION: CF

---

98   DATE: June 6, 1955
PLACE, OPP.: Briggs Stadium,
   Detroit Tigers
SCORE: NY 7, DE 5
SWING, POS. IN ORDER:
   RH, 4th
PITCHER: Bob Miller
MEN ON: 0
STATS: 1 for 5, 1 run, 1 RBI
POSITION: CF

For the Yankees, Eddie Robinson hit a pair of two-run homers, and solo shots were contributed by Billy Hunter, Gil McDougald, and Mantle. Mickey's was a 450-footer that went over the screen in dead-center field, clearing the 440-foot sign. "The first one ever hit into the dead-center stands," said Red Major, a longtime stadium employee.

---

99   DATE: June 17, 1955
PLACE, OPP.: Yankee
   Stadium, Chicago White Sox
SCORE: CH 2, NY 1
SWING, POS. IN ORDER:
   LH, 3rd
PITCHER: Dick Donovan
MEN ON: 0
STATS: 1 for 4, 1 run, 1 RBI
POSITION: CF

Mantle tied the score at 1–1 with a two-out eighth-inning homer 10 rows deep in the right-field upper deck.

---

100   DATE: June 19, 1955
PLACE, OPP.: Yankee
   Stadium, Chicago White Sox
SCORE: NY 5, CH 2
SWING, POS. IN ORDER:
   LH, 3rd

The Yankees wrested away the league lead from Chicago with a double-header sweep. In the nightcap, the Yanks were ahead, 3–2, with a runner on, when Mantle, who was 0 for 7 for the

PITCHER: Sandy Consuegra
MEN ON: 1
STATS: 1 for 4, 1 run, 2 RBIs
POSITION: CF

day, walloped a full-count change-up for a two-run homer about 20 rows back in the right-field seats.

---

101 DATE: June 21, 1955   PLACE, OPP.: Yankee Stadium, Kansas City A's   SCORE: NY 6, KC 2   SWING, POS. IN ORDER: RH, 3rd   PITCHER: Alex Kellner   MEN ON: 0   STATS: 1 for 4, 1 run, 1 RBI   POSITION: CF

---

102 DATE: June 22, 1955
PLACE, OPP.: Yankee
   Stadium, Kansas City A's
SCORE: NY 6, KC 1
SWING, POS. IN ORDER:
   LH, 3rd
PITCHER: Art Ditmar
MEN ON: 1
STATS: 1 for 2, 2 BBs, 2 runs, 2
   RBIs
POSITION: CF

With the game scoreless in the third inning, Mantle hit a 400-foot-plus homer into the right-field bleachers. His homer was hit with a bat belonging to Joe Collins. "I can't seem to get a hit with my own," explained Mickey.

103
104 DATE: July 10, 1955
PLACE, OPP.: Griffith
   Stadium, Washington
   Senators
SCORE: WA 6, NY 4
SWING, POS. IN ORDER:
   RH, RH; 3rd
PITCHER: Dean Stone (2)
MEN ON: 0, 0
STATS: 2 for 4, 2 runs, 2 RBIs
POSITION: CF

A pair of cannon shots by Mantle into the bleachers in left field, the second going about 15 rows deep in the left-center wasn't enough.

105

DATE: July 10, 1955
PLACE, OPP.: Griffith
    Stadium, Washington
    Senators
SCORE: NY 8, WA 3
SWING, POS. IN ORDER:
    LH, 3rd
PITCHER: Ted Abernathy
MEN ON: 1
STATS: 1 for 3, 1 BB, 1 run,
    2 RBIs
POSITION: CF

Mantle completed the double-header with a third home run into the distant bleachers, this one an opposite-field clout to left-center.

106

DATE: July 28, 1955
PLACE, OPP.: Yankee
    Stadium, Chicago White Sox
SCORE: CH 3, NY 2
SWING, POS. IN ORDER:
    LH, 5th
PITCHER: Connie Johnson
MEN ON: 1
STATS: 2 for 3, 1 BB, 1 run,
    2 RBIs
POSITION: CF

Yogi Berra opened the ninth with a single, and Mantle, who earlier tripled, cracked a homer against the third tier in right field to bring the Yanks within a run of the White Sox—as close as they got.

107

DATE: July 31, 1955
PLACE, OPP.: Yankee
    Stadium, Kansas City A's
SCORE: NY 5, KC 2
SWING, POS. IN ORDER:
    LH, 3rd
PITCHER: Cloyd Boyer
MEN ON: 0
STATS: 1 for 3, 1 BB, 1 run, 1
    RBI
POSITION: CF

Of the first eight pitches thrown by Boyer, three were hit for Yankee home runs—by Hank Bauer, Mantle and Yogi Berra.

108

DATE: August 4, 1955
PLACE, OPP.: Yankee
   Stadium, Cleveland Indians
SCORE: CL 6, NY 3
SWING, POS. IN ORDER:
   LH, 3rd
PITCHER: Ray Narleski
MEN ON: 0
STATS: 2 for 4, 1 BB, 1 run,
   1 RBI
POSITION: CF

In the bottom of the ninth, Mantle, who had previously singled, walked, and struck out twice, hit home run No. 24 to go into the league lead ahead of Al Kaline. Yet, the New York fans were unimpressed; Mickey heard mostly boos as he circled the bases.

109
110

DATE: August 7, 1955   PLACE, OPP.: Yankee Stadium, Detroit Tigers   SCORE: NY 3, DE 2   SWING, POS. IN ORDER: LH, LH; 3rd   PITCHERS: Frank Lary, Babe Birrer   MEN ON: 0, 0   STATS: 2 for 4, 1 BB, 2 runs, 2 RBIs   POSITION: CF

111

DATE: August 14, 1955
PLACE, OPP.: Memorial
   Stadium, Baltimore Orioles
SCORE: NY 7, BA 2
SWING, POS. IN ORDER:
   RH, 4th
PITCHER: Eddie Lopat
MEN ON: 1
STATS: 1 for 3, 2 BBs, 3 runs, 2
   RBIs
POSITION: CF

In the first of two games played despite the mud and ankle-deep puddles that Hurricane Connie left behind, Mantle in the fifth ripped a 400-foot cloudbuster deep into the left-field seats to give the Yankees a 5–2 lead. The blast helped beat former teammate Eddie Lopat, waived to Baltimore two weeks earlier.

112
113

DATE: August 15, 1955
PLACE, OPP.: Memorial
   Stadium, Baltimore Orioles
SCORE: NY 12, BA 6
SWING, POS. IN ORDER:
   LH, RH; 4th
PITCHERS: Ray Moore, Art
   Schallock
MEN ON: 2, 0
STATS: 2 for 4, 2 BBs, 3 runs, 4
   RBIs
POSITION: CF

After the Yanks won the first of
two games, Mantle stole the
show in the nightcap, switch-
hitting home runs for a record
second time. His left-handed
shot was a screaming line drive,
and the right-handed homer, a
towering blast. For the day,
Mickey went 5 for 8 and New
York moved back into first
place.

114

DATE: August 16, 1955
PLACE, OPP.: Fenway Park,
   Boston Red Sox
SCORE: NY 13, BO 6
SWING, POS. IN ORDER:
   LH, 4th
PITCHER: Frank Sullivan
MEN ON: 1
STATS: 3 for 5, 1 BB, 1 run, 2
   RBIs
POSITION: CF

Mantle's tremendous opposite-
field shot cleared the high wall
in the left-center near the 379-
foot mark and hit a building
across the street.

115

DATE: August 19, 1955
PLACE, OPP.: Yankee
   Stadium, Baltimore Orioles
SCORE: NY 8, BA 0
SWING, POS. IN ORDER:
   LH, 4th
PITCHER: Jim Wilson
MEN ON: 0
STATS: 2 for 5, 1 run, 3 RBIs
POSITION: CF

Mantle sent a home run 15 rows
beyond the 344-foot sign in
right field; Whitey Ford pitched
a two-hitter.

116 DATE: August 21, 1955
PLACE, OPP.: Yankee
    Stadium, Baltimore Orioles
SCORE: NY 6, BA 1
SWING, POS. IN ORDER:
    RH, 4th
PITCHER: Eddie Lopat
MEN ON: 0
STATS: 1 for 2, 2 BBs, 1 run, 1
    RBI
POSITION: CF

Three Yankee homers: Bill
Skowron blasted a 450-footer,
Hank Bauer sent one 375 feet,
and Mantle hit one a mere 350
feet.

117 DATE: August 24, 1955
PLACE, OPP.: Briggs Stadium,
    Detroit Tigers
SCORE: NY 3, DE 2
SWING, POS. IN ORDER:
    LH, 4th
PITCHER: Steve Gromek
MEN ON: 0
STATS: 1 for 4, 1 run, 1 RBI
POSITION: CF

Yogi Berra and Mantle led off
the ninth with Detroit ahead, 2–
1, and both blasted home runs
into the right-field upper deck.

118 DATE: August 28, 1955
PLACE, OPP.: Comiskey Park,
    Chicago White Sox
SCORE: NY 6, CH 1
SWING, POS. IN ORDER:
    LH, 5th
PITCHER: Connie Johnson
MEN ON: 2
STATS: 2 for 4, 1 run, 3 RBIs
POSITION: CF

New York had a 1–0 lead in the
third inning when Irv Noren
walked, Yogi Berra singled, and
Mantle smote a low liner that
buzzed into the lower deck in
right field.

119 DATE: August 31, 1955
PLACE, OPP.: Municipal
    Stadium, Kansas City A's
SCORE: NY 11, KC 6
SWING, POS. IN ORDER:
    LH, 4th
PITCHER: Cloyd Boyer
MEN ON: 0
STATS: 2 for 5, 2 runs, 1 RBI
POSITION: CF

Mantle's blast was a tremendous wallop way over the 395-foot center-field fence. "We didn't believe what we were seeing," broadcaster Merle Harman recalled years later. "For a second, we thought it was going over the second fence in dead center onto Brooklyn Avenue, and it just missed doing that!"

---

120 DATE: September 2, 1955   PLACE, OPP.: Yankee Stadium, Washington Senators   SCORE: NY 4, WA 2   SWING, POS. IN ORDER: LH, 5th   PITCHER: Bob Porterfield   MEN ON: 2   STATS: 1 for 4, 2 runs, 3 RBIs   POSITION: CF

---

121 DATE: September 4, 1955
PLACE, OPP.: Yankee
    Stadium, Washington
    Senators
SCORE: NY 8, WA 3
SWING, POS. IN ORDER:
    LH, 5th
PITCHER: Pedro Ramos
MEN ON: 2
STATS: 2 for 3, 1 BB, 2 runs, 3
    RBIs
POSITION: CF

Bob Turley escaped a first-inning jam, then gained a nice cushion in the bottom half of the inning when Mantle walloped a three-run homer into the right-field bleachers.

1956

122
123 DATE: April 17, 1956   PLACE, OPP.: Griffith Stadium, Washington Senators   SCORE: NY 10, WA 4   SWING, POS. IN ORDER: LH, LH; 3rd   PITCHER: Camilo Pascual (2)   MEN ON: 0, 2   STATS: 2 for 3, 2 BBs, 3 runs, 4 RBIs   POSITION: CF

124

DATE: April 20, 1956
PLACE, OPP.: Yankee
    Stadium, Boston Red Sox
SCORE: NY 7, BO 1
SWING, POS. IN ORDER:
    LH, 3rd
PITCHER: Ike Delock
MEN ON: 2
STATS: 2 for 3, 1 BB, 2 runs, 4
    RBIs
POSITION: CF

Mantle walked and scored in the fourth inning, crossed up the Red Sox with a two-out drag bunt to drive in a run in the fifth, and lined a three-run homer into the right-field seats in the seventh. Then he retired for the day, after having pulled the hamstring muscle in his right leg in beating out the bunt.

125

DATE: April 21, 1956
PLACE, OPP.: Yankee
    Stadium, Boston Red Sox
SCORE: NY 14, BO 10
SWING, POS. IN ORDER:
    LH, 3rd
PITCHER: George Susce
MEN ON: 1
STATS: 3 for 5, 1 run, 2 RBIs
POSITION: CF

Mantle, playing with right thigh tightly wrapped, hit a tape-measure job which landed 20 rows deep in the far left side of the right-field upper deck, adjacent to the bullpen, a sector that few if any balls had ever reached. It came to rest 415 feet from the plate at a point about 100 feet above the ground: If the ball had been hit directly over the right-field bullpen, it probably would have left the Stadium.

126

DATE: May 1, 1956
PLACE, OPP.: Yankee
    Stadium, Detroit Tigers
SCORE: NY 9, DE 2
SWING, POS. IN ORDER:
    LH, 3rd
PITCHER: Steve Gromek
MEN ON: 0
STATS: 1 for 4, 1 BB, 2 runs, 1
    RBI
POSITION: CF

Mantle gave the Yankees a 1–0 first-inning lead when he sent a full-count pitch just beyond the reach of right fielder Al Kaline and over the wall.

127
DATE: May 2, 1956
PLACE, OPP.: Yankee
  Stadium, Detroit Tigers
SCORE: DE 8, NY 1
SWING, POS. IN ORDER:
  LH, 3rd
PITCHER: Frank Lary
MEN ON: 0
STATS: 1 for 4, 1 run, 1 RBI
POSITION: CF

Lary allowed only three hits, including Mantle's ninth-inning homer.

128
DATE: May 3, 1956
PLACE, OPP.: Yankee
  Stadium, Kansas City A's
SCORE: KC 8, NY 7
SWING, POS. IN ORDER:
  RH, 3rd
PITCHER: Art Ceccarelli
MEN ON: 0
STATS: 2 for 4, 2 runs, 1 RBI
POSITION: CF

Mantle's homer, a 440-footer into the seats in left, was his first batting righty in 1956.

129
130
DATE: May 5, 1956   PLACE, OPP.: Yankee Stadium, Kansas
City A's   SCORE: NY 5, KC 2   SWING, POS. IN ORDER:
LH, LH; 3rd   PITCHERS: Lou Kretlow, Ed Burtschy   MEN
ON: 1, 0   STATS: 3 for 4, 2 runs, 3 RBIs   POSITION: CF

131
DATE: May 8, 1956
PLACE, OPP.: Yankee
  Stadium, Cleveland Indians
SCORE: NY 4, CL 3
SWING, POS. IN ORDER:
  LH, 3rd
PITCHER: Early Wynn
MEN ON: 0

Mantle had a muscle knot in his left thigh and in batting practice hit a foul off his right big toe, but he knocked Wynn's first pitch of the sixth inning into the lower-right-field stands, tying the score at 2–2.

STATS: 2 for 4, 1 run, 1 RBI
POSITION: CF

---

132 DATE: May 10, 1956
PLACE, OPP.: Yankee
    Stadium, Cleveland Indians
SCORE: CL 7, NY 2
SWING, POS. IN ORDER:
    LH, 3rd
PITCHER: Bob Lemon
MEN ON: 0
STATS: 1 for 3, 1 BB, 1 run, 1
    RBI
POSITION: CF

Lemon, breezing, went the distance but in the sixth made the mistake of throwing Mantle a change-up, and the Mick sent it into the right-field bleachers.

---

133 DATE: May 14, 1956
PLACE, OPP.: Municipal
    Stadium, Cleveland Indians
SCORE: CL 3, NY 2
SWING, POS. IN ORDER:
    LH, 3rd
PITCHER: Bob Lemon
MEN ON: 0
STATS: 1 for 4, 1 run, 1 RBI
POSITION: CF

Gil McDougald and Mantle hit back-to-back homers in the fourth inning, but Cleveland overtook New York's 2–1 lead and won.

---

134 DATE: May 16, 1956
PLACE, OPP.: Municipal
    Stadium, Cleveland Indians
SCORE: NY 4, CL 1
SWING, POS. IN ORDER:
    RH, 3rd
PITCHER: Buddy Daley
MEN ON: 0
STATS: 3 for 4, 1 BB, 1 run, 1
    RBI
POSITION: CF

Leading off the seventh, Mantle knocked a Daley knuckleball over the center-field fence to close out the scoring and finish the day batting an even .400 (40 for 100).

135
136 DATE: May 18, 1956   PLACE, OPP.: Comiskey Park, Chicago
White Sox   SCORE: NY 8, CH 7   SWING, POS. IN ORDER:
RH, LH; 3rd   PITCHERS: Billy Pierce, Dixie Howell   MEN
ON: 1, 0   STATS: 4 for 4, 1 BB, 4 runs, 3 RBIs   POSITION:
CF

---

137 DATE: May 21, 1956
PLACE, OPP.: Municpal
    Stadium, Kansas City A's
SCORE: NY 8, KC 5
SWING, POS. IN ORDER:
    LH, 4th
PITCHER: Ed Burtschy
MEN ON: 0
STATS: 2 for 2, 3 BBs, 3 runs, 1
    RBI
POSITION: CF

Mantle felt he hadn't hit it well.
He hit the ball off the bat's
trademark near his fists. Yet it
traveled 450 to 500 feet, clearing an outer wall in right field—
only Larry Doby had done this
since Kansas City went big
league in 1955—and landed on
Brooklyn Avenue.

---

138 DATE: May 24, 1956
PLACE, OPP.: Briggs Stadium,
    Detroit Tigers
SCORE: NY 11, DE 4
SWING, POS. IN ORDER:
    LH, 4th
PITCHER: Duke Maas
MEN ON: 0
STATS: 5 for 5, 1 BB, 3 runs, 3
    RBIs
POSITION: CF

Mickey homered in the second
inning, singled in the third,
fifth, and sixth, got an intentional walk in the seventh, and
singled in the ninth, raising his
batting average to .421, tops in
the majors.

---

139 DATE: May 29, 1956
PLACE, OPP.: Yankee
    Stadium, Boston Red Sox
SCORE: BO 7, NY 3
SWING, POS. IN ORDER:
    LH, 3rd

Nixon, baffling the Yankees
with a tantalizing knuckleball,
had a perfect game going until
he walked Mantle in the seventh. With two out in the
ninth, he lost the shutout when

PITCHER: Willard Nixon
MEN ON: 1
STATS: 1 for 3, 1 BB, 1 run, 2
  RBIs
POSITION: CF

Mantle hit a two-run drive into
the right-field bleachers.

---

140 DATE: May 30, 1956   PLACE, OPP.: Yankee Stadium,
Washington Senators   SCORE: NY 4 WA 3   SWING, POS. IN
ORDER: LH, 3rd   PITCHER: Pedro Ramos   MEN ON: 2
STATS: 3 for 4, 1 run, 3 RBIs, 1 SB   POSITION: CF

---

141 DATE: May 30, 1956   PLACE, OPP.: Yankee Stadium,
Washington Senators   SCORE: NY 12, WA 5   SWING, POS.
IN ORDER: LH, 3rd   PITCHER: Camilo Pascual   MEN ON: 0
STATS: 1 for 4, 1 BB, 1 run, 2 RBIs   POSITION: CF

---

142 DATE: June 5, 1956   PLACE, OPP.: Yankee Stadium, Kansas
City A's   SCORE: KC 7, NY 4   SWING, POS. IN ORDER:
LH, 3rd   PITCHER: Lou Kretlow   MEN ON: 1   STATS: 1
for 4, 1 run, 2 RBIs   POSITION: CF

---

143 DATE: June 14, 1956
PLACE, OPP.: Yankee
  Stadium, Chicago White Sox
SCORE: NY 5, CH 1
SWING, POS. IN ORDER:
  LH, 3rd
PITCHER: Jim Wilson
MEN ON: 0
STATS: 2 for 3, 1 BB, 2 runs, 2
  RBIs
POSITION: CF

In the seventh, Mantle drove a
home run 20 rows up in the
right-field bleachers, breaking a
nine-day long-ball drought.

144   DATE: June 15, 1956
PLACE, OPP.: Municipal
   Stadium, Cleveland Indians
SCORE: NY 6, CL 2
SWING, POS. IN ORDER:
   LH, 3rd
PITCHER: Mike Garcia
MEN ON: 1
STATS: 1 for 5, 1 run, 2 RBIs
POSITION: CF

Mantle swatted an opposite-field homer over the low fence in left field in the first inning, putting him five games ahead of Babe Ruth's 60-homer 1927 pace.

---

145   DATE: June 16, 1956
PLACE, OPP.: Municipal
   Stadium, Cleveland Indians
SCORE: NY 3, CL 1
SWING, POS. IN ORDER:
   RH, 3rd
PITCHER: Herb Score
MEN ON: 1
STATS: 1 for 4, 1 run, 2 RBIs
POSITION: CF

The Yankees trailed, 1–0, in the third inning when Gil Mc-Dougald doubled and Mantle popped the ball way over the left-field fence.

---

146   DATE: June 18, 1956   PLACE, OPP.: Briggs Stadium, Detroit Tigers   SCORE: NY 7, DE 4   SWING, POS. IN ORDER: LH, 3rd   PITCHER: Paul Foytack   MEN ON: 2   STATS: 1 for 4, 1 run, 3 RBIs   POSITION: CF

147
148   DATE: June 20, 1956   PLACE, OPP.: Briggs Stadium, Detroit Tigers   SCORE: NY 4, DE 1   SWING, POS. IN ORDER: RH, RH; 3rd   PITCHER: Billy Hoeft   MEN ON: 0, 0 STATS: 2 for 4, 2 runs, 2 RBIs   POSITION: CF

149
150   DATE: July 1, 1956   PLACE, OPP.: Yankee Stadium, Washington Senators   SCORE: NY 8, WA 6   SWING, POS. IN ORDER: RH, LH; 4th   PITCHERS: Dean Stone, Bud Byerly   MEN

ON: 0, 1   STATS: 2 for 3, 2 BBs, 2 runs, 4 RBIs   POSITION: CF

151

DATE: July 14, 1956
PLACE, OPP.: Yankee
    Stadium, Cleveland Indians
SCORE: NY 5, CL 4
SWING, POS. IN ORDER:
    RH, 3rd
PITCHER: Herb Score
MEN ON: 0
STATS: 1 for 3, 1 run, 1 RBI
POSITION: CF

Mantle unloaded a homer to left that landed in the Indian bull-pen, at least 20 feet beyond the 402-foot sign. With an injured knee acting up, Mantle later left the game, but the Yanks won in 10 innings.

152

DATE: July 18, 1956
PLACE, OPP.: Yankee
    Stadium, Detroit Tigers
SCORE: DE 8, NY 4
SWING, POS. IN ORDER:
    LH, 3rd
PITCHER: Paul Foytack
MEN ON: 0
STATS: 2 for 4, 1 run, 2 RBIs
POSITION: CF

For the first time in two weeks Mantle played without wearing a knee brace, and he beat out a bunt. In the opener, his homer helped the Yanks to an early 3–1 lead, which didn't stand up. In the nightcap, with two on and two out in the ninth, Mickey poked a towering fly to right that Al Kaline leaped above the wall to catch, and Detroit won, 4–3.

153

DATE: July 22, 1956
PLACE, OPP.: Yankee
    Stadium, Kansas City A's
SCORE: KC 7, NY 4
SWING, POS. IN ORDER:
    LH, 4th
PITCHER: Art Ditmar
MEN ON: 1
STATS: 2 for 3, 1 BB, 1 run, 2
    RBIs
POSITION: CF

Lou Boudreau used the Mantle Shift when Mickey led off the sixth, and the Mick easily beat out a bunt. In the seventh, he socked a two-run homer over the auxiliary scoreboard in right field.

154
155

DATE: July 30, 1956
PLACE, OPP.: Municipal
  Stadium, Cleveland Indians
SCORE: NY 13, CL 6
SWING, POS. IN ORDER:
  LH, LH; 3rd
PITCHERS: Bob Lemon, Bob
  Feller
MEN ON: 3, 1
STATS: 2 for 4, 1 BB, 3 runs, 6
  RBIs
POSITION: CF

Mantle had a 6-RBI game—
against two of baseball's greatest
pitchers, Lemon and Feller. In
the second, Mantle hit his first
grand slam of the season, knocking out Lemon; in the fifth,
Mickey hit his only career
homer off Feller.

156
157

DATE: August 4, 1956
PLACE, OPP.: Briggs Stadium,
  Detroit Tigers
SCORE: DE 5, NY 4
SWING, POS. IN ORDER:
  LH, LH; 3rd
PITCHER: Virgil Trucks
MEN ON: 1, 0
STATS: 3 for 3, 2 BBs, 3 runs, 3
  RBIs, 1 SB
POSITION: CF

This was a slugging duel between Mantle and Al Kaline.
Both Mantle and Kaline hit
two-run homers in the first inning. In the third, Mantle singled
(stole a base, and scored) and his
fifth-inning homer, landing in
the right-field upper deck, put
New York ahead, 4–2. But Kaline's three-run homer in the
eighth ruined Mickey's efforts.

158

DATE: August 5, 1956
PLACE, OPP.: Briggs Stadium,
  Detroit Tigers
SCORE: DE 8, NY 5
SWING, POS. IN ORDER:
  LH, 3rd
PITCHER: Jim Bunning
MEN ON: 0
STATS: 2 for 5, 1 run, 1 RBI
POSITION: CF

Mantle and Al Kaline continued
slugging it out. Kaline's three-
run homer helped Detroit to a
4–0 lead, and Mantle's solo
homer in the sixth brought New
York even, at 5–5. Mantle's shot
was no ordinary homer; it hit
the front of the roof of the right-
field upper deck.

159 DATE: August 8, 1956
PLACE, OPP.: Griffith
Stadium, Washington
Senators
SCORE: NY 12, WA 2
SWING, POS. IN ORDER:
LH, 3rd
PITCHER: Camilo Pascual
MEN ON: 1
STATS: 1 for 4, 1 BB, 2 runs, 2
RBIs
POSITION: CF

Mickey put the Yanks ahead in the first inning when he lofted an opposite-field homer into the left-field bleachers, putting him nine games ahead of Babe Ruth's 60-homer pace.

160 DATE: August 9, 1956
PLACE, OPP.: Griffith
Stadium, Washington
Senators
SCORE: NY 15, WA 7
SWING, POS. IN ORDER:
LH, 4th
PITCHER: Hal Griggs
MEN ON: 1
STATS: 2 for 3, 3 BBs, 2 runs, 2
RBIs
POSITION: CF

After receiving three walks, Mantle in the seventh inning capped New York's scoring with his second opposite-field homer in as many days.

161 DATE: August 11, 1956
PLACE, OPP.: Yankee
Stadium, Baltimore Orioles
SCORE: BA 10, NY 5
SWING, POS. IN ORDER:
LH, 3rd
PITCHER: Hal Brown
MEN ON: 2
STATS: 2 for 3, 2 BBs, 1 run, 3
RBIs
POSITION: CF

Mantle hit his first homer against Baltimore this year, breaking the Baltimore jinx and becoming the first Yankee in 19 years to reach the 40-homer mark. He golfed a knuckleball—"my best pitch," said Brown—deep into the upper deck in right field.

162 DATE: August 12, 1956   PLACE, OPP.: Yankee Stadium,
Baltimore Orioles   SCORE: NY 6, BA 2   SWING, POS. IN
ORDER: RH, 4th   PITCHER: Don Ferrarese   MEN ON: 1
STATS: 1 for 2, 1 BB, 1 run, 3 RBIs   POSITION: CF

---

163 DATE: August 14, 1956
PLACE, OPP.: Yankee
   Stadium, Boston Red Sox
SCORE: NY 12, BO 2
SWING, POS. IN ORDER:
   RH, 4th
PITCHER: Mel Parnell
MEN ON: 1
STATS: 3 for 3, 1 BB, 3 runs, 2
   RBIs
POSITION: CF

The highlight of Mantle's perfect day was a homer deep into
the left-field seats. He was 13
games ahead of the Babe Ruth
pace.

---

164 DATE: August 23, 1956
PLACE, OPP.: Yankee
   Stadium, Chicago White Sox
SCORE: CH 6, NY 4
SWING, POS. IN ORDER:
   RH, 3rd
PITCHER: Paul LaPalme
MEN ON: 0
STATS: 3 for 5, 2 runs, 1 RBI
POSITION: CF

The White Sox, led by Nellie
Fox's seven consecutive hits,
beat the Yankees twice, and Fox
took the league's hit lead away
from Mantle, 158 to 155. Mantle went hitless in the opener,
but in the nightcap, he beat out
a bunt, hit a 460-foot triple, and
blasted a tremendous homer 20
rows deep into the left-field upper deck, a shot reminiscent of
the one Mantle hit off Billy
Hoeft in 1953.

---

165 DATE: August 25, 1956
PLACE, OPP.: Yankee
   Stadium, Chicago White Sox
SCORE: CH 4, NY 2
SWING, POS. IN ORDER:
   LH, 3rd
PITCHER: Dick Donovan
MEN ON: 1
STATS: 3 for 4, 1 run, 2 RBIs
POSITION: CF

It was Old-Timers' Day, but everything was overshadowed by the Yankees' release of Phil Rizzuto. Mantle opened the scoring with an opposite-field homer in the fourth, but Chicago's go-ahead run scored on a Mantle throwing error.

---

166 DATE: August 28, 1956
PLACE, OPP.: Yankee
   Stadium, Kansas City A's
SCORE: NY 4, KC 0
SWING, POS. IN ORDER:
   LH, 3rd
PITCHER: Art Ditmar
MEN ON: 2
STATS: 1 for 2, 1 run, 3 RBIs
POSITION: CF

Mantle lifted a modest 360-foot homer that just reached the right-field bullpen in a rain-abbreviated game.

---

167 DATE: August 29, 1956
PLACE, OPP.: Yankee
   Stadium, Kansas City A's
SCORE: NY 7, KC 6
SWING, POS. IN ORDER:
   RH, 4th
PITCHER: Jack McMahan
MEN ON: 0
STATS: 3 for 5, 1 run, 2 RBIs
POSITION: CF

Mantle made a first-inning error that allowed the A's to score four unearned runs, then spent the rest of the game redeeming himself, sending a 410-foot homer into the left-field seats, hitting a run-building single, and singling home the winning run with two out in the ninth.

---

168 DATE: August 31, 1956   PLACE, OPP.: Griffith Stadium, Washington Senators   SCORE: NY 6, WA 4   SWING, POS. IN ORDER: LH, 3rd   PITCHER: Camilo Pascual   MEN ON: 0 STATS: 1 for 4, 1 BB, 2 runs, 1 RBI   POSITION: CF

---

169 DATE: September 13, 1956
PLACE, OPP.: Municipal
  Stadium, Kansas City A's
SCORE: NY 3, KC 2
SWING, POS. IN ORDER:
  LH, 3rd
PITCHER: Tom Gorman
MEN ON: 0
STATS: 2 for 4, 2 runs, 1 RBI
POSITION: CF

Mantle's third-inning homer
gave the Yankees a 3–0 lead.

170 DATE: September 16, 1956
PLACE, OPP.: Municipal
  Stadium, Cleveland Indians
SCORE: CL 4, NY 3
SWING, POS. IN ORDER:
  LH, 3rd
PITCHER: Early Wynn
MEN ON: 0
STATS: 1 for 3, 1 BB, 1 run, 1
  RBI
POSITION: CF

Mantle narrowed Cleveland's
lead to 4–3 in the eighth, hitting a titanic shot into the right-
field upper deck. It was only the
second ball to reach that section
this season; Ted Williams hit the
other.

171 DATE: September 18, 1956   PLACE, OPP.: Comiskey Park,
Chicago White Sox   SCORE: NY 3, CH 2   SWING, POS. IN
ORDER: RH, 3rd   PITCHER: Billy Pierce   MEN ON: 0
STATS: 2 for 5, 1 run, 2 RBIs   POSITION: CF

172 DATE: September 21, 1956   PLACE, OPP.: Fenway Park, Boston
Red Sox   SCORE: BO 13, NY 7   SWING, POS. IN ORDER:
LH, 3rd   PITCHER: Frank Sullivan   MEN ON: 0   STATS:
3 for 5, 1 BB, 3 runs, 2 RBIs   POSITION: CF

173 DATE: September 28, 1956   PLACE, OPP.: Yankee Stadium, Boston Red Sox   SCORE: NY 7, BO 2   SWING, POS. IN ORDER: LH, 3rd   PITCHER: Bob Porterfield   MEN ON: 0 STATS: 1 for 4, 1 run, 1 RBI   POSITION: CF

1957

---

174 DATE: April 22, 1957
PLACE, OPP.: Griffith
  Stadium, Washington
  Senators
SCORE: NY 15, WA 6
SWING, POS. IN ORDER:
  RH, 3rd
PITCHER: Chuck Stobbs
MEN ON: 0
STATS: 2 for 4, 2 BBs, 2 runs, 1
  RBI
POSITION: CF

Mantle in New York's fifth game of the year got his first home run, a 400-foot-plus drive into the center-field seats.

175 DATE: April 24, 1957
PLACE, OPP.: Yankee
  Stadium, Baltimore Orioles
SCORE: NY 3, BA 2
SWING, POS. IN ORDER:
  LH, 3rd
PITCHER: Connie Johnson
MEN ON: 0
STATS: 3 for 3, 1 BB, 2 runs, 1
  RBI
POSITION: CF

Breaking a 2–2 tie, Mantle crushed Johnson's first pitch in the eighth for a game-winning homer; it sailed over 400 feet into the right-field bleachers. And it capped a perfect day for Mickey.

176
DATE: May 5, 1957
PLACE, OPP.: Comiskey Park, Chicago White Sox
SCORE: NY 4, CH 2
SWING, POS. IN ORDER: RH, 3rd
PITCHER: Billy Pierce
MEN ON: 1
STATS: 3 for 3, 1 BB, 1 run, 2 RBIs, 1 SB
POSITION: CF

In the first of two games, New York took the lead for good when Mantle laced a two-run homer into the top tier in left. But Mantle also pulled a groin muscle and, after receiving a fifth-inning intentional walk in the afterpiece, he was through for the day.

177
DATE: May 8, 1957
PLACE, OPP.: Municipal Stadium, Cleveland Indians
SCORE: CL 10, NY 4
SWING, POS. IN ORDER: LH, 3rd
PITCHER: Early Wynn
MEN ON: 2
STATS: 1 for 3, 2 BBs, 1 run, 3 RBIs
POSITION: CF

Mantle gave the Yankees a 3–0 lead with a 440-foot homer to center field. But the Indians parlayed three homers of their own into an easy win.

178
DATE: May 12, 1957
PLACE, OPP.: Memorial Stadium, Baltimore Orioles
SCORE: NY 4, BA 3
SWING, POS. IN ORDER: LH, 3rd
PITCHER: Hal Brown
MEN ON: 0
STATS: 3 for 4, 1 run, 1 RBI
POSITION: CF

Two homers by Andy Carey, good for three runs, had the Yankees in a 3–3 tie. With two out in the eighth, Mantle clouted the game winner deep into the right-field seats. Last year Mantle homered in every league park except Baltimore's Memorial Stadium.

179 DATE: May 16, 1957   PLACE, OPP.: Yankee Stadium, Kansas City A's   SCORE: NY 3, KC 0   SWING, POS. IN ORDER: RH, 3rd   PITCHER: Alex Kellner   MEN ON: 0   STATS: 2 for 2, 2 BBs, 1 run, 1 RBI   POSITION: CF

---

180 DATE: May 19, 1957
PLACE, OPP.: Yankee
 Stadium, Cleveland Indians
SCORE: NY 6, CL 3
SWING, POS. IN ORDER:
 LH, 3rd
PITCHER: Bob Lemon
MEN ON: 0
STATS: 2 for 3, 1 BB, 2 runs, 1
 RBI
POSITION: CF

Lemon was knocked out in the sixth in a rally that included Mantle's sixth, and final, homer off the future Hall of Famer; the Mick sent a curve high into the top tier in right field.

---

181 DATE: May 25, 1957
PLACE, OPP.: Yankee
 Stadium, Washington
 Senators
SCORE: NY 8, WA 1
SWING, POS. IN ORDER:
 LH, 4th
PITCHER: Pedro Ramos
MEN ON: 1
STATS: 2 for 4, 1 run, 2 RBIs
POSITION: CF

Mantle in the fifth lined a homer into the lower stands in right to put the Yankees up, 6–1.

---

182 DATE: May 26, 1957
PLACE, OPP.: Yankee
 Stadium, Washington
 Senators
SCORE: WA 9, NY 7
SWING, POS. IN ORDER:
 LH, 4th

Though the Senators eventually prevailed, the Yankees overcame a 6–0 deficit to tie the game when Mantle laced a two-run homer high into the upper deck in right, the ball disappearing through a runway.

PITCHER: Camilo Pascual
MEN ON: 1
STATS: 1 for 3, 1 BB, 1 run, 2
  RBIs
POSITION: CF

---

183   DATE: May 29, 1957
PLACE, OPP.: Griffith
  Stadium, Washington
  Senators
SCORE: WA 6, NY 2
SWING, POS. IN ORDER:
  LH, 4th
PITCHER: Pedro Ramos
MEN ON: 0
STATS: 2 for 3, 1 BB, 1 run, 1
  RBI
POSITION: CF

Ramos delivered two of the 43 gopher balls he threw in the year, one to Hank Bauer and the other to Mantle. Mantle's caromed off the high center-field wall at the 438-foot mark.

---

184   DATE: June 2, 1957
PLACE, OPP.: Yankee
  Stadium, Baltimore Orioles
SCORE: NY 4, BA 0
SWING, POS. IN ORDER:
  LH, 3rd
PITCHER: Hal Brown
MEN ON: 1
STATS: 1 for 3, 1 BB, 1 run, 2
  RBIs
POSITION: CF

Three first-inning homers, by Mantle, Yogi Berra, and Elston Howard, accounted for all the game's scoring. Mantle's made the upper deck in right.

---

185   DATE: June 5, 1957
PLACE, OPP.: Municipal
  Stadium, Cleveland Indians
SCORE: NY 13, CL 3

Mickey's 450-footer to right was one of four Yankee homers. Gil McDougald hit two.

SWING, POS. IN ORDER:
  LH, 3rd
PITCHER: Early Wynn
MEN ON: 0
STATS: 3 for 5, 2 runs, 1 RBI
POSITION: CF

---

186 DATE: June 6, 1957
PLACE, OPP.: Municipal
  Stadium, Cleveland Indians
SCORE: NY 14, CL 5
SWING, POS. IN ORDER:
  LH, 3rd
PITCHER: Mike Garcia
MEN ON: 1
STATS: 2 for 3, 3 BBs, 3 runs, 4
  RBIs
POSITION: CF

Mantle gave New York a 2–0
first-inning lead with another
450-foot homer; the ball cleared
the center-field fence, landed
on a cinder track, and struck the
bleachers on one bounce (no
ball has ever reached the
bleachers on the fly).

---

187 DATE: June 7, 1957
PLACE, OPP.: Briggs Stadium,
  Detroit Tigers
SCORE: DE 6, NY 3
SWING, POS. IN ORDER:
  LH, 3rd
PITCHER: Jim Bunning
MEN ON: 0
STATS: 1 for 3, 1 BB, 1 run, 1
  RBI
POSITION: CF

Mantle put the Yankees into a
1–0 first-inning lead, stunning a
large crowd with a prodigious
clout that bounced off the facing
of the right-field roof.

188

DATE: June 10, 1957
PLACE, OPP.: Briggs Stadium,
    Detroit Tigers
SCORE: DE 9, NY 4
SWING, POS. IN ORDER:
    LH, 3rd
PITCHER: Frank Lary
MEN ON: 0
STATS: 2 for 3, 1 BB, 1 run, 1
    RBI
POSITION: CF

With his home run, Mantle
gained a 15-to-13 advantage
over Ted Williams in the league
home-run race.

189

DATE: June 11, 1957
PLACE, OPP.: Comiskey Park,
    Chicago White Sox
SCORE: NY 3, CH 2
SWING, POS. IN ORDER:
    LH, 3rd
PITCHER: Jim Wilson
MEN ON: 0
STATS: 2 for 3, 2 BBs, 2 runs, 1
    RBI
POSITION: CF

The second-place Yankees edged
the league leaders, the scoring
beginning with Mantle's first-
inning homer into the right-
field upper deck. Mickey later
doubled and scored the deciding
run.

190
191

DATE: June 12, 1957   PLACE, OPP.: Comiskey Park, Chicago
White Sox   SCORE: CH 7, NY 6   SWING, POS. IN ORDER:
RH, LH; 3rd   PITCHERS: Jack Harshman, Bob Keegan   MEN
ON: 0, 1   STATS: 4 for 5, 2 runs, 4 RBIs   POSITION: CF

192

DATE: June 14, 1957
PLACE, OPP.: Municipal
    Stadium, Kansas City A's
SCORE: NY 10, KC 1
SWING, POS. IN ORDER:
    RH, 3rd
PITCHER: Gene Host

Coming in to relieve, Host, who
posted a career 0–2 record in 28
innings pitched, was greeted by
a Mantle homer.

MEN ON: 1
STATS: 1 for 3, 3 BBs, 2 runs, 2
   RBIs
POSITION: CF

---

193   DATE: June 22, 1957
PLACE, OPP.: Yankee
   Stadium, Chicago White Sox
SCORE: NY 6, CH 5
SWING, POS. IN ORDER:
   RH, 3rd
PITCHER: Jack Harshman
MEN ON: 1
STATS: 2 for 6, 1 run, 2 RBIs
POSITION: CF

With their ninth win in a row—
Yogi Berra won it with a 13th-
inning homer—the Yankees
passed Chicago and moved into
first place. Mantle got them going in the first with a two-run
homer, a low liner the other
way.

---

194   DATE: June 23, 1957   PLACE, OPP.: Yankee Stadium, Chicago
White Sox   SCORE: CH 4, NY 3   SWING, POS. IN ORDER:
LH, 3rd   PITCHER: Dick Donovan   MEN ON: 2   STATS:
2 for 4, 1 run, 3 RBIs   POSITION: CF

---

195   DATE: July 1, 1957   PLACE, OPP.: Memorial Stadium,
Baltimore Orioles   SCORE: NY 3, BA 2   SWING, POS. IN
ORDER: LH, 3rd   PITCHER: George Zuverink   MEN ON: 0
STATS: 2 for 4, 1 BB, 1 run, 1 RBI   POSITION: CF

---

196   DATE: July 11, 1957   PLACE, OPP.: Municipal Stadium, Kansas
City A's   SCORE: NY 3, KC 2   SWING, POS. IN ORDER:
LH, 3rd   PITCHER: Tom Morgan   MEN ON: 0   STATS: 2
for 5, 2 runs, 1 RBI   POSITION: CF

197 DATE: July 12, 1957
PLACE, OPP.: Municipal
Stadium, Kansas City A's
SCORE: NY 4, KC 2
SWING, POS. IN ORDER:
LH, 3rd
PITCHER: Ralph Terry
MEN ON: 0
STATS: 1 for 4, 1 BB, 2 runs, 1
RBI
POSITION: CF

Mantle's first-inning homer was matched by a Vic Power homer in the sixth. Mickey was aboard in the eighth when Harry "Suitcase" Simpson smacked a three-run homer to decide it.

198 DATE: July 21, 1957
PLACE, OPP.: Municipal
Stadium, Cleveland Indians
SCORE: CL 7, NY 4
SWING, POS. IN ORDER:
LH, 3rd
PITCHER: Ray Narleski
MEN ON: 1
STATS: 2 for 4, 1 BB, 2 runs, 3
RBIs
POSITION: CF

Mantle reached base safely 10 consecutive times before popping out in the seventh inning of today's nightcap: two walks in his final trips yesterday, a single and four walks in the opener, and a single, walk, and homer in the afterpiece.

199 DATE: July 23, 1957   PLACE, OPP.: Yankee Stadium, Chicago
White Sox   SCORE: NY 10, CH 6   SWING, POS. IN
ORDER: LH, 3rd   PITCHER: Bob Keegan   MEN ON: 0
STATS: 4 for 5, 2 runs, 4 RBIs, 1 SB   POSITION: CF

200 DATE: July 26, 1957
PLACE, OPP.: Yankee
Stadium, Detroit Tigers
SCORE: DE 3, NY 2
SWING, POS. IN ORDER:
LH, 3rd

Mantle in the ninth wrapped up the scoring with an uncharacteristic left-handed homer—an opposite-field fly ball that hugged the line.

PITCHER: Jim Bunning
MEN ON: 0
STATS: 1 for 4, 1 run, 1 RBI
POSITION: CF

---

201 DATE: July 31, 1957
PLACE, OPP.: Yankee
    Stadium, Kansas City A's
SCORE: NY 2, KC 0
SWING, POS. IN ORDER:
    LH, 3rd
PITCHER: Wally Burnette
MEN ON: 0
STATS: 1 for 2, 2 BBs, 1 run, 1
    RBI
POSITION: CF

Bob Turley didn't permit a runner past second base, and Mantle handed him an insurance
run with an upper-deck homer
to right field.

---

202 DATE: August 2, 1957   PLACE, OPP.: Yankee Stadium,
Cleveland Indians   SCORE: NY 3, CL 2   SWING, POS. IN
ORDER: RH, 3rd   PITCHER: Don Mossi   MEN ON: 0
STATS: 1 for 3, 1 run, 1 RBI   POSITION: CF

---

203 DATE: August 7, 1957
PLACE, OPP.: Yankee
    Stadium, Washington
    Senators
SCORE: WA 3, NY 2
SWING, POS. IN ORDER:
    LH, 3rd
PITCHER: Tex Clevenger
MEN ON: 0
STATS: 2 for 4, 1 run, 1 RBI
POSITION: CF

In the Yanks' last licks, Mantle
knocked a foul off his right foot
and after standing in pain for
some time socked the next pitch
into the lower stands in right.
The Mick made three inspired
defensive plays.

---

204 DATE: August 10, 1957   PLACE, OPP.: Memorial Stadium, Baltimore Orioles   SCORE: NY 6, BA 3   SWING, POS. IN ORDER: LH, 3rd   PITCHER: Ray Moore   MEN ON: 1 STATS: 4 for 5, 2 runs, 2 RBIs, 1 SB   POSITION: CF

---

205 DATE: August 13, 1957   PLACE, OPP.: Fenway Park, Boston Red Sox   SCORE: NY 3, BO 2   SWING, POS. IN ORDER: LH, 3rd   PITCHER: Frank Sullivan   MEN ON: 1   STATS: 3 for 3, 1 BB, 1 run, 3 RBIs   POSITION: CF

---

206 DATE: August 26, 1957
PLACE, OPP.: Briggs Stadium,
  Detroit Tigers
SCORE: DE 5, NY 2
SWING, POS. IN ORDER:
  LH, 3rd
PITCHER: Frank Lary
MEN ON: 1
STATS: 2 for 4, 1 run, 2 RBIs
POSITION: CF

Mantle gave New York a 2–0 first-inning lead with a booming homer into the upper deck in center field, a drive of at least 450 feet.

---

207 DATE: August 30, 1957   PLACE, OPP.: Yankee Stadium, Washington Senators   SCORE: WA 4, NY 2   SWING, POS. IN ORDER: RH, 3rd   PITCHER: Chuck Stobbs   MEN ON: 0 STATS: 3 for 4, 2 runs, 1 RBI   POSITION: CF

1958

---

208 DATE: April 17, 1958   PLACE, OPP.: Fenway Park, Boston Red Sox   SCORE: NY 3, BO 1   SWING, POS. IN ORDER: LH, 3rd   PITCHER: Tom Brewer   MEN ON: 0   STATS: 1 for 3, 1 BB, 1 run, 1 RBI   POSITION: CF

---

209 DATE: May 9, 1958 PLACE, OPP.: Yankee Stadium, Washington Senators SCORE: NY 9, WA 5 SWING, POS. IN ORDER: LH, 3rd PITCHER: Pedro Ramos MEN ON: 0 STATS: 3 for 5, 2 runs, 1 RBI, 1 SB POSITION: CF

---

210 DATE: May 18, 1958 PLACE, OPP.: Griffith Stadium, Washington Senators SCORE: NY 5, WA 2 SWING, POS. IN ORDER: LH, 4th PITCHER: Pedro Ramos MEN ON: 0 STATS: 1 for 3, 1 BB, 1 run, 1 RBI POSITION: CF

Mantle got things going with an opposite-field homer in the fourth inning. The Yanks went on to score five runs in the inning.

---

211 DATE: May 20, 1958 PLACE, OPP.: Comiskey Park, Chicago White Sox SCORE: NY 5, CH 1 SWING, POS. IN ORDER: LH, 4th PITCHER: Dick Donovan MEN ON: 0 STATS: 2 for 3, 1 BB, 2 runs, 1 RBI POSITION: CF

---

212 DATE: June 2, 1958 PLACE, OPP.: Yankee Stadium, Chicago White Sox SCORE: NY 3, CH 0 SWING, POS. IN ORDER: LH, 3rd PITCHER: Jim Wilson MEN ON: 0 STATS: 1 for 3, 1 run, 1 RBI POSITION: CF

Wilson allowed only six hits in going the distance, but three were Yankee home runs—two by Hank Bauer and one by Mantle.

213 DATE: June 3, 1958
PLACE, OPP.: Yankee
  Stadium, Chicago White Sox
SCORE: NY 13, CH 0
SWING, POS. IN ORDER:
  LH, 3rd
PITCHER: Dick Donovan
MEN ON: 2
STATS: 1 for 2, 3 BBs, 3 runs, 3
  RBIs
POSITION: CF

The Yankees routed Donovan
before he retired a batter, helped
by Mantle's liner into the right-
field seats.

214 DATE: June 4, 1958   PLACE, OPP.: Yankee Stadium, Chicago
White Sox   SCORE: CH 7, NY 2   SWING, POS. IN ORDER:
RH, 3rd   PITCHER: Billy Pierce   MEN ON: 0   STATS: 1
for 4, 1 run, 1 RBI   POSITION: CF

215 DATE: June 5, 1958   PLACE, OPP.: Yankee Stadium, Chicago
White Sox   SCORE: NY 12, CH 5   SWING, POS. IN
ORDER: LH, 3rd   PITCHER: Early Wynn   MEN ON: 0
STATS: 2 for 4, 1 BB, 3 runs, 1 RBI   POSITION: CF

216
217 DATE: June 6, 1958
PLACE, OPP.: Yankee
  Stadium, Cleveland Indians
SCORE: NY 6, CL 5
SWING, POS. IN ORDER:
  RH, RH; 3rd
PITCHER: Dick Tomanek (2)
MEN ON: 0, 2
STATS: 3 for 3, 1 BB, 2 runs, 4
  RBIs
POSITION: CF

Mantle hit a hefty first-inning
homer that caromed off the railing in front of the left-field upper deck, and in the fifth, with
the Yankees down, 3–1, he sent
a three-run shot into the lower
seats in left.

218   DATE: June 8, 1958
PLACE, OPP.: Yankee
  Stadium, Cleveland Indians
SCORE: CL 5, NY 4
SWING, POS. IN ORDER:
  LH, 3rd
PITCHER: Mudcat Grant
MEN ON: 0
STATS: 1 for 4, 1 BB, 1 run, 1
  RBI
POSITION: CF

Mantle's one hit on a double-header day was his seventh homer in as many days.

---

219   DATE: June 13, 1958
PLACE, OPP.: Yankee
  Stadium, Detroit Tigers
SCORE: DE 4, NY 2
SWING, POS. IN ORDER:
  RH, 3rd
PITCHER: Billy Hoeft
MEN ON: 0
STATS: 1 for 3, 1 BB, 1 run, 1
  RBI
POSITION: CF

Mantle lofted a rainmaker deep into the left-field seats in the fourth inning to tie it at 1–1.

---

220   DATE: June 24, 1958
PLACE, OPP.: Comiskey Park,
  Chicago White Sox
SCORE: NY 6, CH 2
SWING, POS. IN ORDER:
  LH, 3rd
PITCHER: Early Wynn
MEN ON: 0
STATS: 1 for 5, 1 run, 1 RBI
POSITION: CF

Kicking off a five-run fourth was Mantle's 420-foot homer into the center-field bleachers.

221 DATE: June 29, 1958
PLACE, OPP.: Municipal
   Stadium, Kansas City A's
SCORE: KC 12, NY 6
SWING, POS. IN ORDER:
   LH, 3rd
PITCHER: Ralph Terry
MEN ON: 1
STATS: 1 for 4, 1 BB, 1 run, 2
   RBIs
POSITION: CF

Mantle's homer was his first safety in 17 at bats against the A's; he struck out nine times within the spread.

---

222 DATE: July 1, 1958
PLACE, OPP.: Memorial
   Stadium, Baltimore Orioles
SCORE: BA 7, NY 5
SWING, POS. IN ORDER:
   LH, 3rd
PITCHER: Hal Brown
MEN ON: 0
STATS: 1 for 5, 1 run, 1 RBI
POSITION: CF

Mantle gave the Yankees a 1–0 first-inning lead, slicing an opposite-field 320-foot homer just inside the left-field foul pole.

223 DATE: July 1, 1958
PLACE, OPP.: Memorial
   Stadium, Baltimore Orioles
SCORE: NY 2, BA 1
SWING, POS. IN ORDER:
   RH, 4th
PITCHER: Jack Harshman
MEN ON: 0
STATS: 3 for 4, 1 run, 1 RBI
POSITION: CF

The score was tied, 1–1, when, with two out in the eighth, Mantle cleared the right-center-field fence for a 410-foot homer.

224
225 DATE: July 3, 1958   PLACE, OPP.: Griffith Stadium,
Washington Senators   SCORE: NY 11, WA 3   SWING, POS.
IN ORDER: LH, LH; 4th   PITCHER: Russ Kemmerer (2)
MEN ON: 1, 1   STATS: 2 for 3, 2 BBs, 3 runs, 4 RBIs
POSITION: CF

---

226 DATE: July 4, 1958   The Yankees pounded out 22
PLACE, OPP.: Griffith   hits, one of them a Mantle
   Stadium, Washington   homer.
   Senators
SCORE: NY 13, WA 2
SWING, POS. IN ORDER:
   RH, 4th
PITCHER: Chuck Stobbs
MEN ON: 0
STATS: 2 for 5, 1 BB, 2 runs, 1
   RBI
POSITION: CF

---

227 DATE: July 5, 1958   PLACE, OPP.: Yankee Stadium, Boston Red
Sox   SCORE: NY 3, BO 3   SWING, POS. IN ORDER: LH,
4th   PITCHER: Dave Sisler   MEN ON: 0   STATS: 1 for 2, 3
BBs, 1 run, 1 RBI   POSITION: CF

---

228 DATE: July 6, 1958   The game was decided early,
PLACE, OPP.: Yankee   but those who stayed late got to
   Stadium, Boston Red Sox   see a Ted Williams drive into
SCORE: BO 10, NY 4   the third tier in right and a
SWING, POS. IN ORDER: Mantle blast into the right-field
   LH, 4th   bleachers.
PITCHER: Ike Delock
MEN ON: 1
STATS: 1 for 4, 1 run, 2 RBIs
POSITION: CF

---

229 DATE: July 11, 1958
PLACE, OPP.: Yankee
Stadium, Cleveland Indians
SCORE: NY 11, CL 3
SWING, POS. IN ORDER:
LH, 4th
PITCHER: Ray Narleski
MEN ON: 0
STATS: 1 for 2, 3 BBs, 3 runs, 1
RBI
POSITION: CF

A day of colossal homers—one by Mantle and the other by Cleveland's Larry Doby. Mickey propelled a high 3-and-2 fastball deep into the top tier in right, a drive that might have gone over 500 feet had it been unimpeded. Doby's homer, closer to the foul line, also landed very deep in the same upper deck.

230 DATE: July 14, 1958
PLACE, OPP.: Yankee
Stadium, Chicago White Sox
SCORE: NY 5, CH 0
SWING, POS. IN ORDER:
LH, 3rd
PITCHER: Early Wynn
MEN ON: 0
STATS: 2 for 4, 1 run, 2 RBIs
POSITION: CF

In the seventh, Mantle hit an opposite-way homer that traveled over 400 feet and landed in the box seats adjoining the left field bullpen.

231 DATE: July 15, 1958
PLACE, OPP.: Yankee
Stadium, Detroit Tigers
SCORE: DE 12, NY 5
SWING, POS. IN ORDER:
LH, 3rd
PITCHER: Frank Lary
MEN ON: 0
STATS: 2 for 5, 1 run, 1 RBI
POSITION: CF

Mantle's eighth-inning homer mattered little to the outcome, Lary running his 1958 record against the Yanks to 5–0.

232

DATE: July 23, 1958
PLACE, OPP.: Briggs Stadium,
    Detroit Tigers
SCORE: NY 16, DE 4
SWING, POS. IN ORDER:
    LH, 3rd
PITCHER: Bill Fischer
MEN ON: 1
STATS: 3 for 4, 1 BB, 3 runs, 4
    RBIs
POSITION: CF

The Yankees finally beat Frank
Lary, who had already departed
when Mantle and Yogi Berra hit
back-to-back homers.

233

DATE: July 24, 1958
PLACE, OPP.: Briggs Stadium,
    Detroit Tigers
SCORE: NY 10, DE 7
SWING, POS. IN ORDER:
    LH, 3rd
PITCHER: Paul Foytack
MEN ON: 0
STATS: 3 for 4, 1 BB, 3 runs, 1
    RBI
POSITION: CF

The Yankees were ahead, 6–5,
in the ninth when, with two
out, they scored four runs, including consecutive homers by
Gil McDougald and Mantle,
Mickey's going into the center-
field upper deck.

234
235

DATE: July 28, 1958   PLACE, OPP.: Municipal Stadium, Kansas
City A's   SCORE: NY 14, KC 7   SWING, POS. IN ORDER:
RH, LH; 3rd   PITCHERS: Dick Tomanek, Ray Herbert   MEN
ON: 0, 0   STATS: 3 for 4, 1 BB, 4 runs, 2 RBIs, 1 SB
POSITION: CF

236

DATE: August 4, 1958
PLACE, OPP.: Memorial
    Stadium, Baltimore Orioles
SCORE: NY 9, BA 4
SWING, POS. IN ORDER:
    LH, 3rd

In the ninth, Mantle, who earlier had a key single and a sacrifice fly, rammed a full-count
pitch into the right-field seats.

PITCHER: Charlie Beamon
MEN ON: 0
STATS: 2 for 3, 1 BB, 1 run, 2
  RBIs
POSITION: CF

237

DATE: August 5, 1958
PLACE, OPP.: Memorial
  Stadium, Baltimore Orioles
SCORE: NY 4, BA 1
SWING, POS. IN ORDER:
  LH, 3rd
PITCHER: Connie Johnson
MEN ON: 2
STATS: 2 for 4, 1 BB, 1 run, 3
  RBIs
POSITION: CF

With two on in the third and
New York behind, 1-0, Mantle
poled a 2-and-0 pitch about 400
feet over the barrier in right-
center.

238

DATE: August 9, 1958
PLACE, OPP.: Yankee
  Stadium, Boston Red Sox
SCORE: BO 9, NY 6
SWING, POS. IN ORDER:
  LH, 3rd
PITCHER: Dave Sisler
MEN ON: 0
STATS: 3 for 4, 1 BB, 1 run, 4
  RBIs, 1 SB
POSITION: CF

An Old-Timers' Day turnout of
67,916, the largest Yankee Stadium crowd in seven years, saw
Boston take an early 7–0 lead
and a much-booed Mantle have
a big game: He walked and stole
second in the fourth, put the
Yankees on the board with an
upper-deck homer to right in
the sixth, hit a two-run single in
the seventh, and singled to drive
home another run in the ninth.

239

DATE: August 11, 1958
PLACE, OPP.: Yankee
  Stadium, Baltimore Orioles
SCORE: BA 9, NY 3
SWING, POS. IN ORDER:
  LH, 3rd

Mantle's fifth-inning homer
gave him 32 homers and put
him in a three-way tie for the
league lead with Jackie Jensen
and Roy Sievers.

PITCHER: Connie Johnson
MEN ON: 1
STATS: 1 for 3, 1 BB, 1 run, 2
   RBIs
POSITION: CF

---

240   DATE: August 12, 1958
PLACE, OPP.: Yankee
   Stadium, Baltimore Orioles
SCORE: NY 7, BA 2
SWING, POS. IN ORDER:
   RH, 3rd
PITCHER: Ken Lehman
MEN ON: 0
STATS: 3 for 5, 2 runs, 1 RBI
POSITION: CF

Mantle's homer was off "my best knuckleball" said Lehman years later—it went deep into the left-field seats next to the Oriole bullpen, 425 to 450 feet from home plate.

---

241   DATE: August 16, 1958
PLACE, OPP.: Fenway Park,
   Boston Red Sox
SCORE: BO 7, NY 4
SWING, POS. IN ORDER:
   LH, 3rd
PITCHER: Tom Brewer
MEN ON: 1
STATS: 1 for 4, 1 run, 2 RBIs
POSITION: CF

After his fourth-inning error helped Boston to a 3–0 lead, Mantle, still seething, powered a sixth-inning homer over the bullpen and into the right-field bleachers.

---

242   DATE: August 17, 1958
PLACE, OPP.: Fenway Park,
   Boston Red Sox
SCORE: BO 6, NY 5
SWING, POS. IN ORDER:
   LH, 3rd
PITCHER: Ike Delock
MEN ON: 2

Mantle in the eighth inning launched a homer into the right-field bullpen with two on, bringing the Yanks within a run.

STATS: 2 for 4, 1 run, 3 RBIs
POSITION: CF

---

243 DATE: August 22, 1958
PLACE, OPP.: Yankee
  Stadium, Chicago White Sox
SCORE: NY 8, CH 5
SWING, POS. IN ORDER:
  LH, 3rd
PITCHER: Early Wynn
MEN ON: 0
STATS: 2 for 2, 3 BBs, 2 runs, 2
  RBIs
POSITION: CF

When Mantle scored on his
first-inning homer, he had 99
runs, 99 walks, and 99 strikeouts
for the season. He also had a
key double later in the game.

---

244 DATE: August 27, 1958
PLACE, OPP.: Yankee
  Stadium, Kansas City A's
SCORE: KC 11, NY 7
SWING, POS. IN ORDER:
  LH, 3rd
PITCHER: Tom Gorman
MEN ON: 2
STATS: 1 for 5, 1 run, 3 RBIs
POSITION: CF

In the seventh, Mickey rapped
one into the right-field bleachers
and the earlier boos he was
hearing from having fanned a
couple of times turned to
cheers.

---

245 DATE: September 2, 1958
PLACE, OPP.: Yankee
  Stadium, Boston Red Sox
SCORE: NY 6, BO 1
SWING, POS. IN ORDER:
  LH, 3rd
PITCHER: Dave Sisler
MEN ON: 0
STATS: 1 for 3, 1 BB, 1 run, 1
  RBI
POSITION: CF

An 0–0 tie was broken in the
sixth when Mantle and Yogi
Berra hit consecutive homers.

246 DATE: September 3, 1958   PLACE, OPP.: Yankee Stadium, Boston Red Sox   SCORE: NY 8, BO 5   SWING, POS. IN ORDER: LH, 3rd   PITCHER: Frank Sullivan   MEN ON: 0 STATS: 2 for 4, 1 BB, 3 runs, 1 RBI   POSITION: CF

---

247 DATE: September 9, 1958 PLACE, OPP.: Municipal Stadium, Cleveland Indians SCORE: CL 9, NY 2 SWING, POS. IN ORDER: LH, 3rd PITCHER: Cal McLish MEN ON: 1 STATS: 2 for 3, 1 run, 2 RBIs POSITION: CF

Mantle clouted a tremendous, wind-assisted homer over the 410-foot sign in center field. But the Indians had an eight-run fifth before the game was called because of rain.

---

248 DATE: September 17, 1958   PLACE, OPP.: Briggs Stadium, Detroit Tigers   SCORE: DE 5, NY 2   SWING, POS. IN ORDER: LH, 3rd   PITCHER: Jim Bunning   MEN ON: 1 STATS: 1 for 4, 1 run, 2 RBIs   POSITION: CF

---

249 DATE: September 24, 1958   PLACE, OPP.: Fenway Park, Boston Red Sox   SCORE: NY 7, BO 5   SWING, POS. IN ORDER: LH, 3rd   PITCHER: Tom Brewer   MEN ON: 1   STATS: 2 for 4, 1 BB, 2 runs, 2 RBIs   POSITION: CF

1959

250 DATE: April 21, 1959 PLACE, OPP.: Griffith Stadium, Washington Senators SCORE: NY 11, WA 4 SWING, POS. IN ORDER: LH, 3rd

Mantle finally hit his first homer of the year in the Yankees' eighth game, a towering shot into the dead-center-field bleachers. Later he added a triple.

PITCHER: Pedro Ramos
MEN ON: 0
STATS: 2 for 5, 1 BB, 2 runs, 2
    RBIs
POSITION: CF

251 DATE: April 23, 1959
PLACE, OPP.: Griffith
    Stadium, Washington
    Senators
SCORE: WA 3, NY 2
SWING, POS. IN ORDER:
    LH, 3rd
PITCHER: Russ Kemmerer
MEN ON: 0
STATS: 1 for 4, 1 run, 1 RBI
POSITION: CF

Mantle put the Yankees ahead
for a while, 1–0, with a fourth-
inning homer over the right-
field wall.

252 DATE: April 29, 1959
PLACE, OPP.: Comiskey Park,
    Chicago White Sox
SCORE: NY 5, CH 2
SWING, POS. IN ORDER:
    LH, 3rd
PITCHER: Ray Moore
MEN ON: 1
STATS: 2 for 3, 1 BB, 2 runs, 2
    RBIs, 1 SB
POSITION: CF

Mantle, Hank Bauer, and Bill
Skowron hit homers, Mantle's
going into the lower seats in
right field.

253 DATE: May 10, 1959
PLACE, OPP.: Yankee
    Stadium, Washington
    Senators
SCORE: NY 6, WA 3
SWING, POS. IN ORDER:
    RH, 3rd

Mantle's 410-foot first-inning
homer into the left-field bullpen
put the Yanks ahead to stay in
the first of two. In the second
game, he singled and scored the
winning run in the tenth.

PITCHER: Chuck Stobbs
MEN ON: 0
STATS: 1 for 4, 1 BB, 2 runs, 1
  RBI
POSITION: CF

---

254 DATE: May 12, 1959   PLACE, OPP.: Yankee Stadium, Cleveland
Indians   SCORE: CL 7, NY 6   SWING, POS. IN ORDER:
LH, 3rd   PITCHER: Cal McLish   MEN ON: 0   STATS: 3
for 4, 2 runs, 1 RBI   POSITION: CF

---

255 DATE: May 20, 1959   PLACE, OPP.: Yankee Stadium, Detroit
Tigers   SCORE: DE 13, NY 6   SWING, POS. IN ORDER:
LH, 3rd   PITCHER: Frank Lary   MEN ON: 1   STATS: 3 for
5, 2 runs, 2 RBIs   POSITION: CF

---

256 DATE: May 23, 1959   PLACE, OPP.: Memorial Stadium,
Baltimore Orioles   SCORE: NY 13, BA 5   SWING, POS. IN
ORDER: LH, 3rd   PITCHER: George Zuverink   MEN ON: 0
STATS: 3 for 3, 2 BBs, 3 runs, 2 RBIs, 1 SB   POSITION: CF

---

257 DATE: May 24, 1959
PLACE, OPP.: Memorial
  Stadium, Baltimore Orioles
SCORE: NY 9, BA 0
SWING, POS. IN ORDER:
  RH, 4th
PITCHER: Billy O'Dell
MEN ON: 2
STATS: 2 for 5, 1 run, 4 RBIs
POSITION: CF

Whitey Ford, in complete command, allowed only two hits, and Mantle contributed a three-run, 410-foot homer to center and an RBI-single.

258 DATE: May 30, 1959
PLACE, OPP.: Griffith
  Stadium, Washington
  Senators
SCORE: NY 11, WA 2
SWING, POS. IN ORDER:
  LH, 3rd
PITCHER: Dick Hyde
MEN ON: 1
STATS: 4 for 4, 1 BB, 3 runs, 2
  RBIs
POSITION: CF

The Yankees swept a holiday twinbill with 11–2 and 11–0 routs but are still confined to the league cellar. Mantle, who had five consecutive hits on the day, in the opener boomed a third-inning homer into the center-field bleachers.

259 DATE: June 3, 1959
PLACE, OPP.: Briggs Stadium,
  Detroit Tigers
SCORE: NY 6, DE 5
SWING, POS. IN ORDER:
  LH, 3rd
PITCHER: Ray Narleski
MEN ON: 0
STATS: 1 for 3, 2 BBs, 2 runs, 1
  RBI
POSITION: CF

With the score tied, 5–5, in the ninth, Mickey failed to get all of a Narleski pitch but imparted sufficient charge to the ball to get it over the right-center-field fence.

260 DATE: June 9, 1959
PLACE, OPP.: Yankee
  Stadium, Kansas City A's
SCORE: NY 9, KC 8
SWING, POS. IN ORDER:
  LH, 3rd
PITCHER: Murry Dickson
MEN ON: 1
STATS: 2 for 5, 2 BBs, 2 runs, 2
  RBIs, 2 SBs
POSITION: CF

Mantle gave the Yanks a temporary 6–5 lead with a fourth-inning shot deep into the right-field seats, but New York had to rally to force extra innings, winning on a Hector Lopez RBI single in the 13th

261 DATE: June 11, 1959
PLACE, OPP.: Yankee
  Stadium, Kansas City A's
SCORE: KC 9, NY 5
SWING, POS. IN ORDER:
  LH, 3rd
PITCHER: Ned Garver
MEN ON: 0
STATS: 1 for 4, 1 BB, 1 run, 1
  RBI
POSITION: CF

Garver beat the Yankees for the first time since July 16, 1955, in spite of the home runs he allowed to Mantle, Norm Siebern, and Marv Throneberry.

262 DATE: June 13, 1959
PLACE, OPP.: Yankee
  Stadium, Detroit Tigers
SCORE: NY 6, DE 4
SWING, POS. IN ORDER:
  LH, 3rd
PITCHER: Jim Bunning
MEN ON: 1
STATS: 2 for 3, 1 BB, 1 run, 2
  RBIs, 1 SB
POSITION: CF

The Yankees collected their 1,000th win under manager Casey Stengel, Mantle giving his club a first-inning lead with his homer into the front seats in right field, and helping Don Larsen get his last Yankee win.

263 DATE: June 17, 1959   PLACE, OPP.: Yankee Stadium, Chicago
White Sox   SCORE: NY 7, CH 3   SWING, POS. IN ORDER:
LH, 3rd   PITCHER: Ray Moore   MEN ON: 2   STATS: 1 for
5, 2 runs, 3 RBIs   POSITION: CF

264 DATE: June 18, 1959   PLACE, OPP.: Yankee Stadium, Chicago
White Sox   SCORE: NY 5, CH 4   SWING, POS. IN ORDER:
LH, 3rd   PITCHER: Gerry Staley   MEN ON: 0   STATS: 2
for 4, 1 BB, 1 run, 1 RBI   POSITION: CF

265
266 DATE: June 22, 1959   PLACE, OPP.: Municipal Stadium, Kansas City A's   SCORE: NY 11, KC 6   SWING, POS. IN ORDER: LH, LH; 3rd   PITCHERS: Ray Herbert, Bob Grim   MEN ON: 0, 2   STATS: 3 for 5, 3 runs, 6 RBIs   POSITION: CF

---

267 DATE: June 23, 1959
PLACE, OPP.: Municipal
   Stadium, Kansas City A's
SCORE: NY 10, KC 2
SWING, POS. IN ORDER:
   RH, 3rd
PITCHER: Rip Coleman
MEN ON: 1
STATS: 1 for 5, 1 run, 2 RBIs
POSITION: CF

Mantle, Hank Bauer, and Gil McDougald all hit two-run homers.

---

268 DATE: July 16, 1959   PLACE, OPP.: Yankee Stadium, Cleveland Indians   SCORE: NY 7, CL 5   SWING, POS. IN ORDER: LH, 3rd   PITCHER: Gary Bell   MEN ON: 1   STATS: 2 for 6, 1 run, 2 RBIs   POSITION: CF

---

269 DATE: July 19, 1959
PLACE, OPP.: Yankee
   Stadium, Chicago White Sox
SCORE: NY 6, CH 4
SWING, POS. IN ORDER:
   LH, 3rd
PITCHER: Turk Lown
MEN ON: 0
STATS: 2 for 4, 1 run, 3 RBIs
POSITION: CF

The Yankees swept a double-header, Mantle going 4 for 8, including a nightcap homer. Mantle's homer was the result of an experiment. Lown recalls going against his normal pattern of pitching Mantle—he tried to "turn the ball over and make it sink." The experiment failed.

270

DATE: August 4, 1959
PLACE, OPP.: Yankee
   Stadium, Detroit Tigers
SCORE: DE 4, NY 3
SWING, POS. IN ORDER:
   LH, 3rd
PITCHER: Frank Lary
MEN ON: 0
STATS: 1 for 3, 1 BB, 1 run, 1
   RBI
POSITION: CF

Besides pulling a homer to right, Mantle started a Mantle-to-Richardson-to-Throneberry double play after taking a fly that caught Neil Chrisley off first base.

271

DATE: August 5, 1959
PLACE, OPP.: Yankee
   Stadium, Detroit Tigers
SCORE: NY 3, DE 0
SWING, POS. IN ORDER:
   RH, 3rd
PITCHER: Don Mossi
MEN ON: 1
STATS: 1 for 4, 1 run, 2 RBIs
POSITION: CF

Mantle slammed his homer in the eighth to help decide the pitching duel between Mossi and Bobby Shantz.

272

DATE: August 16, 1959
PLACE, OPP.: Yankee
   Stadium, Boston Red Sox
SCORE: BO 6, NY 5
SWING, POS. IN ORDER:
   LH, 3rd
PITCHER: Jerry Casale
MEN ON: 1
STATS: 1 for 3, 1 BB, 1 run, 2
   RBIs
POSITION: CF

Mantle's first-inning shot went into the upper deck in right, but Boston scored six runs in the second on six singles to center, running Mantle nearly into exhaustion.

273 DATE: August 16, 1959
PLACE, OPP.: Yankee
   Stadium, Boston Red Sox
SCORE: NY 4, BO 2
SWING, POS. IN ORDER:
   LH, 3rd
PITCHER: Bill Monbouquette
MEN ON: 1
STATS: 2 for 4, 2 runs, 2 RBIs
POSITION: CF

In the second game, Mantle hit a long first-inning homer and a booming eighth-inning drive 460 feet to deep center that banged against the bleacher wall, traveling so fast and bouncing back so hard that he had to settle for a double.

---

274 DATE: August 26, 1959
PLACE, OPP.: Municipal
   Stadium, Cleveland Indians
SCORE: CL 5, NY 4
SWING, POS. IN ORDER:
   LH, 3rd
PITCHER: Gary Bell
MEN ON: 0
STATS: 1 for 2, 2 BBs, 2 runs, 1
   RBI
POSITION: CF

Mantle put the Yankees on the board with a first-inning homer that carried about 450 feet, cleared the inner fence, and bounced into the faraway right-center-field bleachers—his only RBI of a 10-game road trip.

---

275 DATE: August 29, 1959
PLACE, OPP.: Griffith
   Stadium, Washington
   Senators
SCORE: NY 9, WA 5
SWING, POS. IN ORDER:
   LH, 3rd
PITCHER: Hal Griggs
MEN ON: 0
STATS: 2 for 4, 1 BB, 2 runs, 1
   RBI
POSITION: CF

Mantle's homer went over 400 feet into the center-field bleachers. But his biggest contribution was a fine catch that killed a Washington rally.

276 DATE: September 7, 1959   PLACE, OPP.: Fenway Park, Boston
Red Sox   SCORE: BO 12, NY 4   SWING, POS. IN ORDER:
LH, 3rd   PITCHER: Jerry Casale   MEN ON: 1   STATS: 1
for 4, 1 run, 2 RBIs   POSITION: CF

---

277 DATE: September 10, 1959   Mantle homered in the first inn-
PLACE, OPP.: Yankee   ing, then added a double and
  Stadium, Kansas City A's   three singles.
SCORE: NY 12, KC 1
SWING, POS. IN ORDER:
  LH, 3rd
PITCHER: Ray Herbert
MEN ON: 0
STATS: 5 for 6, 3 runs, 1 RBI
POSITION: CF

---

278 DATE: September 13, 1959   PLACE, OPP.: Yankee Stadium,
Cleveland Indians   SCORE: NY 2, CL 1   SWING, POS. IN
ORDER: RH, 3rd   PITCHER: Jack Harshman   MEN ON: 1
STATS: 1 for 5, 1 run, 2 RBIs   POSITION: CF

279
280 DATE: September 15, 1959   PLACE, OPP.: Yankee Stadium,
Chicago White Sox   SCORE: CH 4, NY 3   SWING, POS. IN
ORDER: RH, LH; 3rd   PITCHERS: Billy Pierce, Bob Shaw
MEN ON: 1, 0   STATS: 2 for 4, 2 runs, 3 RBIs   POSITION:
CF

1960

---

281 DATE: April 22, 1960   In the home opener, Mantle hit
PLACE, OPP.: Yankee   a fourth-inning towering drive
  Stadium, Baltimore Orioles   upstairs in right.
SCORE: NY 5, BA 0
SWING, POS. IN ORDER:
  LH, 3rd

PITCHER: Hoyt Wilhelm
MEN ON: 0
STATS: 1 for 2, 2 BBs, 2 runs, 1
RBI, 1 SB
POSITION: CF

---

282 DATE: May 13, 1960
PLACE, OPP.: Griffith
Stadium, Washington
Senators
SCORE: NY 7, WA 3
SWING, POS. IN ORDER:
RH, 2nd
PITCHER: Jim Kaat
MEN ON: 0
STATS: 1 for 3, 1 BB, 1 run, 1
RBI
POSITION: CF

Strange to see Mantle batting
second, but behind him were
Yogi Berra, Roger Maris, Bill
Skowron, and Elston Howard!
Mickey slammed an opposite-
field homer over the 31-foot-
high wall in right field, a rare
feat for a right-handed hitter.
But he departed in the eighth
with a slightly pulled groin
muscle.

---

283 DATE: May 17, 1960
PLACE, OPP.: Municipal
Stadium, Cleveland Indians
SCORE: CL 7, NY 6
SWING, POS. IN ORDER:
LH, 2nd
PITCHER: Gary Bell
MEN ON: 2
STATS: 1 for 4, 1 BB, 1 run, 3
RBIs
POSITION: CF

The Yanks knocked out Bell in
the ninth with a four-run rally
capped by a Mantle homer, but
Dick Stigman got the final out
to end the game.

---

284 DATE: May 20, 1960
PLACE, OPP.: Comiskey Park,
Chicago White Sox

Mantle's ninth-inning homer
made it 5–3.

SCORE: CH 5, NY 3
SWING, POS. IN ORDER:
  LH, 2nd
PITCHER: Early Wynn
MEN ON: 1
STATS: 1 for 4, 1 BB, 1 run, 2
  RBIs
POSITION: CF

---

285 DATE: May 28, 1960   PLACE, OPP.: Yankee Stadium,
Washington Senators   SCORE: NY 5, WA 1   SWING, POS.
IN ORDER: RH, 2nd   PITCHER: Jim Kaat   MEN ON: 0
STATS: 1 for 4, 1 run, 1 RBI   POSITION: CF

---

286 DATE: May 29, 1960
PLACE, OPP.: Yankee
  Stadium, Washington
  Senators
SCORE: NY 6, WA 4
SWING, POS. IN ORDER:
  RH, 2nd
PITCHER: Hal Woodeshick
MEN ON: 0
STATS: 3 for 6, 2 runs, 1 RBI
POSITION: CF

Mantle ignited a three-run
sixth-inning rally with a homer
the other way, his third right-
handed homer of the season, all
to the opposite field.

---

287 DATE: June 1, 1960   PLACE, OPP.: Memorial Stadium,
Baltimore Orioles   SCORE: BA 4, NY 1   SWING, POS. IN
ORDER: LH, 2nd   PITCHER: Hal Brown   MEN ON: 0
STATS: 1 for 3, 1 BB, 1 run, 1 RBI, 1 SB   POSITION: CF

288
DATE: June 5, 1960
PLACE, OPP.: Yankee
  Stadium, Boston Red Sox
SCORE: NY 5, BO 4
SWING, POS. IN ORDER:
  LH, 5th
PITCHER: Tom Brewer
MEN ON: 0
STATS: 2 for 3, 1 BB, 1 run, 1
  RBI
POSITION: CF

New York swept a double-header, building a 5–0 lead in the opener on Mantle's homer, a three-run homer by Roger Maris, and an RBI-single by Tony Kubek.

289
290
DATE: June 8, 1960   PLACE, OPP.: Yankee Stadium, Chicago White Sox   SCORE: NY 6, CH 0   SWING, POS. IN ORDER: LH, LH; 3rd   PITCHERS: Bob Shaw, Ray Moore   MEN ON: 0, 1   STATS: 2 for 4, 2 runs, 3 RBIs   POSITION: CF

291
DATE: June 9, 1960
PLACE, OPP.: Yankee
  Stadium, Chicago White Sox
SCORE: NY 5, CH 2
SWING, POS. IN ORDER:
  RH, 5th
PITCHER: Frank Baumann
MEN ON: 1
STATS: 1 for 3, 1 BB, 1 run, 2
  RBIs
POSITION: CF

In the fourth, Mantle boomed a homer into the right-field bull-pen, another opposite-field homer.

292
DATE: June 10, 1960
PLACE, OPP.: Yankee
  Stadium, Cleveland Indians
SCORE: NY 4, CL 3
SWING, POS. IN ORDER:
  RH, 3rd

It was 3–3 in the eighth and Mantle ruined a good Stigman relief effort with a smash into the left-field seats.

PITCHER: Dick Stigman
MEN ON: 0
STATS: 2 for 3, 1 BB, 1 run, 2
   RBIs
POSITION: CF

---

293 DATE: June 17, 1960   PLACE, OPP.: Comiskey Park, Chicago
White Sox   SCORE: NY 4, CH 2   SWING, POS. IN ORDER:
LH, 3rd   PITCHER: Turk Lown   MEN ON: 0   STATS: 2 for
4, 1 run, 1 RBI   POSITION: CF

---

294 DATE: June 18, 1960
PLACE, OPP.: Comiskey Park,
   Chicago White Sox
SCORE: NY 12, CH 5
SWING, POS. IN ORDER:
   LH, 3rd
PITCHER: Bob Rush
MEN ON: 1
STATS: 2 for 4, 2 BBs, 2 runs, 2
   RBIs
POSITION: CF

Long home runs by Mantle, Roger Maris, and Bill Skowron: Mantle homered over the center-field fence, Maris right behind him hit a shot upstairs to right, and Skowron planted one in the left-field upper deck.

295
296 DATE: June 21, 1960
PLACE, OPP.: Briggs Stadium,
   Detroit Tigers
SCORE: NY 6, DE 0
SWING, POS. IN ORDER:
   LH, LH; 3rd
PITCHER: Frank Lary (2)
MEN ON: 0, 1
STATS: 3 for 5, 3 runs, 3 RBIs,
   1 SB
POSITION: CF

Whitey Ford pitched a shutout, and Mantle twice took Frank "Yankee Killer" Lary deep into the right-field stands, then into the left-field seats.

297

DATE: June 28, 1960
PLACE, OPP.: Yankee
  Stadium, Kansas City A's
SCORE: NY 5, KC 2
SWING, POS. IN ORDER:
  RH, 3rd
PITCHER: Buddy Daley
MEN ON: 0
STATS: 2 for 5, 1 run, 1 RBI
POSITION: CF

Mantle's drive into the left-field stands in the third inning tied the score, 2–2.

298

DATE: June 30, 1960
PLACE, OPP.: Yankee
  Stadium, Kansas City A's
SCORE: NY 10, KC 3
SWING, POS. IN ORDER:
  LH, 3rd
PITCHER: Bob Trowbridge
MEN ON: 1
STATS: 1 for 5, 1 run, 2 RBIs
POSITION: CF

Five Yankee homers: two by Bill Skowron and one each by Mantle, Roger Maris, and Tony Kubek. Mantle's went into the right-field bullpen.

299

DATE: July 3, 1960   PLACE, OPP.: Yankee Stadium, Detroit Tigers   SCORE: NY 6, DE 2   SWING, POS. IN ORDER: RH, 4th   PITCHER: Pete Burnside   MEN ON: 2   STATS: 1 for 3, 1 BB, 1 run, 3 RBIs   POSITION: CF

300

DATE: July 4, 1960
PLACE, OPP.: Griffith
  Stadium, Washington
  Senators
SCORE: WA 9, NY 8
SWING, POS. IN ORDER:
  RH, 4th
PITCHER: Hal Woodeshick

Mickey gave the Yankees a first-inning lead of 3–0 when he became the 18th major leaguer to hit 300 home runs.

MEN ON: 2
STATS: 1 for 4, BB
POSITION: CF

---

301 DATE: July 15, 1960
PLACE, OPP.: Briggs Stadium,
  Detroit Tigers
SCORE: DE 8, NY 4
SWING, POS. IN ORDER:
  RH, 4th
PITCHER: Don Mossi
MEN ON: 2
STATS: 1 for 3, 1 BB, 2 runs, 3
  RBIs
POSITION: CF

A Mantle homer into the lower stands in left field got the Yankees off to a 3–0 start.

---

302 DATE: July 18, 1960   PLACE, OPP.: Municipal Stadium,
Cleveland Indians   SCORE: NY 9, CL 2   SWING, POS. IN
ORDER: RH, 4th   PITCHER: Dick Stigman   MEN ON: 2
STATS: 2 for 5, 2 runs, 3 RBIs   POSITION: CF

---

303 DATE: July 20, 1960   PLACE, OPP.: Municipal Stadium,
Cleveland Indians   SCORE: CL 8, NY 6   SWING, POS. IN
ORDER: LH, 3rd   PITCHER: Gary Bell   MEN ON: 0
STATS: 1 for 4, 1 BB, 1 run, 1 RBI   POSITION: CF

---

304 DATE: July 24, 1960
PLACE, OPP.: Yankee
  Stadium, Chicago White Sox
SCORE: NY 8, CH 2
SWING, POS. IN ORDER:
  LH, 5th
PITCHER: Russ Kemmerer
MEN ON: 0

Mantle helped break open a tight game with a fifth-inning homer.

STATS: 2 for 5, 1 run, 2 RBIs,
    1 SB
POSITION: CF

---

305 DATE: July 26, 1960
PLACE, OPP.: Yankee
    Stadium, Cleveland Indians
SCORE: NY 6, CL 1
SWING, POS. IN ORDER:
    RH, 3rd
PITCHER: Dick Stigman
MEN ON: 1
STATS: 1 for 4, 1 run, 2 RBIs
POSITION: CF

Stigman took a 1–0 lead into
the sixth inning, but Roger
Maris (batting first in the order
today) drew a walk, and Mantle
homered to put the Yankees
ahead for good.

---

306 DATE: July 28, 1960
PLACE, OPP.: Yankee
    Stadium, Cleveland Indians
SCORE: NY 4, CL 0
SWING, POS. IN ORDER:
    LH, 6th
PITCHER: Jim Perry
MEN ON: 0
STATS: 1 for 4, 1 run, 1 RBI
POSITION: CF

The big blows of the game were
homers by Tony Kubek, Mantle, and Clete Boyer, and
Whitey Ford and Bobby Shantz
combined on a shutout.

---

307 DATE: July 31, 1960
PLACE, OPP.: Yankee
    Stadium, Kansas City A's
SCORE: KC 5, NY 2
SWING, POS. IN ORDER:
    LH, 5th
PITCHER: Johnny Kucks
MEN ON: 0
STATS: 2 for 4, 1 BB, 1 run, 1
    RBI, 1 SB
POSITION: CF

In the ninth inning of the first
game of a doubleheader, a Mantle homer tied the score at 2–2,
but the A's in the 11th scored
three unearned runs when third
baseman Hector Lopez made
two throwing errors.

308
309 DATE: August 15, 1960   PLACE, OPP.: Yankee Stadium, Baltimore Orioles   SCORE: NY 4, BA 3   SWING, POS. IN ORDER: LH, LH; 3rd   PITCHERS: Jerry Walker, Hoyt Wilhelm   MEN ON: 1, 1   STATS: 2 for 4, 2 runs, 4 RBIs POSITION: CF

---

310 DATE: August 26, 1960
PLACE, OPP.: Yankee
  Stadium, Cleveland Indians
SCORE: NY 7, CL 6
SWING, POS. IN ORDER:
  LH, 4th
PITCHER: Jim Perry
MEN ON: 0
STATS: 1 for 4, 1 BB, 1 run, 1
  RBI
POSITION: CF

The Yankees won on the strength of five solo homers— Yogi Berra's second homer won it in the 11th—and four pinch-hits, tying a league record. Mantle's third-inning solo homer went over the right-field auxiliary scoreboard and into the bleachers.

---

311 DATE: August 28, 1960
PLACE, OPP.: Yankee
  Stadium, Detroit Tigers
SCORE: NY 8, DE 5
SWING, POS. IN ORDER:
  LH, 4th
PITCHER: Phil Regan
MEN ON: 1
STATS: 2 for 1, 1 run, 4 RBIs
POSITION: CF

With the score 3–3 in the fifth, Tony Kubek singled and Mantle and Yogi Berra hit back-to-back home runs.

---

312 DATE: September 6, 1960
PLACE, OPP.: Yankee
  Stadium, Boston Red Sox
SCORE: BO 7, NY 1
SWING, POS. IN ORDER:
  LH, 4th
PITCHER: Billy Muffett

Ted Williams, in his final game at the Stadium, hit his 518th career home run, and Muffett had a two-hit shutout with two out in the ninth, until Mantle slammed a homer into the right-field bleachers.

MEN ON: 0
STATS: 1 for 4, 1 run, 1 RBI
POSITION: CF

---

313   DATE: September 10, 1960   PLACE, OPP.: Briggs Stadium,
Detroit Tigers   SCORE: NY 5, DE 1   SWING, POS. IN
ORDER: LH, 4th   PITCHER: Paul Foytack   MEN ON: 2
STATS: 2 for 4, 1 BB, 1 run, 3 RBIs   POSITION: CF

---

314   DATE: September 11, 1960   Mathias had retired the first two
PLACE, OPP.: Municipal   Yankees in the 11th when Man-
   Stadium, Cleveland Indians   tle swatted a low-and-away
SCORE: NY 3, CL 2   curveball into the wind and over
SWING, POS. IN ORDER: the 380-foot mark in left-center.
   RH, 4th
PITCHER: Carl Mathias
MEN ON: 0
STATS: 2 for 5, 2 runs, 1 RBI
POSITION: CF

---

315   DATE: September 17, 1960   PLACE, OPP.: Yankee Stadium,
Baltimore Orioles   SCORE: NY 5, BA 3   SWING, POS. IN
ORDER: LH, 4th   PITCHER: Chuck Estrada   MEN ON: 1
STATS: 1 for 4, 1 run, 2 RBIs   POSITION: CF

---

316   DATE: September 20, 1960   Mantle smashed a fourth-inning
PLACE, OPP.: Yankee   opposite-field homer to right-
   Stadium, Washington   center that easily cleared the
   Senators   407-foot sign.
SCORE: NY 2, WA 1
SWING, POS. IN ORDER:
   RH, 3rd
PITCHER: Jack Kralick
MEN ON: 0
STATS: 1 for 5, 1 run, 1 RBI
POSITION: CF

---

317 DATE: September 21, 1960
PLACE, OPP.: Yankee
    Stadium, Washington
    Senators
SCORE: NY 10, WA 3
SWING, POS. IN ORDER:
    LH, 4th
PITCHER: Pedro Ramos
MEN ON: 0
STATS: 2 for 3, 1 BB, 2 runs, 1
    RBI
POSITION: CF

Mantle homered in the fourth for New York's first hit. Of the 12 runs the Yanks scored in a two-game sweep of Washington, all were unearned except the two Mantle solo homers.

---

318 DATE: September 24, 1960   PLACE, OPP.: Fenway Park, Boston Red Sox   SCORE: NY 6, BO 5   SWING, POS. IN ORDER: RH, 4th   PITCHER: Ted Wills   MEN ON: 0   STATS: 2 for 5, 1 run, 2 RBIs   POSITION: CF

319
320 DATE: September 28, 1960   PLACE, OPP.: Griffith Stadium, Washington Senators   SCORE: NY 6, WA 3   SWING, POS. IN ORDER: RH, RH; 4th   PITCHER: Chuck Stobbs (2)   MEN ON: 1, 0   STATS: 2 for 4, 2 runs, 3 RBIs   POSITION: CF

1961

---

321 DATE: April 17, 1961   PLACE, OPP.: Yankee Stadium, Kansas City A's   SCORE: NY 3, KC 0   SWING, POS. IN ORDER: LH, 4th   PITCHER: Jerry Walker   MEN ON: 1   STATS: 3 for 3, 1 BB, 1 run, 3 RBIs, 1 SB   POSITION: CF

322
323 DATE: April 20, 1961
PLACE, OPP.: Yankee
    Stadium, Los Angeles Angels
SCORE: NY 7, LA 5

In the opener of a double bill, the first game the new Los Angeles franchise ever played here, he hit two homers against

SWING, POS. IN ORDER:
LH, LH; 4th
PITCHER: Eli Grba (2)
MEN ON: 1, 2
STATS: 2 for 3, 1 BB, 2 runs, 5
RBIs
POSITION: CF

former teammate Grba. The
first homer—a tremendous wallop about 10 rows deep in the
upper tier in right—gave the
Yankees a 2–0 lead. The second
broke a 2–2 tie.

---

324 DATE: April 21, 1961
PLACE, OPP.: Memorial
Stadium, Baltimore Orioles
SCORE: NY 4, BA 2
SWING, POS. IN ORDER:
RH, 4th
PITCHER: Steve Barber
MEN ON: 1
STATS: 1 for 4, 1 run, 2 RBIs
POSITION: CF

Mantle hit his 410-foot rainmaker that went over the fence
in left-center on a bad pitch,
high and away.

---

325 DATE: April 23, 1961
PLACE, OPP.: Memorial
Stadium, Baltimore Orioles
SCORE: BA 4, NY 1
SWING, POS. IN ORDER:
LH, 4th
PITCHER: Chuck Estrada
MEN ON: 0
STATS: 1 for 4, 1 run, 1 RBI
POSITION: CF

The only Yankee dent was Mantle's fourth-inning homer, a shot
landing halfway up in the rightfield bleachers.

326
327 DATE: April 26, 1961   PLACE, OPP.: Tiger Stadium, Detroit
Tigers   SCORE: NY 13, DE 11   SWING, POS. IN ORDER:
LH, RH; 4th   PITCHERS: Jim Donohue, Hank Aguirre   MEN
ON: 1, 1   STATS: 2 for 6, 3 runs, 4 RBIs   POSITION: CF

---

328 DATE: May 2, 1961   PLACE, OPP.: Metropolitan Stadium,
Minnesota Twins   SCORE: NY 6, MI 4   SWING, POS. IN
ORDER: LH, 4th   PITCHER: Camilo Pascual   MEN ON: 3
STATS: 2 for 5, 1 run, 5 RBIs   POSITION: CF

329 DATE: May 4, 1961   PLACE, OPP.: Metropolitan Stadium,
Minnesota Twins   SCORE: NY 5, MI 2   SWING, POS. IN
ORDER: LH, 4th   PITCHER: Ted Sadowski   MEN ON: 0
STATS: 2 for 4, 2 runs, 2 RBIs   POSITION: CF

330 DATE: May 16, 1961
PLACE, OPP.: Yankee
   Stadium, Washington
   Senators
SCORE: WA 3, NY 2
SWING, POS. IN ORDER:
   RH, 4th
PITCHER: Hal Woodeshick
MEN ON: 0
STATS: 1 for 3, 1 BB, 1 run, 1
   RBI
POSITION: CF

Woodeshick had a 3–1 lead and a no-hitter going, when, with one out in the sixth, Mantle ripped a homer into the lower left-field seats.

331 DATE: May 29, 1961
PLACE, OPP.: Fenway Park,
   Boston Red Sox
SCORE: BO 2, NY 1
SWING, POS. IN ORDER:
   LH, 4th
PITCHER: Ike Delock
MEN ON: 0
STATS: 1 for 4, 1 run, 1 RBI
POSITION: CF

Mantle hit a drive into the right-field bullpen in the seventh. With a man on base in the ninth, Mantle drove right fielder Jackie Jensen to the bullpen wall for the final out.

332
333
DATE: May 30, 1961   PLACE, OPP.: Fenway Park, Boston Red Sox   SCORE: NY 12, BO 3   SWING, POS. IN ORDER: LH, LH; 4th   PITCHERS: Gene Conley, Mike Fornieles   MEN ON: 2, 0   STATS: 2 for 5, 2 runs, 4 RBIs   POSITION: CF

334
DATE: May 31, 1961
PLACE, OPP.: Fenway Park, Boston Red Sox
SCORE: NY 7, BO 6
SWING, POS. IN ORDER: LH, 4th
PITCHER: Billy Muffett
MEN ON: 1
STATS: 2 for 3, 2 BBs, 1 run, 2 RBIs
POSITION: CF

Roger Maris hit a 425-foot homer (No. 12) into the right-field bleachers, and Mantle popped No. 14, a 400-foot shot into the bullpen in right-center.

335
DATE: June 5, 1961
PLACE, OPP.: Yankee Stadium, Minnesota Twins
SCORE: NY 6, MI 2
SWING, POS. IN ORDER: LH, 4th
PITCHER: Ray Moore
MEN ON: 1
STATS: 1 for 4, 1 run, 2 RBIs
POSITION: CF

Mantle's eighth-inning homer (his only hit of the day) in the first of two put the Yankees ahead 5–2. The homer, a 420-footer into the right-field bleachers, tied him with Roger Maris and Rocky Colavito for the league lead, with 15 apiece.

336
DATE: June 9, 1961
PLACE, OPP.: Yankee Stadium, Kansas City A's
SCORE: NY 8, KC 6
SWING, POS. IN ORDER: LH, 4th
PITCHER: Ray Herbert
MEN ON: 2

With two out in the third, Tony Kubek and Roger Maris singled, and Mantle sliced a homer to left field. The game was interrupted by rain four times.

STATS: 2 for 2, 2 BBs, 2 runs, 4
  RBIs
POSITION: CF

---

337 DATE: June 10, 1961
PLACE, OPP.: Yankee
  Stadium, Kansas City A's
SCORE: NY 5, KC 3
SWING, POS. IN ORDER :
  LH, 4th
PITCHER: Bill Kunkel
MEN ON: 0
STATS: 2 for 3, 1 BB, 3 runs, 1
  RBI
POSITION: CF

Mantle homered in the eighth, and ex-Yankee Hank Bauer hit an inside-the-parker over Mantle's head to the monuments.

---

338 DATE: June 11, 1961   PLACE, OPP.: Yankee Stadium, Los
Angeles Angels   SCORE: NY 5, LA 1   SWING, POS. IN
ORDER: LH, 4th   PITCHER: Eli Grba   MEN ON: 2
STATS: 1 for 3, 1 BB, 1 run, 3 RBIs   POSITION: CF

---

339 DATE: June 15, 1961
PLACE, OPP.: Municipal
  Stadium, Cleveland Indians
SCORE: NY 3, CL 2
SWING, POS. IN ORDER:
  LH, 4th
PITCHER: Mudcat Grant
MEN ON: 0
STATS: 1 for 5, 1 run, 1 RBI
POSITION: CF

A seventh-inning Mantle homer tied the score at 1–1, and the Yanks won in 11 innings on a pinch-hit single by Johnny Blanchard.

340

DATE: June 17, 1961
PLACE, OPP.: Tiger Stadium,
   Detroit Tigers
SCORE: DE 12, NY 10
SWING, POS. IN ORDER:
   LH, 4th
PITCHER: Paul Foytack
MEN ON: 2
STATS: 1 for 3, 2 BBs, 2 runs, 3
   RBIs
POSITION: CF

With two out and two aboard in the ninth, Mantle sent a rocket into the right-field top deck, but it wasn't enough even with the Elston Howard home run that followed.

341
342

DATE: June 21, 1961   PLACE, OPP.: Municipal Stadium, Kansas City A's   SCORE: NY 5, KC 3   SWING, POS. IN ORDER: LH, LH; 4th   PITCHER: Bob Shaw (2)   MEN ON: 2, 1 STATS: 2 for 3, 2 BBs, 2 runs, 5 RBIs   POSITION: CF

343

DATE: June 26, 1961   PLACE, OPP.: Wrigley Field, Los Angeles Angels   SCORE: NY 8, LA 6   SWING, POS. IN ORDER: LH, 4th   PITCHER: Ken McBride   MEN ON: 0   STATS: 1 for 3, 2 BBs, 2 runs, 1 RBI   POSITION: CF

344

DATE: June 28, 1961   PLACE, OPP.: Wrigley Field, Los Angeles Angels   SCORE: LA 5, NY 3   SWING, POS. IN ORDER: LH, 4th   PITCHER: Ryne Duren   MEN ON: 1   STATS: 1 for 4, 1 run, 3 RBIs   POSITION: CF

345

DATE: June 30, 1961   PLACE, OPP.: Yankee Stadium, Washington Senators   SCORE: NY 5, WA 1   SWING, POS. IN ORDER: LH, 4th   PITCHER: Dick Donovan   MEN ON: 1   STATS: 1 for 3, 1 run, 2 RBIs   POSITION: CF

346
347 DATE: July 1, 1961   PLACE, OPP.: Yankee Stadium, Washington
Senators   SCORE: NY 7, WA 6   SWING, POS. IN ORDER:
RH, RH; 4th   PITCHER: Carl Mathias (2)   MEN ON: 0, 2
STATS: 3 for 3, 1 BB, 3 runs, 4 RBIs, 1 SB   POSITION: CF

348 DATE: July 2, 1961   PLACE, OPP.: Yankee Stadium, Washington
Senators   SCORE: NY 13, WA 4   SWING, POS. IN ORDER:
LH, 4th   PITCHER: Johnny Klippstein   MEN ON: 1
STATS: 1 for 1, 4 BBs, 3 runs, 2 RBIs   POSITION: CF

349 DATE: July 8, 1961
PLACE, OPP.: Yankee
   Stadium, Boston Red Sox
SCORE: NY 8, BO 5
SWING, POS. IN ORDER:
   LH, 4th
PITCHER: Tracy Stallard
MEN ON: 0
STATS: 2 for 4, 1 run, 2 RBIs,
   1 SB
POSITION: CF

Mantle's upper-deck homer to
right in the fifth was his 10th in
support of pitcher Whitey Ford
this year.

350 DATE: July 13, 1961
PLACE, OPP.: Comiskey Park,
   Chicago White Sox
SCORE: NY 6, CH 2
SWING, POS. IN ORDER:
   LH, 4th
PITCHER: Early Wynn
MEN ON: 0
STATS: 3 for 5, 1 run, 2 RBIs
POSITION: CF

Wynn retired only two men in a
first-inning Yankee rally that included back-to-back homers by
Roger Maris and Mantle.
Maris's 34th was one of his best
shots, going upstairs in right
field, but it was dwarfed by
Mantle's 30th, a rising line drive
that crashed into the very top of
the upper stands in center.

351

DATE: July 14, 1961
PLACE, OPP.: Comiskey Park,
   Chicago White Sox
SCORE: CH 6, NY 1
SWING, POS. IN ORDER:
   RH, 4th
PITCHER: Juan Pizarro
MEN ON: 0
STATS: 1 for 2, 2 BBs, 1 run, 1
   RBI
POSITION: CF

Pizarro, whose fastball was smoking, lost his shutout on Mickey's eighth-inning line-drive homer.

352

DATE: July 16, 1961   PLACE, OPP.: Memorial Stadium,
Baltimore Orioles   SCORE: NY 2, BA 1   SWING, POS. IN
ORDER: RH, 4th   PITCHER: Steve Barber   MEN ON: 0
STATS: 2 for 4, 1 run, 2 RBIs   POSITION: CF

353

DATE: July 17, 1961   PLACE, OPP.: Memorial Stadium,
Baltimore Orioles   SCORE: NY 5, BA 0   SWING, POS. IN
ORDER: LH, 4th   PITCHER: Milt Pappas   MEN ON: 0
STATS: 1 for 4, 1 run, 1 RBI   POSITION: CF

354
355

DATE: July 18, 1961   PLACE, OPP.: Griffith Stadium,
Washington Senators   SCORE: NY 5, WA 3   SWING, POS.
IN ORDER: LH, LH; 4th   PITCHER: Joe McClain (2)   MEN
ON: 1, 0   STATS: 2 for 4, 2 runs, 3 RBIs   POSITION: CF

356

DATE: July 19, 1961
PLACE, OPP.: Griffith
   Stadium, Washington
   Senators
SCORE: WA 12, NY 2
SWING, POS. IN ORDER:
   LH, 4th
PITCHER: Dick Donovan

In the long nightcap, Mantle rocketed what may have been a 500-footer. The ball, hit into a wind, cleared the right-field wall with plenty to spare almost before Mickey left the batter's box.

MEN ON: 0
STATS: 1 for 4, 1 run, 1 RBI
POSITION: CF

---

357 DATE: July 21, 1961
PLACE, OPP.: Fenway Park,
   Boston Red Sox
SCORE: NY 11, BO 8
SWING, POS. IN ORDER:
   LH, 4th
PITCHER: Bill Monbouquette
MEN ON: 0
STATS: 2 for 3, 2 BBs, 2 runs, 2
   RBIs
POSITION: CF

In the first inning, the M & M
Boys hit back-to-back homers,
Mantle's a long clout to center,
but it took a two-out, ninth-inning, pinch-hit grand slam by
Johnny Blanchard to settle the
issue.

---

358 DATE: July 25, 1961
PLACE, OPP.: Yankee
   Stadium, Chicago White Sox
SCORE: NY 5, CH 1
SWING, POS. IN ORDER:
   RH, 4th
PITCHER: Frank Baumann
MEN ON: 0
STATS: 2 for 4, 2 runs, 1 RBI
POSITION: CF

The Yankees walloped eight
home runs in a doubleheader
sweep—and four were hit by
Roger Maris, who connected off
four different Chisox pitchers
and finished the day with 40
homers. In the opener, Maris
got the first of his quartet by
yanking a drive against the right-
field foul pole, to be followed by
Mantle's 38th homer off the left-
field pole.

---

359 DATE: July 26, 1961
PLACE, OPP.: Yankee
   Stadium, Chicago White Sox
SCORE: NY 5, CH 2
SWING, POS. IN ORDER:
   LH, 4th
PITCHER: Ray Herbert

The Yankees made only six hits
but four were home runs. Mantle and Blanchard hit back-to-
back first-inning homers—the
Mick's clout landed about 15
rows deep in the right-center-
field bleachers.

MEN ON: 1
STATS: 1 for 4, 1 run, 2 RBIs
POSITION: CF

---

360 DATE: August 2, 1961
PLACE, OPP.: Yankee
    Stadium, Kansas City A's
SCORE: NY 12, KC 5
SWING, POS. IN ORDER:
    LH, 4th
PITCHER: Art Ditmar
MEN ON: 1
STATS: 2 for 4, 1 BB, 2 runs, 3
    RBIs
POSITION: CF

In the first inning, Mantle made it 3–0 with a wallop into the third tier in right. The M & M Boys each had 40 homers.

361
362 DATE: August 6, 1961   PLACE, OPP.: Yankee Stadium,
Minnesota Twins   SCORE: NY 7, MI 6   SWING, POS. IN
ORDER: LH, LH; 4th   PITCHER: Pedro Ramos (2)   MEN
ON: 1, 0   STATS: 4 for 6, 2 BBs, 3 runs, 3 RBIs, 1 SB
POSITION: CF

---

363 DATE: August 6, 1961   PLACE, OPP.: Yankee Stadium,
Minnesota Twins   SCORE: NY 3, MI 2   SWING, POS. IN
ORDER: LH, 4th   PITCHER: Al Schroll   MEN ON: 0
STATS: 1 for 3, 1 BB, 2 runs, 1 RBI   POSITION: CF

---

364 DATE: August 11, 1961
PLACE, OPP.: Griffith
    Stadium, Washington
    Senators
SCORE: NY 12, WA 5
SWING, POS. IN ORDER:
    RH, 4th

The M & M Boys each delivered crushing homers against reliever Burnside; it was No. 42 for Roger and No. 44 for the Mick, a screaming drive that went halfway into the center-field bleachers.

PITCHER: Pete Burnside
MEN ON: 1
STATS: 1 for 3, 1 BB, 1 run, 3
   RBIs
POSITION: CF

365 DATE: August 13, 1961
PLACE, OPP.: Griffith
   Stadium, Washington
   Senators
SCORE: WA 12, NY 2
SWING, POS. IN ORDER:
   LH, 4th
PITCHER: Bennie Daniels
MEN ON: 0
STATS: 1 for 4, 1 run, 1 RBI
POSITION: CF

In the Yanks' farewell to Griffith
Stadium, Maris, frustrated in
the past here, homered in each
game of a twinbill to conclude a
four-homer series. Mantle got
only the one hit of the day—a
homer that kept him tied with
Maris at 45.

366 DATE: August 20, 1961
PLACE, OPP.: Municipal
   Stadium, Cleveland Indians
SCORE: NY 6, CL 0
SWING, POS. IN ORDER:
   LH, 4th
PITCHER: Jim Perry
MEN ON: 2
STATS: 3 for 4, 1 BB, 1 run, 4
   RBIs
POSITION: CF

In the first inning of the opener,
Mantle snapped a week-long
slump by unloading a homer to
give the Yanks a 3–0 lead.

367 DATE: August 30, 1961
PLACE, OPP.: Metropolitan
Stadium, Minnesota Twins
SCORE: NY 4, MI 0
SWING, POS. IN ORDER:
RH, 4th
PITCHER: Jim Kaat
MEN ON: 0
STATS: 1 for 4, 2 runs, 1 RBI
POSITION: CF

With only his second homer in 16 games, Mickey was still two games ahead of Babe Ruth's 1927 pace. In the seventh he homered about halfway into the left-field bleachers: He reached out and with one hand hammered a low change-up, a pitch well out of the strike zone.

368 DATE: August 31, 1961
PLACE, OPP.: Metropolitan
Stadium, Minnesota Twins
SCORE: MI 5, NY 4
SWING, POS. IN ORDER:
RH, 4th
PITCHER: Jack Kralick
MEN ON: 0
STATS: 3 for 4, 2 runs, 1 RBI,
1 SB
POSITION: CF

After arcing a homer just inside the left-field foul pole, Mantle, referring to Lou Gehrig's 47 homers in the Ruth-Gehrig teammate record of 107 homers, told Roger Maris, "Well, I beat my man, now it's up to you."

369
370 DATE: September 3, 1961   PLACE, OPP.: Yankee Stadium,
Detroit Tigers   SCORE: NY 8, DE 5   SWING, POS. IN
ORDER: LH, LH; 4th   PITCHERS: Jim Bunning, Gerry
Staley   MEN ON: 1, 0   STATS: 2 for 4, 2 runs, 3 RBIs
POSITION: CF

371 DATE: September 5, 1961   PLACE, OPP.: Yankee Stadium,
Washington Senators   SCORE: NY 6, WA 1   SWING, POS.
IN ORDER: LH, 4th   PITCHER: Joe McClain   MEN ON: 0
STATS: 2 for 3, 1 BB, 2 runs, 1 RBI   POSITION: CF

372   DATE: September 8, 1961   PLACE, OPP.: Yankee Stadium,
Cleveland Indians   SCORE: NY 9, CL 1   SWING, POS. IN
ORDER: LH, 4th   PITCHER: Gary Bell   MEN ON: 0
STATS: 1 for 2, 2 BBs, 2 runs, 1 RBI   POSITION: CF

---

373   DATE: September 10, 1961   PLACE, OPP.: Yankee Stadium,
Cleveland Indians   SCORE: NY 9, CL 3   SWING, POS. IN
ORDER: LH, 4th   PITCHER: Jim Perry   MEN ON: 0
STATS: 1 for 3, 1 BB, 2 runs, 1 RBI   POSITION: CF

---

374   DATE: September 23, 1961   PLACE, OPP.: Fenway Park, Boston
Red Sox   SCORE: NY 8, BO 3   SWING, POS. IN ORDER:
LH, 4th   PITCHER: Don Schwall   MEN ON: 2   STATS: 2
for 4, 1 run, 3 RBIs   POSITION: CF

1962

---

375   DATE: April 10, 1962   PLACE, OPP.: Yankee Stadium,
Baltimore Orioles   SCORE: NY 7, BA 6   SWING, POS. IN
ORDER: LH, 4th   PITCHER: Hal Brown   MEN ON: 0
STATS: 1 for 3, 1 BB, 1 run, 1 RBI   POSITION: CF

---

376   DATE: April 19, 1962
PLACE, OPP.: Memorial
   Stadium, Baltimore Orioles
SCORE: NY 3, BA 1
SWING, POS. IN ORDER:
   LH, 4th
PITCHER: Chuck Estrada
MEN ON: 0
STATS: 2 for 2, 2 BBs, 2 runs, 1
   RBI
POSITION: CF

Mantle opened the scoring in the second inning with a homer over the 390-foot sign in right-center.

377

DATE: May 5, 1962
PLACE, OPP.: Yankee
 Stadium, Washington
 Senators
SCORE: NY 7, WA 6
SWING, POS. IN ORDER:
 LH, 4th
PITCHER: Bennie Daniels
MEN ON: 0
STATS: 2 for 4, 2 runs, 1 RBI
POSITION: CF

Mantle tied the score at 2–2 in the fourth inning with a home run that landed very high in the right-field third tier.

378

DATE: May 6, 1962   PLACE, OPP.: Yankee Stadium,
Washington Senators   SCORE: WA 4, NY 2   SWING, POS.
IN ORDER: LH, 4th   PITCHER: Dave Stenhouse   MEN ON:
1   STATS: 2 for 4, 1 run, 2 RBIs   POSITION: CF

379
380

DATE: May 6, 1962   PLACE, OPP.: Yankee Stadium,
Washington Senators   SCORE: NY 8, WA 0   SWING, POS.
IN ORDER: RH, LH; 4th   PITCHERS: Pete Burnside, Jim
Hannan   MEN ON: 0, 1   STATS: 2 for 4, 2 runs, 3 RBIs
POSITION: CF

381

DATE: May 12, 1962
PLACE, OPP.: Municipal
 Stadium, Cleveland Indians
SCORE: NY 9, CL 6
SWING, POS. IN ORDER:
 LH, 4th
PITCHER: Barry Latman
MEN ON: 0
STATS: 3 for 3, 2 BBs, 3 runs, 1
 RBI
POSITION: CF

Mantle hit a ninth-inning home run that went perhaps 450 feet and landed in the right-field bullpen.

382 DATE: June 16, 1962   PLACE, OPP.: Municipal Stadium,
Cleveland Indians   SCORE: CL 10, NY 9   SWING, POS. IN
ORDER: LH, PH   PITCHER: Gary Bell   MEN ON: 2
STATS: 1 for 1, 1 run, 3 RBIs   POSITION: Pinch-hitter

---

383 DATE: June 23, 1962
PLACE, OPP.: Tiger Stadium,
  Detroit Tigers
SCORE: DE 5, NY 4
SWING, POS. IN ORDER:
  LH, 4th
PITCHER: Paul Foytack
MEN ON: 0
STATS: 1 for 4, 1 run, 1 RBI
POSITION: RF

In the nightcap Mantle hit a
ninth-inning leadoff homer.

---

384 DATE: June 28, 1962
PLACE, OPP.: Yankee
  Stadium, Minnesota Twins
SCORE: NY 4, MI 2
SWING, POS. IN ORDER:
  RH, 4th
PITCHER: Jack Kralick
MEN ON: 0
STATS: 2 for 4, 1 run, 1 RBI
POSITION: RF

It was 0–0 in the fourth when
Roger Maris and Mantle hit solo
homers. Mickey hit a wide fastball, reaching out to full exten-
sion and pumping the ball into
the right-field bleachers.

---

385 DATE: July 2, 1962
PLACE, OPP.: Yankee
  Stadium, Kansas City A's
SCORE: NY 8, KC 4
SWING, POS. IN ORDER:
  LH, 4th
PITCHER: Ed Rakow
MEN ON: 0

Mantle's sixth-inning homer, a
drive of gargantuan proportions,
landed halfway up the third tier
in right.

STATS: 1 for 1, 3 BBs, 2 runs, 1
RBI
POSITION: RF

386
387

DATE: July 3, 1962
PLACE, OPP.: Yankee
Stadium, Kansas City A's
SCORE: NY 8, KC 7
SWING, POS. IN ORDER:
LH, LH; 4th
PITCHERS: Jerry Walker,
Gordon Jones
MEN ON: 1, 0
STATS: 3 for 5, 2 runs, 3 RBIs
POSITION: RF

The Yankees hit five homers—
two each by Mantle and Roger
Maris and another by Bobby
Richardson. Mantle got New
York on the board in the fifth
with a two-run homer upstairs
in right. His homer in the
eighth broke a 7–7 tie and won
the game.

388
389

DATE: July 4, 1962   PLACE, OPP.: Yankee Stadium, Kansas City
A's   SCORE: NY 7, KC 3   SWING, POS. IN ORDER: LH,
LH; 4th   PITCHERS: Dan Pfister, John Wyatt   MEN ON: 1, 0
STATS: 2 for 2, 2 BBs, 2 runs, 3 RBIs   POSITION: RF

390
391

DATE: July 6, 1962   PLACE, OPP.: Metropolitan Stadium,
Minnesota Twins   SCORE: NY 7, MI 5   SWING, POS. IN
ORDER: LH, LH; 4th   PITCHER: Camilo Pascual (2)   MEN
ON: 0, 0   STATS: 2 for 4, 1 BB, 2 runs, 2 RBIs   POSITION:
RF

392

DATE: July 18, 1962
PLACE, OPP.: Fenway Park,
Boston Red Sox
SCORE: NY 12, BO 4
SWING, POS. IN ORDER:
LH, 4th
PITCHER: Galen Cisco

Mantle's homer went more than
400 feet, over the Boston bullpen in right field.

MEN ON: 1
STATS: 2 for 4, 1 run, 4 RBIs
POSITION: CF

---

393 DATE: July 20, 1962
PLACE, OPP.: Yankee
Stadium, Washington
Senators
SCORE: NY 3, WA 2
SWING, POS. IN ORDER:
RH, 4th
PITCHER: Steve Hamilton
MEN ON: 1
STATS: 3 for 4, 1 run, 2 RBIs
POSITION: CF

Mantle ran his hitting streak to 14 games and raised his on-base average to an amazing .516. In the first inning, Mantle rocketed a homer to left field that rebounded onto the field; it hit either the upper deck's facing or its first rows of seats.

---

394 DATE: July 25, 1962
PLACE, OPP.: Yankee
Stadium, Boston Red Sox
SCORE: BO 4, NY 2
SWING, POS. IN ORDER:
LH, 4th
PITCHER: Earl Wilson
MEN ON: 0
STATS: 1 for 3, 1 BB, 1 run, 1
RBI
POSITION: CF

Mantle, who went 1 for 6 with 5 strikeouts and 2 walks in the doubleheader split, gave the Yankees a short-lived 1–0 lead in the first game with a shot into the right-field bleachers.

---

395 DATE: July 28, 1962
PLACE, OPP.: Yankee
Stadium, Chicago White Sox
SCORE: NY 4, CH 3
SWING, POS. IN ORDER:
LH, 4th
PITCHER: Eddie Fisher
MEN ON: 0

In the seventh, Mantle broke knuckleballer Fisher's spell with an upper-deck homer to right, and Johnny Blanchard followed with a pinch-hit three-run homer, as the Yankees overcame a 3–0 deficit on Old Timers' Day.

STATS: 1 for 3, 1 BB, 1 run, 1
RBI
POSITION: CF

---

396   DATE: August 17, 1962
PLACE, OPP.: Municipal
    Stadium, Kansas City A's
SCORE: KC 7, NY 2
SWING, POS. IN ORDER:
    LH, 4th
PITCHER: Bill Fischer
MEN ON: 0
STATS: 1 for 4, 1 run, 1 RBI
POSITION: CF

Mantle pounded a first-inning
home run some 400 feet over
the left-center-field fence.

---

397   DATE: August 18, 1962
PLACE, OPP.: Municipal
    Stadium, Kansas City A's
SCORE: KC 5, NY 4
SWING, POS. IN ORDER:
    LH, 4th
PITCHER: Diego Segui
MEN ON: 0
STATS: 1 for 3, 1 BB, 1 run, 1
    RBI
POSITION: CF

The Yanks wasted a trio of
homers—Mantle's was a towering 420-foot blast to left-center.

398

DATE: August 19, 1962
PLACE, OPP.: Municipal
  Stadium, Kansas City A's
SCORE: NY 21, KC 7
SWING, POS. IN ORDER:
  LH, 4th
PITCHER: Jerry Walker
MEN ON: 3
STATS: 3 for 4, 3 runs, 7 RBIs,
  2 SBs
POSITION: CF

All 21 Yankee runs were driven in by four players: Elston Howard (8 RBIs), Mantle (7), Bill Showron (4), and Tom Tresh (2). Mantle hit his seventh career grand slam and had an RBI-double and an RBI-single (after which he stole second and third bases). He knocked in his seventh run with a groundout. One of his greatest games ever, it could have been even greater, but he left early (his replacement, Jack Reed, got two more at bats).

399

DATE: August 28, 1962   PLACE, OPP.: Yankee Stadium, Cleveland Indians   SCORE: NY 2, CL 1   SWING, POS. IN ORDER: LH, 4th   PITCHER: Mudcat Grant   MEN ON: 1 STATS: 1 for 2, 1 run, 2 RBIs   POSITION: CF

400

DATE: September 10, 1962   PLACE, OPP.: Tiger Stadium, Detroit Tigers   SCORE: NY 3, DE 1   SWING, POS. IN ORDER: RH, 4th   PITCHER: Hank Aguirre   MEN ON: 0 STATS: 2 for 3, 1 BB, 2 runs, 1 RBI   POSITION: CF

401

DATE: September 12, 1962
PLACE, OPP.: Municipal
  Stadium, Cleveland Indians
SCORE: NY 5, CL 2
SWING, POS. IN ORDER:
  LH, 4th
PITCHER: Pedro Ramos
MEN ON: 2
STATS: 1 for 4, 1 BB, 1 run, 3
  RBIs
POSITION: CF

Mantle and Ford led the way. Mantle's two-out homer in the fifth traveled between 420 and 450 feet to right-center.

402
403
DATE: September 18, 1962   PLACE, OPP.: D.C. Stadium,
Washington Senators   SCORE: NY 7, WA 1   SWING, POS.
IN ORDER: LH, LH; 4th   PITCHER: Tom Cheney (2)   MEN
ON: 2, 1   STATS: 2 for 4, 2 runs, 5 RBIs   POSITION: CF

404
DATE: September 30, 1962
PLACE, OPP.: Yankee
    Stadium, Chicago White Sox
SCORE: CH 8, NY 4
SWING, POS. IN ORDER:
    LH, 1st
PITCHER: Ray Herbert
MEN ON: 0
STATS: 2 for 3, 2 runs, 1 RBI
POSITION: CF

On the final day of the season, Mantle's homer gave him at least 30 homers in eight successive seasons. Mickey left the game having made the required 502 batting appearances to qualify for the batting title. But he fell short of Boston's Pete Runnels, who sat out his final-day doubleheader with the flu, and who bested Mickey .326 to .321.

1963

405
DATE: April 10, 1963   PLACE, OPP.: Municipal Stadium,
Kansas City A's   SCORE: NY 5, KC 3   SWING, POS. IN
ORDER: RH, 4th   PITCHER: Ted Bowsfield   MEN ON: 1
STATS: 2 for 4, 1 run, 2 RBIs   POSITION: CF

406
DATE: April 11, 1963
PLACE, OPP.: Yankee
    Stadium, Baltimore Orioles
SCORE: BA 4, NY 1
SWING, POS. IN ORDER:
    LH, 4th
PITCHER: Milt Pappas
MEN ON: 0
STATS: 2 for 3, 1 BB, 1 run, 1
    RBI
POSITION: CF

Mantle was presented his 1962 MVP Award, then homered deep into the right-field bullpen for the only Yank run and made a great galloping catch in Death Valley in the home opener.

407

DATE: May 4, 1963
PLACE, OPP.: Metropolitan
 Stadium, Minnesota Twins
SCORE: NY 3, MI 2
SWING, POS. IN ORDER:
 RH, 4th
PITCHER: Jim Kaat
MEN ON: 0
STATS: 1 for 4, 1 run, 1 RBI
POSITION: CF

Three solo home runs—two by
Elston Howard and one by
Mantle—were all the runs the
Yankees needed.

408

DATE: May 6, 1963
PLACE, OPP.: Tiger Stadium,
 Detroit Tigers
SCORE: NY 10, DE 3
SWING, POS. IN ORDER:
 RH, 4th
PITCHER: Hank Aguirre
MEN ON: 1
STATS: 3 for 3, 1 BB, 1 run, 3
 RBIs
POSITION: CF

The fourth time Mickey faced
Aguirre (after two singles and a
sacrifice fly), in the seventh, he
reached the upper deck in left.

409

DATE: May 11, 1963
PLACE, OPP.: Memorial
 Stadium, Baltimore Orioles
SCORE: NY 13, BA 1
SWING, POS. IN ORDER:
 LH, 4th
PITCHER: Milt Pappas
MEN ON: 0
STATS: 2 for 4, 1 BB, 3 runs, 3
 RBIs
POSITION: CF

Homers by Mantle and Roger
Maris made this the first game
of the year in which they both
homered.

410

DATE: May 15, 1963
PLACE, OPP.: Yankee
  Stadium, Minnesota Twins
SCORE: NY 4, MI 3
SWING, POS. IN ORDER:
  LH, 4th
PITCHER: Camilo Pascual
MEN ON: 1
STATS: 2 for 4, 2 runs, 2 RBIs
POSITION: CF

Minnesota was leading 3–0 in the bottom of the sixth when Mantle crushed a home run into the right-field third tier, the ball seemingly swallowed up by a ramp opening. He later scored the winning run following a smart baserunning play.

411
412

DATE: May 21, 1963
PLACE, OPP.: Yankee
  Stadium, Kansas City A's
SCORE: NY 7, KC 4
SWING, POS. IN ORDER:
  LH, LH; 4th
PITCHERS: Orlando Pena,
  Diego Segui
MEN ON: 2, 1
STATS: 2 for 4, 2 runs, 5 RBIs
POSITION: CF

In the first inning, Mantle roped a home run about six rows deep in the lower right-field stands, and in the fifth Mantle delivered a ball to the right-field bullpen. Then Maris reached the bleachers, the first time in 1963 that the M & M Boys hit back-to-back homers.

413

DATE: May 22, 1963   PLACE, OPP.: Yankee Stadium, Kansas City A's   SCORE: NY 8, KC 7   SWING, POS. IN ORDER: LH, 4th   PITCHER: Bill Fischer   MEN ON: 0   STATS: 1 for 3, 3 BBs, 2 runs, 1 RBI   POSITION: CF

414

DATE: May 26, 1963
PLACE, OPP.: Yankee
  Stadium, Washington
  Senators
SCORE: NY 7, WA 1
SWING, POS. IN ORDER:
  RH, 4th
PITCHER: Don Rudolph
MEN ON: 0

This was a tight pitchers' duel until the sixth, when Mantle sliced a home run into the lower deck in right, and the Yankees led, 2–1.

STATS: 1 for 3, 1 BB, 1 run, 1
  RBI
POSITION: CF

415

DATE: June 4, 1963
PLACE, OPP.: Memorial
  Stadium, Baltimore Orioles
SCORE: BA 3, NY 1
SWING, POS. IN ORDER:
  RH, 4th
PITCHER: Steve Barber
MEN ON: 0
STATS: 2 for 4, 1 run, 1 RBI
POSITION: CF

Mantle's second-inning homer
was the only run allowed by
Barber, the league's win leader.
The Mick fell away from a full-
count pitch and stroked a lazy
360-foot fly into the opposite-
field bleachers.

416

DATE: August 4, 1963   PLACE, OPP.: Yankee Stadium,
Baltimore Orioles   SCORE: NY 11, BA 10   SWING, POS. IN
ORDER: RH, PH   PITCHER: George Brunet   MEN ON: 0
STATS: 1 for 1, 1 run, 1 RBI   POSITION: Pinch-hitter

417

DATE: September 1, 1963   PLACE, OPP.: Memorial Stadium,
Baltimore Orioles   SCORE: NY 5, BA 4   SWING, POS. IN
ORDER: RH, PH   PITCHER: Mike McCormick   MEN ON: 1
STATS: 1 for 1, 1 run, 2 RBIs   POSITION: Pinch-hitter

418

DATE: September 11, 1963
PLACE, OPP.: Municipal
  Stadium, Kansas City A's
SCORE: NY 8, KC 2
SWING, POS. IN ORDER:
  LH, 4th
PITCHER: Ed Rakow
MEN ON: 2
STATS: 3 for 4, 1 run, 4 RBIs
POSITION: CF

Whitey Ford got all the help he
needed on Mantle's first-inning
homer. The ball hit close to the
right-field foul pole, a lesser
blow than the 421-foot double
Mickey bounced off the center-
field wall two innings later.

419 DATE: September 21, 1963
PLACE, OPP.: Yankee
   Stadium, Kansas City A's
SCORE: KC 5, NY 3
SWING, POS. IN ORDER:
   LH, 4th
PITCHER: Moe Drabowsky
MEN ON: 0
STATS: 2 for 2, 1 BB, 1 run, 1
   RBI
POSITION: CF

Mantle and Yogi Berra homered in the same game for the 50th and last time. It was Yogi's 358th, and final, homer in the majors.

1964

---

420 DATE: May 6, 1964
PLACE, OPP.: D.C. Stadium,
   Washington Senators
SCORE: NY 9, WA 2
SWING, POS. IN ORDER:
   LH, 4th
PITCHER: Bennie Daniels
MEN ON: 0
STATS: 1 for 4, 1 BB, 1 run, 1
   RBI
POSITION: CF

Jim Bouton rode four Yankee homers—two by Hector Lopez and one each by Mantle and Roger Maris—to an easy victory.

---

421 DATE: May 6, 1964
PLACE, OPP.: D.C. Stadium,
   Washington Senators
SCORE: WA 5, NY 4
SWING, POS. IN ORDER:
   RH, 4th
PITCHER: Claude Osteen
MEN ON: 2
STATS: 2 for 4, 1 run, 4 RBIs
POSITION: CF

Mantle's run-producing double in the first inning and his three-run homer in the third staked the Yankees to a 4–0 lead, a lead that didn't hold up.

---

422 DATE: May 8, 1964
PLACE, OPP.: Municipal
Stadium, Cleveland Indians
SCORE: NY 10, CL 3
SWING, POS. IN ORDER:
RH, 4th
PITCHER: Tommy John
MEN ON: 2
STATS: 1 for 2, 3 BBs, 1 run, 3
RBIs
POSITION: CF

Amid tornado warnings, Mantle drilled a homer over the right-field fence.

---

423 DATE: May 9, 1964
PLACE, OPP.: Municipal
Stadium, Cleveland Indians
SCORE: NY 6, CL 2
SWING, POS. IN ORDER:
LH, 4th
PITCHER: Pedro Ramos
MEN ON: 0
STATS: 1 for 3, 1 BB, 1 run, 1
RBI
POSITION: CF

Four Yankees hit home runs off Ramos—Tony Kubek, Mantle (Mickey's 12th, and final, Ramos homer), Joe Pepitone, and Hector Lopez.

---

424 DATE: May 16, 1964
PLACE, OPP.: Yankee
Stadium, Kansas City A's
SCORE: NY 10, KC 6
SWING, POS. IN ORDER:
RH, 4th
PITCHER: Joe Grzenda
MEN ON: 1
STATS: 1 for 5, 1 run, 2 RBIs
POSITION: CF

Mantle's two-run homer in the fourth landed just beyond the left fielder who was standing against the 402-foot sign.

425

DATE: May 17, 1964
PLACE, OPP.: Yankee
  Stadium, Kansas City A's
SCORE: NY 11, KC 9
SWING, POS. IN ORDER:
  RH, 4th
PITCHER: John O'Donoghue
MEN ON: 0
STATS: 2 for 2, 2 BBs, 3 runs, 2
  RBIs
POSITION: CF

Mantle helped New York to a 2–0 first-inning lead with an opposite-field homer deep into the right-field bleachers.

426

DATE: May 23, 1964
PLACE, OPP.: Yankee
  Stadium, Los Angeles Angels
SCORE: LA 9, NY 5
SWING, POS. IN ORDER:
  RH, 4th
PITCHER: Bo Belinsky
MEN ON: 1
STATS: 2 for 4, 2 runs, 2 RBIs
POSITION: CF

Mantle helped the Yanks to a 5–4 lead with a first-inning opposite-field homer that went at least 420 feet into the right-field bleachers.

427

DATE: May 24, 1964
PLACE, OPP.: Yankee
  Stadium, Los Angeles Angels
SCORE: NY 8, LA 5
SWING, POS. IN ORDER:
  LH, 4th
PITCHER: Fred Newman
MEN ON: 0
STATS: 3 for 4, 2 runs, 1 RBI
POSITION: CF

The Angels were up, 2–0, in the second inning when Mantle sent a home run into the upper deck in right field.

428
429

DATE: June 11, 1964
PLACE, OPP.: Fenway Park,
  Boston Red Sox
SCORE: NY 8, BO 4
SWING, POS. IN ORDER:
  LH, 3rd
PITCHER: Bill Monbouquette
  (2)
MEN ON: 1, 0
STATS: 2 for 4, 1 BB, 2 runs, 3
  RBIs
POSITION: CF

Mantle, recently returned from
a two-week injury sidelining,
got back on the beam with two
long homers to right field.

---

430 DATE: June 13, 1964   PLACE, OPP.: Yankee Stadium, Chicago
White Sox   SCORE: NY 6, CH 3   SWING, POS. IN ORDER:
RH, 4th   PITCHER: Frank Kreutzer   MEN ON: 0   STATS:
3 for 3, 1 BB, 1 run, 2 RBIs   POSITION: CF

---

431 DATE: June 17, 1964   PLACE, OPP.: Yankee Stadium, Boston
Red Sox   SCORE: BO 4, NY 3   SWING, POS. IN ORDER:
LH, 3rd   PITCHER: Dick Radatz   MEN ON: 0   STATS: 1
for 4, 1 run, 1 RBI   POSITION: CF

---

432 DATE: June 21, 1964   PLACE, OPP.: Comiskey Park, Chicago
White Sox   SCORE: NY 2, CH 0   SWING, POS. IN ORDER:
RH, 4th   PITCHER: Juan Pizarro   MEN ON: 0   STATS: 1
for 4, 1 run, 1 RBI   POSITION: CF

---

433 DATE: June 23, 1964   PLACE, OPP.: Memorial Stadium,
Baltimore Orioles   SCORE: BA 9, NY 8   SWING, POS. IN
ORDER: LH, 3rd   PITCHER: Chuck Estrada   MEN ON: 2
STATS: 1 for 5, 1 run, 4 RBIs   POSITION: CF

434

DATE: June 27, 1964
PLACE, OPP.: Yankee
  Stadium, Detroit Tigers
SCORE: NY 5, DE 4
SWING, POS. IN ORDER:
  LH, 3rd
PITCHER: Denny McLain
MEN ON: 0
STATS: 1 for 4, 1 BB, 1 run, 1
  RBI
POSITION: CF

Mantle in the fourth brought the Yanks to 4–1 with an arcing homer into the right-field seats.

435

DATE: July 1, 1964
PLACE, OPP.: Yankee
  Stadium, Kansas City A's
SCORE: KC 5, NY 4
SWING, POS. IN ORDER:
  RH, 4th
PITCHER: John O'Donoghue
MEN ON: 1
STATS: 1 for 4, 1 run, 2 RBIs
POSITION: CF

Taxi Day (almost 5,000 cabbies and their families were in the crowd). The Yankees in their half of the first inning took a 3–2 lead on two hits and a 420-foot Mantle homer.

436

DATE: July 4, 1964
PLACE, OPP.: Yankee
  Stadium, Minnesota Twins
SCORE: NY 7, MI 5
SWING, POS. IN ORDER:
  LH, 4th
PITCHER: Al Worthington
MEN ON: 2
STATS: 3 for 5, 2 runs, 4 RBIs
POSITION: CF

In the eighth, with two on and two out and Minnesota ahead, 5–4, Mantle parked a three-run shot in the third tier in right field for the game winner.

437 DATE: July 13, 1964
PLACE, OPP.: Municipal
Stadium, Cleveland Indians
SCORE: NY 10, CL 4
SWING, POS. IN ORDER:
LH, 3rd
PITCHER: Gary Bell
MEN ON: 0
STATS: 1 for 4, 1 BB, 1 run, 1
RBI
POSITION: CF

Four Yankee homers, Mickey's
a liner over the right-field fence.

438 DATE: July 24, 1964
PLACE, OPP.: Tiger Stadium,
Detroit Tigers
SCORE: DE 10, NY 5
SWING, POS. IN ORDER:
RH, 4th
PITCHER: Hank Aguirre
MEN ON: 1
STATS: 1 for 2, 2 BBs, 1 run, 2
RBIs
POSITION: CF

The Yankees jumped ahead, 5–
2, on three homers, Mickey's
hitting the roof overhang.

439 DATE: July 28, 1964
PLACE, OPP.: Chavez Ravine,
Los Angeles Angels
SCORE: LA 3, NY 1
SWING, POS. IN ORDER:
LH, 4th
PITCHER: Dean Chance
MEN ON: 0
STATS: 1 for 2, 2 BBs, 1 run, 1
RBI
POSITION: CF

In the seventh, Mantle took two
strikes, watched three balls, then
lined a homer over the center-
field fence, one of only two hits
off Chance, who had gone 69
innings without allowing a
home run.

440

DATE: August 1, 1964
PLACE, OPP.: Metropolitan
    Stadium, Minnesota Twins
SCORE: NY 6, MI 4
SWING, POS. IN ORDER:
    RH, 4th
PITCHER: Dick Stigman
MEN ON: 1
STATS: 2 for 4, 2 runs, 2 RBIs,
    1 SB
POSITION: CF

The Yanks went up 5–2 in the sixth after Tom Tresh singled and Mantle, on a 3-and-0 pitch, launched a 430-foot homer over the center-field screen.

441

DATE: August 4, 1964
PLACE, OPP.: Municipal
    Stadium, Kansas City A's
SCORE: KC 5, NY 1
SWING, POS. IN ORDER:
    RH, 4th
PITCHER: John O'Donoghue
MEN ON: 0
STATS: 2 for 4, 1 run, 1 RBI
POSITION: CF

The scoring opened with Mantle's sixth-inning homer, a 400-foot line drive over the left-center-field fence.

442

DATE: August 11, 1964
PLACE, OPP.: Yankee
    Stadium, Chicago White Sox
SCORE: CH 8, NY 2
SWING, POS. IN ORDER:
    RH, 4th
PITCHER: Juan Pizarro
MEN ON: 0
STATS: 1 for 4, 1 run, 1 RBI
POSITION: CF

Mantle homered into the lower seats in right with two out in the ninth.

443
444
DATE: August 12, 1964   PLACE, OPP.: Yankee Stadium,
Chicago White Sox   SCORE: NY 7, CH 3   SWING, POS. IN
ORDER: LH, RH; 4th   PITCHERS: Ray Herbert, Frank
Baumann   MEN ON: 0, 0   STATS: 3 for 4, 3 runs, 2 RBIs
POSITION: CF

445
DATE: August 22, 1964   PLACE, OPP.: Fenway Park, Boston
Red Sox   SCORE: NY 8, BO 0   SWING, POS. IN ORDER:
LH, 4th   PITCHER: Jack Lamabe   MEN ON: 1   STATS: 2
for 4, 3 runs, 3 RBIs   POSITION: LF

446
DATE: August 23, 1964
PLACE, OPP.: Fenway Park,
   Boston Red Sox
SCORE: NY 4, BO 3
SWING, POS. IN ORDER:
   LH, 4th
PITCHER: Earl Wilson
MEN ON: 1
STATS: 1 for 4, 1 run, 2 RBIs
POSITION: LF

Mantle unloaded a third-inning
homer to give New York a 2–0
lead.

447
DATE: August 29, 1964
PLACE, OPP.: Yankee
   Stadium, Boston Red Sox
SCORE: NY 10, BO 2
SWING, POS. IN ORDER:
   LH, 4th
PITCHER: Earl Wilson
MEN ON: 1
STATS: 1 for 2, 2 runs, 1 BB, 2
   RBIs
POSITION: CF

Upwards of 40,000 turned out
on Elston Howard Night to see
the Yankees sweep a doubleheader, 10–2 and 6–1. Joe Pepitone hit three homers, including
a grand slam, and Roger Maris
had six singles. Mantle had a
two-run wallop in the opener
and tied Babe Ruth's all-time
career strikeout record in the
nightcap.

448 DATE: September 4, 1964   PLACE, OPP.: Municipal Stadium, Kansas City A's   SCORE: NY 9, KC 7   SWING, POS. IN ORDER: RH, 4th   PITCHER: John O'Donoghue   MEN ON: 1 STATS: 2 for 4, 1 run, 2 RBIs   POSITION: LF

449 DATE: September 5, 1964 PLACE, OPP.: Municipal Stadium, Kansas City A's SCORE: NY 9, KC 7 SWING, POS. IN ORDER: LH, 4th PITCHER: Blue Moon Odom MEN ON: 2 STATS: 2 for 3, 2 BBs, 2 runs, 3 RBIs POSITION: LF

Odom, a 19-year-old bonus baby making his major-league debut, served Mantle an outside pitch in the first inning that Mickey sent over the opposite-field fence to make it 3–0.

450 DATE: September 17, 1964   PLACE, OPP.: Yankee Stadium, Los Angeles Angels   SCORE: NY 6, LA 2   SWING, POS. IN ORDER: LH, 4th   PITCHER: Bob Duliba   MEN ON: 1 STATS: 3 for 4, 3 runs, 2 RBIs   POSITION: RF

451 DATE: September 19, 1964 PLACE, OPP.: Yankee Stadium, Kansas City A's SCORE: NY 8, KC 3 SWING, POS. IN ORDER: LH, 4th PITCHER: Diego Segui MEN ON: 1 STATS: 2 for 4, 1 BB, 2 runs, 2 RBIs POSITION: RF

Mantle walloped a home run deep into the Yankee bullpen in the first.

452

DATE: September 22, 1964
PLACE, OPP.: Municipal
  Stadium, Cleveland Indians
SCORE: NY 8, CL 1
SWING, POS. IN ORDER:
  LH, 4th
PITCHER: Dick Donovan
MEN ON: 1
STATS: 2 for 4, 1 run, 2 RBIs
POSITION: LF

The first-place Yankees swept two from Cleveland, 5–3 and 8–1, getting home runs in the doubleheader from Mantle, Joe Pepitone, Roger Maris, and Phil Linz.

453

DATE: September 27, 1964
PLACE, OPP.: D.C. Stadium,
  Washington Senators
SCORE: WA 3, NY 2
SWING, POS. IN ORDER:
  LH, 4th
PITCHER: Bennie Daniels
MEN ON: 0
STATS: 2 for 5, 1 run, 2 RBIs
POSITION: LF

Mantle tied it, 1–1, with a seventh-inning homer.

454

DATE: September 30, 1964
PLACE, OPP.: Yankee
  Stadium, Detroit Tigers
SCORE: NY 7, DE 6
SWING, POS. IN ORDER:
  RH, 4th
PITCHER: Mickey Lolich
MEN ON: 0
STATS: 1 for 2, 2 BBs, 1 run, 1
  RBI
POSITION: RF

Mantle's leadoff second-inning homer ignited a five-run rally, wiping out a 3–0 Detroit lead.

1965

455

DATE: April 17, 1965
PLACE, OPP.: Municipal
   Stadium, Kansas City A's
SCORE: NY 5, KC 2
SWING, POS. IN ORDER:
   LH, 4th
PITCHER: John Wyatt
MEN ON: 1
STATS: 1 for 2, 2 BBs, 1 run, 2
   RBIs
POSITION: LF

The Yankee infield turned five double plays, and all five Yankee runs came via the home run. The Yankees led, 2–1, in the eighth when Roger Maris walked and Mantle parked his first homer of the season on a hilly pasture in right about 360 feet from the plate.

456

DATE: April 18, 1965
PLACE, OPP.: Municipal
   Stadium, Kansas City A's
SCORE: NY 10, KC 4
SWING, POS. IN ORDER:
   LH, 4th
PITCHER: Moe Drabowsky
MEN ON: 1
STATS: 2 for 3, 2 runs, 1 BB, 2
   RBIs
POSITION: LF

Mantle hit a first-inning homer.

457

DATE: April 21, 1965
PLACE, OPP.: Yankee
   Stadium, Minnesota Twins
SCORE: MI 7, NY 2
SWING, POS. IN ORDER:
   LH, 4th
PITCHER: Camilo Pascual
MEN ON: 0

In the first inning of the home opener, Mantle sent a majestic homer to right that landed far upstairs, putting the Yanks ahead, 2–0.

STATS: 1 for 3, 1 BB, 1 run, 1
   RBI
POSITION: LF

458

DATE: April 25, 1965
PLACE, OPP.: Yankee
   Stadium, Los Angeles Angels
SCORE: NY 1, LA 0
SWING, POS. IN ORDER:
   RH, 4th
PITCHER: Rudy May
MEN ON: 0
STATS: 1 for 3, 1 BB, 1 run, 1
   RBI
POSITION: LF

The only run of a great pitchers' battle between Mel Stottlemyre and May was scored on Mantle's fourth-inning homer into the lower seats in left.

459

DATE: May 10, 1965   PLACE, OPP.: Fenway Park, Boston Red Sox   SCORE: BO 3, NY 2   SWING, POS. IN ORDER: LH, 4th   PITCHER: Jim Lonborg   MEN ON: 0   STATS: 3 for 4, 1 run, 2 RBIs   POSITION: LF

460

DATE: May 11, 1965   PLACE, OPP.: Fenway Park, Boston Red Sox   SCORE: NY 5, BO 3   SWING, POS. IN ORDER: RH, 4th   PITCHER: Arnie Earley   MEN ON: 0   STATS: 1 for 2, 2 BBs, 1 run, 1 RBI   POSITION: LF

461

DATE: May 15, 1965
PLACE, OPP.: Memorial
   Stadium, Baltimore Orioles
SCORE: NY 3, BA 2
SWING, POS. IN ORDER:
   LH, 4th
PITCHER: Dick Hall
MEN ON: 0

Leading off the eighth, Mantle boomed a 400-foot-plus opposite-field homer into the left-field bleachers, breaking a 2–2 tie.

STATS: 1 for 3, 1 BB, 1 run, 1
RBI
POSITION: LF

---

462   DATE: May 30, 1965   Mantle opened the scoring with
PLACE, OPP.: Comiskey Park,   a fourth-inning homer.
Chicago White Sox
SCORE: NY 3, CH 2
SWING, POS. IN ORDER:
RH, 4th
PITCHER: Gary Peters
MEN ON: 0
STATS: 2 for 4, 1 run, 1 RBI
POSITION: LF

---

463   DATE: June 5, 1965   PLACE, OPP.: Yankee Stadium, Chicago
White Sox   SCORE: NY 4, CH 3   SWING, POS. IN ORDER:
RH, 4th   PITCHER: Gary Peters   MEN ON: 0   STATS: 1
for 3, 1 BB, 1 run, 1 RBI   POSITION: LF

---

464   DATE: June 18, 1965   PLACE, OPP.: Yankee Stadium,
Minnesota Twins   SCORE: NY 10, MI 2   SWING, POS. IN
ORDER: RH, 5th   PITCHER: Mel Nelson   MEN ON: 3
STATS: 1 for 3, 1 run, 4 RBIs   POSITION: LF

---

465   DATE: June 22, 1965   PLACE, OPP.: Yankee Stadium, Kansas
City A's   SCORE: KC 6, NY 2   SWING, POS. IN ORDER:
RH, 3rd   PITCHER: John O'Donoghue   MEN ON: 0
STATS: 1 for 3, 1 BB, 1 run, 1 RBI   POSITION: LF

---

466 DATE: July 15, 1965
PLACE, OPP.: Yankee
   Stadium, Washington
   Senators
SCORE: NY 2, WA 1
SWING, POS. IN ORDER:
   LH, 3rd
PITCHER: Phil Ortega
MEN ON: 0
STATS: 1 for 2, 2 BBs, 1 run, 1
   RBI
POSITION: LF

Mantle clipped Ortega for a sixth-inning homer, tying it, 1–1, before giving way to pinch-runner Ross Moschitto late in regulation.

467 DATE: July 25, 1965
PLACE, OPP.: Municipal
   Stadium, Cleveland Indians
SCORE: CL 7, NY 4
SWING, POS. IN ORDER:
   LH, 3rd
PITCHER: Lee Stange
MEN ON: 1
STATS: 2 for 2, 2 runs, 2 RBIs
POSITION: LF

Mickey hit a third-inning two-run homer about 450 feet over the center-field fence.

468 DATE: August 6, 1965
PLACE, OPP.: Tiger Stadium,
   Detroit Tigers
SCORE: DE 5, NY 4
SWING, POS. IN ORDER:
   RH, 3rd
PITCHER: Mickey Lolich
MEN ON: 0
STATS: 2 for 4, 1 run, 1 RBI
POSITION: LF

Mantle, coming off a 7-for-11 series at Chicago, poked an opposite-field homer off the right-field foul screen.

469 DATE: August 7, 1965
PLACE, OPP.: Tiger Stadium,
Detroit Tigers
SCORE: NY 6, DE 5
SWING, POS. IN ORDER:
LH, 3rd
PITCHER: Fred Gladding
MEN ON: 0
STATS: 2 for 4, 1 run, 1 RBI
POSITION: LF

Mantle continued his hot hitting with a fifth-inning homer.

---

470 DATE: August 10, 1965
PLACE, OPP.: Yankee
Stadium, Minnesota Twins
SCORE: MI 7, NY 3
SWING, POS. IN ORDER:
RH, 3rd
PITCHER: Jim Kaat
MEN ON: 0
STATS: 1 for 4, 1 run, 1 RBI
POSITION: LF

Sloppy Yankee fielding handed Minnesota six unearned runs and sealed the outcome by the time Mantle, 14 for 27 in his last seven games, pounded his eighth-inning wrong-field homer into the right-field bullpen.

---

471 DATE: August 18, 1965
PLACE, OPP.: Yankee
Stadium, Los Angeles Angels
SCORE: LA 7, NY 3
SWING, POS. IN ORDER:
LH, 3rd
PITCHER: Dean Chance
MEN ON: 0
STATS: 2 for 4, 1 run, 1 RBI
POSITION: LF

Mantle's homer went deep into the right-field bleachers, at least 425 feet.

---

472 DATE: September 2, 1965
PLACE, OPP.: Chavez Ravine,
Los Angeles Angels
SCORE: NY 8, LA 1

Mantle helped Ford to an early 5–0 lead with a first-inning 400-foot homer into the left-center-field pavilion.

SWING, POS. IN ORDER:
   RH, 3rd
PITCHER: Marcelino Lopez
MEN ON: 2
STATS: 2 for 3, 1 BB, 1 run, 4
   RBIs
POSITION: LF

---

473   DATE: September 4, 1965   PLACE, OPP.: Yankee Stadium,
Boston Red Sox   SCORE: BO 7, NY 2   SWING, POS. IN
ORDER: RH, 3rd   PITCHER: Dennis Bennett   MEN ON: 0
STATS: 1 for 4, 1 run, 1 RBI   POSITION: LF

1966

---

474   DATE: May 9, 1966   PLACE, OPP.: Metropolitan Stadium,
Minnesota Twins   SCORE: NY 3, MI 2   SWING, POS. IN
ORDER: LH, 3rd   PITCHER: Jim Perry   MEN ON: 0
STATS: 1 for 4, 1 run, 1 RBI   POSITION: CF

---

475   DATE: May 14, 1966
PLACE, OPP.: Municipal
   Stadium, Kansas City A's
SCORE: KC 4, NY 2
SWING, POS. IN ORDER:
   LH, 3rd
PITCHER: Fred Talbot
MEN ON: 0
STATS: 1 for 3, 1 run, 1 RBI
POSITION: CF

Mantle's fourth-inning homer
momentarily tied the score at
1–1. It was his longest shot in
some time, traveling between
450 and 500 feet and reaching
the second fence in deepest right
center.

476
477
DATE: May 25, 1966
PLACE, OPP.: Yankee
  Stadium, California Angels
SCORE: NY 11, CA 6
SWING, POS. IN ORDER:
  LH, LH; 3rd
PITCHERS: Dean Chance,
  Lew Burdette
MEN ON: 1, 2
STATS: 3 for 3, 2 BBs, 3 runs, 5
  RBIs
POSITION: CF

Mantle's first two-homer game since August 12, 1964. The first landed near the back of the right-field bullpen, and the second sailed into the left-field stands.

478
DATE: June 1, 1966
PLACE, OPP.: Comiskey Park,
  Chicago White Sox
SCORE: CH 6, NY 2
SWING, POS. IN ORDER:
  RH, 3rd
PITCHER: Juan Pizarro
MEN ON: 0
STATS: 2 for 4, 1 run, 1 RBI
POSITION: CF

Pizarro had a shutout until the bottom of the ninth, when Mantle homered into the center-field bullpen.

479
DATE: June 16, 1966
PLACE, OPP.: Yankee
  Stadium, Cleveland Indians
SCORE: NY 7, CL 6
SWING, POS. IN ORDER:
  RH, 3rd
PITCHER: Sam McDowell
MEN ON: 1
STATS: 1 for 4, 1 run, 2 RBIs
POSITION: CF

Indian right fielder Rocky Colavito leaped at the bullpen gate to rob Mantle of a first-inning homer. But in the third, all Colavito could do was watch as Mantle's wrong-field homer went over his head and into the right-field seats.

480

DATE: June 23, 1966
PLACE, OPP.: Yankee
    Stadium, Baltimore Orioles
SCORE: BA 5, NY 2
SWING, POS. IN ORDER:
    LH, 3rd
PITCHER: Jim Palmer
MEN ON: 0
STATS: 1 for 4, 1 run, 1 RBI
POSITION: CF

Palmer handcuffed Mantle until the eighth, when Mickey unloaded a monstrous third-tier homer to right field.

481
482

DATE: June 28, 1966   PLACE, OPP.: Fenway Park, Boston Red Sox   SCORE: BO 5, NY 3   SWING, POS. IN ORDER: LH, LH; 3rd   PITCHER: Jose Santiago (2)   MEN ON: 1, 0 STATS: 2 for 3, 1 BB, 2 runs, 3 RBIs   POSITION: LF

483
484

DATE: June 29, 1966   PLACE, OPP.: Fenway Park, Boston Red Sox   SCORE: NY 6, BO 5   SWING, POS. IN ORDER: LH, LH; 3rd   PITCHER: Rollie Sheldon (2)   MEN ON: 2, 0 STATS: 3 for 4, 2 runs, 4 RBIs   POSITION: LF

485

DATE: July 1, 1966   PLACE, OPP.: D.C. Stadium, Washington Senators   SCORE: NY 8, WA 6   SWING, POS. IN ORDER: LH, 3rd   PITCHER: Phil Ortega   MEN ON: 0   STATS: 3 for 3, 1 BB, 2 runs, 2 RBIs   POSITION: CF

486
487

DATE: July 2, 1966   PLACE, OPP.: D.C. Stadium, Washington Senators   SCORE: WA 10, NY 4   SWING, POS. IN ORDER: RH, RH; 3rd   PITCHER: Mike McCormick (2)   MEN ON: 0, 0   STATS: 2 for 4, 2 runs, 2 RBIs   POSITION: CF

---

488 DATE: July 3, 1966   PLACE, OPP.: D.C. Stadium, Washington Senators   SCORE: NY 6, WA 5   SWING, POS. IN ORDER: RH, 3rd   PITCHER: Pete Richert   MEN ON: 0   STATS: 1 for 4, 1 run, 1 RBI   POSITION: CF

---

489 DATE: July 7, 1966   PLACE, OPP.: Yankee Stadium, Boston Red Sox   SCORE: NY 5, BO 2   SWING, POS. IN ORDER: LH, 3rd   PITCHER: Don McMahon   MEN ON: 2   STATS: 1 for 4, 1 BB, 1 run, 3 RBIs   POSITION: CF

---

490 DATE: July 8, 1966   PLACE, OPP.: Yankee Stadium, Washington Senators   SCORE: WA 7, NY 6   SWING, POS. IN ORDER: LH, 3rd   PITCHER: Dick Bosman   MEN ON: 0   STATS: 2 for 5, 1 run, 1 RBI   POSITION: CF

---

491 DATE: July 8, 1966   PLACE, OPP.: Yankee Stadium, Washington Senators   SCORE: NY 7, WA 5   SWING, POS. IN ORDER: LH, 3rd   PITCHER: Jim Hannan   MEN ON: 0   STATS: 3 for 3, 1 run, 1 RBI   POSITION: CF

---

492 DATE: July 23, 1966
PLACE, OPP.: Yankee
  Stadium, California Angels
SCORE: CA 7, NY 6
SWING, POS. IN ORDER:
  RH, 3rd
PITCHER: Marcelino Lopez
MEN ON: 3
STATS: 3 for 4, 1 BB, 1 run, 4
  RBIs
POSITION: CF

Old-Timers' Day and Mantle walloped his ninth career grand-slam homer, an opposite-field shot that carried into the upper deck in right.

---

493   DATE: July 24, 1966
PLACE, OPP.: Yankee
  Stadium, California Angels
SCORE: NY 9, CA 1
SWING, POS. IN ORDER:
  RH, 3rd
PITCHER: George Brunet
MEN ON: 0
STATS: 2 for 3, 1 BB, 2 runs, 1
  RBI
POSITION: CF

Mantle rocketed a long opposite-field homer that tied him with Lou Gehrig for sixth place on the all-time home-run list.

---

494   DATE: July 29, 1966
PLACE, OPP.: Comiskey Park,
  Chicago White Sox
SCORE: NY 2, CH 1
SWING, POS. IN ORDER:
  LH, 3rd
PITCHER: Bruce Howard
MEN ON: 0
STATS: 1 for 3, 1 BB, 1 run, 1
  RBI
POSITION: CF

Mickey, passing Gehrig, lifted a pitch into the right-field upper deck—his 14th homer in his last 24 games.

---

495   DATE: August 14, 1966
PLACE, OPP.: Yankee
  Stadium, Cleveland Indians
SCORE: NY 6, CL 4
SWING, POS. IN ORDER:
  RH, 3rd
PITCHER: Jack Kralick
MEN ON: 0
STATS: 2 for 3, 1 BB, 1 run, 1
  RBI
POSITION: CF

Mantle homered in the second game of a doubleheader sweep. The Indians committed six errors in one inning of the nightcap.

496 DATE: August 26, 1966   PLACE, OPP.: Yankee Stadium, Detroit Tigers   SCORE: NY 6, DE 5   SWING, POS. IN ORDER: RH, PH   PITCHER: Hank Aguirre   MEN ON: 1   STATS: 1 for 1, 1 run, 2 RBIs   POSITION: Pinch-hitter

---

1967

---

497 DATE: April 29, 1967   PLACE, OPP.: Yankee Stadium, California Angels   SCORE: NY 5, CA 2   SWING, POS. IN ORDER: LH, 3rd   PITCHER: Jack Sanford   MEN ON: 1 STATS: 2 for 4, 1 run, 3 RBIs   POSITION: 1B

---

498 DATE: April 30, 1967   PLACE, OPP.: Yankee Stadium, California Angels   SCORE: NY 4, CA 1   SWING, POS. IN ORDER: LH, 3rd   PITCHER: Minnie Rojas   MEN ON: 2 STATS: 2 for 4, 1 BB, 1 run, 3 RBIs   POSITION: 1B

---

499 DATE: May 3, 1967
PLACE, OPP.: Metropolitan
  Stadium, Minnesota Twins
SCORE: MI 4, NY 3
SWING, POS. IN ORDER:
  LH, 3rd
PITCHER: Dave Boswell
MEN ON: 0
STATS: 1 for 4, 1 run, 1 RBI
POSITION: 1B

Mantle's first-inning homer opened the scoring.

---

500 DATE: May 14, 1967   PLACE, OPP.: Yankee Stadium, Baltimore Orioles   SCORE: NY 6, BA 5   SWING, POS. IN ORDER: LH, 3rd   PITCHER: Stu Miller   MEN ON: 0   STATS: 2 for 4, 2 runs, 1 RBI   POSITION: 1B

501

DATE: May 17, 1967
PLACE, OPP.: Yankee
   Stadium, Cleveland Indians
SCORE: CL 8, NY 7
SWING, POS. IN ORDER:
   LH, 3rd
PITCHER: Steve Hargan
MEN ON: 0
STATS: 1 for 4, 2 runs, 1 RBI
POSITION: 1B

Down 8–2, the Yanks got five
runs back in a seventh-inning
rally capped by long back-to-
back homers by Tom Tresh and
Mantle into the right-field
bleachers, Mickey's going higher
and farther and more toward
center field.

502

DATE: May 19, 1967
PLACE, OPP.: Tiger Stadium,
   Detroit Tigers
SCORE: DE 4, NY 2
SWING, POS. IN ORDER:
   RH, 3rd
PITCHER: Mickey Lolich
MEN ON: 0
STATS: 2 for 4, 1 run, 2 RBIs
POSITION: 1B

Mantle collected two of the five
hits Lolich allowed and knocked
in both Yankee runs. In the
eighth, he pulled a homer down
the left-field line and through a
20-mph crosswind.

503

DATE: May 20, 1967
PLACE, OPP.: Tiger Stadium,
   Detroit Tigers
SCORE: DE 3, NY 1
SWING, POS. IN ORDER:
   LH, 3rd
PITCHER: Denny McLain
MEN ON: 0
STATS: 1 for 4, 1 run, 1 RBI
POSITION: 1B

McLain allowed only one run—
a titanic Mantle homer. The
ball had a little wind behind it
and was still rising when it
banged into the deepest portion
of the seats upstairs in right-center, the drive falling just short of
reaching the roof. The ball
might have gone 500 feet if unobstructed.

504
DATE: May 21, 1967
PLACE, OPP.: Tiger Stadium,
  Detroit Tigers
SCORE: DE 9, NY 4
SWING, POS. IN ORDER:
  LH, 3rd
PITCHER: Earl Wilson
MEN ON: 1
STATS: 2 for 4, 1 BB, 1 run, 2
  RBIs
POSITION: 1B

Whitey Ford's last major-league game. Mantle's late-inning homer was his fifth in six games.

505
DATE: May 24, 1967
PLACE, OPP.: Memorial
  Stadium, Baltimore Orioles
SCORE: NY 2, BA 0
SWING, POS. IN ORDER:
  RH, 3rd
PITCHER: Steve Barber
MEN ON: 1
STATS: 1 for 3, 1 BB, 1 run, 2
  RBIs, 1 SB
POSITION: 1B

With two out in the third inning, Mantle hit an opposite-field drive that sent right fielder Frank Robinson to the barrier; Robinson leaped and actually had the ball in his glove, but he lost it when his hand hit the fence coming down.

506
DATE: May 27, 1967
PLACE, OPP.: Municipal
  Stadium, Cleveland Indians
SCORE: CL 5, NY 3
SWING, POS. IN ORDER:
  LH, 3rd
PITCHER: Sonny Siebert
MEN ON: 0
STATS: 1 for 4, 1 run, 1 RBI
POSITION: 1B

Breaking a 2–2 tie, Mantle led off the sixth inning with a home run.

507 DATE: May 28, 1967
PLACE, OPP.: Municipal
    Stadium, Cleveland Indians
SCORE: NY 5, CL 0
SWING, POS. IN ORDER:
    LH, 3rd
PITCHER: Gary Bell
MEN ON: 0
STATS: 1 for 3, 1 BB, 1 run, 1
    RBI
POSITION: 1B

Mickey homered over the right-field fence, putting him two games ahead of Roger Maris's 1961 pace.

---

508 DATE: June 5, 1967   PLACE, OPP.: Yankee Stadium,
Washington Senators   SCORE: NY 4, WA 2   SWING, POS.
IN ORDER: RH, 3rd   PITCHER: Darold Knowles   MEN
ON: 0   STATS: 1 for 4, 1 run, 1 RBI   POSITION: 1B

---

509 DATE: June 15, 1967
PLACE, OPP.: D.C. Stadium,
    Washington Senators
SCORE: NY 2, WA 0
SWING, POS. IN ORDER:
    RH, 3rd
PITCHER: Frank Bertaina
MEN ON: 0
STATS: 2 for 3, 1 BB, 1 run, 1
    RBI
POSITION: 1B

In the lineup after missing five games with a pulled right thigh muscle, Mantle untied a scoreless game in the sixth with a 450-foot-plus homer into the second row of the left-center-field upper deck.

---

510 DATE: June 24, 1967   PLACE, OPP.: Yankee Stadium, Detroit
Tigers   SCORE: NY 4, DE 3   SWING, POS. IN ORDER:
LH, 3rd   PITCHER: Fred Gladding   MEN ON: 0   STATS: 1
for 3, 1 BB, 1 run, 1 RBI   POSITION: 1B

511
512

DATE: July 4, 1967
PLACE, OPP.: Metropolitan
  Stadium, Minnesota Twins
SCORE: MI 8, NY 3
SWING, POS. IN ORDER:
  LH, LH; 3rd
PITCHER: Mudcat Grant (2)
MEN ON: 0, 1
STATS: 3 for 4, 2 runs, 3 RBIs
POSITION: 1B

All three Yankee runs were
courtesy of Mantle homers. He
tied and then passed Mel Ott for
fifth place on the all-time
home-run list.

513

DATE: July 16, 1967
PLACE, OPP.: Yankee
  Stadium, Baltimore Orioles
SCORE: BA 2, NY 1
SWING, POS. IN ORDER:
  LH, 4th
PITCHER: Bill Dillman
MEN ON: 0
STATS: 2 for 3, 1 BB, 1 run, 1
  RBI
POSITION: 1B

Mantle got two of the four Yank
hits, one a 420-foot homer to
right-center in this 14-inning
game.

514

DATE: July 22, 1967
PLACE, OPP.: Tiger Stadium,
  Detroit Tigers
SCORE: DE 11, NY 4
SWING, POS. IN ORDER:
  LH, 3rd
PITCHER: Earl Wilson
MEN ON: 0
STATS: 1 for 4, 1 run, 1 RBI
POSITION: 1B

Mantle's homer into the right-
field upper deck broke a personal string of six consecutive
strikeouts, and his 359th *left-
handed* homer meant that he
had hit as many from that side
as the great Johnny Mize, a full-
time lefty.

---

515 DATE: July 25, 1967   PLACE, OPP.: Yankee Stadium, Minnesota Twins   SCORE: NY 1, MI 1   SWING, POS. IN ORDER: RH, 3rd   PITCHER: Jim Kaat   MEN ON: 0   STATS: 1 for 4, 1 run, 1 RBI   POSITION: 1B

---

516 DATE: August 7, 1967
PLACE, OPP.: Anaheim
  Stadium, California Angels
SCORE: CA 8, NY 4
SWING, POS. IN ORDER:
  LH, 3rd
PITCHER: Minnie Rojas
MEN ON: 1
STATS: 1 for 3, 1 BB, 1 run, 2
  RBIs
POSITION: 1B

In the top of the eighth inning, Mantle put New York ahead, 4–1, with a towering homer over the fence in left-center.

---

517 DATE: September 2, 1967   PLACE, OPP.: Yankee Stadium, Washington Senators   SCORE: NY 2, WA 1   SWING, POS. IN ORDER: LH, PH   PITCHER: Bob Priddy   MEN ON: 1 STATS: 1 for 1, 1 run, 2 RBIs   POSITION: Pinch-hitter

---

518 DATE: September 3, 1967
PLACE, OPP.: Yankee
  Stadium, Washington
  Senators
SCORE: WA 6, NY 3
SWING, POS. IN ORDER:
  LH, 3rd
PITCHER: Dick Bosman
MEN ON: 0
STATS: 1 for 4, 1 run, 1 RBI
POSITION: 1B

In the eighth, on a full count, Bosman challenged Mantle, and Mickey parked the ball in the right-field seats.

1968

519

DATE: April 18, 1968
PLACE, OPP.: Anaheim
   Stadium, California Angels
SCORE: NY 6, CA 1
SWING, POS. IN ORDER:
   LH, 3rd
PITCHER: Jim McGlothlin
MEN ON: 1
STATS: 1 for 4, 1 BB, 1 run, 2
   RBIs
POSITION: 1B

Mantle lined a fifth-inning homer over the 406-foot mark in center field. The ball traveled 465 feet, according to *The Sporting News*.

520

DATE: April 24, 1968
PLACE, OPP.: Oakland
   Coliseum, Oakland Athletics
SCORE: OA 4, NY 3
SWING, POS. IN ORDER:
   LH, 3rd
PITCHER: Jim Nash
MEN ON: 0
STATS: 2 for 4, 1 BB, 2 runs, 1
   RBI
POSITION: 1B

In the first inning, Mantle made the Oakland Coliseum the 16th league park to see a Mantle home run.

521

DATE: April 26, 1968
PLACE, OPP.: Yankee
   Stadium, Detroit Tigers
SCORE: NY 5, DE 0
SWING, POS. IN ORDER:
   LH, 3rd
PITCHER: Earl Wilson
MEN ON: 1
STATS: 1 for 4, 1 run, 2 RBIs
POSITION: 1B

Mickey whaled a fastball into the right-field upper deck for his 521st homer, tying him with Ted Williams for fourth place on the all-time list. The fans went crazy, cheering even while the next two batters were hitting.

522   DATE: May 6, 1968   PLACE, OPP.: Yankee Stadium, Cleveland
Indians   SCORE: CL 3, NY 2   SWING, POS. IN ORDER:
RH, 3rd   PITCHER: Sam McDowell   MEN ON: 1   STATS:
1 for 4, 1 run, 2 RBIs   POSITION: 1B

523
524   DATE: May 30, 1968   PLACE, OPP.: Yankee Stadium,
Washington Senators   SCORE: NY 13, WA 4   SWING, POS.
IN ORDER: LH, LH; 3rd   PITCHERS: Joe Coleman, Bob
Humphreys   MEN ON: 1, 0   STATS: 5 for 5, 3 runs, 5
RBIs   POSITION: 1B

---

525   DATE: June 7, 1968   PLACE, OPP.: Yankee Stadium, California
Angels   SCORE: CA 8, NY 4   SWING, POS. IN ORDER:
LH, 3rd   PITCHER: Jim McGlothlin   MEN ON: 1   STATS:
1 for 4, 1 run, 2 RBIs   POSITION: 1B

---

526   DATE: June 11, 1968
PLACE, OPP.: Yankee
   Stadium, Chicago White Sox
SCORE: CH 9, NY 5
SWING, POS. IN ORDER:
   LH, 3rd
PITCHER: Joe Horlen
MEN ON: 1
STATS: 1 for 4, 1 run, 2 RBIs
POSITION: 1B

Home runs by Tom Tresh and
Mantle, good for a total of five
runs, weren't enough.

---

527   DATE: June 16, 1968
PLACE, OPP.: Anaheim
   Stadium, California Angels
SCORE: NY 4, CA 3
SWING, POS. IN ORDER:
   RH, 3rd
PITCHER: Clyde Wright
MEN ON: 1

Wright struck Mantle out on a
curveball the previous year, so
he tried it again, but this time it
didn't work.

STATS: 1 for 2, 2 BBs, 1 run, 2
RBIs
POSITION: 1B

---

528 DATE: June 22, 1968
PLACE, OPP.: Metropolitan
Stadium, Minnesota Twins
SCORE: NY 5, MI 2
SWING, POS. IN ORDER:
RH, 3rd
PITCHER: Jim Kaat
MEN ON: 0
STATS: 1 for 3, 1 BB, 1 run, 1
RBI
POSITION: 1B

Mantle's first-inning 380-foot
homer to left-center gave the
Yankees a 1–0 lead.

---

529 DATE: June 29, 1968   PLACE, OPP.: Yankee Stadium, Oakland
A's   SCORE: OA 5, NY 2   SWING, POS. IN ORDER: LH,
3rd   PITCHER: Blue Moon Odom   MEN ON: 1   STATS: 2
for 3, 1 BB, 1 run, 2 RBIs   POSITION: 1B

530
531 DATE: August 10, 1968
PLACE, OPP.: Yankee
Stadium, Minnesota Twins
SCORE: MI 3, NY 2
SWING, POS. IN ORDER:
RH, RH; 3rd
PITCHER: Jim Merritt (2)
MEN ON: 0, 0
STATS: 2 for 4, 2 runs, 2 RBIs
POSITION: 1B

Mantle's two homers were the
only Yankee runs on Old-Timers' Day. It was Mickey's 46th,
and final, two-homer game—26
two-homer games behind Babe
Ruth's record.

---

532 DATE: August 12, 1968
PLACE, OPP.: Anaheim
Stadium, California Angels
SCORE: NY 5, CA 2

Mantle, after a painful foul off
his foot, stroked a 400-foot
homer over the right-center-
field fence.

SWING, POS. IN ORDER:
RH, 3rd
PITCHER: George Brunet
MEN ON: 1
STATS: 1 for 5, 1 run, 2 RBIs
POSITION: 1B

533

DATE: August 15, 1968
PLACE, OPP.: Oakland
Coliseum, Oakland Athletics
SCORE: OA 4, NY 3
SWING, POS. IN ORDER:
LH, 3rd
PITCHER: Blue Moon Odom
MEN ON: 2
STATS: 2 for 4, 1 run, 3 RBIs
POSITION: 1B

Odom was so upset at a disputed call resulting in a Tresh triple that he walked Jake Gibbs and served a home run to Mantle.

534

DATE: August 22, 1968
PLACE, OPP.: Metropolitan
Stadium, Minnesota Twins
SCORE: MI 3, NY 1
SWING, POS. IN ORDER:
RH, PH
PITCHER: Jim Merritt
MEN ON: 0
STATS: 1 for 1, 1 run, 1 RBI
POSITION: Pinch-hitter

Merritt lost his shutout in the ninth inning when Mantle, pinch-hitting for Dooley Womack—the Mick was getting a rest after playing 9 of 10 games on this road trip—homered, tying him with Jimmie Foxx for third place on the all-time list.

535

DATE: September 19, 1968   PLACE, OPP.: Tiger Stadium,
Detroit Tigers   SCORE: DE 6, NY 2   SWING, POS. IN
ORDER: LH, 3rd   PITCHER: Denny McLain   MEN ON: 0
STATS: 2 for 2, 2 BBs, 2 runs, 1 RBI   POSITION: 1B

536

DATE: September 20, 1968   PLACE, OPP.: Yankee Stadium,
Boston Red Sox   SCORE: BO 4, NY 3   SWING, POS. IN
ORDER: LH, 3rd   PITCHER: Jim Lonborg   MEN ON: 0
STATS: 2 for 4, 1 run, 1 RBI   POSITION: 1B

Yankee Won-Lost Record in Games in Which Mantle Homered

	Won	Lost		Percentage
1st 100 home runs	71	25		.740
2nd 100 home runs	62	27		.697
3rd 100 home runs	62	30	(1 tie)	.674
4th 100 home runs	67	19		.779
5th 100 home runs	62	30		.674
Home runs 501–536	12	20	(1 tie)	.375
Total	336	151	(2 ties)	.690
Yankee record (1951–1968)	1,664	1,165		.588

Yankee Won-Lost Record by Year in Games in Which Mantle Homered

	Won	Lost	Percentage
1951 (13 games)	9	4	.692
1952 (22 games)	14	8	.636
1953 (21 games)	17	4	.809
1954 (26 games)	21	5	.808
1955 (32 games)	25	7	.781
1956 (45 games)	30	15	.666
1957 (33 games)	21	12	.636
1958 (38 games)	24	14	.632
1959 (29 games)	20	9	.690
1960 (36 games)	28	8	.778
1961 (46 games)	37	9	.804
1962 (25 games)	18	7	.720
1963 (14 games)	11	3	.786
1964 (33 games)	23	10	.697
1965 (19 games)	11	8	.579
1966 (19 games)	12	7	.632
1967 (20 games)	9	11	.450
1968 (16 games)	6	10	.375

Locations of Mantle Home Runs

Yankee Stadium, New York..........	266
Briggs Stadium–Tiger Stadium (same park),* Detroit..................	42
Fenway Park, Boston...............	38
Municipal Stadium, Cleveland.......	36
Comiskey Park, Chicago............	30
Griffith Stadium, Washington, D.C. ..	29
Municipal Stadium, Kansas City	26
Memorial Stadium, Baltimore	25
Metropolitan Stadium, Bloomington, Minnesota......................	14
D.C. Stadium,† Washington	10
Shibe Park–Connie Mack Stadium (same park),* Philadelphia.........	6
Sportsman's Park–Busch Stadium (same park),* St. Louis	4
Anaheim Stadium, Anaheim, California.....................	4
Wrigley Field, Los Angeles..........	2
Chavez Ravine,‡ Los Angeles........	2
Oakland Coliseum, Oakland.........	2
Total	536 home runs

*The park was the same but the name changed during Mantle's time. †Renamed Robert F. Kennedy Stadium after Mantle retired from baseball. ‡Better known as Dodger Stadium, but the Angels, tenants of the Dodgers from 1962–65, preferred to call their home Chavez Ravine.

Teams Against Which Mantle Homered

Washington Senators (both)	80
Detroit Tigers	74
Chicago White Sox	73
Boston Red Sox	69
Cleveland Indians	64
Kansas City A's	63
Baltimore Orioles	43
Minnesota Twins	27
Los Angeles/California Angels	23
Philadelphia A's	11
St. Louis Browns	6
Oakland A's	3
Total	536 home runs

Mantle Home Runs by Innings

1st inning	102	
2nd inning	21	
3rd inning	66	
Total	189	home runs hit in first three innings
4th inning	65	
5th inning	43	
6th inning	59	
Total	170	home runs hit in middle three innings
7th inning	53	
8th inning	63	
9th inning	47	
10th inning	9	
11th inning	5	
Total	177	home runs hit in bottom three innings or in extra innings
Grand Total	536	home runs

Number of Men on Base for Mantle Home Runs

Solo home runs	298
2-run home runs	162
3-run home runs	67
Grand slams	9
Total	536 home runs

Mantle and Back-to-Back Home Runs

Mantle, then Berra	11
Berra, then Mantle	1
Total with Yogi Berra	12
Maris, then Mantle	7
Mantle, then Maris	3
Total with Roger Maris	10
Gil McDougald, then Mantle	4
Collins, then Mantle	2
Mantle, then Collins	1
Total with Joe Collins	3
Mantle, then Bill Skowron	2
Mantle then Elston Howard	2
Mantle, then Bill Renna	1
Mantle, then Clete Boyer	1
Bobby Brown, then Mantle	1
Mantle, then Johnny Blanchard	1
Hector Lopez, then Mantle	1
Bobby Richardson, then Mantle, then Joe Pepitone .	1
Grand Total	39

Mantle Home Runs By Month

April	40
May	110
June	113
July	111
August	95
September	67
Total	536 home runs

Pitchers Who Gave Up Most Mantle Home Runs

	Home Runs		Home Runs
Early Wynn	13	Jim Bunning	6
Pedro Ramos	12	Billy Hoeft	6
Camilo Pascual	11	Bob Lemon	6
Frank Lary	9	Jack Harshman	6
Chuck Stobbs	8	Connie Johnson	6
Dick Donovan	8	Steve Gromek	5
Billy Pierce	8	Ike Delock	5
Gary Bell	8	Jim "Mudcat" Grant	5
Jim Kaat	7	Hank Aguirre	5
Ray Herbert	7	Jim Perry	5
Frank Sullivan	7	John O'Donoghue	5
Hal Brown	7	Virgil Trucks	5
Ray Moore	6	Jim Brewer	5
Earl Wilson	6	Ray Narleski	5
Paul Foytack	6		

Left-handed and Right-handed Home Runs By Mantle

	Left-handed	Right-handed
1st 100 home runs	62	38
2nd 100 home runs	75	25
3rd 100 home runs	75	25
4th 100 home runs	77	23
5th 100 home runs	59	41
Home runs 501–536	24	12
Total	372	164

Special Mantle Home Runs

Inside-the-Park Home Runs
No. 52	August 7, 1953, at Yankee Stadium
No. 209	May 9, 1958, at Yankee Stadium
No. 211	May 20, 1958, at Chicago
No. 215	June 5, 1958, at Yankee Stadium
No. 254	May 12, 1959, at Yankee Stadium
No. 345	June 30, 1961, at Yankee Stadium

Total 6

Pinch-Hit Home Runs
No. 49	July 6, 1953, at Philadelphia
No. 382	June 16, 1962, at Cleveland
No. 416	August 4, 1963, at Yankee Stadium
No. 417	September 1, 1963, at Baltimore
No. 496	August 26, 1966, at Yankee Stadium
No. 517	September 2, 1967, at Yankee Stadium
No. 534	August 22, 1968, at Minnesota

Total 7

Grand-Slam Home Runs
No. 28	July 26, 1952, at Detroit
No. 29	July 29, 1952, at Chicago
No. 49	July 6, 1953, at Philadelphia
No. 95	May 18, 1955, at Yankee Stadium

No. 154   July 30, 1956, at Cleveland
No. 328   May 2, 1961, at Minnesota
No. 398   August 19, 1962, at Kansas City
No. 464   June 18, 1965, at Yankee Stadium
No. 492   July 23, 1966, at Yankee Stadium
Total   9

Switch-Hit Home Runs in One Game

Nos. 92, 93, 94   May 13, 1955, at Yankee Stadium
Nos. 112, 113   August 15, 1955, at Baltimore
Nos. 135, 136   May 18, 1956, at Chicago
Nos. 149, 150   July 1, 1956, at Yankee Stadium
Nos. 190, 191   June 12, 1957, at Chicago
Nos. 234, 235   July 28, 1958, at Kansas City
Nos. 279, 280   September 15, 1959, at Yankee Stadium
Nos. 326, 327   April 26, 1961, at Detroit
Nos. 379, 380   May 6, 1962, at Yankee Stadium
Nos. 443, 444   August 12, 1964, at Yankee Stadium
Total   10

Home Runs in Both Games of Doubleheader

Nos. 5, 6   June 19, 1951, at Yankee Stadium
Nos. 23, 24   July 13, 1952, at Yankee Stadium
Nos. 50, 51   July 26, 1953, at Detroit
Nos. 103, 104, 105   July 10, 1955, at Washington
Nos. 140, 141   May 30, 1956, at Yankee Stadium
Nos. 222, 223   July 1, 1958, at Baltimore
Nos. 272, 273   August 16, 1959, at Yankee Stadium
Nos. 361, 362, 363   August 6, 1961, at Yankee Stadium
Nos. 378, 379, 380   May 6, 1962, at Yankee Stadium
Nos. 420, 421   May 6, 1964, at Washington
Nos. 490, 491   July 8, 1966, at Yankee Stadium
Total   11

Opening Day Home Runs

No. 85   April 13, 1955, at Yankee Stadium
Nos. 122, 123   April 17, 1956, at Washington
No. 375   April 10, 1962, at Yankee Stadium
Total   4